ALSO BY BEN DOWNING

The Calligraphy Shop

Queen Bee of Tuscany

Queen Bee
of Tuscany

THE REDOUBTABLE
JANET ROSS

BEN DOWNING

FARRAR, STRAUS AND GIROUX

NEW YORK

Farrar, Straus and Giroux
18 West 18th Street, New York 10011

Owing to limitations of space, all acknowledgments
for permission to reprint previously published
material can be found on page 339.

Library of Congress Cataloging-in-Publication Data
Downing, Ben, 1967–
    Queen bee of Tuscany : the redoubtable Janet Ross / Ben Downing.—First edition.
        pages   cm
    Includes bibliographical references and index.
    ISBN 978-0-374-23971-8 (alkaline paper)
    1. Ross, Janet, 1842–1927.   2. Ross, Janet, 1842–1927—Homes and haunts—
Italy—Tuscany.   3. Ross, Janet, 1842–1927—Friends and associates.   4. British—
Italy—Tuscany—Biography.   5. Women—Italy—Tuscany—Biography.   6. Exiles—
Tuscany—Biography.   7. Tuscany (Italy)—Biography.   8. Tuscany (Italy)—Social life
and customs—20th century.   I. Title.

DG738.79.R67 D69 2013
945'.5084092—dc23
[B]

2012048078

Designed by Jonathan D. Lippincott

www.fsgbooks.com
www.twitter.com/fsgbooks • www.facebook.com/fsgbooks

1   3   5   7   9   10   8   6   4   2

For Cordelia,
for Erika,
and for Grazia Gobbi Sica

CONTENTS

A NOTE ON SOURCES

In the following pages, I quote frequently from three of Janet Ross's books. In the first chapter, most of my quotations are drawn from *Three Generations of English Women*, which successively traces the lives of Janet's great-grandmother, grandmother, and mother. Afterward, most are from her two works of autobiography: *Early Days Recalled*, which covers her first twenty-one years, and *The Fourth Generation*, which takes her from birth to her late sixties. The latter book extensively cannibalizes the former, replicating many passages almost—but not quite—verbatim. As a result, I was often forced to choose, quotation-wise, between two slightly different versions. Since the changes Janet made were, in my opinion, sometimes for the better and sometimes for the worse, I alternate between quoting from *Early Days Recalled* and *The Fourth Generation*. On occasion I specify the source of the quote, but more often I do not.

Queen Bee of Tuscany

INTRODUCTION

Poggio Untoppled

In the summer of 1944 the tide of the war finally turned in Tuscany. By August the Nazis had pulled out of Florence, and by early September they'd retreated from their positions in Fiesole, a few miles to the north. No sooner did the Germans withdraw than another group of foreigners began to edge back in. Mostly British and American, they'd lived in the hills near Fiesole before the war, and were now returning to assess the damage to their properties. One of them, the writer Iris Origo, went to survey the Villa Medici, home of her recently deceased Anglo-Irish mother; as she recalls in her memoirs, not only was the estate "very thoroughly equipped with booby-traps" but its garden house was still on fire, and on venturing into it she fell through a hole in the floor, slightly injuring herself. About the same time, the art historian Bernard Berenson came out of hiding and made his way back to his own villa, I Tatti. Though he didn't take a fall, he had the sensation of one: "As in the twilight . . . I came in sight of the broken-down garden walls and scorched fields, I sank into a pool of despair." To his relief, the house itself had scarcely been touched, and he was amazed to find his "dear and half-forgotten *objets d'art*" lying about unbroken.

While Berenson reacquainted himself with his objets, another inspection took place just uphill. Lt. Col. John Beevor, attached to the headquarters of Field Marshal Harold Alexander in Siena, was in

Florence on official business but had slipped away to check on the castellated villa where his wife, Kinta, had spent much of her childhood. Like Berenson, he was mostly relieved. Though shells had punched several holes in the house and its contents had been looted, he was able to lead off his report to Kinta with this comforting sentence: "Poggio is still standing."

Poggio Gherardo—to give its full name—had in fact been standing since at least the eleventh century. In the fourteenth it was attacked by the celebrated condottiere Sir John Hawkwood and served (or so some scholars believe) as the model for one of the houses where the plague-fleeing characters of the *Decameron* take refuge. But it was only in the late nineteenth century that it acquired a master, or rather a mistress, of real distinction. Her name was Janet Ross. She was Kinta's great-aunt, and she presided over Poggio Gherardo for almost forty years, till her death in 1927. During that time she turned it into one of the outstanding homes in Europe. Though modest in size and short on luxury, the house became, under her reign, a magnet for a colorful miscellany of people, and it rang with polyglot conversation and tales as vivid in their way as those told in the *Decameron*.

She herself was no less exceptional. If she's now all but forgotten, she was once widely known—and feared—as "the redoubtable Mrs. Ross." This book will attempt to show why, to put back on the map a woman who led one of the fullest lives imaginable, whose forceful personality made, for better or worse, a strong impression on all those who met her, and who experienced and understood Tuscany like few outsiders before or since.

Tuscany: by now the word itself is a kind of talisman, its mere pronunciation or even thought triggering a series of images in the mind. These days, the first is bound to feature a backdrop of tawny, rippling, cypress-studded hills. At their base we picture a lone farmhouse, or else, perched atop one of them, a tiny walled town where cap-wearing codgers stroll the winding lanes. Next might come some particular urban treasure—Michelangelo's *David*, the Leaning Tower of Pisa, the Duomo of Florence, Siena's Piazza del Campo—but idyllic country scenes are likely to reassert themselves: perhaps we now see ourselves at that same farmhouse, dining al fresco on rustic fare straight from the surrounding fields.

Not just another fantasy destination, Tuscany has come to stand for one version of the good life, beckoning us to trade our harried, sterile existence for an authentic nirvana of the senses. Its lodestone powers tend, moreover, to hold particular sway over anglophones. So thick on the ground have the British become that a swath of the province is now referred to as Chiantishire, and the success of Frances Mayes and her imitators has led countless Americans to follow suit, snapping up *case coloniche* wherever they can.

None of this is news, and neither is the fact that our obsession goes back a ways: anyone who's read—or, courtesy of Merchant and Ivory, seen—*A Room with a View* is aware that the Edwardians were as mad about Tuscany as we now are. Yet the full scope of the phenomenon has gone oddly underappreciated. The history of our collective love affair with Tuscany, and with Florence in particular, is longer and richer than most people realize, even those who've taken part in it. By many measures, in fact, its current phase pales in comparison to earlier ones. In 1910 the British consul in Florence estimated that there were thirty-five thousand British citizens living in and around the city—about a seventh of its total population at the time. And that's to say nothing of the many Americans, Irish, Canadians, Australians, and New Zealanders. But the statistics barely hint at the full story. In Florence, the English-speaking tribes weren't just scattered among the locals, they formed their own little world, one known, quasi-officially, as the Anglo-Florentine colony.

The colony crystallized in the early 1840s and flourished for almost a century, until it was driven out by Mussolini; after the war it partially reestablished itself, and traces of it lingered into the 1990s, when the deaths of Sir Harold Acton—often named as the last of the Anglo-Florentines—and several other aged stalwarts brought it to a close. Though not a colony in the true imperial sense, it had the ethos of one. More than just an agglomeration of people or a state of mind, it was part of the texture of the city: the Anglo-Florentines had their own churches, graveyards, cafés, clubs, and shops. As a society, it was inevitably somewhat floating, but less so than one might think. Transitory residents were outnumbered by long-termers, many of whom felt an almost umbilical connection to the city; some, Origo recalls, "sank roots so deep that when, at the outbreak of the Second World War, the British Consulate attempted to repatriate them, a number of obscure old ladies firmly refused to leave, saying that, after fifty years' residence in Florence, they preferred the risk of a concentration camp to a return to England." Nor did the colony consist entirely of transplants. Establishing itself over generations, it produced its own natives, such as Acton—"I took pride," he writes, "in being a Florentine by birth."

Predictably enough, the colony had its share of bores, and could be egregiously silly and provincial: smug, insular, dilettantish, riven by pointless quarrels and hypnotized by trivial gossip. It could also be deplorably ignorant and bigoted—too many of its members scarcely bothered to learn a word of Italian and treated the locals with frank contempt. Yet it had a good deal of charm, fascination, even majesty. Over the years, it pulled in hundreds of talented, curious, often eccentric figures, who thrived on the twin stimulations of Florence and each other.

Many were involved in the visual arts, and the special regard in which Florence is now held, as "the cradle of the Renaissance" and as a peerless storehouse of masterpieces, has much to do with their influence. But the tone of the colony was largely set by writers. If Florence was the home of Botticelli and Donatello, it gave the world Dante and Boccaccio too, and English writers as early as Milton made pilgrimages there. In the mid-nineteenth century the city gained a reputation as a sort of literary Shangri-La: if a writer was looking to escape the chilly north, Florence was the obvious place. There were, of course, many hacks, but also many virtuosi, some of whom one is surprised to find turning up there—Mark Twain, for instance. Certain other writers, such as Henry James and George Eliot, were never part of the colony yet maintained close ties with it, used it in their work, and dropped in whenever possible.

They weren't the only ones to drop in. Florence saw a surge of visitors after the Napoleonic Wars, and the rise of the colony only intensified the trend, since many were lured by the prospect of free-loading at a friend's villa or palazzo for weeks or even months on end. Furthermore, other foreign colonies—German, French, Russian—sprang up alongside the Anglo-American one, adding to Florence's revived internationalism.

The combined effect of all this was to make the small city on the Arno, which for centuries had been something of a backwater, once again a cultural capital of Europe, a place that people talked and dreamed about and found unique fulfillment in. Among restless anglophones in search of beauty and cosmopolitan vibrancy, it was surpassed in popularity only by Paris. And it had one quality that Paris, with its fractious and bloody recent history, didn't: a kind of unblemished, Pre-Raphaelite dewiness. Serene yet invigorating, it presented (or at least seemed to present) a bright, clean surface on which quaint or utopian ideals could be projected. It was, in short, a place of the imagination as much as reality. In *A Room with a View*, Lucy Honeychurch thinks of Florence as "a magic city where people thought and did the most extraordinary things." While Forster probably intends a measure of irony here, he's also being faithful to the romantic fancies of the age in having her perceive it through a golden nimbus. And that nimbus, that aura of enchantment, was to a significant degree a creation of the colony.

In 1908, when *A Room with a View* was published, virtually anyone in the colony, as well as quite a few outside it, could have informed Miss Honeychurch that Janet Ross was the doyenne of the Anglo-Florentines. Distinctly matriarchal, the colony never lacked for domineering women, but the redoubtable Mrs. Ross (thus would Miss Honeychurch have heard her mentioned) stood above the rest, a queen bee among queen bees.

Not that she was a "leader of society" in the rather fatuous conventional sense. Her prestige had other sources. Some of it derived from sheer seniority, for she had (along with her husband, Henry) moved to Florence as early as 1867 and would ultimately spend sixty years there, one of the longest terms of residence on record. She was also an expert on everything local: besides having written several books on Tuscan subjects, she was a consummate fixer, someone who knew how to get things done. (When Twain needed a villa, it was she who found him one.) Above all, her regal status emanated directly from her person. Severely beautiful, with penetrating black eyes and thick, expressive brows, she had a voice, an air, an overall presence that everyone registered as commanding and formidable; even those used to dealing with such natures were often cowed by hers. But if she was, in the words of Sir Kenneth Clark (who lodged with her), "a well-known terrifier," she was equally known for her gregariousness and vivacity, which helped win her a huge cohort of friends.

It was at Poggio Gherardo that one saw her in her element. There were many chances to do so, for almost every Sunday she held an open house, where colonists and native Florentines would mingle with whatever visitors happened to be passing through town. One attraction was the delicious food, another the magnificent view. (As Forster's Mr. Eager, "a member of the residential colony who had made Florence their home," remarks to Miss Honeychurch about Settignano, where Poggio Gherardo is located, "The view thence of Florence is most beautiful—far better than the hackneyed view of Fiesole.") But the main draw was Janet herself, who would sing Tuscan folk songs while strumming her guitar and tell stories of her chockablock past. These weekly performances helped make her a creature of legend.

Haughty, imposing, well connected, and authoritative, Janet Ross easily came off as a kind of sovereign, and the fact that she wielded her power from what Twain termed a "stately castle" only added to the impression. But Poggio Gherardo also pointed up how down-to-earth she was—literally. Not just a house, it was an estate with three small farms, each inhabited by a family of peasants who worked the land under a sharecropping system known as *mezzadria*. Normally, foreigners who acquired such estates would either break them up or hire a manager; for them to run the show themselves—a complex and demanding job—was unheard of. Yet the Rosses did precisely that. Before buying Poggio Gherardo, for almost twenty years they'd largely run another mezzadria estate on behalf of a Florentine friend living in Rome. Or rather, Janet had done so, the less assertive Henry hanging back. This too was most uncommon: estates were nearly always run by a *padrone*, not a *padrona*. But Janet turned out to have a feeling for agriculture, as well as a knack for bossing around *contadini* (peasants). By the time she got to Poggio Gherardo, she was proficient in local farming techniques and the customs of mezzadria, and the estate prospered under her direction. Nor did she issue orders from on high, often pitching in alongside her sharecroppers.

All this was markedly uncolonial. "In contrast with the average foreign resident," Harold Acton remarks of Janet, "her energy and enterprise seemed phenomenal." And where most colonists would have blanched at the mere thought of mingling on a daily basis with grubby contadini, Janet did so avidly. Despite her close association with several beaux mondes, she was the furthest thing from a snob, as much at home with Italian peasants as with British dukes, and generally holding them in greater respect. Her affection and regard were, moreover, warmly reciprocated: many of the sharecroppers at Poggio Gherardo came to love her like family.

With her happy immersion in this timeless world of seeds and plows, Janet's true allegiance was, then, less to Florence than to Tuscany at large, and especially to the rural side of the province; she wasn't so much an Anglo-Florentine as (to coin a term) an Anglo-Tuscan. Today this sounds unremarkable—who doesn't prize the Tuscan countryside? But it wasn't always thus. To return to that set of easily triggered mental snapshots, at one time—say, a century ago—an American or Briton daydreaming about Tuscany would likely have conjured them up in reverse order: the urban ones would have led off the phantasmagoria, and while the mind's eye might have roved out into the landscape, the images would have grown increasingly hazy. For the Tuscan countryside wasn't the Mecca it is now. Certain smaller towns, such as San Gimignano,

were touristed, but most of the hinterland remained terra in-
cognita—it's telling that the 1903 edition of *Baedeker's Central
Italy* mentions only the Casentino Valley as a rural escape. As for the
now widespread idealization of Tuscan rural life and the urge to
take part in it—the belief that pressing one's own olive oil constitutes heaven on earth—these fancies would have struck many people
as absurd if not lunatic.

Janet herself held no such notions and went about her business
matter-of-factly. All the same, she was a sort of accidental pioneer.
Where the vision of bliss pursued by the colony had been about pas-
sive absorption, ours today involves action and effort; we tend to
aspire to a kind of rugged self-reliance. So too for Janet, who took
more pleasure from doing things herself than from having them
done for her. In her participatory enthusiasm, her preference for the
rural, her esteem for the peasantry and its traditions, and the fact
that she wrote about all this—she was the first to do so—she was a
prototypical figure.

What makes her Tuscan career compelling has less to do, though,
with its anticipatory qualities than with its premodern ones. Her life
in the province had a richness and complexity no longer available to
us. Mezzadria having been abolished, we couldn't oversee sharecroppers even if we wanted to, nor could we have the intimate satisfactions (and frustrations) stemming from such an arrangement.
Returning from the fields, we wouldn't find Mark Twain or Bernard
Berenson waiting on our terrace. And, perhaps most regrettably, the
view from that terrace wouldn't be of pristine countryside but of
something perilously like suburbia. Even if we lived farther out of
town, we'd be encroached upon by highways, factories, and electric-
ity pylons. The sad fact is that Tuscany, despite its renown as a bucolic
Eden, has become crowded and rather indiscriminately developed.
In Janet's time it was otherwise: the countryside was unblighted,
and the peasantry worked it in ways that, as she pointed out, differed hardly at all from those described in Virgil's *Georgics*. Nestled
between this ancient rusticity and a slower, more gracious Florence
plied not by buzzing Vespas but clopping horse trams, she lived in
what now seems a lost paradise.

Like the colony, Janet Ross had her limitations. Though intelligent and learned, especially for an autodidact, she was by no means brilliant. She had little imagination or inner life, and she made no towering contribution to humanity. Yet her life was singular. For one thing, it was entirely free of longueurs: her first twenty-five years, spent in England and Egypt, were every bit as packed as her sixty in Florence, not excluding early childhood—she hit the ground crawling, as it were. And her life was equally free of isolation. Nobody has ever been more tightly or continuously woven into the social fabric of their age. Janet knew a staggering number and variety of people, many of them famous and nearly all of them in some way noteworthy. Now we might call her a node or hub, and so she was—but on a grand scale, her spokes radiating across the map. Across time too: the wide span of her years, 1842 to 1927, saw momentous changes of every sort, and to follow Janet's progress is to watch, from her enviable vantage point, the whole panorama slowly unfold.

There is, finally, a special coherence and roundedness to her life. Everything is linked, patterned, of a piece—somewhat like, it's tempting to say, the Tuscan landscape at its best. While her life was by no means utterly charmed—Janet endured her share of struggle, anxiety, and loss—it stands as a heartening example of how much can be crammed into one's allotted days, and of the degree to which the patient cultivation of friendships can improve them.

With her dynamism and adaptability, Janet was largely the architect of her own contentment. But she built on a foundation laid down well before, and was very much the product of her family. Neither wealthy nor terribly prominent, never advancing beyond the lowest rungs of the aristocracy nor achieving stupendous feats, it was a remarkable family nonetheless, and one that, being dominated by women, was tailor-made for a headstrong daughter such as Janet. Beginning with her great-grandmother, the women in the family had built up a set of traits and skills and attitudes, blazed a track of stubborn independence, and gathered round themselves a sort of cumulative milieu. All this she inherited, gratefully conscious of it as something rarer than, and quite superior to, a silver spoon. She then took the legacy and ran with it.

Since she never had a daughter of her own, Janet was unable to sustain the female line that produced her. She did, however, hand off the baton—which in her grip had become a scepter—laterally to her niece, Lina, whom she and Henry had adopted. Spending her formative years at Poggio Gherardo, Lina ended up living much of her life in Florence and other parts of Tuscany, which she wrote about as copiously as her aunt. In her memoirs, she also wrote about Janet, evoking her lioness presence and the bustling yet Elysian atmosphere of Poggio Gherardo, which Lina inherited. Nor did the succession end there, for Lina's daughter, Kinta, had her own lifelong relationship with Tuscany, and wrote about Janet and Poggio Gherardo in her own memoirs.

And so Janet was the preserver of one tradition and the founder of another: having benefited from the women who came before her, she passed their blend of self-reliance and connectedness along to those who followed, together with a taste for things Tuscan. The men also felt the pull of Tuscany, and of the looming matriarch who'd rooted the family there. One great-nephew became a chef and cooked from her recipes, while another spent years researching and writing about her. To this day, Kinta's sons (who include the military historian Antony Beevor) remain invested in both Tuscany and, as they call her, "Aunt Janet," despite having been born too late to know her.

All of which might give the impression of unbroken peace and concord within the family. In truth it was not, of course, without dissension, conflict, and vitriol. Still, the image presented by Janet's family tree is one of uncommon symmetry and continuity. Just as she's a central figure in the history of Anglo-Tuscany, she sits perched in the middle of a coherent series of generations. She might almost be thought of as resembling the hilltop Poggio Gherardo: not the largest or most magnificent of houses, but proud, handsome, solid, and perfectly situated, with the best views in the area.

Poggio Gherardo is reached by means of a long, upward-sloping driveway. So too must its chatelaine be approached—from below, from a temporal distance. Even more than with most people, to understand Janet Ross one needs to step back a bit.

ONE

A Dynasty of Sorts

On February 24, 1847, at 8 Queen Square in Bloomsbury, London, there took place a party whose guests included the novelist William Makepeace Thackeray, the controversial author and feminist Caroline Norton, the illustrator Richard "Dicky" Doyle, the playwright Tom Taylor, and the Whig statesman Lord Lansdowne. Everyone in the group already being acquainted, there was nothing odd about their assembly. Somewhat unusual, however, was the occasion itself, for they'd come to celebrate the birthday of a five-year-old girl, who, allowed to draw up the guest list, had invited only adults—she was the only child present. Thackeray, she would later recall, mischievously gave her an oyster, expecting her to find it vile. "But I turned the tables on him, for I liked it, and insisted, as queen of the day, on having two more of his."

Spirited, brassy, imperious: Janet Duff Gordon at age five was already on course to become the queenly Janet Ross. But even the most precocious child doesn't cultivate her own highbrow coterie, and what this little scene also hints at is the nature of the family that produced her, especially on the distaff side. Thackeray and the rest were friends of her parents, Alexander and Lucie, who in fostering a rapport between their daughter and their friends were extending a tradition established by Lucie's grandmother. Later in life Janet would develop a keen interest in this tradition, and in the women behind it. Her fascination amounted in part to mere genealogical pride, but it was driven by a sense of affinity and even destiny, of her own cornucopian life as the outcome of theirs. The child who so regally took three oysters from Thackeray would grow up to make, or at least insinuate, almost dynastic claims for the three generations behind her.

It all began in Norwich, an East Anglian town that by the mid-eighteenth century had become, in Janet's phrase, "a provincial Athens," distinguished for its intellectual liveliness, as well as its political radicalism and religious nonconformity. Among those nurtured by this ferment was a feisty bluestocking named Susannah Cook, who in 1777 married John Taylor, a wool merchant. As Unitarians, the couple placed a premium on reason and learning, and strove to provide a rigorous education to all seven of their children, including their two girls—"A well-educated young woman may always provide for herself," Susannah declared. They also made sure to include their daughters in the erudite talk that flourished in their parlor, where Susannah held a salon.

The youngest of the Taylor children was Sarah, born in 1793. Like the others, she was schooled from an early age, with an emphasis on languages. She was also vivacious and attractive, her coquettish manner and dark-browed good looks making her a favorite with the local beaux. In 1812 she met John Austin, a law student three years her elder from nearby Ipswich. Though devoid of charm and humor, he was handsome and hailed from a well-to-do Unitarian family. And he had one outstanding quality: a crystalline brilliance of mind that, if one caught him at the right moment, blazed forth in an eloquence so virtuosic as to amaze even those jaded by such displays. This, along with his zeal for the philosophy of law, convinced Sarah that he was marked for greatness.

After two years of courtship, John proposed to Sarah in what is surely one of the least romantic letters of its kind ever written. Among other stipulations, he insisted that they both conduct a sort of premarital due diligence by confessing their worst faults, "a self-examination which may perhaps wound your vanity, but which you must triumphantly encounter before I can dare to hang the fate of my feelings upon the chance of your consistency." Once Sarah presented him with the necessary evidence, he would be able to judge whether she was "in truth that volatile, vain and flirting thing . . . submitting its light and worthless affections to the tampering of every specious coxcomb;—or have really *nerve* enough for the deep-toned, steady, and consistent enthusiasm, upon which both my pride and my tenderness might securely rely."

Astonishingly, Sarah not only passed John's test but accepted his pompous proposal. It was her mission, she'd decided, to help him achieve his destined eminence. Not that she meant only to bask in reflected glory. Inspired by the model of her parents, she expected to be treated as a near equal, one who would scale the heights of knowledge alongside her husband. In this assumption she wasn't entirely deluded, for John valued her brains and craved her cerebral companionship—"I shall desire to talk with you," he informed her, "on subjects which engage my attention." To improve herself as a sounding board, she eagerly tackled the arduous reading list—Hume, Malthus, Adam Smith—that John assigned her. Apparently she did have the "nerve" he demanded of her.

At first John himself seemed to have nerve of a kind. In 1818, after being called to the bar, he was introduced to his hero, Jeremy Bentham, by that point age seventy. Following up, he wrote Bentham to offer himself as a disciple. Bentham, intent on seeing his doctrines promulgated, encouraged John to come join him in London. Together with his chief protégé, James Mill, Bentham had recently moved to Queen Square, which automatically became the central shrine of Utilitarianism. When a flat at 1 Queen Square opened up, John swooped down and rented it.* Soon after, in August 1819, he finally married Sarah and took her to London.

---

*Queen Square no longer exists per se: in the 1880s part of it (including the building where the Austins lived) was torn down, and the rest was renamed Queen Anne's Gate.

Immediately made welcome by Bentham, John spent long hours listening to the old sage expound on his "Panopticon" prison design and other ideas while doing gymnastic exercises in his specially adapted coach house; we are to picture the two men discriminating fine points of law, politics, and philosophy as they balance on bars and swing on a trapeze, Bentham's long white hair sailing out behind him. (In portraits, he bears a resemblance to Benjamin Franklin.) Often joining them were James Mill and his wildly precocious son John, then thirteen. In his education, John Stuart Mill was force-fed by his father like a foie gras goose, and John Austin was soon enlisted to help fatten him up; as John Stuart Mill recalls in his autobiography, "Mr. John Austin . . . kindly allowed me to read Roman law with him." For her part, Sarah taught German to the teenage genius, who, unhappy at home, took to her with affection and began referring to her as "Mütterlein" (Little Mother).

This tight little band of Utilitarians was supplemented by visiting acolytes, such as the banker and classical historian George Grote, who, along with his wife, often went to Queen Square to drink from the source. The Grotes and the Austins became fast friends, and Sarah, who'd also won the fondness and admiration of Bentham, was inspired by so much intelligent company to start a salon of her own. In addition to Bentham, the Mills, and the Grotes, regular attendees included the poet Samuel Rogers, the cleric and celebrated wit Sydney Smith, the art historian Anna Jameson, and the future historian Thomas Babington Macaulay, then barely twenty. As Janet puts it, with only minor hyperbole, "Though the Austins were poor, the learning and glowing eloquence of Mr. Austin, and the talents and beauty of his wife, made their house a resort of the most remarkable and cultivated people of that time."

Established in the heart of intellectual London, the Austins seemed to be off to a smashing start, and in the summer of 1821 their luck was crowned by the birth of a daughter, Lucie, by common consent a radiant child; on the surface, all prospects glowed. Underneath, however, ran darker currents, for John was turning out to be a deeply troubled man. Depressive by nature, he was increasingly irascible, solitary, and, most worrisome of all, incapable of sustained work. To become a barrister was out of the question, but even the incandescent legal writing expected of him failed to materialize. Endlessly vacillating and hair-splitting, he lost himself in pointless perfectionism, and by 1824 he'd completed only one essay, on the law of primogeniture.

In 1827 there arose a golden opportunity for him to redeem himself. Motivated by Benthamite ideals, James Mill and others had founded London University (later renamed University College London), and John was invited to be its first Professor of Jurisprudence. Since the school wasn't slated to open till the following year, he decided to spend the interval studying German and Roman law in Bonn, where he and Sarah consorted with the likes of August von Schlegel. After their return John dithered and postponed but finally made his professorial debut in 1829. It was not a success. According to the diarist Henry Crabb Robinson, who sat in on the class, the students "could not attend to the matter of his lecture from anxiety for the lecturer." John's lectures had all the wooden prolixity of his marriage proposal, and most of his thirty-odd students (though not the loyal John Stuart Mill) quickly fled. The fiasco dragged on till 1832, when he at last resigned.

Their savings depleted, the Austins had by that point moved to a cheaper flat near Regent's Park. While John felt the move as a wrenching Edenic expulsion, it did no harm to Sarah's social connections, which in fact multiplied, Thomas and Jane Carlyle being among those added to her circle. But John's gloomy fecklessness greatly distressed her. Taking action, she somehow persuaded John Murray to publish a book of her husband's university lectures. Graced with the scintillating title *The Province of Jurisprudence Determined*, it went precisely nowhere. (Lord Melbourne declared it the dullest book he'd ever read.) Then John managed to squander another opportunity: appointed to the prestigious Criminal Law Commission, he quarreled with his fellow commissioners and soon resigned. With virtually no income coming in, the Austins were forced to move again, to even cheaper lodgings in unfashionable Bayswater. The following year they were priced out of England altogether, taking refuge across the Channel in Boulogne,* where they'd spent part of the previous two summers.

Facing up to John's inadequacy, Sarah resigned herself to becoming, as she phrased it, "the man of business in our firm." Her mother's insistence on female education as a safety net, and especially her stress on languages, proved to be farsighted. Sarah had already begun trying her own hand at writing—her first essay was on the mathematician and explorer Carsten Niebuhr—and now she started to translate as well. Her initial renderings were from the French, including a series of Stendhal's letters for *London Magazine*. (Not knowing her identity, Stendhal sent a thank-you note addressed to "Mister Translator.") Her forte, however, was German, from shorter pieces by Goethe—"I hear the fine silver music of Goethe sound through *your* voice, through your heart," Carlyle effused—to Leopold von Ranke's multivolume *History of the Reformation in Germany* and other doorstoppers.

It was, ironically, through her monkish work as a translator that Sarah came to have an affair of sorts. In 1832 she translated a book under the title *Tour in England, Ireland and France*. Its author, Prince Hermann Pückler-Muskau, was one of the gaudiest erotic swordsmen of his day, a kind of Prussian Casanova. Having run up massive debts, he proposed to his wife that they divorce so he could marry a richer woman and bail out their estate in Silesia. She agreed, and for two years the prince stalked heiresses—mostly in England, which he considered prime hunting ground—before returning home brideless. He salvaged a victory, however, by publishing a book of letters to his ex-wife detailing his futile quest. Boosted by a rave review from Goethe, the book became a bestseller and put the prince in the black. Nor was he, despite his matrimonial failures, at all unpopular with women; smooth, flamboyant, and studiously Byronic, he could (and did) boast of a string of conquests across Europe.

---

*Though these things are difficult to gauge, life in England seems to have been, on average, more expensive than on the Continent through the nineteenth century and well into the twentieth.

Now he set out to add Sarah Austin to the list. A master of the billet-doux, he enticed his English translator—whom he'd never met—into a heavy-breathing correspondence, and before long he had Sarah writing frenzied declarations like this: "I lay entire claim to you, swear I will tear out the eyes of any man or woman who disputes my claim, and will cause you to disavow, disclaim, and 'utterly abjure and renounce' all translators but myself." Over the next few years she and the prince traded hundreds of torrid letters proclaiming their passion, many of them carried, for secrecy, in the diplomatic pouch of the Prussian ambassador. At one point the prince even asked Sarah to mail him some of her pubic hair, just as, he told her, Byron's lover Teresa Guiccioli had once done. (She refused.)

Even though the lovers never once laid eyes on each other during their long postal liaison—it was only years later, in Berlin, that an anticlimactic meeting took place—Sarah's romance with Pückler-Muskau, which John seems never to have suspected, brought to the surface an emotional strain in her nature, one that she saw as fundamentally un-English. "In vivacity, passion and energy I am very little like an Englishwoman," she told the prince. "I ought to have been the wife of a *Norseman*, a sea king—or else of an Arab chief . . . Anything wild and adventurous, and here I am, ye Gods, a Professorin!!! of all tame animals." While she would never get to act on her more exotic yearnings, the next phase of her life was largely played out against a shifting foreign backdrop. Throughout this period, she showed herself to be a woman of great resourcefulness, making the most of every place she went and knitting together a Continental network of friends that would embrace her daughter and granddaughter in turn.

First came Malta. The island had been simmering with discontent, and in 1836 John, along with one of his former students, was sent as a royal commissioner to investigate native grievances. For once he didn't make a hash of things, drawing up a set of policy proposals that showed sympathy for the Maltese without ceding too much British control. Sarah, meanwhile, got to test out some of the educational theories that had come to obsess her—she'd been corresponding with William Gladstone and others about them—by opening ten new village schools, which flourished.

After John was recalled to London in 1838, he found himself widely praised for his work as a commissioner. But when certain of his recommendations were attacked in Parliament, he relapsed into morose lethargy, and the Austins, their meager income coming almost entirely from Sarah's translations, were forced back to the Continent. This time they stayed for almost seven years. The first two were spent mostly in Dresden, then known as "Florence on the Elbe," which Sarah found beautiful and civilized. Ultimately, though, the city was too small for her, while Berlin, where she and John spent the following winter, she found abrasive. So in 1843 the Austins moved to Paris. Here Sarah came into her own, accumulating a large circle of friends that included Alexis de Tocqueville, the sociologist Auguste Comte, the poets Alfred de Vigny and Alphonse de Lamartine, and the hostess Madame Récamier. With two others she became particularly close: the philosopher-statesman Jules Barthélemy Saint-Hilaire, rumored to be an illegitimate son of Napoleon, and François Guizot, whom she'd met in London when he was the French ambassador and who'd since become foreign minister. At the weekly salon she instituted, these French luminaries mingled with foreign residents and visitors; as Saint-Hilaire put it, "The *salon* of Mrs. Austin was a centre where France, England, Germany, and Italy met, and learned to know and appreciate each other." He was also impressed by Sarah's skill at turning away interlopers, who were "eliminated without harshness . . . I have seen executions of this kind done with perfect tact."

The Austins' sojourn in Paris abruptly ended with the revolution of 1848. Once fairly radical in their politics, they'd become, in the usual way, more conservative, and they were appalled at the triumph of—as they saw it—anarchy. They also had a personal reason to deplore the change of regime, for Guizot, who'd become prime minister the previous year, was forced into exile in England. The Austins followed. This time they prudently avoided ruinous London, instead buying a cottage in Weybridge, Surrey. Tucked into their sleepy native countryside, they finally came to rest. For her distinguished work as a translator, Sarah was granted a civil-list pension of £100 per year, which allowed her and John to breathe more easily. And they found a new peace with each other, enjoying one of those late halcyon periods that couples are sometimes granted after decades of strain and strife.

In 1859 John died of a respiratory infection, and Sarah assumed the full panoply of Victorian mourning. Like Victoria herself after Albert's demise, she had John's study frozen in time—not a book was to be shifted, not a pen used. She also took on the role of flame-keeping literary widow, even though there wasn't much of a flame to keep. The great disappointment of her life, as she told Guizot, had been John's "*resolute* neglect or suppression of the talents committed to his care." But with John no longer around to sabotage himself, she could ripen the fruits of those talents and bring them to market. In 1863 she added to *The Province of Jurisprudence Determined* a selection of John's notes and later essays to form the three-volume *Lectures on Jurisprudence*. Her preface to the book concludes by expressing the hope that "the benefits which [John] would have conferred on his country and on mankind" would be posthumously recognized. It seemed a pathetic last illusion, but that, remarkably, is just what happened. Where *Province* had sunk like a stone, *Lectures on Jurisprudence* was well received, in part because John Stuart Mill wrote a long, appreciative review of it. Eventually John Austin came to be regarded as a seminal figure in the history of jurisprudence—the "Austinian theory of law" is studied to this day.

Throughout her remaining years—she died in 1867—Sarah continued to revere John and his genius. "The rise of my husband's reputation and authority," she wrote to a friend, "is the one bright spot of my dark life." She seemed to put little stock in her own achievements. Yet she was surely the better writer of the two (not that John's excruciatingly costive style posed much competition) and probably broader in her learning. Under different circumstances she might have become an English Madame de Staël, a lionized woman of letters. Mill, Saint-Hilaire, and others felt she had unplumbed potential, and she herself once referred to "voluntary abnegations of what I might have attained." Hers was, perhaps, a life of thwarted possibilities. But it was also one rich in books, languages, international experience, and the love and admiration of many friends. And however unfortunate in marriage, in motherhood Sarah struck lucky. Though she had only one child to her own mother's seven, that one was exceptional. Absorbing the best lessons Sarah had to offer, Lucie would also avoid her worst mistakes, and would find for herself both the public happiness her mother had known and the domestic variety she hadn't. Then she was forced to renounce it all and find a wholly different, death-haunted fulfillment in exile.

━━═✣═━━

Her life was unusual from the start. Many children grow up playing in gardens, but not normally in Jeremy Bentham's, where, according to Janet, "[the] flower-beds were intersected by threads and tapes to represent the passages of a panopticon prison." The image might stand for Lucie's entire childhood, which was in certain ways enviable but also sharply circumscribed—all those threads and tapes—and blighted by solitude. Like Sarah's, it was enhanced from an early age by unrestricted contact with intelligent adults. Yet the closest thing she had to a peer was John Stuart Mill, fifteen years her senior. (Nowhere does the serious Mill appear more attractive than in his gay, spontaneous romping with the Austins' small daughter—as a teenager, he wasn't just a babysitter but a playmate to Lucie.)

Whatever the detrimental effects of her upbringing, ignorance and provincialism were not among them. By the time the Austins returned from Germany in 1828, Lucie, now seven, spoke the language fluently and had been, in Janet's words, "transformed into a little German maiden with long braids down her back." This Teutonicism was reinforced by her mother's romance with Pückler-Muskau, into which she was drawn as a sort of innocent conspirator; Lucie herself exchanged letters with the prince, and Sarah boasted to him that Lucie was "more Deutsch than English." But Sarah was also intent on broadening her daughter. While Sarah expressed her-self "quite willing to forego all the feminine parts of her education" (Lucie never learned to draw, sew, or play an instrument), she felt as strongly as her own mother about languages, and personally taught the girl French and Latin. When even this seemed insufficient, she enrolled Lucie, age ten, at a Hampstead boys' school. Despite being the only girl there, she flourished, learning math, philosophy, an-cient history, and Greek; soon she was reading the *Odyssey* in the original.

That Lucie was not only an intelligent child but one of rare ma-turity is clear from the company she kept during her two summer stays in Boulogne. During the first, when she was twelve, she man-aged to strike up a friendship with one of the great poets of the age, Heinrich Heine, whom she and Sarah met at their table d'hôte. "He heard me speak German to my mother," Lucie later recalled, "and soon began to talk to me, and then said, 'When you go back to En-gland, you can tell your friends that you have seen Heinrich Heine.' I replied, 'And who is Heinrich Heine?' He laughed heartily, and took no offence at my ignorance." She and Heine often lingered together on the pier, where he told her "stories in which fishes, mer-maids, water-sprites, and a very funny old French fiddler with a poodle . . . were all mixed up in the most fanciful manner."

The following summer Lucie was befriended by several fisher-men's families, whom she described to her friend Alice Spring-Rice (by then she'd had the chance to make a few friends her own age) with a sophistication and dry wit far beyond her years. "The men are null except at sea," she wrote in one letter. "They bring home their fish, the wives go down to the boat, each takes her husband's share on her back in a basket, trots off to market and sells it, never giving her husband any account of the money: the wife furnishes the house, clothes her husband, children and self, so the husband has nothing to spend at the alehouse and is entirely under the do-minion of his . . . wife, and a very excellent thing for him too." When the Austins moved to Boulogne in 1835, Lucie resumed and then deepened her intimacy with these families. On her departure, they gathered on the pier to bid her farewell—her parting image was of a red hat slowly waved by a tearful fisherman. Back in London, she reminisced—this time to another friend, Janet Shuttleworth—about going to "the *matelot* [sailor] balls and to their houses, mending their nets, playing with their children, learning their songs and their manner of fishing and navigating, and speaking their *patois* to perfection." Her gift for being accepted into rustic traditional cultures would later stand her in good stead when she found herself in places more alien than Boulogne.

Lucie's adaptive skills might have come in handy at her parents' next destination, Malta, but they considered the island too hot and insalubrious to risk bringing her along. Instead, she was sent to a London boarding school, spending her vacations in Hastings with Janet Shuttleworth's family, which was to be intertwined with her own down the generations. Janet Shuttleworth's younger stepsister, Marianne North, was especially in awe of Lucie, and later wrote of her mesmerizing "grand eyes and deep-toned voice." Other accounts from the period testify to her poise, presence, and ripening beauty. Where Sarah had only a standard-issue, rosy-cheeked prettiness, Lucie's features bewitchingly combined classical elegance with romantic volatility—her almost translucent skin, set off by her dark hair and eyes, would flush dramatically when her feelings were inflamed.

In short, she'd become eminently marriageable, and on returning from Malta her parents wasted no time in launching her. That summer, after being presented to Queen Victoria—who, only two years older than Lucie, had just been crowned—she came out for her first London "season." The following winter, at the behest of her cousin Henry Reeve,* she was invited to a ball thrown by Lord Lansdowne. It was a pivotal evening, for she met two people who would play leading roles in her life. One was Caroline Norton, whose poems had earned her the sobriquet "the female Byron" and whose private life was no less stormy or gossip-generating than his. Three

---

*Born in Norwich, Reeve (1813–95) was a friend of Lord Lansdowne's and moved in some of the same circles as the Austins, counting among his acquaintances Liszt, Balzac, and Tocqueville, whose *De la démocratie en Amérique* he was the first to translate into English. He later became the editor of the *Edinburgh Review*.

years earlier, her jealous husband, convinced that her friendship with the prime minister, Lord Melbourne, had crossed over into adultery, had sued Melbourne for "alienating her affections." Even though Melbourne won the case, Norton had been blackballed, and was only now making her first forays back into society, where she was still mostly persona non grata. Under these punitive circumstances, Lucie's youth, open-mindedness, and unconventionality held a strong appeal for the thirty-year-old Norton, and the two quickly became best friends.

Lucie's other encounter was with a young baronet, Sir Alexander Cornewall Duff Gordon, with whom she danced repeatedly. Ten years her senior, he came from a modestly aristocratic background. His mother, Caroline, was the daughter of Sir George Cornewall, an MP for Herefordshire. On the paternal side, his family, largely Scottish, had grown prosperous in the eighteenth century as wine merchants in southern Spain, where they owned a sherry bodega. More recently, however, their fortunes had declined. Alexander's father, Sir William Duff Gordon, had also been an MP but had died young and left heavy debts. His widow had struggled to maintain her four children at the proper level, and to help out Alexander had taken a job at the Treasury immediately after Eton. Unlike many down-at-heel aristocrats, he was unresentful at actually having to work for a living. This good humor was, in fact, perhaps his outstanding quality; despite being tall, handsome, and clever, he had no young-buck arrogance about him, and was instead, by common consent, kind, humble, and affable to a fault. He even shared the Austin fondness for all things German, and had already produced several translations.

Lucie and Alexander fell for each other at once and were engaged the following summer. In May 1840, a month before Lucie turned nineteen, they were married. After a honeymoon in Germany, they set up home at 8 Queen Square, Bloomsbury, and there, some twenty months later, their first child, Janet Anne, was born.

TWO

Successions

O nly a short time ago," writes Janet in her preface to *The Fourth Generation*, published in 1912, "the Miss Berrys were mentioned, and Mr. Berenson, who was sitting next to me, exclaimed: 'How I should like to have known those two dear old ladies.' When I said: 'Well, here is someone who knew them well,' he looked astonished, and replied '*You*, impossible.'" Mary and Agnes Berry were a pair of spinsters known for their connection to the bachelor man of letters Horace Walpole, who in the 1780s took them under his wing and began referring to them as his "twin wives." Though not half as spicy as it sounds, the arrangement set tongues wagging, and the Miss Berrys became minor celebrities of the late eighteenth and early nineteenth centuries. Hence the astonishment of Bernard Berenson: by the second decade of the twentieth century, it seemed hardly more conceivable that one's neighbor had known the Miss Berrys than that she'd known Mozart or Louis XVI. Yet Janet as a child had several times sipped tea with the sisters, who both lived to almost ninety. The fact seemed to her emblematic: "I often feel," she continues, "as though I had a dual personality, at times quite old, at others many years younger than I really am."

It is said of some people that they were born old, possessed of a wisdom or seriousness beyond their years. While this can't be said of Janet, who had her normal share of juvenility, she did slip with remarkable ease into the world at the adult level. Where Lucie had benefited but also suffered from being dropped into a milieu of bookish grown-ups, Janet thrived on her early immersion. This was in part because of her less sensitive nature: sturdy, uncomplicated, and extroverted, she was the ideal child for Providence to set down in such circumstances. But the circumstances were also more stimulating this time around. Janet's parents were busily making a life for themselves, one that harmonized the venerable past with the exciting present. The frame was crowded, the picture teeming with detail, and the Duff Gordons' alert, pleasure-loving daughter was there to take it all in.

Strangely, Janet nowhere explains how the Duff Gordons ended up at Queen Square—whether they just happened to move there or made a point of doing so. The address must have had some resonance for Lucie, who'd come full circle after a life of nomadic displacements. Janet, meanwhile, took interest even as a child in the facts that her grandparents had lived only a few doors away, that her mother had been born there, and that Bentham, the Mills, and others had turned Queen Square into a sort of philosophical commune.

Like Sarah, Lucie swiftly established a salon. But where the Austins' had been prim and earnest, the Duff Gordons' was rollicking and almost bohemian, with Lucie flitting about in flamboyantly gypsylike or masculine clothes and smoking cigars with the men. And where John had retreated into solitary brooding, Alexander was every bit as outgoing as his wife. It was, in fact, the synergetic magnetism of the Duff Gordons that most drew people. Though they had little money or position, their physical beauty, warmth, wit, high spirits—Alexander brought out Lucie's playful side— and obvious love for each other made them one of London's golden young couples.

Not that the old guard was unwelcome. Sydney Smith dispensed his champagne repartee in Lucie's drawing room as he once had in

Sarah's, and the Grotes, the Carlyles, Macaulay, John Stuart Mill, and Samuel Rogers put in appearances. But new friends set the tone, none more so than Caroline Norton, whose presence was enough to repel prigs and attract their opposites. Charles Dickens sometimes showed up, full of contagious mirth, and a variety of men from the worlds of theater and journalism—Dicky Doyle, Tom Taylor, the *Times* editor Mowbray Morris, and C. J. Bayley, one of that paper's liveliest contributors—joined in the badinage. "Laughter was loud and long," Janet recalls, "when Bayley, Tom Taylor, Mowbray Morris and my father were together."

Another cluster of friends originated at Trinity College, Cambridge in the late 1820s and bore a rough similarity to the so-called Brideshead generation at Oxford a century later. Two went on to major careers, namely Thackeray and Alfred Tennyson. As his presence at Janet's fifth birthday party suggests, Thackeray was on intimate terms with the family.* As for Tennyson, he claimed to have been thinking of Lucie when he wrote his long poem *The Princess* and seems to have had a crush on her: "I never loved a dear gazelle but some damned brute—that's you, Gordon—had married her first," he sighed to Alexander. A third ex-Trinity writer was Richard Monckton Milnes, who wrote underwhelming poetry but was otherwise a distinguished man of letters.

The last two of the group followed similar postgraduate trajectories. Eliot Warburton, an Irishman, gave up his career as a barrister and burst onto the literary scene in 1844 with an account of his travels in the Middle East, *The Crescent and the Cross*, which became a bestseller. In the same year, Alexander Kinglake, who'd also dabbled in the law, brought out the equally popular *Eothen*, an account

---

*Besides his hospitality, Thackeray had reason to be thankful for Alexander's diplomatic equanimity, which may have saved him from injury and even death. In June 1847 the novelist became embroiled in a trivial but heated quarrel with Dickens's friend John Forster. Thackeray challenged Forster to a duel, at which Alexander was to serve as Thackeray's second and Dickens as Forster's. Luckily, Alexander managed to persuade both men to put away their muskets. "Nothing could be more frank, sensible, or gentlemanly in the best sense, than Gordon's behaviour through the whole affair," commented Dickens, who afterward arranged a reconciliation dinner for the two antagonists and their seconds.

of the eighteen months he'd spent knocking around the Ottoman Empire. Whereas *The Crescent and the Cross* is now forgotten, *Eothen* is widely held to be the finest travel book of its time, shot through with a wry humor that has proven perennially fresh. In person, Kinglake was shy but engaging—"delicious, sweet . . . as urbane and deferential as Emerson" was how Henry James described him. As a confirmed bachelor, he was much in circulation, but the Duff Gordons were among his closest friends, and he became almost a member of the family.

The Duff Gordons' social web extended well beyond the English-speaking world. While they spent less time than the Austins on the Continent, they were equally in touch with it, in part through their own work as translators. Lucie, having grown up around a mother always engaged in anglicizing some huge tome, picked up translation the way most girls did needlepoint. In 1844, at twenty-two, she struck gold with a translation of Wilhelm Meinhold's *The Amber Witch*. Even though the novel, which concerns a woman wrongly accused of witchcraft during the Thirty Years' War, turned out to be a hoax—Meinhold claimed to have stumbled on an old manuscript containing the story, which he in fact made up—Lucie's translation was immensely popular, and Meinhold was so taken with it that he dedicated his next book to her.

There followed more translations, from both German and French. Several of these Lucie did with Alexander, including Ranke's massive *Memoirs of the House of Brandenburg*—bringing the prolific German historian over into English was now a family business. The Duff Gordons got to know, and often to host, many of the writers they translated, and other accomplished Europeans as well; as Janet puts it, with her usual proud exaggeration, "every foreigner of talent and renown looked upon the Duff Gordon house as a centre of interest."

These, then, were some of the figures who populated the lives of Lucie and Alexander in 1840s London. As her birthday guest list illustrates, the same figures substantially made up the background of Janet's own existence.

Several took an interest in her education, not always with conspicuous success. Though bright, she displayed none of the eagerness to learn that her mother and grandmother had shown. Not even the leading novelist of the age could sell her on the joys of reading: Dickens, she recalls, "pretended to be terribly shocked at my resolute determination not to learn my letters. The truth was that my nurse read fairy tales aloud to me, and it was not till after she married and left us that I began to read, at six years old. Dickens then gave me what he called 'one of the most delightful of books,' the 'Seven Champions of Christendom'" (a chivalric tale by the Elizabethan writer Richard Johnson). Math also eluded her. One of her parents' acquaintances was Charles Babbage, inventor of the difference engine, which is now recognized as the world's first computer. Taken by Babbage to see the machine, Janet "begged hard that he would give it to me" so that she wouldn't have to do her sums.

Along with a resistance to education, Janet displayed, from an early age, a tendency toward cheekiness and skepticism—she was never one to take eminence on faith. August men of letters, with their swollen amour propre, often ran afoul of the Duff Gordons' undeferential young daughter. During a visit to Tennyson on the Isle of Wight, "the great poet's shoe-string came untied, and imperiously pointing to his foot, he said: 'Janet, tie my shoe.' I resented so imperative a command, besides which the strings were extremely dirty, so rudely enough I answered: 'No; tie your own shoe. Papa says that men should wait on women, not women on men.' . . . He afterwards told my father that I was a clever girl, but extremely badly brought up." On another occasion, Carlyle, frustrated at being unable to outflank Lucie in an argument on German literature, called her a windbag, at which point Janet angrily jumped in to reprove him: "My papa says men should be civil to women."

Such friction was, however, more the exception than the norm, and for the most part Janet adored her family's friends. Caroline Norton, whose "glorious beauty and deep rich voice had an extraordinary fascination for me even as a baby," was so steadily present in her life that she became known as Aunt Carrie, while Kinglake was an honorary uncle. Thackeray, a talented draftsman, would sometimes dandle her while drawing: "I still possess a sketch he made for the frontispiece of *Pendennis* while I was sitting on his knee." As for Samuel Rogers, "My father and mother often went to [his] Sunday morning breakfasts . . . and he always asked that his 'baby-love,' as he called me, should be brought later for dessert. A great treat it was, for the old poet kept a bunch of grapes in the sideboard, which I ate perched on a chair . . . by his side."* And with C. J. Bayley, who in 1846 became the Duff Gordons' lodger, she carried on as boisterously as Lucie once had with John Stuart Mill—the journalist was, Janet writes, her "playfellow and slave."

Another lodger-playfellow was from a very different walk of life. Twelve-year-old Hassan el-Bakkeet had been brought by missionaries from his native Nubia to England. He'd gone into service with a friend of Sarah's, but when his eyes began to fail he was heartlessly fired and turned out on the street. The Duff Gordons, returning home one night from a party chez Dickens, found him on their doorstep—it seems that Hassan had met Lucie once or twice and sensed her softheartedness. In a series of scenes straight out of a Dickens novel, Hassan was brought indoors, taken to an oculist who both fixed his eyes and offered him a job, and, after tearfully begging to remain with the Duff Gordons instead, was more or less adopted by the family, though he was given nominal footman's duties.

To Janet, who dubbed him Hatty, he became a beloved older brother—*The Fourth Generation* includes a drawing by Caroline Norton of him reading to Janet, who sits smiling in his lap. Most of the Duff Gordons' friends treated him well, but Janet recalls a visiting American writer, a certain "Mr. Hilliard,"† who was "shocked at seeing me in Hatty's arms." When the man "asked my mother how

---

*Rogers's weekly breakfasts were a long-running institution, and highly popular despite his sharp tongue and alarmingly cadaverous appearance. "How can you go and dine with Rogers in this hot weather?" ran one quip. "He has been dead these thirty-two years and cannot be expected to keep." (Quoted in Althea Hayter's *A Sultry Month: Scenes of London Literary Life in 1846*.)

†Almost certainly a misspelling of the last name of George Stillman Hillard (1808–79), a Boston lawyer and author. If it was indeed Hillard, his bigotry toward Hatty was somewhat ironic, given that his legal partner was Charles Sumner, one of the foremost American defenders of black rights.

she could let a negro touch her child," Lucie "called us to her, and kissed me first and Hatty afterward."

Dote on Hatty though they might, the Duff Gordons were powerless to protect him from the English climate. In March 1849 Lucie gave birth to a son, Maurice. Wanting a break from London, she decided to take the newborn, along with Janet and Hatty, to stay with her parents at Nutfield Cottage, their home in Weybridge. The cottage was clammy and cold, and Hatty caught bronchitis. "The doctor ordered leeches to be applied to his chest," Janet writes, "and my mother told the maid how to put them on. She answered with a toss of her head: 'Lawks, my lady, I could not touch either of 'em.' I can see now the look of pitying scorn with which my mother turned from the girl, who had but lately entered our service, which softened into deep affection as she bent over Hatty, and with her white hands placed the leeches on his black chest." Though he was brought back to London, his condition only worsened. "He died in my father's arms on Christmas Day, from congestion of the lungs, and left a great void, particularly in my young life."

By then Lucie too had developed a bad cough. She shook it off, but not for long. Previously in good health, she fell more and more under the shadow of pulmonary illness. When the bustle of London became too much for her, she again retreated with the children to Nutfield Cottage, despite its permanent damp. In the winter of 1851 the cottage struck again, dealing Lucie a case of severe bronchitis. At last she recognized the need to escape her parents' death-trap, and in the spring of 1851 she and Alexander rented a ramshackle former inn outside Esher, a few miles east of Weybridge. Belvedere House, it was called, but their friends christened it the Gordon Arms, and Lucie and Alexander, who would never have been so pompous as to bestow such a name, played along. Extending the joke, Dicky Doyle devised a mock coat of arms that featured, among its heraldic emblems, a quill, a keg of ale—there was always one on tap—and a fistful of cigars, this last alluding to Lucie's habit of puffing away on horseback.

Horses became, in fact, a big part of family life, for the property included a stable. Nobody was more pleased than Janet, who was "advanced to the dignity of a pony." (She named it Eothen, after the family nickname for Kinglake.) Country life held other attractions for her as well. Something of a tomboy, she was happy to trade stuffy town-house parlors for open fields and the nearby River Mole, where she boated, fished, and sicced her bull terrier on water rats. Complementing these Tom Sawyerish adventures were more civilized boating parties organized by her parents; during one, she recalls, "the wine had been hung over the side of the boat to cool, and a bottle had somehow slipped out of the string, so my father told the ladies to go away, stripped, and dived in to recover it."

Whether to go boating and riding or simply to take a break from city life, friends constantly came to stay at the Gordon Arms. Thackeray liked to herald his arrival with a bit of light verse:

> *A nice leg of mutton, my Lucie,*
> *I pray thee have it ready at three;*
> *Have it smoking and tender and juicy,*
> *And what better meat can there be?*

He goes on to fantasize about how he will lazily "smoke my canaster, / and tipple my ale in the shade."

Mainly a pleasure oasis, the house also served as an infirmary, as when the painter Henry Phillips, after breaking his kneecap, was brought there to convalesce. "A suspension lamp was taken down," Janet recollects, "and to the hook was hung a canvas, on which Phillips, lying on his back, painted a portrait of my mother." On another occasion, the Pre-Raphaelite painter John Everett Millais caught a cold while on the Mole and spent a week recuperating at the Gordon Arms.

Several of the Duff Gordons' friends also lived in the area, or were soon to arrive. Macaulay, who was at nearby Ditton Marsh, "often dropped in for a talk with my mother. They cordially agreed in admiring Miss Austen's novels, and talked about the personages in them as though they had been living friends and acquaintances." By this point Macaulay was a formidable figure in both literature and politics, and about to be elevated to the peerage. Yet he had a way with children. "The wonderful thing about him was the perfect footing of equality on which he seemed to place whomever he was talking to. To me, a young girl, he would say, 'Don't you remember?' as if I had one-tenth of the information he possessed in his little finger!" Unlike some of her parents' other logorrheic friends, he enchanted rather than bored Janet with his torrents of eloquence. "As soon as I heard his voice I installed myself by his knee and imperiously said: 'Now talk.' I rather suspect my mother might occasionally have liked to give a counter-order, for she also talked much and well; but Macaulay was impossible to stop once launched."

She also made new friends, notably among the next-door neighbors. The garden of the Gordon Arms abutted the grounds of Claremont, a large estate. In 1817 it had been the scene of significant tragedy, when Princess Charlotte, daughter of and heir apparent to King George IV, gave birth to a stillborn child and then died. (The ensuing nationwide mourning has been compared to that for the Princess of Wales a hundred and eighty years later.) With the succession to the throne in jeopardy, Charlotte's bachelor uncles scrambled to find brides and produce a new heir—a mating program that eventually yielded Queen Victoria. Despite Claremont's sad associations, Victoria was fond of the house, and when, in 1848, the toppled King Louis-Philippe of France washed up in England with Queen Marie-Amélie and their extended family, she had the lot of them installed there.

By the time the Duff Gordons arrived on the scene Louis-Philippe had died, but his family remained. The Duff Gordons soon became convivial with their new neighbors, especially Janet, who found among them two playmates roughly her own age: the Comte de Paris, whose supporters had once attempted to establish him as King Louis-Philippe II, and the Prince de Condé, son of the Duc d'Aumale. She was to spend a large part of her childhood with these deposed members of the Orléans clan, charging around on horseback.

Rather too large a part, from her parents' point of view. Alexander and Lucie, troubled that Janet (by her own account) "knew little else but how to saddle a horse and how to ride him," decided that her education needed stiffening. In 1852 they got her a German governess, to little effect. An environment more conducive to learning clearly being called for, Janet was sent with the governess to her hometown, Dresden, where for fifteen months she attended a local school. In addition to picking up excellent German, she began to acquire the sense of matrilineal pride that would later loom so large: "For the first time, I learned that my grandmother was known beyond the precincts of Weybridge and Esher. 'Die Austin,' as they called her in Dresden, was remembered by many, including the King and Queen, who asked me to tea." Still, she was relieved when her parents deemed her educated enough to come home.

Though she eagerly resumed her country pursuits at Esher, she was by no means cut off from, or unresponsive to, the riches of London. Her parents weren't in the best position to expose her to them, Lucie because of her reluctance to venture into town, Alexander because he was swamped with work. (Having shone at the Treasury, he became private secretary to the Chancellor of the Exchequer and then, in 1856, a commissioner for Inland Revenue, the British equivalent of the IRS.) But their friends filled the gap. Lord Lansdowne took Janet to a Handel festival at the Crystal Palace and to witness the opening of Parliament by the queen, while Kinglake took her to watch the proceedings at the House of Commons. The debates being mostly "carried on by chorus and anti-chorus, such as 'Hear! Hear!' in approval, or 'Hear! Hear! Hear!' in derision," she was aghast at what she considered "behaviour of the silliest nursery type" and indignantly asked Kinglake why he'd brought her to "such a childish place."

More to her taste was Little Holland House, where George Frederic Watts lived, worked, and hosted a kaleidoscopic salon. One of the top English painters of the age, Watts was an old friend of her paternal grandmother, the dowager Lady Duff Gordon, but had only recently, after returning from a long stay in Italy, gotten to know the rest of the family. Janet, who called him "Signor" (presumably because of his Italian connection), was enraptured by Watts. "Many hours did I spend sitting in his studio, watching those great pictures grow under his hand. One day a young violinist (I believe it was Joachim as a lad) came to play to 'Signor,' who loved music. I was sitting on the floor listening intently, when 'Signor' put his hand on my shoulder and said: 'Sit still, Janet, don't move for a few minutes.'" He then did a sketch of her. The violinist in question must have been Joseph Joachim, a protégé of Mendelssohn who composed and conducted as well. To be drawn by a portraitist of Watts's caliber while enjoying a private concert by a musician of Joachim's is not the sort of experience granted to every child.

In 1857 Lucie and Alexander were seized with another fit of concern over Janet's education and took her to Paris for three months. Their closest friend in the city was Saint-Hilaire, who, appalled at Janet's "methodless way of learning a language," undertook to improve her French, which rapidly became good enough for her to sit in on lectures at the Sorbonne. For her part, Lucie caught up with Alfred de Vigny and other old acquaintances. One of these, however, she pointedly avoided. During his London exile in the mid-1840s, Louis-Napoléon had become friendly with the Duff Gordons, and when the Chartist riots broke out in 1848 he and Alexander had patrolled the streets together as special constables. Soon after, he began his astonishing rise to power, which culminated with him being crowned Emperor Napoleon III in 1852. According to Janet, "the Emperor, to whose credit it must be said he never forgot anyone who had been kind to him . . . in London, sent several times to place a carriage at my mother's disposal." Each time she refused it, largely out of loyalty to Saint-Hilaire, who'd been imprisoned for his opposition to the new regime and referred to Napoleon III "with infinite scorn as 'ce monsieur.'" Perhaps she was also thinking of her Orléans neighbors, who, as Bourbons, had no more love for the emperor than did Saint-Hilaire.*

---

*Given Lucie's distaste for Napoleon III, it is ironic that she bore some resemblance to the founder of the Bonaparte dynasty. Janet recalls that during a trip to the Ardennes in 1847, the Duff Gordons ran into a nephew of Napoleon I, the one commonly known as Plon-Plon. "Prince Pierre Buonaparte, an old acquaintance of my grandmother's, was in the same hotel, and, when introduced to my mother, he burst forth: 'Mais, madame, vous êtes des nôtres, vous êtes une Buonaparte'; and, taking her hand, he led her before a looking-glass. 'I am considered like the great Emperor; but look at your face, madame,—it is the image of him.' In fact Prince Pierre and my mother might have passed for brother and sister."

By the time she left Paris, Janet was essentially trilingual, and the last traces of her insular parochialism had been buffed away. Yet on returning to Esher she plunged into the hearty life of the English shires as never before. In particular, she became fanatical for foxhunting, riding mostly with the Surrey Union Foxhounds and the Duc d'Aumale's Harriers. Because she was considered too young to ride alone and neither of her parents hunted, equestrian chaperones had to be found. One was Lucie's physician, Dr. Izod. Another was Watts, though it was actually Janet who ended up doing most of the anxious supervision: Watts, she writes, "rode well, but always on the curb, and when there was a gate, or a blind ditch, I always insisted on his going around by the road. I did not want to be accused of causing the death of the great painter."

Not only was Janet never injured, she once came valiantly to the aid of a rider who was. In the fall of 1859, while out with the Duc d'Aumale's Harriers, she noticed that the Comte de Paris was having trouble controlling his new horse. A few minutes later, she found the horse riderless. After tethering it, she tore off in search of the count, whom she found "dashed against a tree," his leg broken. When Dr. Izod arrived, he sent Janet to fetch his medical kit. "While galloping to Esher, it struck me that should Queen Marie-Amélie see her grandson carried to Claremont on a hurdle, it might give her a dreadful shock, so I turned into the park gates, rode up to the back door, and told her old servant what had happened." Everyone was impressed by her conduct, including Sarah Austin, who, in a letter to Saint-Hilaire, described her granddaughter's quick-thinking heroism. "When there was nothing more to be done," Sarah added, "she burst into tears, like the child she still is."

A child she may have been in some respects, but she was also edging toward adulthood. The previous spring, she'd been presented by Lucie at court, which she found a rattling experience: "My train was so terribly in the way that my curtsey to Her Majesty must have been very ungraceful, and I let my glove fall just in front of the Queen, and did not dare to pick it up." Despite such moments of awkwardness, she was confidently coming into her full beauty, which was quite different from her mother's yet resembled it in being at once marmoreal and animated. In one of Watts's portraits, she stares forth with huge dark eyes, her thick brows arched in a challenging manner and her jaw firmly set; one can tell that the artist admired her chiseled features, but he seems to have felt a flicker of fear at her Gorgon-like intensity.

Watts and the other grown men close to Janet can't have failed to notice the changes in her as puberty took hold, and one might expect them to have flirted with her, attempted to seduce her, or even tried to marry her—the Victorian code made allowance for vast discrepancies of age between bride and groom. But nothing of the sort seems to have occurred. Some of this purity no doubt had to do with Janet herself, for despite her marked preference for masculine company she was quite without the coquettishness that John Austin had detected in—and then driven out of—Sarah at that age. In fact, Janet appears to have had virtually no prurient or romantic interest in the opposite sex. Yet it also appears that Watts and the rest were content to be friends and mentors, and nothing more. Even Kinglake, who as a well-heeled bachelor might have sought her hand, remained chaste and parental. But now there surfaced, or rather resurfaced, a man with designs on her.

In the spring of 1859, Janet had been riding to the train station to meet Alexander on his way home from work—it was her fixed habit to do so—when she saw a small boy stumble and fall just in front of her. After picking him up and comforting him, she brought him to his father's lodgings in Esher. "A gentleman came out, kissed the child, and looked hard at me. 'Are you not Lady Duff Gordon's daughter?' he asked; and before the answer was out of my mouth he clasped me in his arms, exclaiming: 'Oh, my dear Janet! Don't you know me? I'm your Poet.'" It was George Meredith.

Though he would go on to become one of the major writers of the late Victorian and Edwardian eras (his reputation has since declined), Meredith at this point was just starting to make a name for himself. He and his wife, Mary Ellen, whose father was the satirist Thomas Love Peacock, had met the Duff Gordons nine years earlier, while staying near Weybridge. Janet had often played with their daughter, Edith, and Meredith had carried Janet on his shoulders while telling tales he'd made up, in the vein of the *Arabian Nights*. Taken by these yarns—which were later collected in *The Shaving of Shagpat*—and by his recited verses, she had dubbed Meredith, with typical proprietariness, "my Poet." (There was a family tradition of such tags: George Grote, for instance, was referred to as "the Historian.") Lucie and Alexander had encouraged the literary ambitions of both Merediths—Mary Ellen was interested in becoming what we would now call a food writer—but lost track of them when they moved away.

Now here Meredith was again, at low ebb. The intervening years had brought him a measure of professional success, but also personal humiliation: in 1858 Mary Ellen had run off with the painter Henry Wallis, leaving Meredith to care for their sole surviving child, Arthur. The following year he moved to Esher, where he remained unaware of the proximity of his old friends the Duff Gordons—until, that is, Janet brought the sniffling Arthur to his door. That evening he had dinner with the family, and so quickly did the friendship rekindle that within days Meredith moved to a cottage almost next door to the Gordon Arms.

Meredith had a part-time job at a publishing house in London, and when he was at work Janet often looked after Arthur and taught him German, just as Lucie had once done for John Stuart Mill. But Meredith was interested in her as more than a babysitter: he was, as one of his biographers puts it, "more than a little in love with Janet Duff Gordon." The strongest evidence lies in his portrayal of Janet in *Evan Harrington*. Like his previous novel, *The Ordeal of Richard Feverel*, *Evan Harrington* is substantially autobiographical: for instance, its protagonist is the son of a poor tailor, as was Meredith. Yet it also has an element of wish fulfillment, in that Evan, despite his humble background, ends up marrying the beautiful and aristocratic Rose Jocelyn, who is unmistakably based on Janet, just as Rose's parents are based on Lucie and Alexander; as Siegfried Sassoon writes in his biography of Meredith, the Duff Gordons are "drawn to the life."* In *The Fourth Generation*, Janet crows that *Evan Harrington* "was *my* novel, because Rose Jocelyn was myself . . . With the magnificent impertinence of sixteen† I would interrupt Meredith, exclaiming: 'No, I should have said it like that'; or, 'I should not have done so.' A young Irish retriever, Peter, which I was breaking in and afterwards gave to little Arthur, was immortalized in the pages of the novel as a special request."

However strong his feelings for Janet, in real life Meredith lacked the audacity to make a play for her; both his poverty and the sordid circumstances of his break with Mary Ellen, from whom he was not yet divorced, told against him. His hopelessness is pitifully reflected in a pair of quatrains he wrote for Janet:

> *I dare not basely languish,*
> *Nor press your lips to mine;*
> *But with one cry of anguish,*
> *My darling I resign.*

> *Our dreams we two must smother:*
> *The bitter truth is here.*
> *This hand is for another*
> *Which I have held so dear.*

Her hand was indeed for another, but nobody could have guessed just how soon it would be claimed. Out of nowhere, a dark horse was about to appear.

---

*This wasn't the only time Meredith based a character on Lucie: in *Diana of the Crossways* (1885), she's clearly the model for Lady Dunstane, a friend of the heroine, Diana Warwick, who in turn is based on Caroline Norton. Meredith had first met Norton many years earlier at the Gordon Arms.
†Seventeen, actually. Janet recalls that Meredith came back into her life in 1858, but scholars unanimously agree that it was in 1859.

Back in 1853, Janet had been in the Gordon Arms garden, sitting in a mulberry tree she liked to climb, when a family friend, Lord Somers, appeared on the lawn and asked her to come down, saying, "Here is the man who dug up those big beasts you saw in the Museum." The beasts in question were Assyrian *lamassi*, huge statues of winged bulls or lions with the bearded heads of men; the British Museum had acquired several of them by way of Austen Henry Layard, an archaeologist who'd recently discovered the lost biblical cities of Nimrud and Nineveh.

Whether Layard had previously known Lucie and Alexander is unclear, but he became yet another of those cultivated gentlemen to take an interest in Janet. By 1859 he was in regular correspondence with her and had begun to regard her in a matrimonial light. Not, however, on his own account—it was with the eye of a matchmaker that Layard appraised her.

The eligible fellow Layard had in mind was a certain Henry Ross. Born in Malta in 1820 to an English merchant family, he was as precocious in his way as Janet. At sixteen he left Malta (by chance, it was just after the Austins arrived on the island) and set out for Turkey, where for six years he underwent a sort of informal apprenticeship to the British consular service, working in turn for the consuls of Trebizond, Erzurum, and Kayseri.

In 1844 Ross moved on to Mosul, in modern-day Iraq, where he became the commercial partner to the vice-consul. Excitement was in the air, for the French consul, Paul-Émile Botta, had uncovered what he believed to be Nineveh. Though it turned out to be not Nineveh but Khorsabad, Botta's find sent archaeologists racing to the region. Among them was Layard, who hired Ross as an assistant. He immediately came in handy. Layard having neglected to obtain permission to excavate from the Ottoman authorities, Ross, an avid hunter, brought along his greyhounds, so as to disguise their activities. "After coursing a hare or two," Ross writes in his memoirs, "[we] set to work with the pickaxe, and soon blistered our hands . . . But the sight of a small row of heads revived our energies, and we dug up the first slab of the great palace of Nimrod [*sic*]." By the time they discovered Nineveh in 1847, they'd become best friends.

Wanting to get back into trade, Ross became a commercial partner to the British vice-consul in Samsun, on the Black Sea coast. In 1852 he accepted an offer from Briggs Bank to manage their Alexandria branch, but was frustrated by the bank's timidity— "Mr. Briggs," he complained in a letter, "is too slow and cautious for modern trade when one runs a neck and neck race with Greeks." When the Crimean War broke out in 1853, Ross saw a chance to put his Black Sea expertise to use. Returning to Samsun, he organized supplies for Allied forces, and at war's end was asked to help sell off the horde of pack animals—nearly eight thousand horses, mules, and camels—amassed during the conflict. For three months, Ross, accompanied by a small armed escort, led this motley herd southward like some ragtag Crusader army, stopping in towns where criers would drum up business for the sale of beasts belonging, as they enticingly put it, to the Queen of England. So successful were these impromptu auctions that by the time Ross reached Aleppo every last animal had been sold, and he rewarded himself with a dawdling tour of the Holy Land. Afterward he decided to return to Briggs Bank in Alexandria, lured by the offer of a partnership. Either the bank had grown less timid or Ross no longer cared, for this time he stayed on.

In the summer of 1860, Janet and Alexander went to stay with their friends the Highford Burrs at Aldermaston Court in Berkshire. Layard had also been invited, and he brought along Ross, who was back in England on leave. "Mr. Ross," Janet recalls, "sat next to me at dinner and told me about pig-sticking." Not every young lady is held rapt by tales of boar hunts on horseback, but this was just Janet's sort of thing. Ross also told her of his excavations, "his wild life among the Yezidis" (a shadowy Kurdish tribe often accused of devil worship), and much else. "So wonderfully vivid a *raconteur* I had never met." With his tall, lean frame, hawklike features, and soup-strainer mustache, Ross also looked the part of a Near Eastern adventurer, and this too must have made an impression.

Janet invited Ross to visit her at Esher, and a few months later he showed up. Her account of what happened next is, to say the least, perfunctory: "I took Mr. Ross out with the Duc d'Aumale's Harriers, and was much impressed by his admirable riding, his pleasant conversation, and his kindly ways. The result was that I promised to marry him." Presumably she was already familiar with his ways and conversation, so one guesses that it was his display of horsemanship—a cardinal skill in her scheme of things—that clinched the deal.

Many of Janet's friends were taken aback, not by Ross himself but by his plan to whisk her off to Egypt. "I can't be in a good humour with a marriage which takes you away from England," Kinglake wrote, while Meredith, graceful in defeat, joked that the Duc d'Aumale's Harriers had been reduced to "doleful specters . . . The hunt is queenless evermore." More puzzling was the reaction of Lucie and Alexander. While they approved of Ross and raised no objections, they allowed their daughter's courtship to unfold with virtually no parental oversight—a striking lapse at the time. Also curious is the brevity of Janet's engagement: Ross proposed in November, and the date was set for December. Instead of a waltz, a leisurely ceremonial of wooing and planning, the couple seemed to be dancing a frantic jig to the altar.

What this haste reflects is nothing scandalous—Janet surely remained a virgin—but the fact that her family was in crisis. For Lucie was gravely ill. In November 1858 she'd given birth to her third and final child, Urania. Despite a difficult delivery, her health held steady for a time, but the following autumn her cough returned with a vengeance. John Austin was in even worse shape, and Lucie, disregarding Dr. Izod's warnings, insisted on keeping vigil at treacherous Nutfield Cottage. In December 1859 John died, and soon after, Lucie began coughing blood. Tuberculosis, already strongly suspected, was confirmed nine months later, when she suffered a major hemorrhage. Dr. Izod prevailed on her to spend the winter at Ventnor, on the balmy Isle of Wight.

With her mother in a sanatorium, her father in Ireland on Inland Revenue business, and her brother at Eton, Janet was, except for a few servants, essentially left on her own at the Gordon Arms. Since it would have been unthinkable for her to entertain Ross alone, her great-aunt Charlotte Austin was trucked in to "do propriety," as the phrase went. But her parents, who under better circumstances would have been closely involved in the whole business, had to miss out on it.

The wedding itself couldn't take place in Esher or London if Lucie was to be included. And so it was at St. Catherine's Church in Ventnor, on December 5, 1860, that Janet Duff Gordon became Janet Ross. Other than immediate family, there were few guests— Kinglake, Layard, and the rest had been unable to attend on such short notice. In the end, not even Lucie could be there, as she was too weak to crawl out of bed. It was hardly the sort of wedding that might have been anticipated for Janet. She herself, little given to nuptial fantasies, probably wasn't all that disappointed, but some around her must have felt that the wedding's subdued tone, as well as the haste with which it had been brought off, augured poorly for the marriage to come. Henry was also more than twice Janet's age, and would be taking her to a sweltering land where fortunes could be made but just as quickly lost, and where fearsome diseases could carry one off overnight.

Seen from a certain angle, Janet's future looked rather doubtful. But Lucie, despite the sword of Damocles hanging over her own neck, took a more optimistic view. Writing to Janet Shuttleworth, she described Henry as "excellent and agreeable," pointed out that her daughter had "a new country to see," and predicted that "an interesting life" lay ahead of her. Just how interesting she never could have guessed, nor how poignantly what remained of her own life would intertwine with her daughter's in that same new country.

THREE

Sitti Ross

In *Early Days Recalled*, we find Janet reminiscing about one of her hunts with the Duc d'Aumale's Harriers when out of nowhere, like a fox bolting from the underbrush, comes the following statement: "In December, 1860, I married, and went to Egypt." The transition is so abrupt as to seem a non sequitur—there has been no mention at all of Henry Ross. In *The Fourth Generation*, published over twenty years later, she filled in the gap somewhat, providing a bit of background on her future spouse and a few glimpses of their courtship. But her previous omission, her sudden leap from maidenhood to matrimony and from Esher to Egypt, had been apt. Because her own transition was nearly that quick. By throwing in her lot with Henry, she'd acted out of pure instinct. This was often her way: the same coolheaded decisiveness that got her over blind ditches on horseback allowed her to make momentous choices on the spot. Still, something besides Henry's merits persuaded her to drop her old life and turn on a sixpence.

Lucie's letter to Janet Shuttleworth provides a clue: "I am selfishly sorry to lose her," Lucie wrote, "but am glad to get her away from the depressing influence of illness and anxiety and to know her enjoying her youth." Though loyal and capable of sacrifice, Janet was far from the meekly obedient, self-denying daughter typical of the period; she was indeed determined to enjoy her youth. Marriage to a middle-aged banker might seem an odd way of going about it, but, as Sarah remarked to Saint-Hilaire, "Janet never liked young men." Had she stayed in England, she easily might have become, given her beauty and cleverness and position, the wife of some substantial peer, or else of some writer or artist from the upper reaches of Bohemia. Instead, for over six years, she took on the role of—as the Egyptians called her—*Sitti* Ross,* which was a less conventionally prestigious but more exciting part to play.

—⸺⸺⸺◦⸺⸺⸺—

For all Janet's apparent desire to put some distance between herself and her family, she was hardly about to cut herself off from its far-reaching web of friendships. Just so, when she and Henry went for their honeymoon to Paris, it was less in the nature of a romantic hideaway than a series of calls on almost-relatives like Saint-Hilaire. The couple then moved on to Malta, where Henry's parents and sister still lived, and where, Sarah had predicted, Janet would reap "an inheritance of love and veneration earned and bequeathed by her dear grandfather." Though Sarah was prone to overestimating John's status, Janet did find "the name of Austin" to be an open-sesame to Maltese homes.

After a few weeks in Malta, the Rosses embarked on the last leg of their journey, and in January they stepped off the boat at Alexandria.

Egypt in 1861 was in a state of flux. Throughout the Middle Ages it had been a crucial part of the Islamic world, as the base first of the Fatimid caliphate and then of the Mameluke sultanate. But when the Ottomans captured the country in 1517 it fell into a long provincial eclipse. This backwater status abruptly ended in 1798 with Napoleon's invasion, and from then on Egypt had been closely watched and jealously contested by the European powers, in particular Britain and France. After the French were, with British assis-

---

Sitt is Arabic for "lady," and *sitti* means "my lady." These terms, indicating deference rather than rank, were routinely used to address Western women in Egypt.

tance, expelled in 1801, there followed several years of civil war. When the dust settled, an unlikely figure had taken control: an Albanian mercenary named Muhammad Ali, who turned out to be one of the giants of the nineteenth century. Under his rule, Egypt was swiftly Westernized and converted into a military powerhouse. At first he put Egypt's might at the service of Constantinople, driving the upstart Wahhabis from Mecca and Medina. But in the 1830s he began to chafe at the Ottoman yoke, and his armies twice came within a whisker of toppling the empire, prevented from doing so only by European intervention. Finally he dropped his rebellion in exchange for hereditary rule of Egypt.

When Muhammad Ali died in 1849, he was succeeded as khedive (equivalent to viceroy)* by his xenophobic grandson Abbas Pasha, who resisted Egypt's Westernization. But when in 1854 the reins passed to Said, fourth son of Muhammad Ali, Egypt swung sharply back toward the Occident. Suave, gregarious, and modern, Said delighted in the company of Westerners and was happy to let them meddle. More than ever did the French and British jockey for influence and pieces of the action.

So things stood at the time of Janet's arrival. Only a few months later, Egypt's fortunes would receive a jolt that intensified this trend of development. With the start of the American Civil War, Dixie cotton exports ground to a halt, and Egypt stepped in to take up the slack. Now feeding the ravenous mills of Lancashire, the country found itself the main supplier of one of the world's crucial commodities. A boom was on, bringing with it a gold-rush atmosphere and the usual swarm of con artists and wild-eyed speculators.

A parallel boom, already well under way, involved not the financial possibilities of Egypt's future but the glories of its past. Napoleon's auxiliary army of scholars and scientists had produced a sumptuous encyclopedia, *Description de l'Égypte*, that drew attention to the depth and richness of the nation's heritage. So, even

---

*Though the Ottomans didn't formally recognize the right of the Muhammad Ali dynasty to use the title "khedive" till 1867—before then they were technically *walis*, or governors— Muhammad Ali claimed the title in 1840 and exercised powers commensurate with it.

more, did a series of archaeological finds. Though Egyptology had yet to cohere into a professional discipline, bold men were already at work in the field, such as the Swiss explorer J. L. Burckhardt and the Italian colossus Giovanni Belzoni, a former circus strongman who'd developed a taste for excavation. Their intrepid efforts resulted in the rediscovery of, among other marvels, Abu Simbel and the tomb of Seti I, and Belzoni even managed to lug a seven-ton bust of Rameses II all the way to London, where in 1818 it dazzled visitors at the British Museum. A few years later, Jean-François Champollion, by means of the Rosetta Stone, finally cracked the code of hiero-glyphics. A whole lost world opened up, and Egyptomania, as it was known, infected not only archaeologists and researchers but the general public.

The country was meanwhile becoming ever more accessible, and by the 1840s one could reach the stupendous temples of Upper Egypt in relative comfort and safety. The Scottish painter David Roberts, a protégé of J.M.W. Turner, produced evocative, briskly selling prints of Egyptian scenes that helped cement the country's exotic image and fuel tourism. Other, more pious visitors were drawn by its biblical associations, and still others passed through on their way to India. Egypt was, in short, awash in Westerners. Among them were quite a few literary types, most famously Gustave Flau-bert, who in 1849–50 spent seven months touring the country and sampling its prostitutes. Several of Janet's friends also came, such as Kinglake, whose harrowing visit in 1835 (described in *Eothen*) coin-cided with an outbreak of plague, and Thackeray, whose 1844 visit yielded *Notes on a Journey from Cornhill to Grand Cairo*. In Lon-don bookstores, Egyptian travelogues piled up as fast as Saharan sand against Abu Simbel.

The first place most visitors laid eyes on was Alexandria. If Cairo had been, until the nineteenth century, in a long deep slumber, Al-exandria had been virtually comatose, and for far longer. Its decline was in fact proverbial—no surviving city more epitomized vanished grandeur. After the Muslim conquest in 641 and the subsequent rise of Cairo, Alexandria became a depopulated Podunk, and so re-mained for over a millennium, until Muhammad Ali decided to revive it. Egypt, if it was to join the modern world, needed a major Mediterranean port, and Alexandria fit the bill. The city was rebuilt almost from scratch; as E. M. Forster puts it in *Alexandria: A History and a Guide*, Muhammad Ali "waved his wand, and what we see arose from the modern soil." The results were unimpressive from an aesthetic standpoint. "There is nothing to say about its architecture," Florence Nightingale stated after visiting in 1849, and others were similarly underwhelmed.

However unsightly, Alexandria thrived. It wasn't yet the coffeehouse metropolis evoked by Forster or his poet friend Cavafy (who was born during Janet's tenure in town), let alone the hedonistic wallow of Durrell's *Alexandria Quartet*. But it did have a humming entrepôt vitality—nowhere was Egypt's air of giddy profit more tangible—and a pronounced internationalism: supplementing the established Greek, Levantine, and Armenian communities, Italians, Britons, and French now flocked to the city. The majority of these foreigners lived in what was known as the Frank (i.e., European) Quarter. Centered on a massive square and full of imposing if undistinguished Beaux-Arts buildings, it could make one feel that one was back on the Continent—Thackeray was reminded of Marseilles, while Mark Twain found the Quarter by night reminiscent of Paris.

The Gallic comparison drawn by Janet Ross, disembarking in early 1861, was rather less flattering: Alexandria seemed to her "like a tenth-rate French provincial town." Anticlimax was followed by abandonment, for the very next day Henry was called away to Cairo on business. Feeling "more forlorn than I can say," Janet was left alone with the servants, consisting of a Greek cook, a Maltese maid, and a Berber footman. "I shall never forget the odd and humiliating sensation of being unable to understand a word any of our servants spoke, or making myself understood." Pulling her socks up, she decided to tackle the language problem head-on by having the footman tell her the names of objects around the house. Anyone who has struggled with Arabic knows its difficulty, yet Janet claims to have learned enough within a few weeks "to give many orders—with a superb disregard of grammar."

Not that she was often around to give them. Where most young brides would have resigned themselves to keeping house and making what they could of Alexandria, Janet quickly established the habit of clearing out of town whenever possible. Chiefly she escaped to Cairo, which became, in a sense, her true Egyptian home. Briggs Bank maintained a house in Ezbekieh Square for the use of its employees, and Janet, with or without her husband, never missed a chance to stay in it.

Accompanying Henry on his next trip to Cairo, she found herself "transported bodily into the *Arabian Nights*." She was hardly the first to have this sensation; in fact, it was almost de rigueur for visitors of the period to exclaim over the similarity of Cairo, which remained essentially medieval, to the world conjured up by Scheherazade.* Some of the city's fairy-tale charm derived from its predominant means of transportation: the donkey. As Kinglake notes in *Eothen*, "The usual mode of moving from place to place is upon donkeys; of these great numbers are always in readiness, with donkey-boys attached."

On one of her first visits to Cairo, Janet found a "donkey-boy" (in fact a man several years her senior) whom she liked so much that he became not only her regular chauffeur and guide but her friend. Hassan—his name must have put her in mind of Hatty—was a rich source of local lore, and he claimed to find her more sympathetic than "the other English who laugh at our customs." He took her to the remotest corners of the city and to observances rarely witnessed by Europeans, such as the Doseh (literally, "treading"), a uniquely Cairene dervish ritual in which devotees were trod upon by a mounted sheikh. Janet describes how, after the sheikh's followers "threw themselves flat down in a line close together on their stomachs in the dust," his horse "ambled rapidly over the men's backs . . . A great shout of Allah, la, la, la, la, la! resounded, and to my astonishment the trampled-on bodies sprang up and ran after the Sheykh." Where many would have reviled the rite as barbaric—

---

*This similarity was due in part to the fact that most nineteenth-century translations of *The Thousand and One Nights* were based on the so-called Egyptian recension, into which had crept many details of local life.

indeed, the Egyptian authorities suppressed it in 1884—Janet deemed it "a wonderful sight." Her openness to traditions very different from her own was already declaring itself.

Even as she was starting to develop, through Hassan, a feel for the life of ordinary Egyptians, she was also gaining entrée to Cairo's more rarefied strata. These were almost exclusively Turkish. Despite all the trouble Muhammad Ali had given the Sublime Porte, Egypt was still dominated by Turks, who set themselves apart from the Arab natives. Not from Westerners, however, particularly under Said. The American consul general, Edwin de Leon (who would shortly be sent by Jefferson Davis to Britain and France to plead the cause of the Confederacy), likened Said to Henry VIII for his stocky, bearded appearance and bluff heartiness, and fondly remembered his "grand *fêtes* . . . to which all European men were free to come." From the khedive on down, the ruling class rubbed along smoothly with Westerners, who couldn't help admiring the urbanity and exquisite manners of the true Turkish gentleman.

Janet's first encounter with this debonair breed came when, on her initial visit to Cairo, Henry brought her to meet his most important client, Said's brother Halim Pasha, who considered Henry a friend. Already Halim had sent Janet one of his prize Arabian horses as a wedding gift. He now greeted her warmly and took her to meet his wife and daughter in his harem. It was there that her blood began to simmer.

Harems were places of titillating mystery at a distance but numbing monotony up close, at least to those Western women who got inside them (something their menfolk, seething with concupiscent curiosity, could never hope to do). Florence Nightingale wrote of Said's harem that its ennui would make it "stand in my memory as a circle of hell." Janet's reaction to Halim's harem and others she penetrated was less intense, but she did conceive "a deep pity for the stunted lives circumscribed within them." Like her mother, she took strong exception to any sort of glaring injustice, and she now began to nurture an aversion to the Turks. Besides their misogyny, she was nettled by their lack of respect for medieval Arab architecture. "I could never pass the ancient mosque of Tooloon without a feeling of rage at seeing such an edifice neglected and falling to pieces, while the Viceroy squandered such vast sums on hideous barracks, miscalled palaces, and European furniture." Hassan loved hearing her uncork "imprecations against the Turks," but she had to bite her tongue around Halim and the rest, given their importance to Henry and his bank. Still, she began to feel that these conceited pashas and beys were in need of a little humbling. An opportunity soon arose.

No less than England, Egypt was horse country, and the local grandees, with their easy access to the bloodlines of Arabia, were justly vain of their steeds. Halim was no exception: "The Prince boasted so much about the superior fleetness of Arab horses as compared to English that my patriotism was aroused, and I challenged him to a race between his mare and an English thoroughbred I had just bought in the square at Alexandria for £40." Tauntingly, she invited him to bring not only his mare but as many horses as he liked "to help him beat an English racer." In the spring of 1861 he showed up in Alexandria with ten additional horses and a squad of Mamelukes to ride them. The two-mile race took place in the desert outside town. For Janet there was a bad moment near the middle, when her horse, Companion, was nearly driven into a patch of prickly pear, but he recovered, put on a burst of speed, and beat Halim's mare by, Janet claims, "about a hundred yards," with the Mamelukes even farther behind. "They did not like it—particularly being beaten by a woman." Halim himself, however, was gracious in defeat, and gave her as a prize a beautifully worked gold bracelet, which stayed on her wrist the rest of her life.

This race is one of the few Alexandrian experiences related in Janet's memoirs; if Cairo was poetry, Alexandria was humdrum prose, and she has little to say about it. Yet some sense of her life there can be gleaned from a young woman named Marguerite Power, who stayed with the Rosses for a time. In her predictably titled memoir *Arabian Days and Nights*, Power, a niece of the Irish novelist Lady Blessington, describes the Rosses as living in a large ("twelve or thirteen rooms") waterfront apartment filled with curios from Henry's nomadic past, including a Kurdish carpet made in part from feathers and human hair. They had a rooftop garden-cum-menagerie, complete with pigeons, parrots, flamingos, and "a charming little monkey, hardly so big as a cat." Power also serves up several comic vignettes of Janet about town. When the two women went to pay their respects to the wife of the khedive, they found her perched on a divan, languidly smoking a chibouk. Taking a pause from her pipe, the vicereine expressed admiration for Janet's equestrian skills, "which had greatly amazed Alexandria, where a woman on horseback is a rare sight," and asked her for riding lessons. These never came about, and Power scoffs at the notion of "the lounging, nerveless, Eastern woman, who I do not suppose ever walked a quarter of a mile in her life" trying to emulate someone like Janet, "always among the first at the death, in the stiffest hunting counties in England."

Bored by the expatriate scene in Alexandria, with its Raj-like round of clubs and parties, Janet gave most of her fellow anglophones a wide berth. One exception was William Sydney Thayer, who'd been appointed by his friend William H. Seward, the new U.S. secretary of state, to replace Edwin de Leon as consul general. Thayer took up his post in July 1861, dividing his time between Cairo and Alexandria. A former editor at the *New-York Evening Post*, the thirty-two-year-old Thayer was also a lively writer, and his Egyptian diary—never published, but fortunately preserved by his family— includes many eagle-eyed entries on Janet, whom he met soon after his arrival. Already knowing of her mother and grandmother, Thayer was immediately intrigued by Janet, who, detecting his enthusiasm, regaled him with anecdotes: he was amused to hear that Lucie had been "a great aggravation to Carlyle," and as a Massachusetts native he relished her story about Tennyson putting a roomful of people to sleep with an interminable recitation of Longfellow's *Evangeline*. Astutely, he took these stories with a grain of salt: "Mrs. R's likes and dislikes are very *pronounced*," his diary notes, "and she is often inaccurate without intention."

Though she bothered to make few friends beyond Thayer, Janet was no hermit in Alexandria. A saving grace of the city was that, as the gateway to Egypt and points east, it saw a steady stream of visitors, and there would often surface, at random, some worthwhile character bearing a letter of introduction. One was the historian Henry Thomas Buckle, whose *History of Civilization in England* had just appeared to much fanfare. Passing through Alexandria in late 1861, Buckle called on the Rosses, and Janet was so impressed by his Macaulay-like cataracts of erudition that she brought him together over dinner with an Armenian friend of hers, Hekekyan Bey, a mild-mannered scholar also known for his talk. Hoping for synergistic fireworks, she was mortified to watch Buckle aggressively and pedantically overwhelm the gentle Armenian.

Far better mannered was the hero of empire Sir James Outram, who also turned up at her door. A retired general honored for his bravery during the Indian Mutiny, Outram was one of the growing number of British valetudinarians who, "ordered south" (as the phrase went) by their doctors, chose to push past the Mediterranean to the even drier climates of North Africa. Stooped almost double and racked by coughing, he was a shadow of his former virility, but Janet found his stoicism and quiet gravitas deeply appealing. The liking was mutual, and she spent many hours either distracting Outram with chatter about common acquaintances or riding along-side his carriage on excursions around town, "proud of forming the escort of the Bayard of India." When he moved on to Cairo, Janet went with him, saw him installed in a *dahabeah* (a traditional Nile-plying boat) for a trip to Upper Egypt, "and said good-bye with rather a heavy heart."* Her ability, at only nineteen, to entertain and comfort this broken-down old warrior speaks volumes.

Another new friend was as far as possible from having a foot in the grave. The idea of linking the Mediterranean with the Red Sea by means of a canal across the Isthmus of Suez had been in the air for years; aside from the practical and strategic value of creating a shortcut to Asia, there was something almost godlike about such a work. The French became especially fixated: Napoleon ordered his

---

*Hardly more than a year later, Outram succumbed to his ailments and was buried in West-minster Abbey. The honorific "Bayard of India" had been bestowed on him by Sir Charles Napier and referred to Pierre Terrail, seigneur de Bayard, the knight immortalized as "le chevalier sans peur et sans reproche."

engineers to investigate its feasibility (impossible, they said), and in the 1840s the utopian Saint-Simonians, envisioning a mystical "marriage between the East and the West," went to Cairo to pitch their scheme (the Egyptians declined). Then along came Ferdinand de Lesseps. While filling a series of consular posts in Egypt in the 1830s, he'd both caught the canal bug and gotten on chummy terms with Muhammad Ali and his son Said. When Said became khedive in 1854, de Lesseps, spying his chance, hastened to Cairo with his engineers. The canal they proposed would have to run for over a hundred miles and be wide and deep enough for modern ships, more behemoth with each passing year—the obstacles were daunting. But Said, trusting de Lesseps, granted him a concession, and in 1859 the first shovel went into the sand.

That de Lesseps would eventually cross paths with Janet was almost inevitable, given that Sarah Austin was an old friend of his and that Saint-Hilaire had been the secretary of an early incarnation of the Suez Canal Company (he even wrote a book, *Egypt and the Great Suez Canal*, that propagandized for the project). The two met in the spring of 1861, de Lesseps repeatedly calling on the Rosses. The following February, Janet ran into him while out riding. On a whim he invited her to join the canal inspection tour he was about to start, and the very next morning she set out with him and several of his staff.

After spending the night at the oasis of Tel-el-Kebir, where the company maintained an outpost, they continued eastward by dromedary and riverboat, at one point fighting through a dense swarm of locusts, which the imperturbable de Lesseps "flicked off . . . as they alighted on him with his lavender-coloured kid gloves." Near Lake Timsah, where work was then concentrated, Janet came face-to-face with the full immensity of his undertaking. Though dredgers and steam shovels would be brought in to dig the southern stretches of the canal (which wasn't completed till 1869), the northern ones were dug by hand. In approving de Lesseps's plan, Said had agreed to provide free manual labor, and the pharaonic spectacle that greeted Janet was of "twenty thousand men . . . swarming up and down the steep banks, chanting a sad, monotonous song as they carried the sand in small rush-baskets from the bottom of the cutting to the top of the bank."

For two more days Janet accompanied de Lesseps on his inspection, marveling at his energy: he could "go all day on a handful of dried dates," and his sleep consisted mostly of ten-minute naps, after which he awoke "a giant refreshed . . . I never saw such a man." On horseback, they headed north along a stretch of canal as yet no wider than a ditch, Janet leaping repeatedly across it, "so in years to come I can say that I have jumped the Suez Canal." They happened to reach Port Said on her twentieth birthday, and she was fêted at the home of de Lesseps's chief engineer.

Getting back to Alexandria proved tricky—when their steamer caught fire near Mansourah, they had to requisition horses from the local authorities and gallop sixteen miles across the desert to where a private train awaited them—but this only added to the fun. Janet's letter to Lucie describing the tour fairly bursts with exuberance, and for good reason: she'd been granted a privileged, up-close view of one of the great (if also most ethically dubious—the canal was essentially being built by slave labor) enterprises of the century, and of the steely yet charismatic man behind it.

By this point Janet had been continuously in Egypt for some fifteen months—a long time by "Frank" standards, since most Europeans fled the country's infernal summers. But one hot season in Egypt had been enough for her, and the following year she joined the general migration, heading for England in April 1862.

Though pleased to see old friends, she found her family more than ever at sixes and sevens. In Janet's absence, Lucie had suffered another hemorrhage and gone for relief to South Africa. Janet and the rest got to see her in July, when, apparently much improved, she came back home. But she almost immediately began coughing again, and again was ordered south. This time she decided to try Egypt, sailing for Alexandria in October. Neither of the Rosses was in town when she arrived—Janet was still in England, and Henry had recently joined her there—but she recuperated from the voyage in their apartment before continuing up the Nile.

With Lucie away indefinitely, Alexander decided, with great reluctance, to give up the Gordon Arms. "I passed a sad and weary time," Janet recalls, "packing up pictures, china, etc., for my father." Now homeless, Alexander went to lodge with Tom Taylor. As for the two younger children, Maurice was still at Eton, and Urania, now four, was sent to live with Lucie's spinster aunt Charlotte Austin.

But Urania wasn't the only child farmed out to Aunt Charlotte. Besides escaping the heat, Janet had a second motive for coming back to England: she was pregnant, and had no wish to carry the baby to term in Alexandria. On September 8 she gave birth to a son, christened Alexander Gordon Ross but known as Alick. He was to be the Rosses' only child. And when, in January 1863, they at last returned to Alexandria, he didn't go with them.

This in itself is unremarkable—Britons living in India and other hot climates routinely left their children behind for safety's sake, as the Austins had done while in Malta. In the case of Alick Ross, though, there was a strange and troubling quality to the arrangement. While his parents kept faint tabs on him, they seemed unpained by his absence. In *Early Days Recalled* Janet merely records the fact of his birth, and in *The Fourth Generation* he's omitted altogether. Her lack of maternal feeling is hardly surprising, given her youth and appetite for thrills—a friend likened her to "a salmon which swims up river to spawn and then swims out to sea again." More baffling is Henry's indifference; especially in view of his relatively advanced age, he might have been expected to prize a son, if for no better reason than as a means of perpetuating his name.

The Rosses' apathy toward Alick makes one wonder about the state of their relationship. Sexually it seems to have been less than a smoldering success. Janet openly preferred the pleasures of the saddle to those of the bedroom, and while pregnant was heard to say she couldn't imagine how she'd gotten that way—a joke, clearly, but a pointed one. Henry can't have been all that libidinous himself, to judge from his acceptance of the erotic failure of the marriage. This in turn can be deduced from the absence of turmoil or estrangement: the Rosses showed no sign of losing patience with each other and bifurcating into separate lives, like so many couples before and since.

Janet was, admittedly, known to make outrageous remarks about Henry, as when she told Thayer "she did not love him more than her horse." But Thayer knew better than to take her seriously: "These sayings doubtless mean nothing," he observed in his diary, "and are but eccentricities of expression, for no woman loves her husband one tenth more than Mrs. R." If the wisecrack came to Henry's attention—given Janet's penchant for hard teasing, she may have hurled it straight at him—he too, being thick-skinned, probably laughed it off; besides, Janet loved her horses with abandon, and to be on a par with them was no mean thing.

Another of Henry's virtues was his lack of jealousy. Young, brash, and beautiful, Janet inevitably caught the eyes of other men. Thayer once noted that a certain Dumreicher of Alexandria "has been making love to her, mistaking her somewhat open hospitality for a special compliment to himself . . . Continental Europeans and Levantines usually misconstrue the freedom of an Englishwoman, especially one who like Mrs. R has lived among men and who has followed the hunt with them." Given her frigidity, Henry had little reason to fear being cuckolded. Of the hopeful Dumreicher, for instance, Thayer reports that Janet "soon cooled him." Still, many husbands in the same position would have grown nervous and possessive, or even begun to mutter darkly of demanding satisfaction. That Henry did none of this was a great relief to Janet, who hated such behavior. Another relief was that Henry, in his calm self-sufficiency, didn't require constant proofs of adoration. What he needed Janet gave him, apparently, and vice versa; the partnership worked because neither made large demands of the other.

Back in Alexandria, Janet found she had a new reason to be grateful for Thayer, who'd been a tremendous help to her mother. Savoring not only Lucie's reminiscences of Boston literati—"She remembers hearing Margaret Fuller talk nonsense in London, and going with Tom Taylor and R. W. Emerson to Cambridge"—but her entire character, Thayer had put himself at her service. Since she couldn't afford a proper dragoman for her planned trip to Upper Egypt, he recommended a young man of his acquaintance, Omar Abu Halaweh. His unusual surname, meaning "Father of the

Sweets," alluded to the fact that he was from a family of pastry chefs. Omar's skill as a cook would come in handy on remote stretches of the river, but he had other, more human qualities that would make him indispensable to Lucie.

After being escorted by Thayer to Cairo, where Omar found her an affordable dahabeah, Lucie sailed up the Nile as far as Abu Simbel. There, among the graffiti on the temple's huge statues of Rameses II, she was startled to see a name familiar from her childhood: that of Prince Pückler-Muskau, who'd carved his entire coat of arms into the rock. "I wish someone would kick him for his profanity," she wrote.* Except for this and a few other discordant moments, though, she found herself taking to Egypt like a crocodile, and not only to its monuments and riverscapes but to its people; with the fellahin she met along the Nile she felt as comfortable as she once had with the matelots of Boulogne.

All the same, she was eager to return home. Her health having responded nicely to the desert air—"I can walk four or five miles . . . and the blood-spitting [is] almost forgotten"—she decided to risk doing so in the spring of 1863. It was a mistake: the English damp soon had her hemorrhaging again, and by October she was scurrying back to Upper Egypt. This time the Rosses were in Alexandria when she arrived, and she spent two weeks with them before continuing southward.

The Rosses had been in Egypt since the previous winter, Janet having again mustered the courage to ride out the summer heat. For her, the highlight of the season was a return to Tel-el-Kebir, at the invitation of de Lesseps's manager there, Jules Guichard. The occasion was the sixth-hundredth anniversary of a miracle involving the Muslim saint Abu Nishab. After he was buried near Aswan, one of his arms was stolen and interred in a shrine near Tel-el-Kebir. But Abu Nishab, writes Janet, "being a saint, did things in topsy-turvy

---

*Pückler-Muskau had spent much of the 1830s wandering around North Africa and writing copiously. While in Egypt he produced the three-volume *Aus Mehemed Alis Reich* and fell in love with his Ethiopian slave. After traveling with the girl through Asia Minor and Greece, he tried to introduce her into fashionable Viennese society before bringing her home to Silesia, where she soon died of tuberculosis.

fashion, and instead of recalling his arm, transported his body to where the stolen limb had been put." A festival had sprung up in commemoration of the miracle, and in 1863 flocks of Bedouin—five or six thousand, she estimates—came from as far as Syria to take part in it.

In a letter to Alexander, Janet describes her first sight of them: "A cloud of dust in the distance, shots, and faint shouting heralded seventy to eighty horsemen. They charged down on us at full gallop, and then circled round and round, firing into the air, and shaking their long spears, tipped with a tuft of ostrich feathers, above their heads." Where many would have run screaming, Janet knew better than to take alarm at this martial jubilation. Sure enough, a comic moment followed. "They eyed me curiously, and at last expressed their sorrow at my having lost a leg, and their wonder at my being able to sit a horse"—she was riding sidesaddle, a practice unknown to them.

That evening, though, when Guichard invited several sheikhs for coffee in his tent, the mood suddenly soured. Guichard's Berber servant, schooled in European customs, served Janet first, and one of the sheikhs, Mohammed Hassan, "rose and walked away in high dudgeon, saying: 'Who is this, a creature without a soul, that she should be served before one who can summon a whole people to arms?'" Guichard tried to mollify him by explaining "that the Sultan of the English was a woman, and that women were highly honoured in Europe," but Janet was left feeling, for once, distinctly uncomfortable.

The next morning she awoke to find that her horse had somehow injured himself during the night. Guichard asked Mohammed Hassan to lend Janet his "well-known and vicious" horse Sheitan (Satan), and he grudgingly agreed. "Visions of a disgraceful spell rose before me," she admits, and Sheitan, when she mounted him, showed "the whites of his eyes in ominous fashion." Despite his evil reputation, she decided to ride him in a race that was about to start. Immediately he began to rear up, "but was bucked by the martingale, and when he felt a light hand humouring him soon settled down into a swinging gallop."

Though she didn't win the race, afterward Mohammed Hassan rode up to her, salaamed, and, in a stunning reversal of his previous contempt, said, "O lady, by Allah, thou ridest like ten *bedaween*, and Saoud [her groom] tells me thy conversation is such that thy husband would not need to go to the coffee-shop for entertainment or knowledge. When tired of thy white master come to the tent of Mohammed Hassan. By the head of my father, O lady, I will stand before thee like thy mameluke and serve thee like thy slave." Sarah Austin had once fantasized about marrying an "Arab chief," and now here was one groveling before her granddaughter. Back at Guichard's tent, the sheikh demonstrated his devotion to "the Rose of Tel-el-Kebir," as he'd dubbed her, by personally serving her coffee. At dinner—a whole roast sheep stuffed with raisins and pistachios—he insisted on feeding her by hand, tenderly putting pieces of mutton in her mouth.

The next day she and Guichard hunted with hawks and greyhounds. When they came across a lost baby gazelle, she decided to adopt it. "A goat was procured as foster-mother, and Guichard promised to send it to Alexandria when it was old enough." The day after that she returned to Alexandria, presumably followed by the gazelle.

If Janet's trip to the canal zone had put her on the cutting edge of modern Egypt, this one represented timeless desert romance. *Early Days Recalled* (published when she was almost fifty) concludes with it, and her decision to stop there is telling—with this whirlwind Saharan adventure, she seems to suggest, the curtain rang down on her youth. While it would be an exaggeration to say that she now crossed over from innocence to experience, the remainder of her time in Egypt had a very different flavor. The country was headed for trouble, and the Rosses with it. Even before that, Janet turned a corner, succumbing to Alexandria's boomtown cynicism and guile. Her instrument of deceit was the pen, which she now took up for the first time.

In early 1863 the outgoing Egyptian correspondent for the London *Times* suggested Henry Ross as his replacement, and Alexander's old friend Mowbray Morris, who by that point was the paper's managing editor, wrote to offer Henry the job. He accepted, and officially it was he who served as correspondent for some twenty months thereafter. (Though the articles were unsigned, the paper's internal records list Henry as their author.) It would seem, however, that he did little or none of the actual writing, which was instead produced by Janet. The facts surrounding the episode are murky in the extreme. "Mowbray Morris proposed that I should be the *Times* correspondent," Janet states in *The Fourth Generation*. This wasn't the case, and her retrospective fudging might appear to undermine her claim of authorship. Yet there is a great deal of circumstantial evidence in support of that claim, and ultimately no good reason to doubt it. Whether or not Morris was aware of it, he now had a twenty-one-year-old woman rather than a forty-three-year-old man turning out the majority of the paper's dispatches from Egypt.*

Regardless of how Janet wound up becoming the de facto Egyptian correspondent for *The Times*, it was a plum of a commission, and an especially juicy one at that particular moment. In January 1863 Said had died and been replaced by Ismail Pasha, a grandson of Muhammad Ali. Sharing his grandfather's energy and ambition (if not, as would later become clear, his shrewdness), Ismail was determined to loosen what remained of Ottoman control over Egypt and to firmly align the country with the West. As the U.S. Civil War dragged on and markets continued to clamor for Egyptian cotton, huge profits were being made, and the accession of a big-spending, forward-thinking khedive seemed to promise more of the same. Investors and power players would be keeping a closer eye than ever on Egyptian affairs, which meant that *Times* bulletins "FROM OUR OWN CORRESPONDENT," as the byline had it, were sure to be followed religiously.

Janet made her debut in March 1863, and thereafter her articles

---

*For a fuller discussion of these ambiguities, which have provoked some dispute, see the appendix.

(most of them miscellaneous rather than dealing with a single topic) appeared on a semiregular basis, sometimes only a week apart but on occasion more than a month. Several of the earliest ones were largely devoted to elaborate state receptions for Sultan Abdülaziz—it was the first time an Ottoman monarch had visited Egypt since Selim I conquered the country in 1517—and Prince Napoleon, the same "Plon-Plon" she'd met as a child in the Ardennes. The explorers who were then unlocking the stubbornest mysteries of the "Dark Continent" also popped up in her columns. "Captain Speke is expected here soon, as the Viceroy has sent a steamer to meet him," she reported; this was, of course, John Hanning Speke, who'd just confirmed Lake Victoria as the source of the Nile. A few months later she noted that the Italian explorer Giovanni Miani, who'd raced Speke to find the river's origin, "is now in Cairo, preparing another expedition with the aid of the Emperor of Austria. He denies that the true source has been found."

Somewhat surprisingly, Janet rarely mentioned the Suez Canal. Her coziness with de Lesseps had certainly caught the attention of her friends in government: both Kinglake (then an MP) and Layard (who, after entering politics in the early 1850s, had risen to become under-secretary for foreign affairs) pumped her for information. But the prime minister, Lord Palmerston, was strongly opposed to the project, and Mowbray Morris shared his suspicion of French motives; it therefore seems likely that Janet was told to keep her enthusiasm for de Lesseps and his damn canal to herself. Instead, she often reported on an even more important body of water, the Nile, which, as she reminded her readers, "is master of every one's fortune, from the Viceroy down to the meanest fellah." In the fall of 1863 the river rose catastrophically, wiping out most of the millet and cotton crops, and her articles included harrowing eyewitness descriptions of the damage.

"I read *The Times*' Alexandrian correspondent diligently," Meredith wrote her, "and catch the friend's hand behind the official pen." For those in the know, that hand was especially evident in the disproportionate attention paid to horseflesh. "Your racing readers may be interested in hearing that the much-vexed point as to the merits of English and Arab horses has just been tried in Cairo," began a September 1863 article, which went on to say that a certain Companion had dealt "a crushing defeat" to his rivals and had thereby "taken all courage out of the partisans of Arab horses." (Apparently some bigwig had made the same mistake as Halim by agreeing to race Janet.)

For a correspondent to ride her hobbyhorse, as it were, across the pages of *The Times* showed dubious judgment, but was ultimately harmless and forgivable. The same cannot be said of another transgression. Henry had recently started a new business venture, and Janet, flagrantly violating every principle of objectivity and avoidance of conflict of interest, tried to use her column inches to attract investors for it.

The first hint of this ploy came in her second article, which stated that Ismail "desires to develop the trade between Egypt and the Soudan." A few weeks later she announced that trade would be handled by a new company, established "with the approbation of His Highness" and backed by some of "the first merchants and bankers of Alexandria." Readers were next told that the company had "brilliant prospects," that it planned to reach all the way into Abyssinia, and that it would deal in "gums in very large quantities, elephants' teeth, ostrich feathers, bees-wax, ox-hides, and gold-dust." Though she didn't name it till several months later, this brilliantly prospected new entity was the Egyptian Commercial and Trading Company, of which Henry was a founder and director. In fairness, Janet wasn't the only one raving about its potential: the *Money Market Review* compared it to the East India and Hudson's Bay companies and predicted a rosy future. Yet there was something inherently shady about such an enterprise, an odor of Conradian nefariousness. Nominally under Egyptian control, the Sudan remained a lawless wilderness, and while Janet assured readers that the company would practice "fair traffic with the black population," it probably had no such intention. It was also causing alarm among other British merchants in Egypt, who saw it as a cartel shamelessly exploiting its ties to the ruling family. Banding together, they sent a letter of protest to *The Times*, which published it.

Thus began, in the spring of 1864, a running public battle between Janet and the merchants. "It is greatly to be regretted that a
portion of the English here should place themselves at open war
with the Government," she wrote in her opening salvo, "as it
will . . . drive the Viceroy to ally himself with other nationalities."
The merchants, who may or may not have guessed her identity, shot
back with another open letter. Her dispatch of May 12 acknowl-
edged that her previous attention to the company had "given offence, because I did not notice the hostility of a portion of the
British merchants toward it." Yet their hostility, she insisted, had
been based on a misunderstanding, and they'd since come to their
senses: "No difference of opinion now remains between them and
myself."

With that pat—and patently false—statement, Janet washed her
hands of the whole business. But for a *Times* correspondent to have
to defend himself, let alone herself, in this way was highly irregular,
and Mowbray Morris (who, again, may have been unaware that Janet
was essentially ghostwriting for Henry) was surely embarrassed and
annoyed. While Henry was allowed to keep his commission, *The
Times*'s Egyptian correspondent henceforth kept silent about the
Trading Company and its foes. Only four more articles appeared
before Henry finally resigned the commission in November 1864.

Besides serving as the nominal holder of the commission, what
part did Henry play in the Trading Company imbroglio? Did he egg
Janet on? Or did he, with his more temperate nature, try to restrain
her? Lacking all evidence, one can't say. Clearly, though, both Rosses
were swept up into the financial delirium that had taken hold of
Egypt; spotting a chance at a quick killing, they charged out rough-
shod in pursuit of it.

Not that Janet's sins entirely invalidate her record as a correspondent. She reported objectively and vigorously on many other matters,
and was more sympathetic to the native point of view than most of
her contemporaries, often taking Westerners in Egypt to task for
their arrogance and ignorance; in fact, the twenty-odd articles she
wrote have been said to constitute "the best journalistic record of
the Egypt of the period." But she unmistakably compromised herself.

"The longer you live in the East," Layard had predicted, "the more your eyes will be opened to the disgraceful intrigues and petty interests which distort and influence every question, public and private." Now she and Henry had become complicit in such machinations. For the time being, the sole consequence was strife with the merchants, but not for long.

Though she continued to take pleasure from Cairo, Janet had become utterly bored with Alexandria. In a *Times* article of February 1864, she enjoined the European colony to contribute toward a new racetrack and thereby to support "the Viceroy's efforts to afford them some change from our usual dull routine of existence, the present excitement being restricted to the ups and downs in the value of cotton and cereals." She still received the occasional visitor, such as Henry Phillips, who came to Egypt to execute a series of paintings for Halim's garden pavilion. (Halim had complained to Henry Ross that "a French artist he had picked up at some bathing-place did not satisfy him" and asked him to suggest a replacement.) But there were fewer distractions than before, and her feud with the merchants must have made Alexandria more unappealing than ever.

In June she bolted for England, returning only in November. By this point she'd become so blasé about life in Egypt that *The Fourth Generation* skips right over the months before her next trip home, in the summer of 1865. When she came back to Alexandria later that year, boredom was no longer a concern, having been replaced by fear. For the Egyptian bubble was about to burst.

By early 1865, with the U.S. Civil War winding down and American cotton poised to come back on the market, Egyptian cotton prices dipped, and the following year they went through the floorboards, dragging the economy down with them. As Janet frankly puts it, "1866 was a disastrous year." Briggs Bank had been absorbed into the Trading Company, of which Henry was appointed manager—and into which he'd sunk his whole fortune. It was struggling to get off the ground, and just when Henry's stewardship was most needed he came down with severe bronchitis.

As he lay wheezing in bed, Janet received a telegram from Alexander "begging me to come if possible to London as he had heard that

the Trading Co. intended to make a call of three pounds a share."
Afraid of worsening Henry's condition, she kept him in the dark and,
at the suggestion of his doctor, took him to Sicily to recover. "At
Messina I invented a story that my father had been suddenly taken ill
and wanted me, and went straight to London via Marseilles."

On arrival in London another blow fell, for there began the
international banking crisis now known as the Panic of 1866. On
May 11, "Black Friday," when several large banks collapsed, Janet hurried to the Trading Company's office in the City, where she found
"five or six old gentlemen sitting around looking very lugubrious."
They told her that if the khedive, who'd borrowed heavily from the
company, didn't pay up promptly, the company was sure to fail. When
Janet asked what steps were being taken, they went blank. Though
she was, by her own admission, no businesswoman, she felt compelled to act. " 'Well, gentlemen,' I said, 'as you can do nothing,
perhaps you will allow me to try?' " They agreed, and Janet raced off
to the Foreign Office to beg for help from Layard, who in turn in-
structed the British consul general in Cairo to lean on the Egyptian
government to pay Ismail's debt. The pressure worked, and for the
moment the company was saved.

In the meantime, Henry had recovered and hastened back to
Alexandria to try to shore up the company. Now it was Janet's turn
to fall ill—the protracted, white-knuckle anxiety had taken its toll.
Her father pleaded with her to take a break before plunging back
into the Egyptian maelstrom, and his insistence proved, in a round-
about way, to be life-changing.

The Kingdom of Italy, which had come into being only five years
earlier, had joined the winning side in the recent Austro-Prussian
War and been rewarded with the province of Venetia, ceded by the
Austrians. King Victor Emmanuel II planned to make his triumphal
entrance into Venice in November, and a group of Janet's friends,
organized by Layard, was going for the occasion. Why not join
them? Other than dropping Henry off in Sicily, she'd never set foot
in Italy—a glaring gap for a woman of her worldliness. And since
afterward she could easily scoot from Venice to Trieste and catch a
boat to Alexandria, it seemed only a small extravagance.

Crossing the Italian border at Susa by means of an "odious dili-gence," the group stopped at Turin, Vicenza, and Padua before reaching Venice. The king's entrance was a rousing spectacle: "Vic-tor Emmanuel, ugly as he was, looked every inch a king as he stood on the prow of the *Bucintoro,* hailed with the wildest enthusiasm from the fleet of gondolas on the Grand Canal and by the crowd on the shore. All the palaces had magnificent sheets of damask or em-broideries hanging from their windows, and even in the poorest quarters of the town something had been suspended, a counter-pane, a shawl, or a small flag, the tricolour waved everywhere, and patriotic songs resounded on all sides." In the Piazza San Marco a military review took place, and when "the agile little Bersaglieri* tore round the Piazza the people positively danced with excitement and shouted themselves hoarse."

Suddenly, above the roar of the crowd, she heard her name being called. She turned around, and there was "my Poet." George Mer-edith had covered the Italian front of the Austro-Prussian War for *The Morning Post* and then decided to linger, so as to pick up some local color for a novel set in Italy. Though he and Janet hadn't known of each other's presence in Venice, they were still on excel-lent terms. He'd been one of her steadiest correspondents through-out her years in Egypt, regularly sending bulletins on the latest doings in Esher and London, and if he still carried a torch for Janet it had probably been dimmed by his recent remarriage.† Falling in with each other, they spent a whole day at Torcello, "and talked of the dear old Esher days, and of the novels he had written and was going to write. I tried to persuade him to come with me to Egypt, but alas, he could not."

---

*The Bersaglieri originated as an infantry corps in the Piedmontese Army, served in the Crimean War, and were later incorporated into the Italian Army. They are distinguished to this day by their jaunty, wide-brimmed hats, plumed with extravagant black feathers.

†Meredith's second wife, Marie Vulliamy, was (quite unlike his first) a garden-variety En-glish rose, sweet, domestic, and unintellectual. When her father balked at Meredith as a suitor, Alexander Duff Gordon helped bring him round. Both Alexander and Janet attended the wedding in 1864, but she never so much as mentions Ms. Vulliamy in *The Fourth Generation*—in the words of Siegfried Sassoon, "One imagines she regarded the chosen of her poet with a somewhat critical eye."

Back in Alexandria, the situation remained bleak. The directors of the Trading Company had voted to close up shop, and as major shareholders the Rosses took a frightful hit. Their next decision was easily reached: "We determined to leave Egypt with what remained of Henry's hard-earned fortune." They'd never planned to stay forever—at the time of their wedding, Sarah had written to Saint-Hilaire that they meant "to settle in England in the course of a few years," presumably in some delectable corner of the shires where they could ride and hunt. But this certainly wasn't how they'd envisioned things, limping home half broke. The short-term plan was to return to England and take stock; beyond that, the future was a blank. First, however, they wanted to see Lucie down south, and to take in the surprising new life she'd made for herself there.

Since October 1863, when she'd rushed back to Egypt with her lungs in tatters, Lucie had hardly left the country. After rehiring Omar Abu Halaweh, she'd headed for Luxor, where Janet had arranged for her to stay rent-free in a disused house belonging to the French government. Though derelict, the Maison de France enjoyed a choice position atop Luxor Temple and was very much a place with a past: several of the titans of Egyptology, such as Belzoni and Champollion, had stayed there while going about their work, as had Flaubert and Maxime Du Camp while engaged in less toilsome activities. ("The stairs give on a rubbishy part of the village," Flaubert observed, "with the brothels at the far end." He often walked to the far end.)

After arranging her collection of carpets and divans in the empty house and rigging up a kitchen of sorts, Lucie began to meet and receive the locals. Before long she was "on visiting terms with all the 'country families' resident in Luxor" and had started a salon. One of her frequent guests, an imam, gave her Arabic lessons and discoursed on matters of faith. Though she seems never to have thought of converting, her interest in and respect for Islam were plain to see, and this further disarmed the Luxorites, who took the extraordinary step of inviting her to a mosque to have the first sura of the Koran read for her as a blessing. "I think . . . I must have the 'black drop' and that Arabs see it," she wrote to Tom Taylor, "for I am always told that I am like them." (Presumably the "black drop" is Arab blood.)

Lucie had been writing voluminously to other friends as well, and to her family. She'd done the same from South Africa, and after her return Alexander had convinced her that her travel jottings might have mass appeal. The book that resulted, *Letters from the Cape*, had confirmed Alexander's hunch, and its success emboldened Lucie to line up a similar book of Egyptian letters. Aware of her wider audience, she began to think in terms of good copy, and this may have contributed to a decision she made in the spring of 1864: to stay in Luxor through the hot season. For Westerners, such a thing was unheard of—Cairo and Alexandria summers were positively alpine compared to Upper Egypt's. By late March the last tourists vanished, and the heat became so intense that Lucie spent afternoons lying on a mat in a "dark, stone passage"—the only spot in the house where she could breathe. But shared hardship bonded her to the community. When an epidemic broke out (of what is unclear), she was, by virtue of her English medicine chest, thrust into the role of "*hakeemah* (doctoress) of Luxor." A woman whose son she'd cured "kissed my feet and asked by what name to pray for me. I told her my name meant *Noor* (light—*lux*), but as that was one of the names of God I could not use it. 'Thy name is *Noor-ala-Noor*,' said a man who was in the room. 'That means something like "God is upon thy mind," or "light from the light," and *Noor-ala-Noor* it remains.'" The name stuck, and added to her aura.

The following summer Lucie took the risk of going to a German spa town, Bad Soden, to celebrate her silver wedding anniversary with Alexander, and with Sarah, Janet, Maurice, and Urania as well. Exposing her lungs to the damp north once again proved a mistake, and she hemorrhaged horribly. As soon as she stabilized, she fled Europe for the last time, heading for Cairo. In her new dahabeah, which she named the *Urania*, she sailed for Luxor, where her health soon improved—a fact she chalked up largely to a regimen of camel's milk. ("I expected it to have a twang, but it is more delicate than cow's milk.")

Her friends and neighbors were, however, struggling to get by: already bled white by taxes, they were now beginning to feel the effects of Egypt's financial crisis. To Lucie, the blame fell squarely on the khedive and his cronies, whom she pilloried for their "blind rapacity" in a letter to Alexander. Her book *Letters from Egypt*, which had recently appeared to glowing reviews and excellent sales, also contained some blistering passages on Egyptian officialdom, and Ismail ordered that its pesky, dissident author be closely watched and her mail intercepted. (Lucie eventually figured this out and avoided sending her letters through the Egyptian post.) Where the Rosses had hopped brazenly into bed with the ruling family, Lucie proclaimed her allegiance with ordinary Egyptians ground down by kleptocracy.

Over the next few years her life settled into a seasonal rhythm. One summer in Luxor had been plenty, so when the mercury spiked each spring she would—accompanied by Omar—take the *Urania* up to Cairo, where she'd live in the moored boat till Luxor cooled down. (Previously she'd stayed at Thayer's house whenever in Cairo, but in 1864, a few days shy of thirty-five, he'd died, probably of malaria.)* Heading back to Luxor each fall, she'd reinstall herself in the Maison de France and pick up where she'd left off with the locals. "When I go and sit with the English [tourists]," she confessed to Alexander, "I feel almost as if they were foreigners to me too, so completely am I now a *Bint el-Beled*—a daughter of the country."

She did, however, enjoy entertaining the occasional English visitor, usually one passing through Luxor on their way up or down the Nile. Edward Lear, who had perhaps been referred by their mutual friend Tennyson, stopped by to make her acquaintance; "he has done a little drawing of my house for you," she reported to Alexander.

---

*The *New-York Evening Post*, where Thayer had been an editor, ran a long obituary that included this melancholy detail: "But a few days ago we recorded in these columns the death of Mr. Abijah W. Thayer, an eminent New England editor, and the father of the late Consul-General. Father and son have thus passed away within a few days of each other, though almost at opposite ends of the globe."

Frederick North, the stepfather of her old friend Janet Shuttle-worth, and his daughter Marianne also turned up at her door. Having walked in just as Lucie was playing Arabophile *salonière*, North "looked rather horrified at the turbaned society in which he found himself." But Marianne, who as a child had idolized Lucie, was as smitten as ever: "The natives all worshipped her," she would later write in her memoirs, "and she doctored them, amused them, and even smoked with them." On her side, Lucie was much impressed by Marianne's sketches of Egypt, and rightly so: she would later achieve fame as a painter.

Janet, meanwhile, still hadn't visited her mother in Luxor; she'd been there briefly in 1861, when she joined her cousin Sir Arthur Gordon on a cruise up the Nile, but not since Lucie's arrival. And so in February 1867 she and Henry—along with their terrier, Bob, whom they planned to leave with Lucie to keep her company—finally made the trip, riding in a government steamer provided by Nubar Pasha.

Reaching Luxor, they were stunned at the extent of Lucie's popularity. "You have no idea what a power she is in the land," Janet told Alexander. "Henry, who knows the East, is astonished." Villagers had "stuck palm branches about the entrance [to the Maison de France], and the *sakka*, or water-carrier, had been at work since dawn sprinkling a path from the river's bank." Right under Lucie's balcony, a fantasia (a sort of pantomime of mounted combat) was staged in their honor, and that evening they were feasted by the magistrate and other notables. "Our procession to dinner was quite Biblical. Mamma on her donkey, which I led, while Henry walked by her side. Two boys in front had lanterns, and Omar in his best clothes walked behind carrying some sweet dish for which he is famous, followed by more lantern bearers. As we went through the little village the people came out of their mud huts and called on Allah to bless us, the men throwing down their poor cloaks for my mother to ride over and the women kissing the hem of her dress."

A few days later the Rosses embarked with Lucie for a cruise to Aswan. When they returned to Luxor, they witnessed further demonstrations of love and reverence for Sitti Noor-ala-Noor. To prolong the visit a bit, Lucie planned to accompany the Rosses as far as Qena, some thirty miles downriver. But the *Urania*, which she'd rented out to a group of English tourists, hadn't been brought back in time. Hearing of this, a Nubian trader offered his own boat, which (as Janet tells it) "now belonged to the *Sittee* who had saved his nephew's life when ill of cholera last year." Lucie tried to pay him for the boat, but the man wouldn't hear of it.

On March 21 the Rosses' steamer and Lucie's boat set out in tandem. "Our departure from Luxor was very touching," Janet reported to Alexander. The locals lined up to present them with food—"one woman had sat up all night to bake so as to give us fresh bread"—and a man whose son had learned English and German from Lucie tried to give them an ancient alabaster jar with "faint traces of kohl" still inside; Janet politely refused the gift, but when the steamer pulled away she found that the man had left it in her cabin. Nor was he alone in forcing generosity on the Rosses: one woman brought them a lamb, "and when we declared we could not possibly take it she ran away leaving her lamb on board."

At Qena, the magistrate threw a lavish dinner for the three of them. The next morning it was time to part ways. Janet's account of the moment is terse: "I said good-bye to Mamma and we steamed away down the Nile."

Heading back to Lower Egypt, Janet must have had a good deal on her mind. Though Lucie's tuberculosis had plateaued, Janet can't have been confident of seeing her again, and the thought of her being marooned in permanent exile was surely a painful one, even if softened by the knowledge that she was cradled on all sides by deep affection and respect. And then Janet's own future was again looking rather hazy. Before leaving Alexandria, she and Henry had given up their apartment and arranged to have their furniture auctioned off—they were returning to the city like tourists.

Henry needed to remain in Alexandria for a bit to wrap up his affairs, but Janet itched to clear out of town. While in Venice she'd linked up with a distant cousin, Sir Henry Elliot, who happened to be the British ambassador to Italy, and who'd invited her to come stay with him and his wife in Florence, then the nation's capital.

Her short visit to Italy a few months earlier had whetted her appetite for the country; besides, she reasoned, "it would be warmer than England."

In April she hopped on a steamer to Brindisi, from where she continued to the city she thought would merely serve as a pleasant stopover, little realizing that it would dominate and transform the rest of her life.

The Anglo-Tuscans

When Janet Ross casually rolled into Florence in April 1867, not only did she have no idea that she was to assume a distinctive place in Anglo-Tuscan history, she was only dimly aware that such a thing existed. But something should be said about that history before her convergence with it. In order to appreciate the place Janet found for herself and the nature of the British presence there, we must go back—far back, briefly, before lingering on the tumultuous years preceding her arrival.

※

Like most parcels of European territory, what we now know as Tuscany has gone through endless slicings and dicings, expansions and contractions, changes of name and possession. Much of it was, of course, home to the Etruscans. Their realm, Etruria, after being annexed by Rome, came to be called Tuscia, which in the sixth century was made a duchy by the conquering Lombards, with Lucca as its capital. This entity metamorphosed, under the Franks, into the Margravate of Tuscany, which in the eleventh century produced the first Tuscan of real historical stature: Matilda of Tuscany, one of the shrewder military leaders of the Middle Ages and among the period's most formidable women.

After Matilda's death in 1115, there ensued a long struggle between popes and Holy Roman emperors for control of the margravate, and the lack of firm external rule allowed for the rise of the great city-states, above all Florence. For more than three hundred years there was no Tuscany per se. Florence, though, had been gradually extending its dominion over one *comune* after another, and in 1569 the House of Medici capped this consolidation by inducing Pius V to create the Grand Duchy of Tuscany, with Cosimo I as its first ruler. Except for a brief Napoleonic hiatus, the grand duchy was to survive right up to 1859, when it was absorbed into the United Provinces of Central Italy, which in turn was folded into the new Kingdom of Italy.

Despite these geopolitical fluctuations, some sense of an underlying Tuscan identity held steady over the years. In addition to countless cultural similarities, Tuscans shared a tradition of prickly independence and, above all, a language. The cousin dialects of Tuscany (with Florentine leading the way) not only drew their speakers together but won them collective glory. Virtually at a stroke, the melodious triumvirate of Dante, Petrarch, and Boccaccio put the local vernacular in the front rank of European tongues, and set it on course to become the standard language of a nation.

Among those who sat up and took note of the literary splendor emanating from Tuscany in the fourteenth century were the English, whose own great poet of the period, Geoffrey Chaucer, quite possibly went there: Chaucer visited Italy in 1372–73, primarily on a mission to Genoa, and he may also have swung by Florence. Those scholars who believe he did so often go a tantalizing step further, pointing out that he would have arrived just in time to hear Boccaccio deliver the first of his lectures on Dante.* At the very least, the meeting between the two writers is (to use an old Italian expression) *ben trovato*—if it didn't happen, it certainly should have.

Many other, less momentous meetings unambiguously did take place, for throughout the later Middle Ages and Renaissance there

---

*Florence's governing body, the Signoria, had established a chair for the exposition of the *Divine Comedy* and appointed Boccaccio as the inaugural professor.

were close commercial ties between England (as well as Scotland) and the major Tuscan comuni. The first Briton truly to leave his mark was not, however, a merchant traveler but a man involved in one of the cities' less savory activities: constant warfare. As the French chronicler Jean Froissart put it, "There was in Tuscany a right valiant English knight, called Sir John Hawkwood, who had there performed many most gallant deeds of arms." Among the most sought-after condottieri of his time, Hawkwood fought for a number of Italian powers but ultimately swore allegiance to Florence, which put him in charge of its campaign against Milan. The campaign triumphed, and so grateful were the Florentines that they made Hawkwood—or Giovanni Acuto, as they dubbed him—a citizen of the city, where he spent his remaining years. After his death in 1394, Florence wanted to honor him with a tomb in the Duomo, topped by an equestrian statue. Though the plan had to be scrapped when Richard II of England demanded the return of Hawkwood's ashes, Paolo Uccello's fresco of the proposed tomb remains in the Duomo to this day.

Hawkwood wasn't the only one to find congenial military employment in Tuscany. There was, for instance, Sir Robert Dudley, an Elizabethan courtier and naval genius who in 1606 moved to Florence and entered the service of the Medici, for whom he designed warships and fortifications, including the mole for the harbor of the new city of Livorno; spending the last forty-odd years of his life in Tuscany, he was trusted and valued by a whole series of grand dukes, who made him a chamberlain and showered him with riches.

Increasingly, though, Britons went to Tuscany not to find an outlet for their skills or products but to broaden their minds and stir their souls. Florence's reputation as the "new Athens on the Arno" made it irresistible to men like Hobbes and Milton. Both went to pay their respects to its most famous dissident thinker, Galileo, and Milton's encounter inspired an early passage in *Paradise Lost*: Satan's shield is said to have "Hung on his shoulders like the Moon, whose Orb / Through Optic Glass the *Tuscan* Artist views / At Ev'ning from the top of *Fesole* [*sic*]." During his two visits in 1638–39, Milton also met, as he put it, "many persons eminent for their rank and learning" and read his work before the august Accademia degli Svogliati, in whose minutes he's described as "molto erudito." By the time he left he'd come to feel a real affinity for the city— years later he wrote to one of his Florentine friends, Carlo Dati, that his visits had "planted strings in my heart which now rankle there deeper."

As the seventeenth century gave way to the eighteenth, more and more Britons went clattering across the Alps in their coaches. It was the heyday of the Grand Tour, and Italy was all the rage. "There is evidently no place in the world where a man may travel with greater pleasure and advantage than in Italy," wrote Joseph Addison in *Remarks on Several Parts of Italy*, which inspired thousands of milords to follow suit. (Unable to afford the journey, Dr. Johnson wistfully observed that "a man who has not been to Italy is always conscious of an inferiority.") Much of Tuscany got short shrift from the Grand Tourists, but Florence was considered a highlight, deserving of an extended visit. Often these visits stretched out far longer than anticipated—it took fifteen months for Horace Walpole and Thomas Gray, of "Elegy Written in a Country Churchyard" fame, to tear themselves loose.

Others never left at all, for by midcentury a bona fide residential community had taken shape. Unlike the more heterogeneous colony that was to follow, it was largely rich and aristocratic, a pleasure-loving smart set. At its center was Sir Horace Mann, British minister in Florence from 1738 to 1786. The consummate suave bachelor, Mann regularly held salonlike *conversazioni* at his elegant house in Oltrarno, Casa Manetti, where he also lodged visitors of quality. (Gray and Walpole mooched off him for their entire stay.) Another representative figure was Mann's friend and neighbor Thomas Patch, who settled in Florence after being banished from Rome for a homosexual indiscretion; though an expert on Masaccio and Fra Bartolomeo, Patch made his living banging out romanticized views of Florence for the tourist trade. Then there was George Nassau, third Earl Cowper, who during his Grand Tour fell in love with a Florentine *marchesa*; despite failing to win her, he remained in Florence for the rest of his life, installing himself in the sumptuous Villa

Palmieri, collecting art, and conducting experiments with leading Italian scientists at his private laboratory.

All three men—Mann, Patch, and Cowper—appear in *The Tribuna of the Uffizi* (1778), by the German painter Johann Zoffany. Reluctant to visit Florence but longing to see its art, Queen Charlotte of England had asked Zoffany to produce a single massive painting that would show the Uffizi's greatest works. Brandishing this royal commission, Zoffany was allowed to take paintings and statues from all over the museum into the hexagonal room known as the Tribuna, which he additionally filled with twenty-odd periwigged Englishmen. The result is a kind of emblem of eighteenth-century Anglo-Florence: we see Mann and the rest pointing out to each other the sublimities of the Venus de' Medici* and other treasures, their bearing expressive of nonchalant sophistication.

Not everyone was quite so glossy and contented. Charles Edward Stuart, alias Bonnie Prince Charlie and the Young Pretender, spent the last fourteen years of his life in Florence as an alcoholic wreck, his behavior so uncouth that his wife left him for the dramatist Count Vittorio Alfieri, regarded as the founder of Italian tragedy. Another Scot, James Boswell, had his 1765 visit to Florence spoiled by an outbreak of gonorrhea—not even Mann's joviality could cheer him. The general impression among upper-crust Britons, though, was of Florence as an oasis of beauty and calm, an essential place to visit and the obvious choice for those in search of a southerly new home.

So things would have continued had Napoleon not come along to ruin them. By the time the French marched into Florence in 1799, most of its British residents had already fled, and the remainder wasted no time in doing so. The French dissolved the Grand Duchy of Tuscany (by this point under Austrian control) and replaced

---

*It is difficult to exaggerate the regard in which this Praxitelean statue, transferred from Rome to Florence in 1677, was held at the time. Just as all nineteenth-century Britons visiting Cairo invoked the *Arabian Nights*, their seventeenth- and eighteenth-century predecessors dependably went into raptures over the Venus de' Medici.

it with the so-called Kingdom of Etruria, which in turn was absorbed into France as the *département* of Arno.

In 1814 the grand duchy was restored, and the British, like the Austrians, came rushing back. For fifteen years or more, not just Tuscany but most of Europe had been no place for the compatriots of Nelson and Wellington, and when they again began to venture abroad it was with an eagerness bred by having been too long pent up on their island. This, combined with the middle-class prosperity brought about by the Industrial Revolution, made for an unprecedented wave of pasty-skinned invaders. No longer was Italy the exclusive preserve of toffs putting the final polish on their educations; it beckoned ordinary people. But it also attracted a new, more restless and troubled breed of literary traveler. The Romantic generation was at hand, fated to live out their tangled destinies down the length of the Italian peninsula. Rome, Venice, Ravenna, Naples, and Genoa all figured in their wanderings, but it was more than anywhere in Tuscany that they converged.

Not all of them cared for Florence. Despite never having spent more than a few days there, Byron bracketed the city with Naples as a place spoiled by the rabble of his native land: "Florence and Naples are their Margate and Ramsgate," he hissed in one letter, and in another, "Florence & Naples are their Lazzarettos [quarantine stations] where they carry the infection of their society." To the Shelleys, Florence proved more congenial, and also lucky: during their four-month stay in 1819–20, Mary gave birth to their only surviving child, Percy Florence Shelley, his middle name a tribute to the city,* and her husband, after walking in the park known as the Cascine on a blustery day, wrote one of his greatest poems, "Ode to the West Wind." Yet Florence couldn't hold the footloose couple any more than Livorno or Bagni di Lucca, through which they also flitted. Instead it was sleepy Pisa, where they based themselves for eighteen months, that became something like a home, and that served as a gathering place for an extraordinary set of characters, including

---

*It was not uncommon for anglophone children born in Florence to be named after it, another example being Florence Nightingale, who was born there in 1820.

Byron, Teresa Guiccioli (whose pubic hair Pückler-Muskau would mention in trying to obtain some of Sarah Austin's), the Irish *dantista* John Taaffe, and the pseudo-piratical fantasist Edward Trelawny.

The melodramas and escapades of the so-called Pisan Circle were, of course, brought to a sudden, ghastly end by the drowning of two of its members, Shelley and Edward Williams. The rest soon scattered, except for Leigh Hunt. Left to shift for himself when Byron hared off to Greece with Trelawny, Hunt decided in 1823 to move to Florence with his wife and seven children. While his two-year sojourn was, for personal reasons, often unhappy, it stands out as something new and different.

Dreamy, feckless, and broke, Hunt was no sleek milord going about his fixed rounds of galleries and conversazioni; he was, rather, an expat in the loose modern mold, fumbling his way half-homesick through foreign life yet also taking sharp, spontaneous, unprescribed pleasures from it. That these were largely rural also makes him notable. Following what he called his "old rustic propensities," Hunt rented a villa in Maiano—a hamlet near, as he put it, "the Fiesole of antiquity and of Milton"—and became a kind of countryside flâneur. Like Keats, he was besotted with Boccaccio, and loved to explore spots associated with him, such as the "Valley of the Ladies" evoked in the *Decameron*. He also amused himself by translating *Bacco in Toscana* (*Bacchus in Tuscany*), a seventeenth-century mock-heroic dithyramb to Tuscan wines by Francesco Redi, and by observing the local peasants, one of whose dances at the village hall he declared "the most energetic ball I ever beheld."

Nor did Hunt lack for company. Whenever he tired of mooning about his "Boccaccio haunts," he could head into town and mingle with friends "of the right sort." The reason he could easily do so was that Florence had acquired a fresh anglophone contingent. While it was still of modest size—"In the year 1825," Hunt states, "two hundred English families were said to be in residence in Florence"—it had more variety than its antebellum precursor, as well as a gathering energy and sense of itself. Even its nobs and statesmen tended to be of a creative bent: the new British minister, Lord Burghersh, was a composer whose operas and ballets were often performed in town, while Lord Normanby wrote a novel called *The English in Italy*, as well as producing and acting in performances of Shakespeare plays. It was, in short, the colony in chrysalis form.

Hunt's main entrée to it was by way of another recent arrival, Keats's old friend Charles Armitage Brown, who'd fallen in with two of Florence's most colorful characters. One was the painter and antiquarian Seymour Kirkup. A friend of William Blake's, Kirkup was every bit as peculiar and given over to the occult. He certainly looked the part. Austen Henry Layard, who spent part of his childhood in Florence, writes in his memoirs that Kirkup's "long white locks hung over his shoulders. His sharply chiseled features, hooked nose and bright, restless eyes gave him the aspect of one who practised the black arts. When he sallied forth in his battered felt hat . . . the street boys pointed to him as the *stregone*, the magician." He was even rumored to possess the secret of the Philosopher's Stone. Yet he was also a walking encyclopedia of Florentine lore, and once brought off an ingenious piece of art-historical detective work. Together with another dantista, the former U.S. congressman Richard Henry Wilde, Kirkup theorized that a lost fresco portrait of Dante by Giotto lay hidden in the Bargello, at the time not yet a museum but Florence's police headquarters. Having obtained permission to look for the portrait, Kirkup found it concealed beneath whitewash, exactly where he and Wilde had predicted.* This coup won him considerable acclaim, but he was already well regarded for more personal reasons: far from having the sinister quality of an Aleister Crowley, *lo stregone* was sweet-tempered and gregarious, Florence's favorite English eccentric.

Eccentric in a more alarming manner was the poet and belletrist Walter Savage Landor, who, though little read today, was once sometimes mentioned in the same breath as his contemporaries Words-

---

*Determined to trace the portrait before restorers got their hands on it, Kirkup surreptitiously arranged to have himself locked in the Bargello overnight. He then sent his tracing to an old friend and fellow dantista back in London, Professor Gabriele Rossetti, who passed it along to his painter-poet son, Dante Gabriel, who in turn was inspired to produce the watercolor *Giotto Painting Dante's Portrait* (1852).

worth and Coleridge. Landor was a titanic personality brimming with impulsiveness and rage. "I strove with none, for none was worth my strife" runs the first line of his best-known poem, but nothing could be further from the truth, for he locked horns with nearly everyone. After being kicked out of both Rugby and Oxford—the latter for firing a shotgun at a fellow student—he tried to convert a ruined Benedictine abbey in Wales into a country estate. When this squirearchical fantasy went down in debt and lawsuits, he bolted for Italy. He spent three years in Pisa, where he pointedly spurned the Shelleys (a piece of conceit he later regretted), before moving to Florence in 1821.

The city's serenity did nothing to tame his temper. Landor had a mania for defenestration, and was constantly hurling things from windows. Anecdote has it he once became so incensed with his Florentine cook that he shoved him out the kitchen window, realizing too late that his prize flowers lay just beneath. "Damn," came his bellow of dismay, "I forgot about the violets!" Small wonder he once overheard, to his delight, one local mutter to another, "Tutti gli inglesi sono pazzi, ma questo poi . . . !" (All the English are crazy, but *this* one . . . !)

Landor was, in short, impossible in every way, but possessed of such brilliance and charisma—a charisma accentuated by his leonine head, sonorous voice, and infectious booming laugh—that most not only forgave him but sought him out. This he at first made difficult, aloofly keeping to himself. Finally, in 1825, the visiting William Hazlitt marched up to his door uninvited and bearded him in his den. Flattered and mollified, Landor allowed Hazlitt to socialize him, and from then on he was the toast of the town.*

Among the colony, that is. Toward most Florentines Landor was contemptuous, describing them as "a treacherous tricking mercenary race," and he was so truculent in his dealings with authority

---

*Yet Landor's reputation for ferocity remained. When Emerson, during his 1833 visit to Florence, went to pay his respects, he was braced for "Achillean wrath,—an untameable petulance." To his relief, "on this May day his courtesy veiled that haughty mind, and he was the most patient and gentle of hosts." (Emerson's recollection of Landor appears in *English Traits*.)

that he was briefly banished from the grand duchy. But as a deeply learned and historically minded writer he couldn't help drawing inspiration from the place: his prose series *Imaginary Conversations* includes colloquies between Petrarch and Boccaccio, Galileo and Milton. And he got along far better with the peasantry, whom he found "frank, hospitable, courteous." Like Hunt, he preferred the countryside, and lived in a series of houses around Fiesole, culminating in the Villa Gherardesca, which an admirer bought for him. The young Layard, who lived nearby, often played with Landor's four children, who, he recollects, "were allowed to run wild, nearly barefooted, and in peasant's dress, amongst the *contadini*."

An exotic addition to the colony was the picturesquely raffish Edward Trelawny, who surfaced in 1829 after several years fighting with the klepht guerrillas in Greece. In no time he beguiled Landor, Kirkup, and Brown, just as he once had Shelley and Byron. Brown was moved to put him up, Kirkup to paint a heroic portrait of him (Trelawny is shown with turban and scimitar in his cave on Mount Parnassus), and Landor to make him the star of one of his imaginary conversations. But Trelawny now had the itch to write his own story. As he reported to Mary Shelley, "Brown and Landor are spurring me on, and are to review it sheet by sheet." The resulting book, *Adventures of a Younger Son*, is one of the most swashbuckling autobiographies in English—and one of the most mendacious, for to his genuine adventures in Greece Trelawny added wholly fictitious ones in Asia. Thus one of the first productions of the colony was both something of a group effort and a work of notorious mythomania.

Trelawny stayed in Florence for three years, eventually moving from Brown's digs into yet another villa in Fiesole, which had become the location of choice for British literati. Growing restless again, he decided in 1832 to try his luck in the United States. A few years later Landor pulled a similar vanishing act. His relations with his wife were, unsurprisingly, strained, and in 1835 he decided he'd had enough. Not content simply to find his own villa or move into town, he went off fuming all the way to England, where he remained for many years. While Landor was far from finished with Florence, the colony temporarily found itself deprived of its snarling but much-petted mascot—"the royal animal," Kirkup called him— and there followed a period of relative sleepiness.

Then, in the early 1840s, the colony roared to life as never before. Its character underwent another distinct change: where it had been, if not exactly macho, predominantly masculine, it now became more feminine.

Women had, of course, been an integral part of the scene all along, and some of them had been as self-assured as their male counterparts, especially in the higher reaches of society. Though she wasn't actually British—German, rather—the strong-willed Countess of Albany, former wife of the Young Pretender, exerted a spell over the colony and lived as she pleased right up to her death in 1824. Equally devil-may-care was Lady Blessington, the aunt of Janet's friend Marguerite Power and the author of numerous "silver-fork" novels. In 1822 she'd embarked on a tour of the Continent with her husband, a filthy rich earl, and the Count d'Orsay, one of the top dandies of his day; for years this threesome—Lady Blessington and the count were lovers, the earl a *mari complaisant*—drifted about Italy, and while they never stayed anywhere for long, they spent a good deal of time in Florence, where Lady Blessington made a conquest of Landor just as she had of Byron. But these were exceptions. Women of lesser means were bound to have less fun—for instance, the wives of Landor and Hunt, left to tend their broods all day while the poets went lollygagging across the fields discoursing about Boccaccio.

Frances ("Fanny") Trollope would have had no truck with such an arrangement. A woman of uncommon mettle, she too found herself saddled with a useless husband. But then, determined to provide for her seven children and to make a life for herself, she took the reins. Like Trelawny, she decided to try her luck in the United States, with disastrous results. After catching malaria at the Nashoba Commune in Tennessee, a utopian experiment gone wrong, she embarked on a series of maverick business ventures in Cincinnati, including a waxwork attraction based on the *Divine Comedy* (she was yet another dantista).* The last of these, an architecturally fanciful shopping bazaar that has been described as America's first mall, left her bankrupt. Returning to England, she took revenge on the country that had disillusioned her by writing *Domestic Manners of the Americans*, a scathing account that became a succès de scandale. To keep the family afloat, she followed up with a long series of novels and travelogues produced at speed. In 1841 she went to Italy for the first time. One result was her potboiler *A Visit to Italy*, another her decision to settle in Florence. By now a widow of sixty-three, she was joined by her bachelor eldest son, Thomas Adolphus, himself a writer.

Both Trollopes were zestful veterans of the drawing room, and within weeks of arrival their rented house, Casa Berti, became the new colonial hot spot, with a salon held every Friday. One guest who turned up in 1847 was a young poetess named Theodosia Garrow, hailed by Landor as a modern-day Sappho. Part Indian and part Jewish, high-strung and of delicate health, she was an orchidaceous sort of creature, and Tom soon fell for her. The two married, and Theodosia's inheritance allowed them to move, along with Fanny, to a stately house in the Piazza dell'Indipendenza, dubbed the Villino Trollope, which was for years at the heart of anglophone Florence, serving as the type of hub that Horace Mann's Casa Manetti had once been. Moreover, it doubled as a factory: Tom and Fanny produced books at an astonishing pace (though not quite as fast—or as well—as Fanny's younger son, Anthony, who often came to visit), while Theodosia, a gifted linguist, translated Italian poetry and plays and indited her own rhapsodic odes by the dozen.

But the Trollopes weren't the only game in town, for 1847 also saw the arrival of the Brownings. If anyone was ever destined for Italy it was Robert Browning, who'd been infatuated with the coun-

---

*This widespread exaltation of Dante may now seem unsurprising, but it represented a reversal of eighteenth-century conventional opinion. Horace Walpole, for instance, held Dante to be "extravagant, absurd, disgusting, in short a Methodist parson in Bedlam." Like Boccaccio, Dante was undergoing a major rediscovery.

try from an early age and had visited twice before. (His second journey, in 1844, was largely in the nature of a Shelley pilgrimage.) After eloping with Elizabeth Barrett, Robert took her to Pisa, where the couple spent the winter before heading on to Florence. Together with their famous cocker spaniel, Flush, they settled at Casa Guidi, just opposite Palazzo Pitti, which became the main alternative to the Villino Trollope, its atmosphere more earnest and intellectual.

The Trollope women were viewed askance by the Brownings: Theodosia was too much like Elizabeth, while Fanny, whose roly-poly heartiness was the opposite of Elizabeth's birdlike frailty, had a reputation for satirizing her salon guests in her novels—"people say," Elizabeth wrote in a letter, "she snatches up 'characters' for 'her so many volumes a year' out of the diversity of masks presented to her on these occasions." (Fanny admitted as much, though with a qualification: "Of course I draw from life—but I always pulp my acquaintance before serving them up. You would never recognize a pig in a sausage.") But a surface cordiality obtained between the two households, particularly after the Brownings' son, Pen, and Tom and Theodosia's daughter, Beatrice, became playmates, and they had many friends in common.

Foremost among these was a certain Isabella Blagden. Of mysterious origin—she was rumored to be, like Theodosia, part Indian—this tiny, olive-skinned spinster appeared in Florence around 1850 and rented the Villa Brichieri, in Bellosguardo, a hillside neighborhood south of the Arno that was gaining in popularity. Isa, as she was known, wrote novels and poems, but not even her friends could muster much enthusiasm for them. She herself, however, was universally adored for her sweetness and hospitality—Henry James, who knew her in later years, refers to her "kindly little legend." A sort of den mother to the Anglo-Florentines, she made her villa a gathering spot where coteries could cautiously mix.

Another convivial host was Charles Lever, an Anglo-Irish doctor-turned-novelist who moved to Florence in 1847. Lever loved to recount how he and his family, arriving by way of the Alps, had ridden into town on piebald ponies, with Tyrolese pointed hats on their

heads and their mastiff loping alongside; so quaint was their appearance that they were taken for a circus troupe and offered an engagement. This kind of lighthearted extravagance was par for the
course with Lever. His palatial dwelling, Casa Standish, included a
private theater, and he often threw parties based around amateur
theatricals, to which the colony was much addicted. For him, as for
Fanny Trollope, such entertainments were a source not only of
amusement but of material. "My receptions are my studies," he confessed. "I find there my characters, and pick up a thousand things
that are to me invaluable. You can't keep drawing wine off the cask
perpetually, and putting nothing in."*

While literati dominated the colony, there were also representatives of other walks of life, such as Mary Somerville, one of the most
respected scientists of her time (Oxford's Somerville College is
named after her). Like Earl Cowper before her, she found Florence's
scientific community wonderfully welcoming: the optical designer
Giovanni Battista Amici—"whose microscopes," Somerville writes,
"were unrivalled at that time"—gave her the run of his instru-
ments, and the grand duke himself loaned her rare treatises from
his collection. Somewhat improbably, Somerville became close
friends while in Florence with Frances Power Cobbe, the Irish social reformer, suffragette, and antivivisectionist. Cobbe is hardly
the sort of figure one would have expected to find living in idyllic
Bellosguardo, but there she was, writing her strident tracts amid
the greenery.

Then there was the American contingent, whose forte was the
visual arts. Painters such as George Inness and Thomas Cole, the
founder of the Hudson River School, spent productive time in Flor-

---

*Lever even managed to draw out one of the colony's few recluses. A poor man's Sir Walter
Scott, G.P.R. James (1799–1860) was among the bestselling novelists of his day and probably the top earner in town. Because many of his novels led off with a lone rider galloping
into view, he was nicknamed the "Solitary Horseman"—no piebald ponies for him. James
was equally aloof in person: despite having lived for years at the Villa Palmieri (previously
owned by Earl Cowper), he'd befriended only one other colonist, the equally proud Landor.
But he had a weakness for treading the boards, and Lever's plays enticed him into occasionally showing his face.

ence, and John Singer Sargent was born there in 1856. But it was the sculptors who truly thrived. The mid-nineteenth century was a golden age for grandiose molders of marble, and to those born on the wrong side of the Atlantic a sojourn in Italy was a hajj-like obligation. Rome was their ultimate Mecca, but Florence, with its proximity to the quarries of Carrara, was a firm second favorite.

The dean of American sculptors was Horatio Greenough, who arrived in 1827, converted a disused chapel into a studio, and spent his last quarter-century chiseling out colossi such as *George Washington*. (Commissioned for the Capitol rotunda, the bare-chested statue proved an embarrassment and was shunted to the east lawn.) A fluent writer as well, Greenough was friends with Landor, Kirkup, and several other American sculptors. The most prominent of these was Hiram Powers, who arrived in 1837 and never left. Powers had collaborated with Fanny Trollope on her waxwork *Divine Comedy* in Cincinnati, and when she resurfaced in Florence they renewed their friendship. The following year Powers completed *The Greek Slave*, which was modeled on the Venus de' Medici and became an international sensation. Like Greenough, he found himself sought after not only by colonists but by tourists; as George Stillman Hillard, the Boston writer who (one assumes) recoiled at Janet's embrace of Hatty, observed in his bestselling *Six Months in Italy*, "No American went through Florence without visiting the studios of these distinguished sculptors."

The colony also boasted a growing number of art critics, dealers, and collectors. A gradual shift in taste was taking place across Europe, away from Neoclassicism and Mannerism and toward the so-called primitive painters of the tre- and quattrocento. So out of favor had these early masters become that, as one scholar notes, "when the Italians brought back to Italy the pictures that Napoleon had carried away they left Fra Angelico's 'Coronation of the Virgin' behind," along with works by Cimabue, Giotto, and even Botticelli— none was considered worth the trouble. The pendulum began, however, to swing slowly back, thanks in part to a group of German painters known as the Nazarenes, who in 1810 moved to Rome to pursue an aesthetic program modeled on the later Middle Ages and early Renaissance. Inspired by his meeting with the Nazarenes, the French critic Alexis-François Rio promulgated a similar set of values, and he in turn swayed fellow critics Lord Lindsay, who spent much of his life in Florence, and Anna Jameson.*

But these three critics were only stepping-stones to the far more widely read John Ruskin. Though Ruskin's most famous Tuscan book, *Mornings in Florence*, wasn't to appear until 1877, he first visited Tuscany in 1840, and soon after that his adamantine doctrines—he was one of the most polemical and ferociously opinionated critics who ever lived—began to exert their influence.

One of Ruskin's earliest followers was James Jackson Jarves. Raised in Boston, Jarves began his career as a newspaperman in Hawaii. Then, while visiting the Louvre on his first trip to Europe, he had a road-to-Damascus epiphany and was violently converted to High Art. Falling under the spell of Ruskin, he moved to Florence in 1852 in pursuit of "primitive" masterpieces. Yet Jarves was one of those expatriate Americans who keep their native shores always in view. Determined to refine the tastes of his countrymen, he began writing accessible primers on Italian art. He also assembled a large collection of paintings, focusing on the followers of Giotto, whose works, little appreciated at the time, he ferreted out of their hiding places. These treasures he dreamed of placing in a purpose-built gallery in Boston. The plan never came off, and neither did a bid to sell his collection to the Metropolitan Museum in New York (it went instead to Yale, for a song). But if Jarves was by his own measure a failure, he was also an admirable connoisseur and educator, and his example would prove inspiring to the more successful experts who followed.

Though Jarves was on the retiring side, many other Americans, such as Powers, were more outgoing, and a signal feature of the colony from the 1830s onward was the free and easy mingling of

---

*Jameson (1794–1860), who attended Sarah Austin's salon in London, was Irish by birth but lived mostly in England, Canada, and Continental Europe. She is now remembered chiefly for her *Sacred and Legendary Art*, and for having accompanied the Brownings— whom she often visited in Florence—on their elopement to Pisa.

the English-speaking peoples. Americans and Britons meeting on each other's turf were prone to reflexive postures of superiority and resentment, the former laboring under a sense of barbaric inferiority that the latter did little to dispel. But Florence had the capacity to set them at ease: it was neutral ground, and they could submerge their differences in a shared enthusiasm for the place. While there were still plenty of snubs and raised hackles, there were also many instances of fruitful cooperation (as with Kirkup and Richard Henry Wilde), mutual influence, and friendship. The American journalist Kate Field, who lived in town for several years, wrote in her *Atlantic Monthly* article "English Authors in Florence" that Blagden's Villa Brichieri and the Villino Trollope—where she got to meet, among others, George Eliot, then doing research for her Florentine novel, *Romola*—constituted "spiritual asylums to many forlorn Americans," and she might have said the same of Casa Guidi, where she'd been made equally welcome.*

Indeed, the Brownings were exemplary in their openness toward Americans. Powers became a close friend, and Elizabeth wrote a sonnet about *The Greek Slave*. They were even closer with another American sculptor, William Wetmore Story, who lived in Rome but often visited Florence. Word spreading, Casa Guidi became known as a haven for intelligent Yanks. When Margaret Fuller turned up in 1849 with her new Italian husband, the aristocratic revolutionary Giovanni Ossoli, and their young son, colony tongues—Elizabeth's included—clucked at the scandal. "Nobody even suspected a word of this underplot," she gasped in a letter. But she and Robert ended up being deeply impressed by Fuller during the winter she spent in town, and they were grieved to hear the following summer that she and her family had perished when the ship bearing them to New York sank off Fire Island.

Harriet Beecher Stowe, who was in town for several months in

---

*Now forgotten, the indefatigable Kate Field (1838–96) was once ubiquitous, known not only for her journalism but her ventures into acting, dramaturgy, public relations, and newspaper-founding. She ended up writing a whole series of articles on the Anglo-Florentines for *The Atlantic*, and she is thought to be a model for Henrietta Stackpole in James's *Portrait of a Lady*.

1857, was also befriended by the Brownings, and so was Nathaniel Hawthorne the following year. In fact, the Hawthorne family's four-month stay points up many of the pleasures and benefits to be had from colonial Florence. Their first house, the Casa del Bello, was found for them by Powers, whose nearby studio they delighted to visit. Before the summer heat set in, Isa Blagden found them the cooler Villa Montauto in Bellosguardo. When Hawthorne wanted company, he could stroll across to Blagden's terrace and chat with the likes of Tom Trollope. And while his wife, Sophia, and their three children traipsed about the picture galleries and Boboli Gardens, he settled down to work as he hadn't in years. ("Here I find him again as in the first summer in Concord," Sophia exulted.) There was just the right balance of quiet and stimulation, and his surroundings readily contributed to his new novel, *The Marble Faun*: thus the Montauto became Monte Beni, while Blagden and Theodosia Trollope, with their exotic looks, went toward the character of Miriam. There was even material to be used in a later novel, for Kirkup made such a strong impression on Hawthorne as to inspire, at least partially, Dr. Dolliver in *The Dolliver Romance*.

Though the Hawthornes ultimately moved on, many others did not, succumbing to the city's pull and staying far longer than they'd planned. Their reasons for doing so have been partially indicated but should now be considered more fully.

First off, Florence provided comfort and safety. Its climate could be harsh, especially in summer—Dostoyevsky wrote, with reference to the French and British, of being unable to "conceive of why these people, *who had money to get away with*, would voluntarily stay in such a hell"—but was often pleasant. And the city was, for its time, clean and healthy. Whereas Rome remained a notorious malarial deathtrap, Florence had a reputation as a good place for sufferers of tuberculosis and other lung ailments; the French Riviera was gradually becoming the preferred destination of British coughers, but Florence still claimed its share. It had, moreover, virtually no crime and a reasonably functional bureaucracy.

But these factors were, of course, outweighed by more romantic and intangible ones. The concentration of beauty and history could be overwhelming, as Stendhal famously discovered,* and the city's riches were now inspiring awe as perhaps never before, thanks to Ruskin, Jacob Burckhardt—whose *The Civilization of the Renaissance in Italy* appeared in 1860—and other champions. In certain ways, however, Florence was the opposite of daunting. Where Rome was a jumble, and where the amphitheater setting of Naples was vast and volcano-menaced, Florence was tidy, compact, comprehensible. Leigh Hunt describes walking with Hazlitt outside town and stopping to admire how "Florence lay clear and cathedralled before us." Its quality of tight, focused, orderly grandeur was especially attractive to the British, with their fondness for what might be termed the village sublime—a fondness that only intensified as the Industrial Revolution caused their own cities to sprawl. But Americans were also vulnerable. New Englanders in particular were often put at ease by the sense that Florence was, as Margaret Fuller phrased it, "more in its spirit like Boston, than like an Italian city." (Even a century later, Robert Lowell was to describe it as "Bostonish.")

Britons and Americans alike also responded to Florence's peculiar blend of cheerfulness and severity. Few visitors to the so-called City of Lilies fail to find certain of its narrow streets claustrophobic and intimidating, squeezed as they are between fortresslike palazzi with walls of almost crocodilian rustication. This duality can even be discerned in the city's best-known figures: "To some," writes the expatriate American painter Elihu Vedder, "the shade of Savonarola and of Dante may seem to hang over Florence; to me the merry spirit of Boccaccio was a living presence." While many, like Vedder, enjoyed the city's surface buoyancy, its underlying seriousness and restraint struck a chord somewhere in their Anglo-Saxon souls.

In fact, a sense of ideal balance, of having the best of both worlds, pervaded the colonial view of the place. To Hunt's thinking, Florence allowed him to "possess, as it were, Italy and England together." Elizabeth Barrett Browning relished the fact that it was

---

*In 1817, emerging from Santa Croce, the novelist was so stunned by what he'd just seen that he almost fainted. Over the years, many other visitors have been stricken by (and even sought medical attention for) "Stendhal syndrome," as it is known.

"within the limit of civilization but not the crush of it." There was virtually no sacrifice involved, certainly not of good company. Tom Trollope observed that Florence was "of all the cities of Europe that in which one might be likely to see the greatest number of old, and make the greatest number of new, acquaintances." The colony was self-augmenting: as more members joined, still more were encouraged to do so. Before long its presence was impossible to miss. When the brothers Goncourt visited Florence in 1855, they described it (presumably with some disgust) as "une ville toute anglaise."

As their numbers grew, the colonists increasingly built up amenities, institutions, and rituals for themselves. The Via Tornabuoni, an elegant shopping street, catered to their tastes in food, clothes, pharmaceuticals, even umbrellas. They had several churches and clubs—both sport and social—to choose among, and could send their boys to Doctor Broomback's Academy for the Sons of Gentlemen. Their favorite haunt was Gran Caffè Doney, on Via Tornabuoni. ("Something good might be written" about the café, Herman Melville concluded after a day spent people-watching there.) They could catch up on news from home at the Gabinetto Vieusseux, a lending library and reading room stocked with an excellent selection of English-language periodicals. On pleasant days their carriages wound north of town to Pratolino, a park where they loved to picnic, or east to the abbey of Vallombrosa, immortalized by Milton. By night they flocked to see opera and ballet at the Teatro della Pergola, where, as Jarves recalls, "representatives of all the nations of Europe [met] in social rivalry, each striving to outshine the other." There were even paranormal diversions, especially during the several months in 1855 that Daniel Dunglas Home, one of the most famous mediums of the day, held séances at the Villino Trollope. Attended by, among others, the Brownings, Powers, Lever, Jarves, and of course Kirkup, the séances electrified the colony and made believers of many skeptics, an exception being Robert Browning, who skewered Home in his poem "Mr. Sludge, 'The Medium.'"

All this leisure and luxury might give the impression of wealth, and there certainly were colonists with deep pockets. The majority, however, were of modest means. Astounding though it may now seem, Tuscany at this time was not only affordable but a downright steal, offering a high quality of just about everything at rock-bottom prices—a "paradise of cheapness," Hawthorne called it. Those who just scraped by at home could breathe easier, the middle class found itself nouveau riche, and the affluent could live like kings, indulging every whim. "We dine our favourite way on thrushes and chianti with a miraculous cheapness," Elizabeth Barrett Browning wrote in a letter. In another letter, she reported that Frederick Tennyson (brother of Alfred), a music aficionado, routinely hired entire orchestras to play for him at home—"He says he likes Florence chiefly for having as much music as you please with very moderate means."

But the true bargain was real estate. The local aristocracy had fallen on hard times, and many an old Florentine family was forced to rent out the *piano nobile* of its palazzo. Layard recalled that his father obtained the piano nobile of the Alberti-designed Palazzo Rucellai for "a sum which would appear these days absurdly small." Outside the city center one got even more square feet for one's money. "We were both of us poor," writes Frances Power Cobbe of herself and a friend, "but in those days poverty in Florence permitted us to rent fourteen well-furnished rooms in a charming villa, and to keep a maid and man-servant." A successful author like Hawthorne could end up with a positive Versailles: setting him back the equivalent of $28 per month, Villa Montauto was "big enough to quarter a regiment . . . and there are vast wildernesses of upper rooms into which we have never yet sent an exploring expedition."

On top of all this, there were extraordinary opportunities for sponging. In Tom Trollope's words, Florence was "an especially economical place for those to whom it was pleasant to enjoy during the whole of the gay season as many balls, concerts, and other entertainments as they could possibly desire, without the necessity, or indeed the possibility, of putting themselves to the expense of giving anything in return." Best of all, from a skinflint's point of view, were the balls thrown by the grand duke at Palazzo Pitti; these were open to everyone and provided "a very handsome and abundant supper, at which . . . the guests used to behave abominably. The English would seize the plates of bonbons and empty the contents bodily into their coat pockets." ("I never saw an American pillaging the supper table," Trollope adds, though "American ladies would accept any amount of bonbons from English blockade runners.")

The free feasts at Palazzo Pitti were just one manifestation of a surprising phenomenon that must also be counted among the reasons for Tuscany's popularity: its decent government. In 1737, with the Medici on their last legs, the problem of the so-called Tuscan Succession had been settled in favor of the House of Habsburg-Lorraine, from which Tuscany's grand dukes had ever since been drawn. For almost thirty years Tuscany was indifferently ruled from Vienna, until in 1765 Grand Duke Leopold I took charge. Pointedly living in Florence, not Vienna, and sincerely dedicated to the welfare of his domain, the enlightened Leopold introduced many improvements and reforms (in 1786 Tuscany became the first state in Europe to abolish the death penalty), and the son who followed him, Ferdinand III, was equally benign.

Ferdinand's own son, Leopold II, assumed the throne in 1824. Though by all accounts a dull dog—his nicknames included "il Broncio" (the Sulker) and "il Gran Ciuco" (the Great Ass)—he preserved the established liberties and was entirely unpretentious; in fact, he prided himself on maintaining, as he put it, "the worst drawing-room in Europe." The more snobbish colonists were aghast at his lack of discrimination,* but almost everyone appreciated the nonoppressiveness of his policies. So easygoing was Tuscany that even Leigh Hunt, a lifelong radical, was moved to say, "I loved the Government itself . . . for at that time it was good-natured and could 'live and let live.'" Nor was it any different in the 1840s: Fanny Trollope referred to it as a "mild and truly paternal Government," while to Charles Lever it was "a government so mild as to be no government at all."

---

*One British minister, George Hamilton, intent on exercising some quality control, tried to persuade Leopold II to receive only those Britons who had already been presented at court back home. But the grand duke resisted, and the minister gave up. "Oh!" sneered Hamilton, "that's what he wants! À la bonne heure! He shall have them all, rag, tag and bobtail." (The anecdote is related by Tom Trollope.)

Politically speaking, Tuscany looked particularly good compared to the twin powers of southern Italy, the Kingdom of the Two Sicilies and the Papal States (which in fact stretched to north of Bologna). These had become notorious as bastions of despotism, repression, and backwardness. That both states were deeply Catholic made them, to the Protestant mind, sinister redoubts of "Popishness" as well. Here again Tuscany shone by contrast, remaining relatively Laodicean and tolerant of rival faiths. Not that there weren't sectarian tensions. Ever since 1835, when Count Piero Guicciardini, descended from one of Tuscany's most illustrious families, founded a group of Plymouth Brethren in Florence, the authorities had been watchful of suspected proselytizers, and in 1852 they swooped down on Francesco and Rosa Madiai, a Florentine couple who'd been converted by the English family they worked for; both were given long prison sentences, which provoked furor in Britain, with everyone from Lord Palmerston to Charles Dickens taking up the cudgels. For the most part, however, Anglo-Saxons in Tuscany felt free to worship as they pleased, and were grateful not to feel themselves in the belly of the papist beast, as they might have in Naples and, even more, Rome.

Tuscans, and Florentines in particular, were reassuring in other ways as well. Sober, hardworking, somewhat phlegmatic, they came off as Italian but not *too* Italian, people as much of the north as of the south. And their city, despite its economic hardships, continued to deliver a high standard of living.

Florence was, in short, something perilously close to a utopia, and its very perfection almost ruined the colony. With so much cut-rate hedonism at their disposal and so little to trouble them, colonists were dangerously tempted toward indolence, superficiality, and navel-gazing; it was all too easy for them to stay within their anglophone bubble. Too few made close friends among their Florentine neighbors or became fluent in their language, even after long periods of residence. To a degree this had always been the case, but the self-isolation had intensified, at least among the upper social strata. In the days of the Grand Tour, British and Italian aristocrats had often hobnobbed, gambling together, playing *cicisbeo* or *cavaliere servente* to each other's ladies, and so forth. (Rumor had it that Earl Cowper's wife had been bedded by Leopold I himself.) By the mid-nineteenth century, however, their fortunes had diverged, the Italian nobility struggling while their British counterparts, nearing the peak of their imperial prosperity, grew ever more arrogant, insular, and priggish; as a result, there was less contact between the two groups than previously.

"The English, more than all other people," Lady Blessington acutely observed in *The Idler in Italy*, "carry with them the habits and customs of their own country. It would appear that they travel not so much for the purpose of studying the manners of other lands, as for that of establishing and displaying their own." This chauvinism could be so extreme as to be laughable: the writer Mary Boyle recalls of a "staunch John Bull" she met in Florence that "no power on earth could persuade him . . . he could possibly be called a foreigner. 'No, ma'am,' he used to say, 'the Italians are foreigners, but I am an Englishman!' "

The flip side of pride is contempt, and Britons often turned up their long, straight noses at their aquiline hosts. A favorite sport was to pityingly deride them as historical has-beens: "They pelt us with great names; they look down on us because there is no Michelangelo now in Florence, and Savonarola no longer preaches there," complained the Florentine scholar Enrico Nencioni. Italians in general were often viewed (in the words of Giuliana Artom Treves, whose *The Golden Ring: The Anglo-Florentines, 1847–1862* is the prime Italian source for the period) as "unworthy custodians of unappreciated treasures." Some of the ugliest slurs on Italy's people came from those most deeply in thrall to its art. Ruskin was especially virulent: "I detest the Italians beyond measure," he spat in a letter. "They are Yorick's skull with the worms in it, nothing of humanity left but the smell." Nor were Americans immune to this kind of disdain. "I am sorry to say," reported Margaret Fuller, "that a large portion of my countrymen here take the same slothful and prejudiced view as the English, and after many years' sojourn betray entire ignorance of Italian literature and Italian life . . . They talk about the corrupt and degenerate state of Italy as they do about that of our slaves at home."

To be sure, there were plenty of exceptions among the colonists. Specialized professionals like Mary Somerville automatically connected with their Florentine counterparts. Greenough was intimate with luminaries like the dramatist Giovanni Battista Niccolini, the poet Giuseppe Giusti, and the statesman and historian Gino Capponi, whose bust he sculpted. Jarves came to relish "the Tuscan *patois*," as he called it, and in particular "the wit and the humor of the street *gamins*." And Tom Trollope was exemplary in his embrace of all things Tuscan. Despite having no background as an Italianist, he immersed himself in his environment so completely that he was soon publishing novels and histories with Tuscan themes and settings, including the massive *A History of the Commonwealth of Florence*. Nor did his reverence for the past engender scorn toward the present; to the contrary, he found himself fascinated by the persistence of certain Florentine characteristics down the centuries, and had many Italian friends.

The colony's predominant tendency, however, was to hang back, to stay cocooned within itself, and, insofar as it paid any heed to the status of Italy per se, to write the place off as a hopeless basket case. So things would no doubt have remained had history not intervened.

———◈———

Ever since the eviction of the French in 1814, the larger forces of history had dealt lightly with Florence and the rest of Tuscany, the once-swift current of events growing lazy as the Arno in midsummer; indeed, this drowsy stasis was part of the allure of the place. But in the later 1840s that began to change, as the grand duchy was drawn into the whirlwind of Italian nationalism. That the shift happened to coincide with the crystallization of the colony turned out to be highly fortunate, both for the colony itself, which was saved from lotus-eating triviality, and for Florence, Tuscany, and the new nation that was soon to incorporate them. For the eventual triumph of the Risorgimento, as it came to be called, depended not insubstantially on British (and to a lesser degree American) support, and much of that support was whipped up by the colony.

In a sense, the early headquarters of the Risorgimento was London. Drawn in part by the presence of the patriotic poet Ugo Foscolo, members of the secret revolutionary society known as the Carbonari escaped to London in the early 1820s after the rebellions they'd fomented sputtered out, and it was to London that the movement's first true leader, Giuseppe Mazzini, exiled himself in 1837. While Mazzini soon won friends and supporters among the intelligentsia—the Carlyles in particular—the government, wary of his destabilizing potential, kept him under close surveillance. In 1844 Mazzini ingeniously turned the tables by providing proof that it had spied on his mail. Among his correspondents were the revolutionary brothers Attilio and Emilio Bandiera, who, with Mazzini's encouragement, had launched a doomed insurrection in Calabria. When it came out that British authorities had learned of the plot by opening Mazzini's mail and then tipped off their Neapolitan counterparts, who in turn foiled the plot and executed its leaders, the public was outraged. The result was a bonanza of support for Mazzini and his cause.

Tuscany also nurtured the movement early on. So secure in its liberalness was the grand duchy that it allowed a measure of agitation within its borders, and Florence in the 1820s and 1830s became a minor hotbed of nationalism, with writers and radicals meeting at the Gabinetto Vieusseux to vent grievances and lay plans. (The library's founder, Gian Pietro Vieusseux, was a Swiss scholar with a progressive bent.) Though occasionally cracking down, the government mostly upheld this permissiveness in the following decade. In 1847, in fact, it loosened the reins still further. The new pope, Pius IX, was proving to be—to the horror of the old guard—a humane reformer, and Leopold II, inspired by this softening in the Vatican, decided to scale back on censorship and to reinstate the civil guard.

Both men soon had reason to rue their lenience, for the wave of revolution that swept through Europe in 1848 caught up with them the following year. Leopold fled for Gaeta, near Naples, where he joined Pius, who'd been driven out of Rome. Like Rome, Florence became a republic, ruled by a triumvirate that included Mazzini. The republican experiment was, however, short-lived in both cities. In Florence, there were growing fears that the Austrians would invade and restore Leopold by force; he was therefore invited to return, which he did in July 1849. But if invasion had been avoided, a clampdown was inevitable, and before long the city was swarming with Austrian troops—neither Leopold nor Emperor Franz Joseph was taking any chances.

These dizzying developments provoked much excitement in the colony. The first to espouse the nationalist cause were Tom and Theodosia Trollope, who took advantage of the easing of censorship in 1847 to launch a weekly paper, *The Tuscan Athenaeum*. This curious little publication ran for only thirteen weeks but set a benchmark for Anglo-Italian cooperation.* Theodosia had begun translating a number of Florence's best-known patriotic poets, and both Trollopes had become friends with them, as with other members of the pro-Risorgimento intelligentsia. And so *The Tuscan Athenaeum* featured, alongside colonial advertisements (a merchant selling "good black tea" and Bass Ale) and arts coverage (a review of a Niccolini play), polemical and satiric poems by the likes of Giuseppe Giusti and Francesco Dall'Ongaro, as well as Theodosia's verse anthems and Tom's clarion calls for unification.

When Leopold was ousted, the Trollopes, like many others, took pride in the lack of accompanying violence. "If ever there was a revolution 'made with rose-water,'" Tom later wrote in his memoirs, "it was the revolution which deposed the poor *gran ciuco*. I don't think it cost any human being in all Florence a scratch or a bloody nose." When Leopold was restored, however, disillusion set in. The grand duke was now a far more draconian ruler, summarily abrogating all the liberties he'd once sponsored. More offensive still was his new obedience to Vienna. Unlike other parts of northern

---

*The New York Public Library has the only complete run of *The Tuscan Athenaeum*. To flip through its brittle pages is as close as one can get to time-traveling back to the colony.

Italy, Tuscany had gone largely unmolested by the Habsburgs. No longer: from the summer of 1849 onward, Austrian troops were an obnoxious presence in the city.

Though scarcely affected by them, many colonists were furious at these retrograde changes. Greenough found the new order so unpalatable that he pulled up stakes and returned home. Few followed his example, but there was widespread hatred for the Austrians, and solidarity with those who longed to send them packing. Not that the colonists were uniformly engagé or of one voice. The conservative Lever denounced "the rule of the stiletto and the rabble" and lamented the advance of Italian liberalism in the *Fortnightly Review.* He was, though, very much in the minority. Even Fanny Trollope, whose friendship with the great Metternich made her soft on the Austrians, came round to advocating Tuscan independence.

Then there was Elizabeth Barrett Browning. With their house directly across from Palazzo Pitti, the Brownings had enjoyed a catbird view of recent events. Robert, whose cerebral nature and immersion in the Renaissance precluded any sort of fiery activism, was only moderately stirred. His wife, however, was galvanized utterly. The immediate fruit of her invigoration was *Casa Guidi Windows,* a book-length poem whose first part praises Leopold and Pius but whose second is a bitter record of hopes crushed. The fact that she was among the most popular authors of the day meant that her eyewitness account reached a wide audience, causing readers on both sides of the Atlantic to sympathize with the counter-despotic aims of the Risorgimento.

But not even she could make much of a difference for the moment. With Italy again under the firm control of the Habsburgs in the north and the Bourbons in the south, the independence movement was reduced to a smoldering ember, its leaders forced to bide their time in exile. For the colony, life largely reverted to its former patterns, except that Leopold no longer threw open the gates and larders of Palazzo Pitti. The more politicized colonists remained loyal to the cause and did what they could to support it, but most Anglo-Florentines slipped back into a parochial, self-satisfied trance.

In 1858 the colony was again jolted awake, this time not by a revolution but a Rip van Winkle–like resurfacing. For out of no-where appeared Walter Savage Landor. Though he'd been away for twenty-three years, he was by no means forgotten; "there still lingered," as Tom Trollope put it, "a traditional remembrance of him—a sort of Landor legend." Even in his absence Villa Gherardesca had drawn pilgrims: when Charles Dickens, with whom Landor had become close friends (and who'd cast him as Boythorn in *Bleak House*), visited Florence in 1845, he made a special trip out to the villa, from which he plucked an ivy leaf to bring back to the old poet.

Now here was the prodigal himself, age eighty-three. In England, a particularly scurrilous satire of his had provoked a libel suit, and he'd decided again to seek refuge in Italy. Amazingly, his wife allowed him to move back in. But they were soon at daggers drawn, and Landor once again went storming out of the house. Later that day, he was found stumbling about Florence by Robert Browning, who brought him back to Casa Guidi. For the next two years Landor would live largely with or near the Brownings, a kind of honorary grandparent. Still pugnacious and devoted to defenestration, he did not make their lives easy—more than one dinner, judged unsatisfactory, was sent sailing through Casa Guidi's famous windows. Yet they found him irresistible, and didn't mind constantly having to (in Robert's words) "explain away the irritations and hallucinations as they arise."

In 1859 the Brownings brought Landor along to a rented house outside Siena, where they were to spend the summer with William Wetmore Story and his wife. Also joining the group for part of the season were Isa Blagden and the twenty-one-year-old Kate Field, whose flirtatious attentions Landor, four times her age, found just the thing for his vanity. (Field wrote a profile of the old lion for *The Atlantic Monthly*.) When not writing or sculpting separately, the group often discussed Italian politics, and did so with an excitement not felt since ten years earlier. For the Risorgimento had flared back up.

It was now spearheaded by the plucky little state of Piedmont-Sardinia, led by the warlike King Victor Emmanuel II and his

diplomatically brilliant prime minister, Camillo Cavour, who'd persuaded Napoleon III to help dislodge the Austrians. In April 1859
the fighting began, and in June the Franco-Piedmontese coalition
scored major victories at the battles of Magenta and Solferino.*
Though Napoleon betrayed his allies the very next month, going
behind their backs to sign the Treaty of Villafranca with Franz
Joseph, enough momentum had been generated to keep events
surging forward. Tuscany, in fact, had already taken advantage of
the turmoil. After a series of demonstrations in Florence, at which
nationalist *tricolore* flags were waved by the thousand, Leopold had
decided to abdicate; the last of his grand-ducal line, he made his
way to exile in Bologna.

All this the Brownings and their friends hashed over together,
with Landor directing particular venom at Napoleon III and Elizabeth feverishly versifying the latest developments in her new book,
Poems before Congress. But what most exercised the group was the
reemergence of Giuseppe Garibaldi.

Garibaldi had been lying low since making his appearance on the
world stage in 1849, when he'd led the doomed defense of the Roman Republic. Now, like Landor, he was suddenly back on the scene,
in command of a private corps, the Cacciatori delle Alpi (Hunters of
the Alps), that was fighting alongside the Piedmontese.

Outside Italy, nobody was more intoxicated by his return than
the British. Fearless, gallant, modest, soulful, ruggedly picturesque,
and capable of stirring eloquence (Churchill's "I have nothing to
offer but blood, toil, sweat, and tears" was lifted from his Italian pre-
decessor), Garibaldi had overwhelming romantic appeal, and of a
kind tailor-made to capture British hearts. A few Britons, such as
Colonel Hugh Forbes, a former officer in the Coldstream Guards
who'd moved to Siena and become an Italian patriot, had fought
with him in 1849, and in subsequent years Garibaldi's cross-Channel
reputation had only grown, enhanced by his monthlong visit to Tyne-

---

*Solferino represented a turning point not only for Italy but for humanitarian causes: it was
after witnessing the battle's carnage that the Swiss activist Henry Dunant was inspired to
found the International Red Cross.

side in 1854 and by the advocacy of Jessie White Mario, an Englishwoman who, à la Margaret Fuller, married an Italian revolutionary and began barnstorming on Garibaldi's behalf, her lectures and
articles winning droves of supporters.

Some of these supporters were moved to put their lives on the
line, just as an earlier generation (most famously Byron and Trelawny) had done in the Greek War of Independence, and as a later
one would do in the Spanish Civil War. They soon had a chance.

When, in April 1860, revolts broke out in Palermo and Messina,
Garibaldi seized the occasion and invaded Sicily with his new corps
of volunteers, the Redshirts. The Expedition of the Thousand, as it
came to be called, included a British-led regiment, which played a significant part in one of history's most rousing David-versus-Goliath
upsets. After the Redshirts invaded the Italian mainland in August
1860, so many Britons rallied to Garibaldi's banner that he formed
the British Legion (also known as the Garibaldi Excursionists), led
by the gargantuan Colonel John Peard, whose beard and commanding presence often caused him to be mistaken for Garibaldi himself.
Those who were injured, British and Italian alike, could count on
the ministrations of Jessie White Mario, who'd become a sort of
Florence Nightingale to the campaign, just as Margaret Fuller had
been to the Roman campaign in 1849.

Though no prominent members of the colony went off to fight
for Garibaldi—most were too long in the tooth—a number had
been backing his efforts, as well as those of the Piedmontese in the
north, in the best way they knew how: not with swords but with
pens. "We were all equally 'Italianissimi,' as the phrase went then; all
equally desirous that Italy should accomplish the union of her *dis-
jecta membra*," Tom Trollope recalled,* and to help her do so he and
his fellow writers fired off persistent volleys of partisan journalism.
There were plenty of venues for it, thanks in particular to Charles

---

*Another testament to the universality of this sentiment can be found in *The Education of
Henry Adams*. Adams's sister Louisa Kuhn lived in Florence with her husband for some
months in 1859–60, and Adams remarks that "like all good Americans and English [she
was] hotly Italian."

Dickens, who once declared, "I feel for Italy almost as if I were an Italian born."

As the editor of (successively) *The Daily News*, *Household Words*, and *All the Year Round*, Dickens often commissioned and published pro-Risorgimento articles, many of them by Tom Trollope—with whom he'd struck up a warm friendship during his 1845 visit to Florence—and other colonists. Thackeray did something of the same as editor of the *Cornhill Magazine*. American periodicals, meanwhile, carried Kate Field's plugs for unification. Even Landor got into the act, donating the proceeds from his latest imaginary conversation to a Garibaldi fund. But the writer most valuable to the cause was, of course, Elizabeth Barrett Browning. "It is incredible to see the effect which your wife's book *Poems before Congress* has made," the British foreign minister, Sir Odo Russell, told Robert. So much clout was she perceived as wielding that the Piedmontese statesman Massimo d'Azeglio came to enlist her help in swaying the British government.

By that point it needed little swaying. The potent trio of Lord Palmerston (then prime minister), William Gladstone, and Lord John Russell kept Britain on a pro-unification tack despite the dissent of Queen Victoria.* Though the British officially remained on the sidelines, their diplomatic support was crucial, and Victor Emmanuel now made bold to sweep down the peninsula with his army, easily defeating the forces of the Papal States. Meanwhile, Garibaldi dealt a final blow to the Kingdom of the Two Sicilies at the Battle of Volturno. On October 26, 1860, the leaders linked up near Naples and enacted the climactic scene of the Risorgimento, the "handshake of Teano," with Garibaldi putting aside his republican aspirations to hail Victor Emmanuel as the prospective King of Italy.

Though two of the most important pieces of the jigsaw—Venice and Rome—still lay in enemy hands, the rest had come splendidly

---

*Russell became especially impassioned, and was consequently revered in Italy. According to George Macaulay Trevelyan, "Once, in 1869, when [Russell] and his family were staying at a villa in San Remo, they found the ceiling of the principal room frescoed with portraits of four national heroes. The four turned out to be Mazzini, Garibaldi, Cavour, and, to their surprise and delight, Lord John himself!"

together, through either conquest or plebiscite: the previous spring, Tuscany and the other northern duchies had voted to throw in their lots with Piedmont-Sardinia and be absorbed into a new constitutional monarchy. At long last, on March 17, 1861, Victor Emmanuel was proclaimed the first King of Italy in Turin, which became the capital.

The colony had reason to be proud of its role in bringing the nation into being. Though its contributions ultimately amounted to no more than a tributary to a tributary to the main river of the Risorgimento, it had helped to redraw the map of Europe.

Sadly, several of its most engaged members barely lived to see their efforts bear fruit. The first to go was Elizabeth Barrett Browning, whose body-and-soul involvement had eclipsed all others. The closeness of her identification may, in fact, have hastened her death. When Cavour, whom she idolized, keeled over from a stroke on June 6, 1861, the loss may have been, as William Wetmore Story remarked to Charles Eliot Norton, "the last feather that broke her down." While she certainly suffered from one or more serious maladies (Pott's disease is now thought the likeliest culprit), the volatility of unification also took its toll, and she followed Cavour to the grave less than a month later, on June 29.

Unable to bear remaining in Florence without Elizabeth, Robert moved back to London. The loss of the Brownings marked the beginning of the end of the heroic age of the colony. The next to fall away was Fanny Trollope, who died in 1863, her tongue sharp but playful till the end. The following year it was Landor's turn. Before leaving town, Browning had gotten Landor settled with a pair of Florentine caretakers. But his long Indian summer was nearly over, and in September 1864 he too passed on. Seven months later it was Theodosia Trollope's turn. They were all buried in the so-called English Cemetery, which had actually been founded by Swiss Protestants. Around Elizabeth Barrett Browning's ornate tomb were clustered those of her friends and rivals, the little graveyard now a sort of shrine to a whole generation.

If the English Cemetery represented the colony's memorial to itself, Florence and the new nation of Italy were quick to pay their own respects. On the death of Elizabeth Barrett Browning, many Florentine shops closed for a day in tribute, and municipal authorities affixed to Casa Guidi a plaque stating that she "fece del suo verso aureo anello fra Italia e Inghilterra" (made of her verse a golden link between Italy and England). A similar plaque was placed on Villino Trollope to commemorate Theodosia. Nor did the living go without recognition. Thomas Trollope received a thank-you visit from Garibaldi himself, as well as the Order of Saints Maurice and Lazarus, the highest honor conferred by Victor Emmanuel's House of Savoy. For his contributions as a dantista, Kirkup got the same honor in 1865, on the six-hundredth anniversary of Dante's birth. In knighting Kirkup, Victor Emmanuel accidentally addressed him not as "cavaliere" but "barone," and the rapturous old necromancer seized on the slip, thereafter styling himself Baron Kirkup. Dante's ghost, contacted by Kirkup via a medium, deemed the title just.

By the time he inadvertently made Kirkup a baron, Victor Emmanuel wasn't visiting the City of Lilies but ruling from it. For the city had been awarded an honor of its own, albeit one that was very much a mixed blessing: the capital of Italy, it had been decided, should no longer be Turin but Florence. On February 3, 1865, the king made his formal entrance into the city and took up residence in Palazzo Pitti.

Not unlike Alexandria under Muhammad Ali, Florence—which at that time had a population of about a hundred fifty thousand—found itself abruptly thrust into an unfamiliar role, forced to accommodate an administration far larger than that of the grand dukes and to serve as the center of a forward-looking nation. Inevitably, a makeover began. The city had undergone modest changes during the previous decades, with streets widened and monuments revamped,* but now more extensive alterations were felt to be needed. Hired to oversee them was the architect Giuseppe Poggi,

---

*One of the larger and more controversial of these projects, the affixing of a polychrome neo-Gothic façade to the austere front of Santa Croce, was single-handedly financed by a member of the colony, Sir Francis Sloane, a pious Catholic who'd made his fortune mining in Tuscany.

who drew up a plan that, while nowhere near as ambitious as Hauss-mann's for Paris, would reshape the city over the coming years. By the summer of 1865 the most radical of Poggi's plans, which called for the destruction of the city's ancient circuit of walls, was already being implemented. For centuries a self-enclosed, essentially medieval town, Florence was becoming a modern metropolis with a ring road.

Unlike its walls, Florence's hulking gates were spared by Poggi and allowed to stand in lonely grandeur around its perimeter. Similarly, a certain number of human relics remained from the Anglo-Florentine glory years: among others, Kirkup, Blagden, Powers, Lever, and Tom Trollope were still in town. But the essential character of the colony was evolving as a new generation moved in. One of the first to arrive was Janet Ross.

FOUR

La Padrona di Castagnolo

One of Janet's earliest memories, dating from 1846, was of a Leghorn hat—a kind of straw bonnet for which Livorno (Leghorn
to the British) was then known—that the dowager Lady Duff Gordon had brought her from Tuscany. Because the hat flapped in her
face with the least gust of wind, she hated it with a passion, until one
day in St. James's Park she threw it in a puddle and trampled it in
front of her horrified nanny.

This little incident, which she recalls in the opening pages of *The
Fourth Generation,* must in retrospect have struck her as ironic: her
petulant destruction of a Tuscan souvenir could not have been less
predictive of her later attitude toward the province. It was, however,
in some ways a harbinger. By the time of her arrival, a whole body
of Anglo-Tuscan precedents had been laid down, a set of outlooks
and expected behaviors. Much of this she unthinkingly perpetu-
ated, following well-worn grooves like thousands of others. Yet she
also branched off in new directions and turned her back on custom.
While she never committed improprieties equivalent to public hat-
flattening, some of her compatriots' entrenched habits seemed to
her as silly, confining, and impractical as a flimsy bonnet on a breezy
day, and these she left lying in a ditch. Her sixty years in Tuscany
were to constitute, in a sense, one long rejection of Leghorn hats in

favor of whatever rough-and-ready headgear would allow her to go unhindered about her business. And, as it turned out, that business would include a good bit of stomping: instead of bonnets, she was soon to crush grapes.

— = =◦= = —

It cannot be said of Janet—unlike, say, Robert Browning—that destiny had been pointing her toward Italy all along. Except for her paternal grandmother, none of her close relatives seems even to have visited Italy, oriented as they were toward Germany and France. But there were hints of Italy always floating about her, like notes of fragrance from a citrus grove; as ever, the family network saw to it that she had connections to the place long before she got there.

Some of these originated with Sarah Austin, who knew a number of Italian exiles in London, including Ugo Foscolo and the Count of Santa Rosa, who'd led an insurrection in Piedmont. Sympathetic to their cause, touched by their loneliness, and able—thanks once again to her mother's emphasis on languages—to converse with them in their native tongue, Sarah warmly befriended these émigrés and went out of her way to help them, directing several to Norwich, where her parents helped them find work; one, a certain G. Pecchio, proclaimed her "the protecting saint of the refugees."

In the next generation, Lucie learned Italian as well, and while neither she nor Alexander was markedly Italophile, they had friends who were, including Samuel Rogers, whose hugely popular long poem *Italy* (1822–28) was once the vade mecum of British tourists. But the figure who probably first piqued Janet's curiosity about Italy, and Florence specifically, was George Frederic Watts. "Signor" had gone to Florence for a visit in 1843 and ended up staying four years, a more or less permanent guest of the British minister, Lord Holland. Sitting in Watts's studio while he painted, Janet must have heard at least the occasional anecdote about Florence and those members of the colony, such as Kirkup and Powers, with whom Watts had consorted. She may also have picked up stories from the dowager Lady Duff Gordon, who during her 1846 tour of Italy—the one that yielded the infamous Leghorn hat—had spent much time with Watts in Florence.

Another likely source of alluring tidbits about Florence and the colony was Layard, whose childhood in the city was, to judge from his memoirs, nothing short of paradisal. Layard maintained a strong interest in Italian affairs, and in 1859 he wrote Janet several long letters about his recent travels in the country. Given that he was a busy man of the world and she a mere girl, they are surprising and rather touching documents, avuncular but never condescending; Layard wades right into the political situation, describing his visit to the Tuscan parliament and voicing his reasoned optimism about the Risorgimento. Janet must have been especially flattered by his account of a meeting with Lord Clanricarde in Florence: "He seems quite delighted with Garibaldi (whom I hope to see on my way back), and declares that a dinner with the General reminded him of a day at the Gordon Arms." (Presumably what the experiences had in common was a certain relaxed bonhomie, for Garibaldi was renowned for his unpretentiousness.)

How closely Janet followed Garibaldi's campaigns, or those of the Piedmontese, is hard to say. Essentially apolitical, she was always more inflamed by local conflicts and injustices than large-scale ones. Also, the endgame of the Risorgimento happened to coincide with compelling changes in her own life: the Expedition of the Thousand took place during her courtship and engagement, and Victor Emmanuel's coronation occurred just as she was making her first discovery of Cairo. But if marriage and Egypt were more on her mind in the early 1860s than the struggle for Italian unification, she surely kept track of it, and had friends who cared deeply about it, such as Meredith.*

In short, when Janet arrived in Florence at the age of twenty-five, she had a number of associations with the city, the colony, and Italy

---

*A late convert to Italophilia, Meredith made his first trip to Italy in 1861 and went on to publish two novels with an Italian heroine: *Emilia in England* (later retitled *Sandra Belloni*) and its sequel, *Vittoria*, which he'd been working on when he ran into Janet in Venice, and which has an early-Risorgimento theme and setting.

at large; according to Thayer, she also spoke at least some Italian even when she lived in Alexandria. Janet herself says nothing of these matters in *The Fourth Generation*, and she may have given them little thought. Preoccupied with finances and somewhat at loose ends, she wound up in Florence almost by accident, with no intention of remaining. Only gradually did she knit herself to the place.

———

In his memoirs, Tom Trollope refers to the "migratory nature of such a society as that which was gathered together on the banks of the Arno," and to the "quicksand-like society" of the Anglo-Florentines. Of course there were many exceptions, Trollope himself among them. But the tendency was for colonists to drift in and out of town; even the Brownings, for all their love of Florence, were constantly sneaking off to Rome, Siena, Bagni di Lucca, or even England. For several years, the Rosses epitomized this transitoriness, always coming and going without putting down real roots.

Janet's initial stay was short indeed, about two months in the spring of 1867 while waiting for Henry to catch up with her. Even so, she managed, with her usual social alacrity, to get straight into the thick of things.

Like Watts, she took full advantage of her consular connections. Sir Henry Elliot had filled several posts in Italy during the Risorgimento—he once conferred with Garibaldi aboard a British warship off Naples—before being appointed ambassador in 1863, and he was on easy terms with the local dignitaries.* At the embassy, Janet met Ubaldino Peruzzi, a former mayor of Florence, and through him his uncle Simone, with whom she hit it off. Simone Peruzzi served as her introduction to the great families of Florence, for whom the Middle Ages were as yesterday, and as a reminder of the ancient ties between the city and her homeland: "Often with a sigh [he]

---

*Elliot's official title was Minister to the King of Italy, but the post was virtually identical to an ambassadorship.

would tell how his family had been ruined by Edward III of England, who repudiated his debts in 1339."

She was also befriended by an even more hallowed family, the Strozzi, in the person of the Marchese Luigi Strozzi, then in his last year of life. Though handsome and distinguished, he was a rather pitiful figure, hopelessly carrying a torch for Napoleon's niece Princess Mathilde Bonaparte, to whom he'd once been engaged. The princess had instead married the boorish Count Demidov, perhaps Florence's richest man.* According to Janet, "One day [Strozzi] showed me her bust on a pedestal at the foot of his bed, saying no woman was ever so clever or so handsome. Princess Mathilde would have been a happier woman had she married charming, courtly Marchese Strozzi."

Strozzi, who bred horses at his estate near Mantua, gave Janet entrée to Florence's equestrian scene, such as it was. It certainly didn't match that of Egypt or England, and there was one unique hazard, at least according to the writer Charles Weld, who in *Florence: The New Capital of Italy* (1867) advises riders to proceed with caution, as the local youth "are very fond of playing a game called Ruzzola [that] consists in rolling a cheese on a road, generally downhill, by means of a broad string wrapped around the cheese . . . Such a missile, striking your horse's legs, is very likely to bring steed and rider to sudden grief." But at least there was superb riding of the see-and-be-seen variety in the Cascine, Florence's answer to Rotten Row. "Now, the Cascine is to the world of society what the Bourse is to the world of trade," Charles Lever wrote in the 1840s. "It is the great centre of all news and intelligence, where markets and bargains of intercourse are transacted, and where the scene of past pleasure is revived, and the plans of future enjoyment are canvassed."

---

*Anatole Demidov (1813–70), who belonged to what was probably the wealthiest family in Russia after the Romanovs, lived outside Florence in the Villa San Donato, a Palladian house built by his father. Mathilde Bonaparte (1820–1904) was the daughter of Napoleon's youngest brother, Jérôme Bonaparte, who settled in Florence in later life, and the sister of "Plon-Plon." Their brief union was as wretched as that of the Young Pretender and the Countess of Albany, and in 1846 she scarpered to Paris with her lover. There is a portrait of her by Watts, who painted it in Florence.

Nothing had changed by the 1860s, except that one was now likely to cross paths not with the Grand Duke of Tuscany but the King of Italy. Janet did so while riding with Elliot on a "raking young Irish hunter, a very useless horse for Florence," which she'd volunteered to break in for him. Persistently bucking, the horse drew the attention of Victor Emmanuel, who, pulling his carriage alongside Elliot's, curiously questioned the ambassador about Janet. Seizing the opportunity, Elliot asked whether she might visit the royal stud near Pisa. "Il Re Galantuomo," as he was known, readily agreed.

A few days later a royal usher escorted Janet to the farm, where the head groom told her that the "small Arabs" in which it specialized "were the King's favorite mounts when he went hunting in the Alps, and that they climbed like chamois. His Majesty must have weighed something like seventeen stone, and I pitied the poor wee things." She was also intrigued to see camels, "laden with pine cones and firewood, stalking along on the grass under trees. The first was brought to Tuscany more than 300 years ago I was told, and have not degenerated, only their coats struck me as thicker and rougher than those I had been accustomed to in Egypt."

In Egypt itself, meanwhile, Henry had straightened out his affairs, and by June he was in Florence. He and Janet proceeded to England, staying at Nutfield Cottage with Sarah. In August the Rosses went to a German spa on account of some ailment of Henry's, and there they received news that Sarah had died at age seventy-four. Tributes poured in from Guizot, Saint-Hilaire, and other old friends, and the obituaries were properly fulsome. Janet dutifully documents this posthumous praise in *The Fourth Generation* but makes no show of grief. Certainly she was grateful to her grandmother for her matrix of friends, and respected her intellect, tenacity, and skill as a translator. (Janet had in fact recently taken over a translation job— a book of essays by the Belgian diplomat Jules Van Praet—that Sarah had been too unwell to complete.) But Sarah had always been put off by her granddaughter's careless joie de vivre, while Janet, on her side, seems to have found Sarah humorless and excessively earnest— as Kinglake once commented, "a joke of any kind was to her a detestable interruption of serious reasoning and statements." Overall,

Sarah was more appealing to her as a forebear than a relative, so to speak.

Back in England, Janet had a brush with death herself when she caught severe bronchitis. Fearing the clammy English winter, she decided to return to Florence. Henry briefly joined her but then had to attend to a fresh round of troubles in Egypt—the Trading Company debacle refused to go away. This time around Janet couldn't stay with the Elliots, who'd been reposted to Constantinople, so she rented an apartment on the Lungarno Acciaiuoli. Though she doesn't say so in *The Fourth Generation*, which gives the impression of childlessness, she'd brought along five-year-old Alick, temporarily collected from Charlotte Austin. (The only proof of his presence is a letter from Lucie that remarks on a picture of Alick taken in Florence.) While the colony had of course never been devoid of children— Landor, the Brownings, and the Trollopes had all delighted in their offspring—it was more of a grown-ups' world, and one guesses that Janet wasted no time finding a nanny. At any rate, her memoirs tell us almost nothing about the months that followed, except that she became friends with Giovanni Morelli, important in art history for having devised a new, more subtle method of attribution.

The highlight of this interim period took place not in Florence but Venice. When previously in Venice, Janet had met a celebrated local character named Rawdon Brown. A historian and collector, Brown had lived some thirty years in Venice and was known for giving detailed tours of both the city and his home on the Grand Canal, Palazzo Gussoni Grimani della Vida. Among his friends were Ruskin, Morelli, and, later, Robert Browning, who wrote a sonnet about Brown's inability to tear himself away from La Serenissima for even a day. Over time he became almost as eccentric as Kirkup, and also something of a curmudgeon.

These qualities became evident in the spring of 1868, when Brown invited Janet to stay with him. In accepting, she committed a grave faux pas: recalling that Brown had once "been obliged to hire a big bath for a lady guest," she asked whether she should bring a portable tub. "In reply I received a cold and sarcastic note to say that as evidently I did not consider his house as properly furnished I had better not come." After telegraphing to apologize, she decided to go anyway, hoping that Brown's fit of pique would pass. He met her train, brought her home, and coolly showed her to her bedroom, which she found "filled with baths of every shape and size." This wild caprice seems to have been part apology and part joke, but really more of a dig, "a sort of punishment for my impudence in daring to imagine that he did not possess them." Despite Brown's needling, "he was the most delightful of hosts, and I learnt more about old Venice during my week's visit than a whole library of books could have taught me."

With Henry still pinned down in Egypt, Janet decided to return to England for the summer, taking a novel route back. Great strides were being made in European transportation at the time. To get from Florence to Britain in the 1840s, one could either take a steamship to Livorno or travel overland by means of a hired carriage, known in Italy as a *vetturino*. The latter option was agonizingly slow—in 1844, Fanny Trollope spent ninety-seven hours just getting from Florence to Turin. By the mid-1850s, however, one could go by rail all the way from Calais to Marseilles, and in the following decade the lines crept toward Italy. While the first Alpine tunnel was being dug, a temporary means of traversing the mountains was devised by the British engineer John Barraclough Fell. Known as the Mont Cenis Railway, it opened in June 1868, and Janet was among its very first passengers. She'd been given a letter of introduction to Fell, who had his son take her over the pass in a train consisting of a single carriage and an engine. Alick must have been with her, and was probably thrilled—one can imagine few things more exciting to a five-year-old boy. For Janet, it was a privileged sneak preview to go with her Suez Canal tour.

In November 1868 she returned to Florence, where her new favorite companion was the Pre-Raphaelite artist William Holman Hunt. Hunt was at his nadir. In 1866 he'd recklessly decided to take his pregnant young wife, Fanny, to Egypt and the Holy Land, where he'd happily traveled and painted twelve years earlier. A cholera outbreak in Marseilles throwing a spanner into their plans, the couple wound up instead in Florence. Given the Pre-Raphaelites' rapturous identification with Botticelli and other Florentine painters, it seems surprising that he found his way there only by accident. But the detour wasn't a lucky one, for Fanny, after giving birth to a boy, came down with miliary fever and died. The stricken Hunt poured his grief into a ghoulishly themed painting, *Isabella and the Pot of Basil*—based, like Keats's poem, on a tale from the *Decameron*—and into sculpting the ark-shaped tomb he'd designed for Fanny's grave in the English Cemetery, which was his main preoccupation at the time Janet crossed paths with him.

To judge from his *Self-Portrait* of 1867 (now hanging in the Uffizi), Hunt had one of the great Victorian beards, and gentle features expressive of kindness and melancholy—one can see why Janet was drawn to him. The fact that their common friend Henry Phillips had just died prematurely made for a sad bond between them, and Janet often kept Hunt company in his Fiesole studio, where he was working up a study of "big Egyptian pigeons" he'd done years earlier; the sight of the birds gave her a pang of "*heimweh* [homesickness] for the land of sun."

As she may have disclosed to the aching Hunt, the land of sun had recently become a scene of mortal struggle for her mother. Since the Rosses' visit to Luxor, Lucie had—except for a brief, failed stab at living in Beirut—maintained her pattern of seasonal migration between Luxor and Cairo. The Maison de France having partially collapsed, the *Urania* became her only home, her life reduced to a ceaseless sailing of the Nile.

In late 1867 the monotony lifted somewhat with the arrival of her son, Maurice, now eighteen. After graduating from Eton, Maurice had been sent to study with a tutor in Brussels, with a view toward entering the diplomatic service, but had become increasingly dissolute. Lucie felt a spell in Egypt would do him good. To her dismay, he charged straight into the fleshpots of Cairo, patronizing the city's brothels with Flaubertian relish, and she found herself giving him (as she confessed to Alexander) "a pound or two to have a good dancing girl rather than a lot of four-penny women." In Luxor he continued his whoring but also began to show an appreciation for local folkways. "Living among the Arab *canaille* has greatly improved Maurice's manners, which were terribly strong of [*sic*] the billiard room and brandy," Lucie wrote. "He has all my faculty for getting on capitally with savages."

For over a year Maurice remained with her. All this time her health held steady, but in early 1869 it abruptly worsened. So ill was she that, while in Aswan, she had to turn down an invitation to visit the Prince and Princess of Wales (the future Edward VII and Queen Alexandra) aboard their dahabeah; graciously, the royal couple instead came to see her aboard her own. Realizing that her days were numbered, she stopped briefly in Luxor to say goodbye to her friends. A crowd of hundreds—made up of sheikhs, prostitutes, and everyone in between—saw her off, and she sailed downriver for the last time. Once in Cairo, she insisted that Maurice go home to England; the end was close, and she didn't want him to witness it. Never leaving the moored *Urania*, she hung on for another few weeks. On July 13 she filled out a telegram to Alexander to inform him of her death, leaving the date blank. The next day she died, at forty-eight.

By then Janet was back in England, where she and Alexander, hoping to see Lucie once more, had been about to head for Egypt. But now there seemed little point, and they left it to Omar to arrange her burial, next to Thayer in Cairo's European cemetery.

By the time of her death, Lucie had become something of a celebrity—"Egypt's most famous invalid," as one scholar puts it. *Letters from Egypt* had shown her to be a woman of exemplary compassion and broad-mindedness, and nearly everyone who sought her out or ran into her along the Nile, from the Prince of Wales on down, came away moved by the encounter. In a sense, her final phase echoed that of her old friend Heine, who'd spent twelve years stoically wasting away in Paris on what he called his "mattress-grave," and who, as one biographer writes, was "an obligatory stop for visitors from beyond the Rhine."*

---

*Shortly after Lucie's death there occurred a haunting, rather uncanny incident involving another departed friend. In 1852 Eliot Warburton (who'd just finished editing the memoirs of Horace Walpole) had been headed to Panama on the steamer *Amazon* when the ship caught fire and sank; along with more than a hundred others, he perished in the disaster, remaining with the captain on deck till the end. As he helped a fellow passenger into one of

But if Lucie had become a sort of Heine-on-the-Nile, a public and even universal figure, her loss of course fell hardest on the family. The extent of Janet's sorrow is difficult to gauge. Certainly she felt far more in tune with her mother than her grandmother, both for the high spirits of which Lucie was capable and for the quiet moral force and dignity that Janet, even in her flippancy, recognized and revered. Even harder to fathom are Alexander's feelings. Mysteriously, he'd visited Lucie in Egypt only once, and even then had cut his visit short; on some level he'd given up on her. But however much he'd resigned himself to losing his wife, her death came as a terrible blow.

"My father was so unhappy," Janet recalls, "that I insisted on his coming abroad with me, away from condoling friends who did him no good." She took him to the Alpine region of Val d'Aosta. On a drive through the area, they were enchanted by the Château de Fénis, a fabulous medieval pile prickling with towers and turrets. Learning that it was for sale, they gave in to a mad spasm of fantasy, presumably born of the mountain air and the shock of their bereavement. "We counted up our pennies, made wild plans to buy the Château de Fénis, and at Aosta sought out the lawyer who was charged with the sale." But the scheme soon evaporated: "Perhaps fortunately our castle had been sold two hours before for an absurdly low price." Janet's dream of castle ownership would have to wait.

Instead of sharing a château in the Italian Alps with Alexander, the Rosses finally committed to Florence in the fall of 1869. Frustratingly, Janet nowhere explains this momentous decision. The city, which she'd been darting in and out of for over two years, had obviously grown on both of them, but it would also seem that money played a role: whatever the amount that Henry had ultimately salvaged from the ruins of the Trading Company, it wasn't enough to fund the English country-house life they'd hoped for. And so, like

---

the few lifeboats, Warburton handed her a portrait of Lucie he'd brought with him, asking her to return it to the Duff Gordons. But the woman forgot the name, and the portrait remained with her in the West Indies. Seventeen years later, a visitor recognized it, at which point the woman obtained Alexander's address and sent it to him. It happened to arrive just after Lucie herself died on the *Urania*.

many Britons before, they probably came to the conclusion that it was better to live comfortably in Tuscany than frugally in Surrey or Kent. Moving into a rented apartment on the Lungarno Torrigiani—the stretch of Oltrarno riverfront just east of the Ponte Vecchio, more or less opposite the Uffizi—they put an end to their long, trying period of uncertainty and nomadism and began their new lives.

Whether because she'd decided to settle in Florence or because by this point she had substantial experience of the place, Janet grew increasingly curious about Tuscany and its traditions. Of particular interest to her were its songs, which filled the air at the time. "Life was not so strenuous forty years ago," she asserts in *The Fourth Generation*. "The Florentines were pleasanter and far gayer than they are now.* Singing was to be heard nearly every evening, particularly on our side of the river, as there was considerable rivalry between the young men of San Niccolò and San Frediano [two of the city's sixteen *gonfaloni*, or districts]." She was especially impressed by a laborer named Ulisse, who often strolled down her street belting out *canzoni*. With his superb tenor voice, this latter-day Odysseus might have turned the tables on the Sirens: "At last I could not resist opening my window and calling out *Bene, Bravo*," Janet recalls. They became friends, and Ulisse taught her the hits of the day, some adapted from Neapolitan versions "to suit the Tuscan taste." She found it tricky to learn a song from him, "as he seldom sang it in exactly the same way. But I had a good ear and generally mastered even his *girigogoli*, as '*fioriture*' [flourishes] are called in common parlance in Tuscany . . . The words I could always buy at the corner of the street for five centimes." In exchange she occasionally saved Ulisse from himself: whenever he got dead drunk ("a rare failing among Florentines in those days") and wound up in jail, Janet would "go to my friend the Syndic [mayor] and beg him off." That she was already able to *dare una spintarella*—to practice, that

---

*Nostalgia is par for the course with writers about Tuscany, as elsewhere; the golden age is always in the past. In *What I Remember* (1888), Tom Trollope sighs over the demise of "*Firenze la Gentile*," graced by "little old-world sights and sounds which are to be seen and heard no longer."

is, the crucial Italian art of string-pulling—testifies to how quickly she'd gotten up to speed; most colonists went decades without mastering such skills.

If her grasp of etiquette and love of musical ephemera were unusual, in another of her enthusiasms, namely art collecting, she was entirely typical. The colony's appetite for pictures had grown over the previous decades, in tandem with the vogue for "primitives." The market was scoured by professionals like Jarves and Kirkup but also by amateurs like Layard's father, who'd placed an altarpiece by Filippino Lippi over his son's bed.* An especially voracious collector was Landor, one of whose many vanities was an absolute faith in his eye for painting. Colonists liked to joke about the ease with which forgers and unscrupulous dealers tricked him into buying worthless daubs, but he also ended up with some authentic masterpieces— Richard Monckton Milnes, who saw his collection, reported that "amid some pretenders to high birth and dignity his walls presented a genuine company of such masters as Masaccio, Ghirlandaio, Gozzoli, Filippo Lippi and Fra Angelico."

Today such a collection would be worth millions, and the fact that Landor was able to amass it on a minuscule budget says less about his shrewdness than the affordability—not to mention the availability—of great art at the time. On the other hand, even those more skeptical than Landor stood more chance than they would now of being duped. Jarves expressed his wonder at the "amount of trash annually palmed off on . . . discerning critics" and noted that "Italy, which has given birth to the finest works of art, has also produced the most ingenious race of imitators." The risk of being hoodwinked was well known, and *The Tuscan Athenaeum* featured ads for *The Lions of Florence*, an art-and-monuments guide by the English painter and dealer William Blundell Spence that included advice on how to guard against it.

As for the Rosses, their first major venture into picture buying

---

*The altarpiece is now in the National Gallery in London. According to the editor of Layard's memoirs, it "still bears traces of a wound inflicted by the heel of [his] shoe, flung at his brother in a childish quarrel."

(they'd already made some smaller ones) in October 1869 was an extraordinary piece of beginner's luck. "An old man from whom I had bought frames," Janet writes, "came one day with an air of mystery to tell me that a wonderful picture, one of *the* pictures of the world, could be bought for *un pezzo di pane* [a piece of bread]." Along with Henry, she was taken to the studio of a restorer named Tricca, where they met with an astonishing sight: a large panel, over six feet tall and eight wide, containing one of the more unique paintings of the Renaissance, Luca Signorelli's *The School of Pan*.

Best known for his frescoes of the Last Judgment in Orvieto Catherdral, Signorelli was also an accomplished panel painter, and *The School of Pan* (c. 1490) is widely considered to be his masterpiece in the genre. It depicts a group of nude and scantily clad figures gathered around the goat-legged Pan; several have flutes and are, as the title suggests, being taught pastoral music. "In no other work," one scholar contends, "is the never-never land of classical antiquity . . . so idyllically re-created." Be that as it may, the picture also has a certain decadence, a hint of the orgiastic.

Standing before it in Tricca's studio, Henry said to Janet in Arabic (to which they often resorted for encrypted communication), "What a fine thing, we must try and buy it." The asking price, however, was so low that they "suspected there must be something wrong." Sensing their wariness, Tricca related the work's troubled history. Painted for the Medici, it had come as part of a dowry into the Corsi family, one of whose members, a cardinal, was so shocked by its naked figures that he had clothes painted over them. Later it was consigned to an attic, until a nineteenth-century descendant of the family had it restored and discovered it to be a Signorelli. But he too was offended by it, and so brought it to Tricca, who tried unsuccessfully to sell it to the Louvre. Evidently Tricca was now in a hurry to unload it, and the Rosses had come to his attention as possible buyers. A price of fifteen thousand francs (Janet tends to quote prices in French terms) was agreed on, and just like that the Rosses had the giant thing in their dining room, the only place it would fit.

While the painting was unquestionably genuine, there now began a curious series of events suggesting that the Rosses had been caught up in a shady little web of art-world maneuvering. Out of nowhere, William Blundell Spence stopped by and mentioned to Janet "what I already knew, that my old friend Sir William Boxall was expected in Florence." Spence had been hoping, he continued, to persuade Boxall, the director of the National Gallery in London, to buy *The School of Pan* for the museum, "but unfortunately some Hungarian with mustachios had just bought it." The mustachioed mystery man was, of course, Henry. "My husband had been very little in Florence," Janet explains, "and was not known by sight, and there was so strong a resemblance between him and General Türr that occasionally officers saluted him in the street."*

Guessing that Spence had been tipped off to the true identity of the "Hungarian," Janet showed him the rest of her pictures but kept him out of the dining room, and he went away empty-handed. Soon afterward Boxall arrived, and at dinner Janet mischievously sat him opposite *The School of Pan*. "He was so much occupied in talking to me about common friends that for some minutes he did not look up. Suddenly he dropped his knife, exclaiming, 'Eh, why good gracious, that's the picture Spence has been telling me about.' Rather to my dismay, my husband offered Boxall the *School of Pan* for the price we had given, plus 10 per cent which had been promised to Tricca in case we ever sold it. The dear old man hemmed and hawed, said it was rather undressed for the British public, and to my relief did not accept Henry's offer."

What to make of all this? As National Gallery archives reveal, in 1866 Boxall had been sent by the previous director, Sir Charles Eastlake, to look at *The School of Pan*, which he concluded was too lubricious for the museum. But this only complicates the puzzle. It would seem that some tangle of bungled schemes yielded a comedy of errors. At any rate, the Rosses kept the painting for the moment.

---

*The Hungarian revolutionary István Türr (1825–1908) led a brigade of his countrymen during the Expedition of the Thousand and was possessed, as portraits show, of a truly magnificent soup strainer.

Two years later, Tricca brought over Wilhelm von Bode, founder of the Kaiser Friedrich Museum in Berlin (which has since been renamed after him), to inspect it. Bode expressed interest in buying it but said he'd first have to send a photograph of it to Berlin for consideration by his colleagues. In true Prussian style, he barked at his assistant to take the picture down from the wall and have it photographed, only to have Henry countermand the order. "Evidently Dr. Bode was not accustomed to be thwarted," Janet notes. "He looked astonished and angry." Despite his vexation, Bode agreed to buy the painting on the spot, "for 66,000 francs, 6000 of which went as promised to Tricca." Even if the Rosses hadn't bought it with a view toward a quick profit, they ultimately made one.

Meanwhile, the map of Italy had again been redrawn, thanks indirectly to Bode's compatriots. A few years earlier, in 1867, Garibaldi had made another attempt to capture Rome but had been repulsed, in large part because the papal army was reinforced by French auxiliaries. But with the outbreak of the Franco-Prussian War in the summer of 1870, the French, needing every available soldier, recalled their garrison. When Pius IX rebuffed Victor Emmanuel's offer of a negotiated settlement, Italian troops took Rome in September. In Florence, Janet recalls, "*Roma Capitale* was the cry all through the city. I admired the patriotism of the Florentines, for they must have foreseen what a loss this would mean for Florence." The city's days as seat of government were numbered, and on July 1, 1871, the transfer took place. Though many Florentines felt they could afford the loss of prestige and were glad to be rid of so much cumbersome bureaucracy, the abrupt drain of population and money brought the city to the brink of bankruptcy.

For Florentines serving in Victor Emmanuel's administration, the change also meant having to move to Rome. Janet had become friends with one of these uprooted functionaries, and it made all the difference. His shoes needed to be filled, and in filling them she discovered an unforeseen vocation, one far removed from the slick, shifty demimonde of art dealing.

The Marchese Lotteringo della Stufa belonged to an old and moderately prominent Florentine family, commemorated to this day by the Via della Stufa, near the Medici tombs, and the Palazzo della Stufa in the Piazza San Lorenzo. Born in 1829 but still a bachelor, he'd served in the Tuscan parliament before becoming a chamberlain to Victor Emmanuel. Lotto, as his friends called him, was an Italian nobleman in the classic mold, handsome, debonair, amiable, and with a dash of Renaissance multifacetedness—he liked to invent gadgets in his spare time.

How and where he first met the Rosses is unclear, but by 1870 he knew them well enough to offer them, as a summer rental, Castagnolo, his farm estate seven miles to the southwest of Florence. They both loved the place, and the following year, with the king's relocation imminent, Lotto made them a proposal: the Rosses could indefinitely occupy part of the villa and largely have it to themselves, since most of the time he'd be at court in Rome. He planned to return home whenever possible, but would stay in his own quarters. The Rosses may already have been hankering to move outside town, or perhaps they merely decided to give it a try. In any event, they wound up staying at Castagnolo for seventeen years.

The comune where they now found themselves was Lastra a Signa, a fortified town with only two small claims to fame: that Sir John Hawkwood had helped the Pisans destroy it in 1364, and then, switching sides, persuaded the Florentines to rebuild it for defensive purposes; and that its Spedale di Sant'Antonio, built in 1411, had served as the model for Florence's foundling hospital, which put Brunelleschi on the map as an architect. These scraps of glory were far in the past, and for centuries Lastra a Signa had been an ordinary, unsung burg. In an essay published some years later, Janet wrote that there was, except for the now disused hospital, "nothing remarkable in the village," and that its population, "squalid and miserable enough," was largely employed in producing Leghorn hats—"the clatter of the hopper used for sorting the straw is incessant."

While the racket can't have softened her animus toward Leghorn hats, it was no more than a distant sound at Castagnolo. The house had begun as a simple loggia belonging to the Arte della Lana

(Wool Guild), which used it to dry their wool. In the fifteenth century it was acquired by the della Stufa family, who renovated and expanded it into a proper villa, as well as buying the surrounding acres for use as a vineyard. (Supposedly Lorenzo de' Medici was partial to their wine and would often come to sip it.) The completed villa was a long, L-shaped, mostly two-storied structure with deep eaves and a porte cochere. One room had a ceiling with Raphaelesque frescoes, and Lotto's collection of Roman and Etruscan statues was scattered about.

In addition to Lotto, who came and went, the house accommodated a *fattore* (farm manager) named Andrea and his family. But since it measured many thousands of square feet, there was more than room enough for everyone, and the Rosses took over an entire wing, intermingling their possessions with Lotto's. Apparently Lotto encouraged them to make free with the grounds as well, for Henry laid out a garden and built orchid houses. (Orchids were to become an obsession of his, but whether he'd previously cultivated them or was embarking on a long-dreamt-of hobby is unclear.)

One benefit to having so much space was that the Rosses could host friends from abroad. Their first guest was Saint-Hilaire, who'd become secretary to the new French president, Adolphe Thiers. Just before Victor Emmanuel decamped from Florence, Thiers sent Saint-Hilaire to him on a private mission (surely one of some delicacy, given the awkward pavane that France, Italy, and the Vatican had been dancing with each other). With appealing unpretentiousness, the aging philosopher-statesman chose to stay not in Palazzo Pitti or a fancy hotel but with the granddaughter of his old friend Sarah Austin in her makeshift country lodgings. Before his appointment with the king, Saint-Hilaire asked whether he could hitch a ride with Andrea, who was headed into town in his two-wheeled gig for market day. "*Come, un tal pezzo grosso con me nel baroccino?* (What, such a great personage in the gig with me?)," Janet quotes the flustered fattore as responding. "So at about six in the morning the French envoy started in the *baroccino* and drove up to the Palazzo Pitti." At first the guards refused to admit him, doubting the credentials of a man who arrived with a peasant in a cart full of vegetables. Moments later, a personal attendant rushed out to apologize and escort Saint-Hilaire to his meeting with the king.

The Rosses' next guest was Alexander, who arrived later that summer. During his weeks at Castagnolo he seemed to be in pain, and Janet was nagged by forebodings. These proved to be well-founded, for on returning to England Alexander was diagnosed with cancer of the tongue. Somehow he was persuaded to cross the Atlantic and "drink the waters" at a spa in Vermont—the first time a member of the family had visited the United States. The waters of course did nothing for his cancer, and by the summer of 1872 he was rapidly failing. He'd been living at Nutfield Cottage, but his brother, Cosmo, insisted on moving him into his London flat, where Janet went to keep vigil. "For five and a half months I watched by the bedside of him I loved more than anyone in the world." Flocking to his side, Alexander's friends were shocked "at the sight of his thin, sad face, and at being greeted by a word scrawled with difficulty on a slate"— the cancer had left him mute. He died in late October, at sixty-one.

Unlike Sarah Austin, the dowager Lady Duff Gordon hadn't had the good fortune to predecease her child, and her last few years—she died in 1875, at eighty-six—were embittered by the conviction that Lucie had ruined his life. Hers was an unfair view, but fate *had* turned implacably against the once-charmed couple, and where Lucie had been transformed into a saintlike, Nile-haunting legend, Alexander had suffered in humdrum obscurity, plugging away at his Inland Revenue job while trying to care for his motherless children. He'd once seemed destined for something better.

For Janet's part, whatever she'd felt at the loss of her mother, that of her father was devastating; more at ease with men in general, she was especially so with Alexander, who understood and enjoyed her vigorous character like nobody else in the family. "Life was never the same again," she writes, "without that dear friend and companion"—a bland statement, but one of unquestionable sincerity.

There were, however, consolations, for her new existence at Castagnolo, to which she gratefully returned in late 1872, was a source of deepening happiness. The arrangement with Lotto was working out brilliantly. If the Rosses paid any rent at all, it was surely very low, even by Florentine standards. Better yet, their nominal landlord had become the closest of friends. Fleeing Rome and the stiff punctilios of court whenever he could, Lotto would return for long stretches to his beloved estate. The furthest thing from an aloof or lazy patrician, he would roll up his sleeves, eagerly pitching in on whatever needed doing. He also knew a great deal about farming and viewed the peasants who worked his acres with an almost Tolstoyan benevolence. But since he had to be in Rome most of the time, he began putting Janet in charge. (Henry preferred to fuss over his garden and orchids.) The exact terms of the understanding are unclear, but within a year or two she was considered to stand in loco whenever he was away. This she did with gusto, authority, and ever-increasing competence.

Like virtually all Tuscan *tenute* (estates), Castagnolo was run on the mezzadria system, also known as *mezzeria*.* Both terms are derived from the Italian *mezzo*, for "half," the basic principle being that each harvest was evenly split between the padrone and the contadini who farmed his land. The contadino gave his labor, while the padrone supplied, in addition to land and housing, all necessary equipment and capital for the purchase of livestock, seeds, and fertilizer. During lean years, the padrone was also supposed to absorb the loss and lend the contadino enough to see him through. Another feature of the system was that the tenuta was divided into small *poderi* (farms), each typically worked by a single family.

For foreigners to acquire a tenuta wasn't unheard of, but neither was it their style to participate in or oversee farming, let alone to interfere with the archaic methods of the contadini. At the Ricorboli estate owned by Tom Trollope and his second wife,† the contadini farmed the land in, as he put it, "precisely the fashion of their

---

*In her writings, Janet uses "mezzeria," but "mezzadria" came over time to be more widely used, and therefore seems preferable here.
†Trollope hadn't remained a widower for long. In 1866, Frances Ternan, the sister of Dickens's mistress Ellen Ternan, came to Florence to serve as governess to Tom's daughter, Bice, and within a few months married the father of her charge, twenty-five years her senior. As he had with Theodosia, Tom often collaborated on books with Frances, including *The Homes and Haunts of the Italian Poets.*

grandfathers and great-grandfathers, and strenuously resisted any suggestion that it could, should or might be cultivated in any other way." At Castagnolo, Janet wasn't yet in a position to challenge peasant orthodoxy. She did, however, begin to confidently assert herself as a sort of deputized padrona, and this in itself was radical, since women—even Tuscan women—were no more in the habit of running estates than were foreigners. One can only guess what Andrea initially made of this freakish imposition, though he seems to have come round to it.

Some sense of Castagnolo's agricultural life can be gathered from Janet's description of the 1874 *vendemmia* (grape harvest), in which Tom Taylor participated. Taylor, who was one of Janet's oldest friends—he'd attended her fifth birthday party—was a literary jack-of-all-trades: in addition to writing plays (including *Our American Cousin*, the play Abraham Lincoln was watching when he was assassinated), he churned out biographies and art criticism, and had just taken over as editor of *Punch*. He arrived in September with his composer wife, Laura, and their two children, and the whole family joined their hostess in the vineyards. Janet's account of the harvest in *The Fourth Generation* evokes a Brueghelesque charm and beauty:

All day long the handsome white oxen, their heads gaily decked with scarlet and yellow tassels, dragged the heavy red cart with a large vat, full of the grapes we had picked tied on it, from the vineyard to the villa. There the grapes were transferred into huge vats in the *tinaia* [barrel room] to ferment. Every twelve hours the peasants, after rolling up their trousers and carefully washing their legs and feet, stamped down the fermenting mass to prevent the top layer from becoming acrid by too long a contact with the air. This must be thoroughly done, or the contents of the vat, many hectoliters, would turn to vinegar. The scene in the *tinaia* in the evening was most picturesque. In the large building, dimly lit by little oil lamps shaped like those out of old Etruscan tombs, stood rows of enormous vats, up and down which the men scrambled with purple-stained legs singing *stornelli* [folk songs] at the top of their voice as they danced about vigorously on the grapes. Many of the tunes were noted down in the evening by Laura Taylor, who was an admirable musician. A certain Beppe, a famous *improvvisatore*, wove the names of Laura, Lucia, and Antonio (Tom, he said, could not possibly be a name as it had only one syllable) into his verses, paying them high-flown compliments. Tom declared he did not recognize himself as the clever, handsome, stalwart Antonio who performed such wonderful feats.

Though she doesn't mention it here, Janet often joined the men in the vats, her legs as purple as theirs from grape-squashing, and she always sang lustily along with (or even initiated) the stornelli. If Tuscany's ephemeral canzoni piqued her interest and challenged her technique, its folk songs—ancient, rooted, dense with peasant philosophy—exerted a stronger and more lasting fascination. Not only did she learn a large repertoire of them, she took up playing the guitar so as to accompany herself and others. Over the years, her earthy performances would become, among her fellow anglophones, one of the things for which she was best known. More important, her fluency in the musical lingua franca of the land made for an instant rapport with all but the most surly and suspicious contadini.

In addition to singing with the local peasants, Janet routinely sang stornelli with several neighbors higher up the social scale. Living at a nearby villa were the three Orsi brothers, all of whom "sang delightfully and often came in with their guitars." She became especially fond of the youngest, Carlo, who was in his early twenties and just starting out as a painter. Later he would illustrate several of her books, but first she posed for him. He did at least two portraits of her, one of which was eyebrow-raising. Janet is shown lying on a chaise longue in the nude, with a sheet draped across her legs but her buttocks half exposed; turned away from the viewer, she has her head propped on one arm and is reading a book, like a sort of literate odalisque. Even more surprising than the painting itself is the fact that Janet hung it above her bed. With some people, this would suggest narcissism, exhibitionism, or a wish to provoke. In Janet's case, a likelier explanation is simply that she was pleased with the portrait, which has a lovely intimacy, and wanted to keep it in view. Still, one wonders how Henry felt about her hindquarters being displayed for all to see.

What Janet's English visitors made of the portrait is unknown. A number of them did, however, set down their general impressions of her at Castagnolo.

One was the now obscure but once-ubiquitous Augustus Hare. Born in Rome, Hare was a social butterfly who spent much of his life fluttering about the Continent, all the while writing at speed; as prolific as Tom Taylor, he specialized in sophisticated, rather long-winded guidebooks. In his memoirs, he describes Castagnolo, which he visited several times in the 1870s, as an assemblage of "charming old halls and chambers, connected by open arches, and filled with pictures, china, books, and beautiful old carved furniture. A terrace lined with immense vases of tulips opens on a garden with vine-shaded pergolas and huge orange-trees in tubs." Hare liked Lotto but thought Janet "the presiding genius of the place." "All the small-nesses of life, which make a thoroughly anglicised character igno-ble," he writes, had been "washed out" of Janet's, leaving the "higher qualities . . . to be mingled with the Italian frankness and kindly simplicity, which *English* English do not possess." Her stornelli he found "rendered with all the verve which a *contadina* herself could give them. It is no wonder the Italians adore her."

A few months before Hare's second visit, Janet received two other forgotten Victorians. Elizabeth Thompson (later Lady Butler) was, of all unladylike things, a military painter, and a highly suc-cessful one; dubbed "the Florence Nightingale of the brush," she showed a rare concern with the suffering of ordinary soldiers. (One of her depictions of the Crimean War, *The Roll Call*, was a particu-lar favorite of Queen Victoria, who strong-armed its owner into sell-ing it to her.) She first met Janet in 1875 at Aldermaston, where both were guests of the Highford Burrs, and when she mentioned that a magazine had commissioned her to go to Florence later that year to illustrate the festivities for the four-hundredth anniversary of Michelangelo's birth, Janet invited her to stay at Castagnolo. When the time came, Elizabeth asked whether she might bring along her sister, who would later, under the name Alice Meynell, become known as a poet and woman of letters. Janet agreed.

At Castagnolo, Janet welcomed the Thompson sisters and led them through, as Elizabeth recalls in her memoirs, "frescoed rooms and passages, dimly lit with oil lamps" to their bedrooms, "enormous, brick-paved, and airy."* Entertained by musical evenings with the Orsi brothers and finding "endless subjects for sketching" around the estate, they so enjoyed themselves that they arranged to come back the following year for the vendemmia. On that occasion, Janet struck Elizabeth as having "assimilated the sunshine of Egypt and Italy into her buoyant nature, and to see the vigour with which she conducted the vintage at Castagnolo acted as a tonic on us all; so did the deep contralto voice and the guitar, and the racy talk." On going back to England, she and Alice asked themselves, "How could we have had the fullness of Italian delights, which our kind hosts afforded us, in some pension or hotel in Florence?" Many of Janet's guests asked themselves the same question, more or less, and she and her bucolic retreat began to gain a reputation for providing what the city and the colony couldn't.

Not that the colony was remotely in abeyance. By the mid-1870s, the last remnants of its old guard were gone—Blagden and Powers had died, the Trollopes had moved to Rome, and Kirkup had been

---

*During the sisters' visit, Janet also took in an unexpected guest: Sir Frederick Burton (1816–1900), an Irish painter who'd recently taken over from Boxall as director of the National Gallery. Janet's account of his arrival is one of the funnier moments in *The Fourth Generation*: Burton "suddenly appeared one day and asked whether we could give him a bed. He had fled from Florence because at the table d'hôte he had been worried by two gushing English spinsters who asked his opinion on Botticelli, Fra Angelico, etc. etc., and talked nonsense. So he expatiated on the enjoyment he had experienced from the works of two great masters, *Mortadella di Bologna* and *Coteghino di Modena* [two types of sausage], which he was sure they would like. Next day they told him their search in the Pitti Gallery had been fruitless, but that a friend who knew the director was to take them next day to the Uffizi. Alarmed at the prospect of their indignation, he packed his bag and came to us."

advised by spirits to move to Livorno—and it had no dominant or quintessential figure, no Landor or Elizabeth Barrett Browning. Yet it remained a melting pot of strong and quirky personalities, one thickened by an influx of newcomers. Jessie White Mario had settled in Florence, where she served as a reminder of the glory days of the Risorgimento. Lucy Baxter, daughter of the "Dorset poet" William Barnes, arrived about the same time as Janet and began publishing learned works on Italian art and history under the nom de plume Leader Scott. (Her father's friend and admirer Thomas Hardy spent much of his 1887 visit with her.) The socialite Lady Walpurga Paget, whose husband had replaced Elliot as British ambassador, was often in Florence even after it lost capital-city status, and she eventually moved back. There were artists galore. John Roddam Spencer Stanhope, Marie Spartali Stillman, and Charles Fairfax Murray were second-wave Pre-Raphaelites of some standing. Among the American painters, Elihu Vedder was still around, and so were the portraitist Francis Alexander and his daughter, Francesca, who was to bowl over Ruskin with her illustrated collection of Tuscan ballads.* Fresh faces included Henry R. Newman, a watercolorist also much admired by Ruskin, and Frank Duveneck, hailed as a genius by Henry James and popular as an art teacher; establishing himself in Florence, Duveneck had a subcolony of his own, and his exuberant protégés, known as "the Duveneck boys," became a familiar sight in town.

As for Janet's relationship to the colony, it's somewhat difficult to pin down. Despite her pride in old family ties, she wasn't a name-dropper, and *The Fourth Generation*, the main source for these years, is pell-mell and almost arbitrary: Janet stuffed into the book

---

*Francesca Alexander (1837–1917) had lived in Florence since she was a teenager, and like Janet had become interested in stornelli, especially the longer ones. Gaining the trust of a celebrated old *improvvisatrice*, she copied out the songs in the woman's repertoire and compiled them into an album, adding her own drawings. During his 1882 visit to Florence, Ruskin happened to be shown the album, and was stunned at the originality of Alexander's illustrations. He urged her to publish the album as a book and provided a glowing preface. *Roadside Songs of Tuscany*, as the opus was titled, ran to four volumes and brought Alexander brief but widespread fame.

whatever letters she had at hand, interspersed with, it seems, whatever memories happened to pop into her head, so that a chance
meeting might be mentioned but a long friendship neglected. As a
result, the extent of her involvement with the colony and her attitude toward it remain rather obscure. What can be safely asserted is
that there was a degree of mutual ambivalence involved, and even of
paradox, for she was becoming at once a fixture of the colony and a
dissenter from it.

Even after moving to Castagnolo, Janet continued to know many
colonists, and to attend the occasional ball or party. But much of
colonial life held little appeal for her. In his Anglo-Florentine novel
Indian Summer, William Dean Howells writes that his protagonist,
Colville, "objected that the barbers should offer him an American
shampoo; that the groceries should abound in English biscuit and
our own canned fruits and vegetables." Janet might not have shared
Colville's objections, but neither did she give a damn about English
biscuit. Nor did she wish to surround herself with anglophones.
Vedder recalls that the denizens of Bellosguardo "seemed to live a
little, fussy, literary life filled with their sayings and doings," and
that "a few lived their own lives, but most of them seemed to be living up to the great ones of their acquaintance or up to each other—
somewhat like the inhabitants of that Irish village where they lived
by taking in each other's washing." Janet shared Vedder's distaste
for this enclave mentality, which must have reminded her of Alexandria. Besides, she already had many Italian friends. With her fluent
language skills and cosmopolitanism, she could also fraternize at
will with the Germans and French in town.*

There was, though, one English colonist with whom Janet had a
very intense—albeit largely unilateral—relationship. Over the years
she'd rubbed plenty of women the wrong way, but now she made a
bona fide, almost rabid enemy.

---

*The German colony was especially vibrant at this time. Among its key figures was the
sculptor Adolf von Hildebrand (1847–1921), who lived in the Villa San Francesco di Paola
and held (as R.W.B. Lewis puts it in *The City of Florence*) "one of the most celebrated salons
in Europe"—Wagner, Liszt, and many others dropped in on it.

Born in 1839 to an English mother and a French father, Marie Louise de la Ramée, who wrote under the pen name Ouida, became one of the most popular novelists of the 1860s and 1870s, her fame resting in particular on *Under Two Flags*, the prototype of French Foreign Legion adventure stories. Many of her forty-odd novels were, like *Under Two Flags*, highly colored historical romances with swaggering Byronic heroes. In person she was just as flamboyant, living in an expensive London hotel and often dressing up as her own heroines. The ravishing beauty of these heroines was, however, lacking in Ouida. Slathering over her harsh features with gallons of makeup, she struck most people as grotesque—an impression not softened by a pushy manner and, as someone put it, "a voice like a carving knife." Despite all this she commanded a salon of sorts and exerted a queasy mesmerism over many. Henry James was intrigued by her "most uppish or dauntless little spirit of arrogance and independence." She was, in short, a kind of painted, spinster Fanny Trollope, only with less charm and a more florid imagination.

In 1871, tiring of England, Ouida moved to Florence with her beloved mother and bought the Villa Farinola, not far from Lastra a Signa. She was soon introduced to Janet, and at first the two got along, to the extent that Ouida, a dog fanatic, gave Janet a Maremma sheepdog (a handsome local breed). But the amity didn't last. Almost on arrival in Florence, Ouida had met and, in a *coup de foudre* straight out of one of her own novels, fallen instantly in love with a dashing Italian aristocrat. He was none other than Lotto. While Lotto didn't reciprocate her ardor, neither did he discourage it, and Ouida became fixated, even trailing him to Rome. A proposal of marriage couldn't be long in coming, she felt. When it failed to materialize, she concluded that a rival was blocking Lotto's otherwise clear path to the altar. At last the awful truth dawned on her: Janet and Lotto were lovers, and Janet, having cast a spell over the marchese, had turned him into a kind of cat's paw for the sole purpose of toying with and humiliating her, Ouida.

Was there any truth to all this? Ouida's theory about Janet's sadism was of course absurd, reflective only of her own paranoia, thwarted matrimonial ambitions, and envy of a woman who, though just three years younger, was infinitely more attractive. One also assumes that nothing much happened between Ouida and Lotto, and that he tolerated her attentions out of some mixture of fondness and pity. But Ouida was by no means alone in thinking that he and Janet were sleeping together. Indeed, widespread colonial gossip had planted the idea in her receptive brain. Nor, on the surface of things, was it ridiculous. That Castagnolo was the scene of a ménage à trois not only in the domestic but the carnal sense, that Mrs. Ross and the Marchese Lotteringo della Stufa had struck up a long-term, eighteenth-century-style liaison: to the colony, these were perfectly logical deductions, especially given that both the supposed lovers were good-looking and that Mr. Ross was more than twenty years older than his wife.

All this is to reckon without either Janet's apparent frigidity or the fact that she enjoyed many close yet blameless friendships with men; to anyone with knowledge of her, it seems highly improbable that she and Lotto ever so much as kissed. But to Ouida their fornications were a blazing reality. Unable to get past her obsession with Lotto, she became increasingly berserk in her hatred of Janet, and wild rumors began to circulate: Ouida had, some said, taken a potshot at Janet through one of Castagnolo's windows. While this seems unlikely, Ouida truly was out for revenge. Being a novelist, she resorted to her profession's weapon of choice, the roman à clef. Not surprisingly for such a nosy, incestuous community, the Anglo-Florentines specialized in poison romans à clef, but there was none so virulent as the novel Ouida now wrote as payback against Janet Ross.

Published in 1878, *Friendship* centers on Lady Joan Challoner, her husband, Robert, and Prince Ioris, who shares Fiordelisa, his estate near Rome, with the Challoners. Lady Joan is a "handsome, black-browed woman" with a "classic head, fitly shaped for a bust of Athene." Whether "sending her horse at racing pace across the grass that covers the dead Etruscan cities, or waltzing at topmost speed down the vast palace ballrooms . . . or swinging through the feathered maize to call the peasants to their duties," she tackles life "with zest and force, and with a reality of enjoyment that [is] contagious."

But she is also a villainess supreme, corrupt to the core. This is made clear by her backstory. Before moving to Italy, the Challoners lived for six years in Damascus, where Robert worked as an export merchant and Joan amused herself by manipulating powerful men— "She had Asiatic ministers for her henchmen, and Turkish pashas for her obedient slaves"—and by having affairs: whenever a "good-looking wayfarer" turned up, "she would have her Arab steeds saddled and scamper away with him over the Syrian Desert."* Because of Robert's inept chicaneries, his business went bankrupt and the Challoners fled Syria. (Clearly Ouida had gotten wind of the Trading Company disaster.)

At Fiordelisa, Joan weaves a web around Ioris, taking him for a lover and insinuating control over his property. But then Ioris falls in love with Étoile, a young French painter of meteoric talent and unblemished virtue who lives in Rome. Learning of their plans to wed, Joan drives a wedge between them. She and Robert have launched a new swindle, which involves bilking investors by means of a wholly fictitious plan to build a bridge to Sicily across the Straits of Messina. The trusting Ioris is drawn into the plot, and when the Challoners' designs are exposed, his fear of scandal allows Joan to blackmail him into renouncing Étoile.

If Ouida's biographers are to be believed, *Friendship* ignited a firestorm among the Anglo-Florentines, dividing them, like a sort of Dreyfus affair avant la lettre, into "Ouidaites" and "anti-Ouidaites"; one biographer claims that "marriages were ruined, engagements broken, life-long associations smashed to smithereens—all in the cause of *Friendship*." This seems as preposterous as the novel itself, but clearly there *was* much colonial chatter on the subject. Most concluded that Ouida, hoist with her own petard, had done far less damage to Janet's reputation than her own.

Just so, Ouida's star now began to dim, first socially—she had,

---

*In shifting the Rosses' backstory from Egypt to Syria, Ouida may have been thinking of her friends Sir Richard and Isabel Burton, who'd lived in Damascus for a spell. She may also have conflated Janet with the scandalous Jane Digby El Mezrab (1807–81), who married a Syrian sheikh and knew the Burtons in Damascus.

after all, made an ass of herself—and then professionally: her later novels sold poorly. Ever more prickly and peculiar, she holed up in Villa Farinola with only her dogs for company, her mother having died. Lady Walpurga Paget recalls finding her there in squalor: "Eight dogs kept up an infernal noise, and went on mistaking the lace frill of her nightdress for a lamp-post . . . Mrs. Spencer Stanhope, whom I saw later, told me that Ouida firmly resists burying her mother and keeps her in a room upstairs in her villa. Ouida is now by her own folly denuded of everything." Her final years, until her death in 1908, were spent in even deeper filth, and with even more dogs, in Viareggio, on the Tuscan coast.

Janet, meanwhile, cannot have been pleased with her portrayal as Lady Joan Challoner, a rather less flattering character to have inspired than Rose Jocelyn in *Evan Harrington*. Colonial scuttlebutt had it that she'd horsewhipped Ouida in retaliation, either at Villa Farinola or in a Florentine street. More plausibly, she was said to be considering a libel suit. In the event, she did nothing, and seemed to shrug off the whole ludicrous episode—nowhere in her memoirs does she so much as mention Ouida. ("Who is Ouida?" she once replied in mock ignorance when asked about her.) Her one small gesture of reprisal was to place a copy of *Friendship*, stripped of its binding, in the lavatory at Castagnolo, implicitly inviting her guests to use it as toilet paper.

—————

By the time Ouida's literary career began to disintegrate, Janet's was, in its modest way, thriving. Precocious in many respects, she wasn't especially so as a writer. As early as 1860 she'd begun doing the occasional translation, getting into the family trade at an even earlier age than Lucie,* and her *Times* articles, which date from her

—————

*In 1860 George Meredith persuaded Chapman and Hall to let Janet translate Heinrich von Sybel's *History and Literature of the Crusades*. She did most of the work herself, but Lucie helped her polish the translation, and for marketing reasons it appeared under Lucie's name, not Janet's.

early twenties, have a certain maturity about them (if also several kinds of immaturity). For more than a decade, though, she wrote nothing for publication, perhaps because she was first too unsettled and then too absorbed by learning the ropes at Castagnolo. By her midthirties she was at last ready to take up the pen in earnest. Her first efforts were small-scale and sporadic, but she quickly gained momentum, and by the end of her life had written or edited over a dozen books.

In truth, none of these is a masterpiece, and most of them display to some degree the same set of flaws: jarringly abrupt transitions, large chunks of quotation thrust crudely into the text, and a general slapdashery. Her memoirs are also so doggedly chronological as to suggest a total lack of structural initiative and creativity—she plows through the years like a blinkered donkey through a field. Flaubert she was not. Her vices, however, not only mirror her blunt, impatient character but lend a distinctive flavor to her work; for better or worse, a page of Janet Ross is quite unmistakable. She wrote as she lived, and more specifically as she rode to hounds: with reckless confidence and brio, plunging ahead in linear pursuit of her quarry. And since her quarry was rarely commonplace, the roughness of the pursuit is almost immaterial.

One vein of the writing that now began to emerge was genealogical. Janet's family history, especially its matrilineal wing, had always been of interest to her, and with her parents in the grave she felt it incumbent on her to preserve and enshrine that history. Her first effort was the forty-page sketch of her mother that she wrote as an introduction to *Last Letters from Egypt*, an expanded version of *Letters from Egypt* published in 1875. (Sarah had been editing the book at the time of her death, after which it was briefly taken over by Alexander.) But this was a mere dry run for a more ambitious project. Alexander had left her a thick sheaf of Sarah's correspondence, which she meant to edit. Distracted, she put it aside. When she returned to it a decade later, she found herself so riveted that she resolved to hunt down additional material pertaining not only to Sarah but to Lucie, Susannah Taylor, and the rest, with a view toward a multigenerational epistolary biography.

It didn't come together easily. Her cousin Henry Reeve, whom she sounded out because of his detailed knowledge about the family's Norwich roots, tried to discourage her at the start, informing her that as she knew "nothing of the life of the Austins in Queen Square" and even less of the preceding years, she might as well scrap her silly plans. "It requires," Reeve pronounced, "to have lived among all these people and things to describe them." (Small wonder he was known in London literary circles as "il Pomposo," and within the family as "Count Puffendorf.") Nothing daunted, she pressed ahead, pumping the old-timers for facts, anecdotes, and, most important, letters. Many letters turned up, but she often had to translate them from German or French, or go fetch them in person. (Saint-Hilaire had over two hundred from Sarah but wouldn't risk mailing them.) Nor did the headaches end there: "Mrs. Austin *never* dated a letter," she groaned to Kinglake, "& others had the same bad habit, so I can only manage them by referring to their contents, & my head swims with votes on the Ballot etc."

In the end her efforts paid off, for when, in 1888, *Three Generations of English Women* was published by John Murray in two thick volumes, it was widely and for the most part positively reviewed. The *Pall Mall Gazette* observed that the "power of heredity is strikingly revealed" in it and foretold that it would serve as "a stimulus to women, and a rebuke to all men who scoff at learned ladies." One suspects Janet took particular pleasure at the thought of Henry Reeve reading that prediction.

Her primary topic, though, wasn't her family but the world at her doorstep. Few, if any, foreigners had so intimately participated in the rural life of Tuscany, and none (at least in English) had written about it from up close.

Beginning in 1875, Janet published a series of essays in the magazines *Macmillan's* and *Fraser's*. The first, "Vintaging in Tuscany," opens with a description of Castagnolo and goes on to an account of the previous year's vendemmia. Somewhat vaingloriously, Janet has us picture the harvesters setting out "each armed with a rough pair of scissors, and our *padrona* leading the way, with her guitar, pouring out as she went an endless flow of *stornelli, rispetti,* and *canzoni.*" Yet she also evinces a firm grasp of country ways, tossing out many pungent details. We learn, for instance, that after the first pressing an inferior grade of wine called *acquarello*—"distributed to the poor in winter"—is made by fermenting *vinaccia* ("skins, grape-stones, and stalks") with water, and that "the perfume of the must is the best medicine, and people bring weakly children to tread the grapes and remain in the *tinaia* to breathe the fume-laden air."

Next came a companion piece, "Oil-Making in Tuscany," which centers on the olive harvest in November. Among other details, Janet explains that a good olive crop depends on an almost sculptural attentiveness to form: "The trees are most carefully and severely pruned, hollow in the middle, to form a cup-shaped tree. *Agli olivi, un pazzo sopra e un savio sotto* (A mad man at the top of the tree, and a wise one at the roots), says the proverb."*

These two essays were followed by a longer one, "Popular Songs of Tuscany," which gathers lyrics (translated by Janet) and music for some twenty songs, mostly stornelli and rispetti. The rispetto, she writes, is "a love song, in six, eight, or ten lines, and some of its old airs are like a recitative, the end notes being drawn out as long as possible." As for the stornello, it "generally starts with an invitation or defiance, to induce [the singer's] companions to reply to his song"; more adaptable than the rispetto, it is "pressed into every variety of service. The lover serenades his mistress with burning words of love; the disappointed suitor, as he passes the house of his successful rival, or of the faithless fair one, insults or upbraids with a *stornello*; two women quarrel—they instantly begin to *stornellare* each other, ridiculing personal defects, or voiding [*sic*] family quarrels in the choicest Tuscan."

Interwoven with these characterizations and the songs themselves are some fine bits of lore. In the fifteenth century, for exam-

---

*Some years later, in a letter to Kinglake, Janet glossed this cryptic proverb as meaning that one should "prune hard back and manure heavily."

ple, Burchiello, "the celebrated barber of the Via Calimala, where the rich cloth merchants of Florence had their shops, used to challenge his friends to sing"—these friends happening to include Ghiberti, Brunelleschi, and Luca della Robbia. "Gifted with a fine voice and feeling for music, with a biting tongue and ready wit, the barber's songs were the terrors of his enemies and the delight of the people. To this day a certain class of songs are called *Burchielleschi*."

While some of the essay was worked up from books, it mostly reflects Janet's own experience and journalistic efforts; we catch a glimpse of the difficulties involved when she writes that peasants "will not believe that anyone can care for their *roba antica*, or old stuff; as to repeating the words—'*Questo va in canto, in discorso non si può dire*' (This does for *singing*, but one cannot *say* the words), will be their answer." Janet was by no means the only colonist to take an interest in Tuscan songs—Theodosia Trollope had translated stornelli, and Francesca Alexander was soon to publish an extensive study of them—but she approached them from the unique perspective of someone immersed in the peasant milieu.

Last came an essay inspired by Kinglake, with whom she'd recently resumed correspondence. After complimenting her previous pieces, Kinglake said he could imagine Janet producing a "capital book" under the title "Farm Life on the Arno," and suggested she have a look at Virgil's *Georgics*, which he thought might strike her as still relevant. Reading the poems, she had just the reaction he'd predicted, to the extent that the resulting essay, "Virgil and Agriculture in Tuscany," opens by declaring, "Agriculture in Italy, at least in Tuscany, has changed so little since old Virgil sang, that his descriptions would pass muster with any peasant of the present day." She proceeds to list some of the methods, tools, and shards of flinty farming wisdom still around since Roman times, their survival a testimony to the profound conservatism of the contadini: "Tuscans do not like change, and are apt to quote: '*Chi lascia la via vecchia per la nuova / Sa quel che lascia, non sa quel che trova*' ('Whoso leaves the old road for the new, / Knows what he leaves, but not what he may find')." She also harnesses the authority of the *Georgics* to assail her bêtes noires, namely sheep and goats (later denounced in *The Fourth Generation* as "the curse of Italy"). Virgil's "warning against the 'poison of the hard tooth' of sheep and goats still holds good," she tells us, and goes on to rail against the Tuscan habit of keeping the animals "at your neighbours' expense. Hedges are ruined, forests denuded of underwood and young trees." She even permits herself a barbed comment on local horseflesh: "As to the horses, so beautifully described by Virgil that one recognises at once a first-class breed, their descendants are indeed degenerate! The Italian horse, generally speaking, is a wretched animal. Small, ill-made, cow-hocked, overworked and underfed . . . he is the type of what a horse ought not to be."

This quartet of essays represents an original achievement of sorts; where Lucie, in *Letters from Egypt*, had unveiled the textures of everyday life in Luxor, Janet did the same for a representative Tuscan tenuta. Her purview wasn't exclusively rural, though, for she was also writing the kind of town-based pieces more typical of the colony. Some of these are rather old hat, such as her essay on the Misericordia, a charitable institution hymned by Tom Trollope and others. But she often catches details that most colonists would miss, for instance in her account of the Scoppio del Carro (Explosion of the Cart), an Easter pyrotechnic spectacle in which a flaming mechanical dove "speeds her fiery course down the centre of the [Duomo] and sets fire to the wonderful erection of squibs, crackers, and catherine wheels outside the great front door, piled up on an old triumphal chariot." While the Scoppio is staged even today, the superstition attached to it—the quality of the dove's flight is said to be an omen—was taken more seriously at the time, and Janet reports that, on this particular Easter, "the *contadini* returned home joyfully, spreading the glad tidings as they went—'*La colombina è andata bene*' (The dove has flown well)."

Another essay, "The Ghetto of Florence," is notable for being one of the last evocations of the place. Established in 1571, the ghetto was later abandoned by nearly all the Jews once forced to live in it, and by the nineteenth century had become a hive of riffraff and thieves—"the very scum of Florence," as Janet puts it. Along with the Mercato Vecchio, it was finally razed and replaced by the

Piazza Vittorio Emanuele II (a change referred to by many Florentines as *lo sventramento*, or "the disemboweling"). Janet went to
poke around the ghetto in the time between its evacuation and its
demolition, and her essay is a kind of anticipatory elegy for an atmo-
spheric little warren-world with its neck in the noose.

She was developing a real feeling for the history of her adoptive
province, and essays like "Old Florence and Modern Tuscany" and
"The Municipal Palace, Poppi"* make clear how much she'd been
reading up on it. The former considers sumptuary laws—and the
ways in which display-loving Florentines flouted them—from the
quattrocento forward, while the latter is an excursion into eighteenth-
century Freemasonry starring Tommaso Crudeli, a freethinker persecuted by the Inquisition, and Philipp von Stosch, a foppish Prussian
antiquarian known less for his studies than for having kicked off a
Europe-wide fad for monocles. Both pieces display considerable learning, and "The Municipal Palace, Poppi" brings to light an obscure
figure of Anglo-Tuscan history: Charles Sackville, second Duke of
Dorset, who founded Florence's first Masonic lodge and was an im-
presario of the Pergola theater. Clearly Janet's fingers hadn't only
been picking grapes and strumming guitars but riffling dusty pages
in libraries and archives.

In 1887, fourteen of these essays were collected and published
by Kegan Paul as *Italian Sketches*, with winsome etchings by Carlo
Orsi. "Some will think my pictures of the Tuscan peasants flattering
and highly coloured," Janet writes in her preface. "I can only say that
I have lived among them for eighteen years, and that nowhere does
the golden rule, 'Do as you would be done by,' hold good so much
as in Italy." As an example, she tells of a "noted ne'er-do-well" for
whom she'd once performed a favor. Late one night, "My *obbligato*
(obliged one), as he calls himself, came to tell me that a raid was intended on all the henroosts of the country, and knowing that I valued
my Cochins and Brahmas, wanted to warn me and the gamekeeper,
adding that he should try and prevent them from paying a visit. Next
morning lamentation was general, for many had lost their fowls."

---

*Poppi is a small comune east of Florence and northwest of Arezzo.

(Why she didn't bother to warn her neighbors goes unexplained.) "I could tell other such stories," she concludes, "for, as my mother says in her *Letters from Egypt*, I 'sit among the people,' and do not 'make myself big,' a proceeding an Italian resents as much as an Arab." If this comes across as a rather boastful assertion of her own modesty, it provides an accurate foretaste of the sensibility governing the rest of the book. At once cocky and straightforward, opinionated and respectful, Janet makes a less than transparent but ultimately engaging guide. Most readers seem to have felt something of the same, for *Italian Sketches* was well reviewed and sold respectably.

Tuscan Sketches, the book might have been called, except that its last two essays have nothing to do with Tuscany. In fact, they concern a part of Italy that to most Tuscans seemed remote as the moon and barbaric as darkest Africa. Puglia, "the heel of the Italian boot," is relatively poor and isolated even today and was far more so at the time. Yet Janet fell deeply in love with the place, which for years was her favorite escape. Except for Venice, she generally showed an odd lack of interest in the rest of Italy; even Rome, closer to Florence than Cairo to Alexandria, she seems to have visited only a handful of times. But Puglia was another matter, in large part because she had a friend who helped her appreciate its neglected glories.

Born in the Puglian town of Manduria in 1813, Giacomo Lacaita became a lawyer in Naples, where he wound up serving as legal adviser to the British legation. The turning point in his life came in 1850, when William Gladstone (then a mere MP) brought his ailing daughter to town for a cure. Outraged at the tyranny of the Bourbon regime, Gladstone began collecting evidence against it, and his main source was Lacaita. The following year Gladstone published two open letters to Lord Aberdeen on the wickedness of King Ferdinand II (known as "il Re Bomba"—King Bomb—for his repressive violence) and his government. Learning of Lacaita's assistance to Gladstone, the Neapolitan authorities briefly jailed him. On his release he fled for London, where he found himself a hero of the liberal intelligentsia. Also qualified as a dantista, he taught Italian literature for a time, served as private secretary to Lord Lansdowne, and was eventually naturalized and knighted as Sir James. Yet his Italian patriotism never diminished. Having carried out diplomatic missions during the Risorgimento, he afterward returned to Italy and became a senator, all the while maintaining close ties with Britain. He was, in short, an Anglo-Italian, or Italo-Briton, of eminence and great moral stature, not to mention likeability—his friends in both countries were legion.

Presumably by way of Lord Lansdowne, Janet had known Lacaita as a child. In 1883 she met him again in Florence, where he kept an apartment, and invited him to Castagnolo. In turn, he invited her and Henry to visit him at his Puglian estate, Leucaspide, a converted sixteenth-century monastery. Despite the dire warnings of their Tuscan friends—"those *Meridionali* [southerners] are all thieves and robbers, you may very likely be captured by brigands and murdered"— they accepted, making the long, slow journey in the spring of 1884.

To Janet, Puglia was a revelation, its wide-open spaces reminding her of the Sahara. She also found herself intrigued by its people, architecture, history, and superstitions, such as tarantism.* For the moment she produced only the two essays in *Italian Sketches*, "Tarentum" and "Leucaspide," along with a dreadful poem, "A View Near Taranto," published by Oscar Wilde in his magazine *The Woman's World*. (If she wasn't Flaubert, still less was she Keats.) But the hook had been set, and she began to meditate an entire book on Puglia.

Nor was it to be a mere travelogue. While visiting the province she'd become curious about Manfred, King of Sicily, a thirteenth-century figure closely associated with Puglia and still venerated by many locals. Ambitiously, she decided to interweave a study of him with her own impressions of Puglia. Toward this end she made several more trips there, including one with Carlo Orsi, who did etchings for the book. When Florence's materials proved inadequate, she spent several weeks at the British Museum Library, boning up on Manfred and the other Hohenstaufen rulers of

---

*Her description of the Puglian response to spider bites suggests that the victims could be surprisingly finicky: "Musicians are called, and begin playing; if the air does not strike the fancy of the *tarantata*, as the patient is called, she moans louder, and says, 'No, no, not that.' The fiddler instantly changes, and the tambourine beats fast and furious to indicate the difference of the time. When at last the *tarantata* gets an air to her liking, she springs up and begins to dance furiously."

southern Italy—a punishingly complex topic even for a professional historian.

While *The Land of Manfred*, as the book was titled, was completed only several years later, its research and writing ate up a significant portion of Janet's final years at Castagnolo. Putting the last touches on *Three Generations of English Women* devoured still more, as did a new series of Tuscan essays, to be published in a follow-up volume; she was setting an almost Trollopian pace for herself. But writing wasn't her only new activity: she also branched out into painting. Characteristically, an old family friend had much to do with it.

Marianne North, whose Egyptian sketches had bewitched Lucie in Luxor, had become a flower painter of genius. Encouraged by the Royal Botanic Gardens at Kew, she'd spent years traveling in Asia and the Americas (she would later go to Oceania at the urging of Charles Darwin), and so lifelike were the studies she brought back that a dedicated space, the Marianne North Gallery, was built to house them. She and Janet met at Aldermaston in the summer of 1879, North's admiration for Lucie making for an instant bond. That autumn North went for the vendemmia to Castagnolo, where she sketched the local grape varieties and enthused over Henry's orchids. She also had nice things to say about the watercolor renderings of these same orchids that Janet had hesitantly begun to produce. Encouraged, Janet kept at it, in part to help Henry catalog his collection but also for pleasure. The quality—not to mention quantity—of her work can be judged by the fact that in 1917 Kew acquired about seven hundred and fifty of her watercolors, which it described in its bulletin as being "very faithfully executed." Along with an aptitude for delicate brushwork, the paintings of course required painstaking concentration and attention to detail—things one might not expect Janet to have been capable of, given her perfunctoriness as a writer.

If all this writing and painting gives the impression of a woman with a growing yen for solitude, such was not the case. The flow of

guests at Castagnolo never subsided, and Janet was constantly urging friends to take advantage of the house, whether as a base for
exploring the area or as a place to buckle down to their own work.
"Why not dearest Eothen pack up & come here," she tempted
Kinglake, "I'll be yr. amanuensis,* & make you work and finish yr.
history . . . I will give you a south room, with a fireplace, & very
quiet, & you need not be at all proper here . . . I will even promise
not to sing to my guitar anywhere near you." Kinglake, who'd become a bit of a homebody after his adventurous youth, didn't take
her up on the offer, but other figures from her childhood found
their way to Castagnolo.

Among them were the Duc d'Aumale and the Duc de Chartres,
younger brother of the Comte de Paris, to whose assistance she'd
raced when he broke his leg riding at Esher. (She'd been of further
service to the Orléans family in the early 1860s, when she repeatedly
smuggled letters from Paris to Claremont House.) While the two
had never stopped angling for restoration—after the collapse of the
Second Empire, the Comte de Paris had briefly been a serious con-
tender for kingship—they weren't your standard drifting pretenders, self-pitying and useless, but duty-minded military men with a
surprising streak of democratic idealism. In fact, the Duc de Chartres was something of a hero in Italy, having served as an officer in
the Piedmontese dragoons during the Risorgimento and been dec-
orated for his valor by Victor Emmanuel. (Along with the Comte de
Paris, he'd also fought on the Union side in the U.S. Civil War.)
Both dukes had at points been allowed to take up arms for mother
France as well, but the nation had recently entered a fresh phase of
anti-Orléanism, and in 1886 they were exiled once again. The following year they turned up at Castagnolo, where their talks with
Janet must have been nostalgic and wide-ranging.

Another set of royal visitors had been out to Castagnolo several

---

*For many years Kinglake had been at work on his magnum opus, *The Invasion of the
Crimea*, published in eight volumes between 1863 and 1887. Back in 1860, when he was
just starting the book, he'd stayed for a time at the Gordon Arms, where, because his eyes
were giving him trouble, Janet persuaded him to dictate and let her do the writing. Thus
her offer to play secretary harked back to old times.

years earlier. A granddaughter of George III and cousin of Queen Victoria, Princess Mary Adelaide of Cambridge grew up in Germany and married the Duke of Teck. Settling in London, the couple was granted a small parliamentary annuity that didn't begin to cover their extravagant lifestyle. After running up huge debts, they decided, like Landor and many others, to flee their creditors and take refuge in economical Florence, where Janet soon came to their attention. As a child Janet had once met the duchess, and they now renewed their acquaintance. "I found [Janet] very pleasant, and not so loud as I had been led to expect," the duchess remarked to the colonial painter Henry Jones Thaddeus, who reported it in his memoirs.* The liking was mutual, and Janet invited the Tecks to dinner, along with their two children, who went on to become the Earl of Athlone and Queen Mary, wife of George V. The duke, Janet writes, "fell in love with my cockatoo," while the duchess "sang some old German *Studenten lieder* with wonderful verve and go." Presumably Janet countered with stornelli.

Where the Tecks were entertaining but negligible figures, the opposite was true of William Gladstone, who came to visit in 1888. Though between premierships at the time, Gladstone remained a luminary in Italy as in Britain, and his visit to Florence was an event; Thaddeus, who painted him, recalls that he was "the subject of much respectful attention from the authorities and the people, who gratefully remembered his active sympathy with their cause in the days of Garibaldi." He and his family stayed in Lacaita's apartment, and presumably it was Sir James who brought him together with

---

*The Irish painter Henry Jones Thaddeus (1859–1929) had a colorful career. A child prodigy, he studied in Dublin, London, and France before moving in 1882 to Florence, where he established himself as a portrait painter specializing in the nobility. Later he was court painter to the khedive of Egypt, and later still lived in San Francisco, where he became friends with Jack London and wrote his lively *Recollections of a Court Painter*. Those who sat for him included the Tecks, Franz Liszt, Pope Leo XIII, and the Irish patriot Michael Davitt.

By chance, among Thaddeus's students in Florence was Henry Savage Landor (1865–1924), grandson of the writer, who had an equally colorful career as a painter, explorer, and author of books about Tibet and other remote places before returning, like his grandfather, to Florence at the end of his life.

Janet. At any rate, her first impression of Gladstone (who'd once corresponded with her grandmother) wasn't especially favorable. As she reported to Layard, he "talked immensely" despite being hoarse— "I think it is a pity he does not lose his voice entirely," she added. Nevertheless, she invited him and his family to Castagnolo for lunch.

By this point one could get from Florence to Lastra a Signa by horse tram, and the Gladstones frugally chose to do so. When their tram broke down halfway, Janet somehow learned of the mishap and dispatched another of her guests, Frances Hodgson Burnett (author of *Little Lord Fauntleroy* and *The Secret Garden*), to fetch the stranded family in a carriage. By the time Gladstone arrived he was, according to Janet, "rather irate." His mood brightened when the talk turned to mezzadria, land tenure being one of his interests. But the topic soon became a minefield: "He thought I was wrong in several things, and I saw by dear Mrs. Gladstone's face that she was rather nervous lest I should contradict him too flatly."

After lunch Gladstone had "a long talk" with Lotto, just back from Rome. He then tackled Janet anew and said (for once with some humor) that "it was partly my fault that his knowledge of the *mezzeria* was not more exact. 'You ought to have written an article about it as you have done about other Italian matters and then I should have known.'" Eventually she was to do so. For the time being, she had to deal with a "Radical Scotch" friend (living where she neglects to say) who "wrote a most indignant letter asking why I had not telegraphed to tell him to come. Did I not know his great wish in life had been to meet the great statesman? He never really forgave me."

It says something about the fullness of Janet's life that Gladstone's visit merits only a paragraph in *The Fourth Generation*; most memoirists of her era would have simpered over such a proof of their own status for pages on end. Equally telling is her response to the three-day visit in 1887 of someone as eminent in the literary world as Gladstone in the political: Henry James. Nowhere in her writings does she so much as mention James. This is the supreme example of her omissions, of the names she doesn't bother to drop. One wishes she *had* bothered, for the details of James's visit are both scant and one-sided, coming entirely from him. Still, it is a meeting, a collision of sensibilities, worth trying to reconstruct.

James, who was almost exactly Janet's contemporary, had, like her, first encountered Italy in his midtwenties, and had responded with an ecstatic, almost symphonic joy that brought him back thirteen times over the years. While Florence had to contend in his affections with Rome and Venice, he felt for the city a distinctive love, doting, sentimental, almost parental. Its smallness never ceased to disarm him: on his first visit in 1869, he wrote of "the beautiful hills among which it lies deposited, like an egg in a nest"; on the next he found it "the same rounded pearl of cities—cheerful, compact, complete—full of a delicious mixture of beauty & convenience"; and by 1890 he was sighing over "this tender little Florence." The city features many times in his writings: in *Italian Hours* and other works of nonfiction; in *Roderick Hudson* and *The Portrait of a Lady*; and in the tales "The Pupil," "The Diary of a Man of Fifty," and "The Madonna of the Future."

James was also keenly aware of the colony and knew a number of figures from its heyday, such as Robert Browning, Isa Blagden, and Kate Field. (When he later came to write a biography of William Wetmore Story, his research enveloped him in the Florentine lives of Landor, the Brownings, and others.) That he'd formed a strong impression of this golden age and regretted having missed it is clear from "The Autumn in Florence," an 1874 essay: "I first knew Florence early enough . . . to have heard the change for the worse, the taint of the modern order, bitterly lamented by old haunters, admirers, lovers—those qualified to present a picture of the conditions prevailing under the good old Grand-Dukes, the two last of their line in especial, that, for its best reflection of sweetness and mildness and cheapness and ease, of every immediate boon in life to be enjoyed quite for nothing, could but draw tears from belated listeners."

From December 1886 to July 1887, James "gave himself up to Italian romanticism," as Leon Edel puts it. His sojourn included two long stays in Florence, one in the winter and one in the spring.

During both, James spent much time with his closest friends in town, the Bostonian composer Francis Boott, his daughter, Lizzie, and the troubled novelist Constance Fenimore Woolson, who'd met the Bootts through James and ended up living near them in a Bellosguardo villa (the Brichieri, previously occupied by Isa Blagden). Also living with the Bootts was the painter Frank Duveneck, who'd recently married Lizzie. Among these artsy villa-dwellers James happily settled himself, thrilled, according to Edel, to "realize a very old dream: he would actually reside on Bellosguardo."

At first James was determined to avoid the colonial scene, and even asked Woolson and the Bootts to keep his arrival a secret, since, writes Edel, "he did not wish to be drawn into the complications of Florentine society." His letters are full of deprecations on the subject: he refers to "that little simmering social pot—a not very savoury human broth—into which Florence resolves itself today," and of "the queer, promiscuous, polyglot (most polyglot in the world) Florentine society." But in fact he sometimes let himself be sucked into the whirlpool, taking in the atmosphere at Adolf von Hildebrand's musical sanctum and calling on two other visitors to Florence, the notoriously timid Civil War general George B. McClellan and his wife. The McClellans' daughter had recently kicked up a scandal by publishing racy gossip pieces about the haut monde of Venice, so James must have been all ears.

Posterity is fortunate that James allowed himself to be put into circulation, since as a result he lucked into one of his juiciest données. How it came about is a story in itself, one that begins with another of those strong-natured women who were the backbone of the colony. Born in 1856, Violet Paget had, along with her family, moved to Florence as a young woman. Adopting the pseudonym Vernon Lee, she began turning out fiction, essays, and works on travel, history, music, and aesthetics—she was an exemplar of the scholarly Englishwoman in Italy. Despite being belligerent, awkwardly lesbian, and, like Ouida, of an appearance unanimously deemed repulsive, she was so smart, and such a good talker, that many were drawn to her, including James, who'd known her for several years and now declared her "the most intelligent person in Florence."

James also enjoyed her half brother, Eugene Lee-Hamilton, an invalid ex-diplomat and poet whose Heine-like paralysis kept him in bed, where he was fussed over by Vernon and her parents.

In January 1887 James visited the family at their Via Garibaldi apartment, where he met the Countess Gamba, "a *putative* natural daughter of Giuseppe Giusti, the satiric Tuscan poet," as he wrote in a letter, and the undisputed niece of Byron's former mistress Teresa Guiccioli, who'd spent her last years in Florence. When the countess left, Vernon told James that she was said to be sitting on a trove of Byron's salacious letters to her aunt, and this prompted Eugene to relate an anecdote about another of Byron's mistresses, Claire Clairmont. After decades of wandering, Clairmont had returned in her old age to Florence, where she lived reclusively for some years before dying in 1879. Her presence in Florence came to the attention of an American Shelley fanatic known as Captain Silsbee, who believed her to be in possession of reams of his hero's letters. Renting an apartment in her building, he lay in wait, hoping to pounce on the treasure posthumously. But Clairmont died when he was briefly out of town, and he raced back to Florence to find her homely niece in control of the letters. Having long hankered after Silsbee, she agreed to surrender them in exchange for his hand in marriage. This was too high a price even for him, and he fled.

So, at least, the story went—as with the meeting of Chaucer and Boccaccio, whether it was true or apocryphal was almost beside the point. James jotted it down in his notebook, and when he returned to Florence in the spring he loosed his imagination on it, transposing the action to Venice and teasing out the comic possibilities of the situation. The result, of course, was *The Aspern Papers*. Just as the tale is one of James's most successful, his windfall acquisition of it stands as an epitome of how the social life of the colony, despite its frivolity, could provide a writer with choice material. Like Browning coming across the homeless Landor in the street and spontaneously adopting him, the bedridden Eugene Lee-Hamilton telling James about Clairmont and the captain is one of the great Anglo-Florentine moments.

As for Janet, where James first crossed paths with her is unknown— he may have met her in some colonial drawing room, or else have been urged by a common friend (Meredith, perhaps) to get in touch with her. In any event, only weeks after the *Aspern* premise fell into his lap, on February 5, he reported, "Today I go . . . to have the day with Mrs. Ross at Castagnola [*sic*]." Apparently the day went well, for he soon returned. This we know because, on February 27, by then in Venice, he wrote that in Florence he'd seen "a good deal of Vernon Lee, who . . . possesses the only mind I could discover in the place—unless the famous Mrs. Ross, whom I spent three days with at her picturesque old villa (or rather the Marchesa [*sic*] Stufa's) of Castagnola, might be said to have another." Though flattering, this comparison to the intensely cerebral Vernon Lee is also quite a stretch. In fact, James scoots away from it in the very next sentence: "But I am not so sure of Mrs. Ross's mind as of her eyes, her guitar, and her desire to sell you bric-a-brac!* She is awfully handsome, in a utilitarian kind of way—and an odd mixture of the British female and the dangerous woman—a Bohemian with rules and accounts."

Like many Jamesian formulations, these are both arresting and ambiguous; what James means by "utilitarian" handsomeness, "the British female," and "the dangerous woman" is less than clear. Though he can't have wasted his time on such drivel as *Friendship*, perhaps he'd heard of Janet's role in it, which might have fostered his perception of her as a femme fatale, or as a duplicitous operator on par with his own Madame Merle (an upmarket cousin to Lady Joan Challoner). But his final descriptor is the most interesting. Janet's "rules and accounts" are plain to see—she was, after all, a part-time padrona—but that James should find her bohemian is unexpected. Certainly she didn't view herself this way. Then again, he'd met plenty of the breed, and we should perhaps allow the epithet to take its place among others, another brushstroke toward the picture of a woman who was both staunchly orthodox and blithely unconventional.

While Janet clearly intrigued him, James doesn't seem to have tapped her, even fractionally, as a character; three days with her probably didn't suffice to make a strong enough impression, and his

---

*This desire will be explained momentarily.

mind may have already been busy transmuting Claire Clairmont into Juliana Bordereau. Years later, though, Vernon Lee made a remark on Janet's meeting with James that is like an unrealized tale in miniature: James, she said, "would never use her. She would tumble in like a great red flamingo among his grey sparrows."

A great red flamingo she may have been, but as the decade wore on a new wave of worries brought a darker coloration.

One problem was money. While opaque as ever, the Rosses' finances were manifestly becoming strained, in part because of Alick. Throughout their years in Italy, Alick had remained a shadowy, intermittent presence. He visited a few times but never for long, presumably continuing to live with Charlotte Austin. His parents did, however, see to his education, and in 1886 the sore topic of his Oxford fees surfaces in Janet's letters. (Alick would then have been about twenty-four, so perhaps he took time off before college.) To supplement their income, Janet started a sideline in, as Henry James discovered, producing and selling bric-a-brac, specifically painted fans. These, she reported to Layard in 1887, had been selling briskly, "as I struck out a new line, & put music [sic], which I illustrated with the flowers mentioned in the songs. Altogether I hope to make about £80 by my pen and my brush this year." Not long after, she asked Layard, by then settled in Venice, to be on the lookout for potential buyers for an Andrea del Sarto sketch that she and Henry needed to sell.

Even as they overcame the financial shortfall, the Rosses faced another problem. For Lotto was gravely ill. With what is unclear, but in the mid-1880s, still only in his fifties, he'd begun to falter. He continued for a time to fill his post in Rome—where, in 1878, Victor Emmanuel had died and been replaced by King Umberto I— but did so with increasing difficulty. Finally he resigned and came home for good. By 1888 the writing was on the wall, not just for Lotto but the Rosses' tenancy at Castagnolo. At least some of the della Stufa clan bought into Ouida's steamy theories about the nature of Lotto's relationship with Janet, and whichever relative stood to inherit the estate was sure to be less than keen on continuing to accommodate the pestiferous *inglesi* who'd brought such notoriety to the family.

After two decades in Tuscany, Janet was in her later forties. On one level she exhibited the same curious agelessness as ever; still youthfully attractive and tireless, she was hardly different from the preternaturally self-possessed five-year-old toasted by Thackeray and the rest. The burdens (and rewards) of motherhood she'd largely sidestepped. And yet her years in Tuscany, especially those at Castagnolo, *had* matured her, turning her from a brassy but callow young woman short on skills and accomplishments into a middle-aged career author with unusual sorts of knowledge at her fingertips and a wealth of practical experience under her belt. If there was one thing she'd learned, it was how to run not just a house but an estate, a tenuta, with its overlapping realms of villa and podere. It was time to move on; it was time, at long last, to find a place of her own.

FIVE

Castle Ross

"Some months ago," begins the first chapter of *The Fourth Genera-tion*, "I made a pilgrimage to a corner of London once very familiar." Janet goes on to describe her visit to what used to be Queen Square. "Part of the dear old square has entirely vanished. The ponderous bulk of Queen Anne's Mansions has crushed it out of sight, and buried under its foundations the houses of John Austin, Jeremy Bentham . . . and the pleasant garden of the sage in which my mother used to play as a child." While a few houses, including the one rented by her parents, still had the carved porches she recalled from her own childhood, most of the "delightful old irregularities which gave the place its quaint charm" were gone.

By leading off her memoir with this plaintive little *ubi sunt*, Ja-net presumably meant only to strike an appropriate opening note of nostalgia. But it also calls attention to her curious relationship to houses. Even in middle age, she'd never lived in one that wasn't rented or borrowed, and therefore provisional. She'd often stayed at the grand properties of friends—Lansdowne House, Aldermaston, Leucaspide—but the closest she'd come to having her own was when she and Alexander missed out on the Château de Fénis. This houselessness was out of step with the rest of her life, and when she finally remedied it, she did so with a vengeance. The house she now acquired was to become such an integral part of her, such a well-spring of her mystique, that, in retrospect, one can hardly imagine her without it.

⚬

By the fall of 1888 Lotto was on his last legs, and the Rosses had no choice but to begin their search. Besides their small budget, they were constrained by a specialized requirement: Henry's orchids had to have just the right balance of shelter and exposure. Several otherwise suitable places were rejected for lack thereof, and as the weeks dragged by the Rosses sank into the peevish despondency of those thwarted by real estate.

Then they learned of a house near Settignano, a few miles from Florence. "I did not like it," Janet recalls, "but my unfortunate husband was so weary of house-hunting that I said: 'Buy.'" Before they could follow through with this halfhearted plan, serendipity stepped in. "Driving down the hill we passed under an old machico-lated castle with fine trees close by. 'There,' I exclaimed, 'if you bought that I should be quite content.'" They learned that it was called Poggio Gherardo, and got the impression it was for sale. Back at Castagnolo, Lotto punctured their hopes: when Janet mentioned Poggio Gherardo, "He smiled and asked me whether I would not like to buy Palazzo Pitti." He knew of the place and was quite certain it wasn't on the market. There the matter seemed to rest. Then, the very next morning, Janet got a letter from a friend "saying that friends of his were in *villeggiatura* [on vacation] in an old castle he was sure I would admire, and that they thought if properly managed it might be bought. Its name was Poggio Gherardo. I waved the letter in Henry's face and exclaimed: 'There! There's my villa.'"

That Janet refers to Poggio Gherardo as both a castle and a villa may sound contradictory. Strictly speaking, the only architectural features that might earn it the former description are its small tower and the merlons ringing its roof (Janet seems to have hallucinated its machicolations). With its hilltop position, though, it does have something ineffably castlelike about it, and one can understand why the Rosses and their friends preferred the more romantic term, which it would be churlish to resist.

The property came with about sixty sloping and terraced acres, including two poderi and a small *bosco* (wood) of ilex and umbrella pines. Its imposing main gate was topped with busts representing the four seasons. Most seductive of all, the views from the house were tremendous, taking in not only Florence below but, as Janet wrote to Kinglake, "a great rich plain all dotted with villas and farm houses, and then tier upon tier of rolling hills as far as one can see, each crowned by some old church or monastery."

After inspecting the place, the Rosses were sure they wanted it. Inquiries revealed that it still belonged to the eponymous Gherardi. (As for the other half of its name, *poggio* is Italian for "hillock" or "knoll.") An old aristocratic family, the Gherardi were nearly extinct, the end of their line consisting of three decrepit countesses, spinsters all. The eldest, the Contessa Gherardi Uguccioni, owned the estate and, as Janet's friend had divined, was willing to sell it. But the Rosses had to play their cards carefully. "We were advised not to appear as buyers, for being English the price would be raised." Instead, one of the Orsi brothers, fronting for the Rosses, approached the countess and, striking a deal, bought the property *"per persona da nominarsi* [for a person to be named later], as the saying is." In January 1889 the Rosses took possession.

Initially Henry moved into Poggio Gherardo on his own while Janet remained at Castagnolo to nurse the fading Lotto. He died in late February, and while *The Fourth Generation* merely notes the fact, her letters make clear that she was shattered. Whatever the exact nature of their relationship, it had been one of the most gratifying of her life, and in a sense the most influential, since Lotto, in his capacity as benign and forward-looking padrone, had helped set her on a new course.

The area where Janet was about to resume that course was significantly closer to Florence than Lastra a Signa, and increasingly popular with colonists. For decades, those who preferred to live not in central Florence but in greener, less crowded surroundings had clustered either in Bellosguardo or around Fiesole. In recent years, though, the realm of "Villadom," as Aldous Huxley was later to dub it, had been expanding into the area around Settignano, northeast of Florence and southeast of Fiesole.

The earliest and most prominent of these settlers was John Temple Leader, who dwelt in splendor on the tallest local hill. In 1844 the wealthy Temple Leader had abandoned a promising parliamentary career for a life of pleasure and independent scholarship on the Continent. After several years in Cannes he moved to Florence and bought the ruined Castello di Vincigliata, which he lavishly restored according to the Gothic Revival aesthetic in vogue at the time. Henry James, while allowing that it was a "massive *pastiche*," found himself beguiled by Temple Leader's pseudo-medieval confection, and most others—including Queen Victoria, who came to inspect it in 1888, during the first of her three visits to Florence—had the same reaction.

An expert on the early Anglo-Tuscans (his books included biographies of Sir John Hawkwood and Sir Robert Dudley) and local history in general, Temple Leader had a huge antiquarian library. Shortly after the Rosses became his neighbors he dropped by to lend them an item from it, namely a monograph about Poggio Gherardo, written by one of the Gherardi around 1740. Drearily longwinded though Janet found the work, it established some intriguing facts. Poggio Gherardo, originally known as Palagio del Poggio, had been around since at least the eleventh century. In 1433 the Zati family sold it to the Gherardi, who imposed their own name on it. An especially satisfying discovery was that in 1363 the house had been attacked by Hawkwood and his White Company, causing heavy damage; Hawkwood had flattened Lastra a Signa as well, and Janet must have smiled at the coincidence. She also learned that Poggio Gherardo had a ghost. One of its early owners was a hardline Guelph whose daughter fell in love with a boy from a Ghibelline family. When this Romeo came to whisper sweet nothings beneath his Juliet's window, her brothers caught and killed him, and the girl died of grief. Her spirit had supposedly haunted her bedroom ever since.

But the most thrilling revelation afforded by the monograph had to do with one of Hawkwood's contemporaries, Giovanni Boccaccio. The characters of the *Decameron* take refuge in two successive houses. In the first, Pampinea is crowned queen and two days' worth of tales are told. The new queen, Neifile, then suggests that two days of rest be observed, after which the group should switch to a new hideout. Her proposal is accepted, and on Sunday the *lieta brigata* (merry band) moves on to the second house. Because Boccaccio neglects to name these houses and describes them only vaguely, there had been much speculation about their identity. One house often put forward—usually as the band's second destination—was the Villa Palmieri, which had been owned by Earl Cowper and G.P.R. James and now belonged to the astronomer and politician Earl Crawford and his wife, a distant cousin of Janet's. The leading candidate for the first destination was Poggio Gherardo, though it was often referred to by a different name. (As with those of people, the names of Italian houses can be maddeningly variable.) In his 1806 *Life of Boccaccio*, Count Baldelli referred to "Villa Gherardo," while Leigh Hunt wrote of "Villa Gherardi, in which Boccaccio laid the scene of his first four days."

While Janet seems to have been unaware of this *Decameron* connection before reading of it in the monograph, she was quick to embrace it. In *The Fourth Generation* she quotes Boccaccio's description of the "palace" in question, which he specifies as standing on a hill two miles from Florence and as featuring arcades, "a pleasant and large courtyard," and "jocund paintings" on the walls. Mention is also made of the palace's "marvelous gardens," "wells of purest water," and "cellars full of precious wines more suited to curious topers than to sober and virtuous women." Even though this description fits many places better than Poggio Gherardo, which has only a small inner courtyard and no arcades, Janet was persuaded, and was soon campaigning to have her house recognized as the inspiration for one of the key settings in world literature. Some were skeptical, for opinion was already shifting toward the view that Boccaccio had no particular models in mind. But she certainly convinced the American writer Laurence Hutton, whose 1896 *Harper's* article "Literary Landmarks of Florence" (later expanded into a book of the same title) includes the following: "Mr. and Mrs. Ross prove very conclusively, from local tradition, and from Boccaccio's own description of the Villa Gherardo . . . that theirs is the 'stately palace' . . . to which the story-tellers repaired on the now famous Wednesday." Janet can't have minded that Hutton several times refers to the stately palace as "Villa Ross."

However gratifying it was for Janet to learn the history of her new home, it was also rather depressing, because Poggio Gherardo had obviously come down in the world since Boccaccio's day. "Of the 'marvellous gardens' no trace remained, save that in digging we sometimes came upon bits of old masonry which might have belonged to anything—walls, arbours, pedestals for statues." As for the "jocund paintings," they too had disappeared: "The rooms had all been papered, and with what paper!" Besides these cosmetic deteriorations, there were more serious structural ones. "The condition of the villa was deplorable. On trying to kill a wasp on the front door my stick went straight through." Even worse were the poderi: "The peasants' houses were wretched—there were not even windows—only heavy wooden shutters, which . . . were half rotten." The land itself was "covered with that terrible pest crouch-grass, ditches had not been cleaned out for years, and the carriage drive was a stony watercourse."

A renovation of the whole estate was clearly in order. The Rosses were, however, in no position to throw bushels of money at it as Temple Leader had done with Vincigliata. Fortunately, they'd learned at Castagnolo how to economize, and instead of hiring contractors and other middlemen they decided to oversee the job themselves. Word went out that they were looking for workers, and dozens of men turned up. With room to spare, the Rosses converted one wing of the house into lodgings for the workers, who, living on site, quickly transformed the place. Once the leaky roof and other damages had been fixed, several walls were knocked down to create bigger rooms and extra doors added between them—this to give the place a lighter, airier feel. The Gherardi family chapel was turned into a bathroom, to somewhat odd effect: when soaking in the bathtub, one gazed up at the Holy Ghost (in the form of a dove) painted overhead.

Turning their attention to the grounds, the Rosses had many dead trees cut down and over a hundred new ones planted. The larger podere, which they judged too big to be properly worked by a single family, was divided in two, and a new cottage built. The existing cottages were repaired, a cistern dug, the rocky carriage drive smoothed over, and ditches unclogged. (Janet supervised this last job: "I have taught my sixteen men how to drain ditches with loose stones set on end," she reported to Kinglake.) A rabbit pen and poultry yard were set up, and the latter was stocked with chickens, ducks, and resplendent golden and silver pheasants. The *orti* (vegetable plots) were reconfigured and planted with delicacies like purple artichokes.

Some of the Rosses' instructions were baffling to their hired hands, such as the one Janet issued about the wallpaper: "When I ordered it to be all scraped off, and the walls to be simply washed a light grey stone colour, the workmen exclaimed: *Ma Lei sa che è carta di Francia?* (But do you know that it is French paper?), in tones of respect and dismay." She also met with resistance over converting an ox stable into one for horses. As she wrote to Kinglake, the masons she hired couldn't comprehend "my insisting on the floor being flat; here the fashion is to put the unhappy beasts on a sharp inclined plane, so that their heads are ½ a foot at least higher than their heels, & I need not tell you how bad that is for their backsinews [*sic*]." The masons protested that, standing on a slanted floor, "the animals *present* themselves so much better. They look taller and grander." In the end, the Italian penchant for *la bella figura* at all costs went down before brute Anglo-Saxon pragmatism.

But the Rosses were far from indifferent to the look of their new home or severe in their aesthetic. They left intact one rather gaudy part of the house: its so-called Poodle Room, dominated by a trompe l'oeil portrait of Pippo, an eighteenth-century pet so cherished by the Gherardi that he was buried near the bosco in his own marble tomb. Shown intricately groomed and with one paw aloofly raised, Pippo had a heraldic gravitas, and the dog-loving Rosses elected to preserve him, along with the rest of the room's ornamentation. As a contemporary photograph shows, they added to the room an octagonal chandelier of perforated metal and stained glass, of a type common in the Middle East—a souvenir, presumably, of their years in Egypt. Elsewhere in the house they similarly mixed idioms with a free hand, retaining the scagliola floors and other typically Italian features but introducing eclectic touches of their own, such as an Asian dinner gong suspended between twin demon statues.

Almost as important to the Rosses as the house itself was the terrace, whose stirring views were sure to make it the center of life in good weather. Its flagstones and marble banquettes were repaired, the pergola on its perimeter replanted with grapevines. Striking an exotic note, the Rosses populated its fountain with a breed of chiffon-tailed goldfish that Lotto, during a visit to Burma some years back, had obtained from the royal tanks at Mandalay. More goldfish cruised the grotto beneath the wisteria-covered double staircase, which led from the terrace to a parterre boasting a variety of fragrant and fruit-bearing trees, including a medlar, a persimmon, and, as Janet described it to Kinglake, "a big camphor tree whose flowers smell like lime bloom mixed with violets."

Though she and Henry chose not to create (and couldn't have afforded to maintain) the sort of elaborate formal garden common to Villadom, Poggio Gherardo teemed with greenery and flowers. In particular, they introduced roses of many kinds and in terrific profusion; especially numerous were those along the driveway, so that visitors wound their way up to the castle through a quarter mile of pink, red, and white. (Roses led, as it were, to Rosses.) But pride of place went to Henry's orchids, for which several glass-roofed conservatories were built, with pools between the rows of orchids and still more Burmese goldfish languidly patrolling them. Already a formidable collection, it continued to grow, and a few years later *The Gardeners' Chronicle*, a leading English periodical, declared it "the finest ever got together in Italy."

No less abundant than the plant life at Poggio Gherardo was the animal life. At Castagnolo, Augustus Hare had been struck by Janet's way with animals—"the creatures, like the people, seemed to regard Mrs. Ross as one of themselves"—and Henry also had a Saint Francis streak in him. Now that they had a place of their own, they could let their zoological proclivities run wild. Besides the goldfish and chickens, ducks, pheasants, and rabbits, there were at least two dogs, a Maremma sheepdog (descended, perhaps, from the one Ouida had given Janet) and a fox terrier. Henry kept guinea pigs, for which he had a soft spot. Though Janet, for reasons of economy, denied herself a proper riding steed, the Rosses maintained several work and carriage horses. Above all, there were birds, to the point that the house resembled an aviary. In addition to a flock of budgies and several larger parrots, there was Cecco the nightingale, who as a nestling had been rescued by Henry and was desperately attached to him; one visitor recalls that the bird would "come into Mr. Ross's hand to be fed and caressed, and after its meal would perch on his shoulder and pour out a wondrous flood of melody." But the king of the birds—and of the house—was the cockatoo, unimaginatively known as Cockie, who kept everyone in stitches with his incessant clowning.

Made to resound with squawks and chirps and barks, lapped in rainbow vegetation, revamped, spruced up, and generally overhauled, Poggio Gherardo was transformed from a derelict house into a loved, active, cheerful one, and in a remarkably short time—most changes were pushed through within two years. The Rosses' energy and diligence, their distinctly uncolonial willingness to put their shoulders to the wheel, clearly sped things up. "All my English acquaintance here are open-mouthed at the amount of work I get done," Janet bragged to Kinglake. Yet even she couldn't keep the place running without a great deal of help. Like real estate, servants came cheaply in Tuscany. It's hard to make out just how many the Rosses employed, but it seems never to have been less than ten. Some had been with them at Castagnolo, including Beppe the gardener and odd-job man, Fortunato the butler and majordomo, Janet's maid Teresa, and a cook, Giuseppe Volpi, whose name she was later to make rather famous.

While the Rosses depended heavily on servants, their more crucial—and potentially vexed—relationship was with their share-croppers. To enter into a mezzadria contract was a serious business, one intimately binding the fortunes of patron and peasant. It was therefore with some wariness that both sides approached the new situation—a wariness heightened for the contadini by the bizarre circumstance of their being under the thumb of not just a woman but a foreigner. Luckily, the Contessa Gherardi Ugaccioni was no hard act to follow. "The former owner of this place imagined that gentlefolk and peasants are made of different clay," Janet told Kinglake, with reference to the sorry condition of the Poggio Gherardo cottages. Those dwelling in them must have been reassured by the Rosses' attention to their living conditions, and by the fact that an entire family, headed by a certain Bencio, had followed them from Castagnolo to work the new podere—which presumably helped persuade the other families that this overbearing Englishwoman actually knew what she was doing.

To an extent they had nothing to fear. A respecter of most traditions, Janet wasn't about to tamper with the basic protocols of mezzadria. She also spared her tenants the feudalistic *patti colonici* (bylaws) inflicted by some estates. In an essay on mezzadria that she was soon to write—Gladstone's suggestion had fallen on fertile soil—she lists some examples: "One peasant of each *podere* is hereby bound to work gratis ten days in the year for the *padrone*, and to do a certain amount of haulage; two women of each family are to come to the *fattoria* to wash linen one day every three months; at Christmas and Easter every *podere* must give a pair of capons, and four dozen eggs during the year as compensation for the damage done by the poultry to the crops."

At Poggio Gherardo there were to be no such grasping seigneurial demands. There were, however, to be modifications and novelties, and these spelled trouble. "Ogni muta, una caduta" ("Every change is a disaster," in Janet's rather loose translation) runs one of the Tuscan proverbs she most often quotes in her books and letters, and her new tenants clearly took it to heart. "The 'English ideas' of the *Padroni* were a source of great wonder to the *contadini*," she writes in *The*

Fourth Generation. "Henry's objections to bits of paper littering the carriage drive and to clothes being hung out to dry on the rose hedges they found inconvenient; and my insisting on air and cleanliness in the cow stables was met with dismay, and evasion wherever possible."

Far more alarming than the hygienic hang-ups of the padroni were their agricultural opinions. "I stood over the peasants," Janet claims, "to see that they dug deep enough to destroy the roots of the wild tulips, anemones, and irises in the fields. This they did unwillingly because their children got a few pence by selling the flowers; never calculating that wheat and potatoes properly grown paid far better." In her view, wheat tended to be particularly mishandled: "It is customary in Tuscany to grow wheat two, or even three years running on the same land, with little or no manure, and the yield is, of course, miserable." Intent on a better yield, she decided to try out some new strains, including an Australian one recommended by Marianne North, who sent her the seeds.

Janet was just as meddlesome when it came to viniculture. In "Virgil and Agriculture in Tuscany," she'd argued that grapes in Tuscany were "picked too soon, with a consequent loss of saccharine and alcohol in the wine," and she also took issue with the Tuscan practice of spur pruning, which seemed to her inferior to cane pruning, a Burgundian technique. When she proposed a later harvest and the use of cane pruning to her new sharecroppers, they were aghast. She therefore decided, as she informed Kinglake, "to make a contest of it. I have told them this year they shall make their share their own way and then we'll see whose wine is best."

While she'd picked up some of these innovations from Lotto, she was trying out others for the first time; after helping to run someone else's estate for many years, she leapt at the opportunity to run her own exactly as she saw fit, and to use it as a kind of laboratory. But these were no idle experiments. To a degree, the Rosses' own welfare was at stake, since they counted on turning at least a small profit from the estate and couldn't afford to keep pouring cash into it. They were also anxious not to alienate their sharecroppers.

For these reasons, the second round of harvests under their ownership (the first was largely of crops planted before they arrived) was crucial. Unhelpfully, the summer of 1890 was drier than usual, and by August an apprehensive note crept into Janet's letters to Kinglake: "We are anxiously scanning the skies for rain." When the drought finally broke later that month, relief flooded from her pen: " 'It is raining wine,' said one of the contadini, & in fact the grapes have swollen in a wonderful way." In the end, the grape harvest was "not very abundant, but very good in quality," and the other crops also produced a solid yield, culminating with the olives in November. One can imagine Janet's pleasure at helping to gather olives from the terraces cut into her very own hillside, and at watching her Val di Chiana oxen—a handsome white breed that is almost a mascot for rural Tuscany—haul them to her *frantoio* (olive press) and, slowly circumambulating, crush them into oil.

With the year's cycle completed, she felt sanguine enough to crow to Kinglake, "The peasants have now a great respect for the Padrona's agricultural knowledge." While this may or may not have been true at the time, it seems that most of them did come to feel not only respect for Janet (as well as for Henry) but affection and gratitude. To be a sharecropper at Poggio Gherardo was in many ways preferable to being one at a normal, Tuscan-run tenuta. Even the alien methods that at first put the contadini on edge proved to be blessings, for the estate consistently outperformed others of its size, and its wine—all produced à la Janet: her tenants had had no chance in that contest— was widely held to be excellent. They were also, despite the occasional scolding, treated with respect and kindness. Eventually Janet would set up a school for their children, and from the start she tended to anyone sick or injured. "The 'Padrona' is said to be a better doctor than the medico of the village," she reported to Kinglake, though she added, "This is not very high praise as he is a drivelling idiot."

Once the contadini had taken half of each crop, the Rosses got the remainder. They put half their oil in barrels beneath the house for personal use and sold the rest. They also sold fruit: "I sowed a whole field of melons," Janet wrote to Kinglake, "& send in 50 or 60 at a time to Florence, & get 2^d or 3^d each! Figs go in baskets, about 300 or 400 every morning." Though the income derived from these products was modest, she took satisfaction in bringing them to market—where the vast majority of Anglo-Florentines were mere consumers, she was now part of the local agrarian economy.

As 1890 came to a close, Janet could look back on the previous two years with pride and contentment, and on the future with optimism. The period had not, however, been without losses and setbacks.

For one thing, her Puglia book, *The Land of Manfred*, published by John Murray in 1889, had received mixed reviews and sold poorly. The book is an agreeable hodgepodge of history and travel, and stands as an interesting counterpart to her Tuscan writings, from its cataloging of superstitions ("No peasant woman will comb or brush her hair on a Friday, unless she desires the death of her husband") and traditional songs to its comic vignettes of contadino stubbornness: "I tried in vain to convince a peasant at Leucaspide of the merits of a wheelbarrow, but he thought it would be 'troppo complicato' (too complicated), and ended with the true conservative reason: 'My forefathers used baskets; what was good enough for them is surely good enough for me.'" Still, one can't help agreeing with the reviewer who complained about its "total want of arrangement"— Janet's habit of leaping abruptly between subjects is more problematic here than elsewhere. To her credit, she took the book's relative failure philosophically.

Harder to shrug off was the death of one friend and the impending death of another. In August 1890, Marianne North, who'd recently contributed to Janet's wheat-growing experiment, died at fifty-nine. And Kinglake was mortally ill. The year before he'd been diagnosed, like Alexander Duff Gordon, with cancer of the tongue. "I can't tell you how miserable I am," Janet wrote to Layard on hearing the grisly news. "All my poor Father's sufferings come before me again redoubled." Somehow Kinglake, half his tongue lopped off and in terrible pain, had hung on, and Janet poured out to him all the excitements and frustrations of her initial grapplings with Poggio Gherardo, writing over forty letters in eighteen months. But now, just as she was getting on top of the estate, Kinglake's end approached. He died in January 1891, at eighty-one. Afterward, Janet wrote to his sister-in-law of his "marvelous mixture of pride and humility, of daring and intense shyness, of affection and cynicism."

She regarded him as a master of English prose (his occasional jabs at her own prose she absorbed with meek gratitude) and as a beau ideal of the early-Victorian gentleman. He was one of the last surviving members of her parents' generation, and therefore a precious link to the past—a link now broken.

With her attachment to auld lang syne, Janet was, for all her zest and stamina, in some danger of premature fogeyism. She was coming up on forty-nine, Henry on seventy-one, and the two of them might easily have spent the rest of their lives rattling around their castle with friends their own age or older, interacting with the young only in the form of their sharecroppers' children. Their own child, Alick, did make one appearance, coming to stay for a month in the fall of 1890. Perhaps because he'd recently established himself as a stockbroker in London, this visit seems to have gone better than previous ones. Janet told Kinglake how excited her sharecroppers were to meet the "padroncino," and described taking him to the Uffizi and other museums—"I have been awakening a love for pictures in Alick." But Alick was now twenty-eight, and would have been unlikely to remain at Poggio Gherardo even if his parents had wanted him to. The rejuvenated castle seemed destined to become a domain of the graying. Fate, though, had other plans: if there was to be no padroncino about the place, there was to be a padroncina.

———— ⚜ ————

After leaving Egypt, Maurice Duff Gordon had returned to England, and in 1872 had married a widow six years his senior, Fanny Ball Hughes. She was already something of a hard-luck case: when her first husband was killed in a riding accident, she'd found in his pocket an unposted love letter to her closest friend, with whom he'd been scheming to run off. Initially her fortunes improved with Maurice. The couple first lived in Saint-Germain-en-Laye, near Paris, where in 1874 they had a daughter, christened Caroline but known as Lina. Two years later they moved to London, where they hobnobbed with Oscar Wilde, James Whistler, and others, and where Maurice, like Alick, traded stocks in the City. In 1884 came a windfall: a Scottish cousin of Maurice's died childless and left him Fyvie Castle, a thirteenth-century pile in Aberdeenshire where Robert the Bruce once held court. Pinching themselves, Maurice and his family moved into the enormous house, and for a time all went swimmingly. But then Maurice fell in love with another woman, Sophie Marie Steer, and turned his back on his wife and daughter. The twice-betrayed Fanny took shelter with relatives and, apparently too distraught to cope with Lina, put her in a Brighton convent school (Fanny was a pious Catholic).

These developments were followed with anger and dismay by Janet, who'd taken an interest in Lina from the start. She and Henry had even gone to France for her christening, bringing a vial of water that Henry had drawn from the River Jordan twenty years before. Over the next few years Janet saw Lina now and then, but the first time the two truly connected was in 1884, when Janet went to visit the newly inherited Fyvie. Characteristically, she decided then and there to write a history of the castle, holing up for long hours in its library with the pertinent books and documents.* But she also made time for her ten-year-old niece, whom she often took riding. During these jaunts Lina began to realize what a commanding woman her aunt was. As Lina would recall many years later in her autobiography, *Castle in Italy*, Janet, dissatisfied with Maurice's horses, noticed a butcher making deliveries with a "frisky little cob," and twisted the man's arm into selling it to her on the spot. "I learnt that day," Lina writes, "how difficult it would be to oppose her wishes once she had made up her mind." Just how difficult she would eventually learn the hard way. For the moment, though, she felt herself to be in the presence of a superior being. On her side, Janet came away from her Fyvie visit with a settled affection for Lina.

In the fall of 1889 the strength of that affection began to be put to the test, for Lina's situation became truly precarious. Her father had gone from bad to worse: slipping back into the dissolute hedonism of his youth, Maurice had racked up such huge debts that he'd been forced to sell Fyvie and retreat with Sophie, whom he'd since

---

*The resulting essay was first privately printed and later published in *Macmillan's*.

married, to a humble lodging in London. For a time Lina stayed
with them, but she hated her stepmother, and Maurice was unfit to
care for her. Nor was her mother able to do so: jinxed to the end,
Fanny had been diagnosed with terminal cancer.

In desperation and poverty, Fanny asked Janet whether she
might pay for Lina to go to a convent school in Paris. Even though
Janet was hard up herself and had little regard for convents, she
agreed. But this was only the beginning of her involvement. Rapidly
sickening, Fanny was determined to find a stable home for her daughter before she died, and in December 1889 she made a desperate
pilgrimage to Poggio Gherardo, where she pleaded with the Rosses
to become Lina's guardians. "My poor sister-in-law is here," Janet
reported to Kinglake. "I am getting her doctored . . . but even my
energy pales at the task of rousing her. I wish I could take a good
thick stick and belabour Maurice!" Appalled at her brother's cal-
lousness, Janet also found her sympathies and family feeling stirred,
and she and Henry agreed not only to house Lina but to adopt her.

Two months later Fanny died at forty-six. Around Easter the
fifteen-year-old Lina came to Florence on a trial visit. Though this
went well, for some reason it was decided that she should remain in
the convent for the time being. About six months later, Lina wrote
in a panic to say that she was under intense pressure to become a nun.
Janet, who had a horror of this kind of coercion, urged her to come
immediately. In December 1890 Lina returned to Poggio Gherardo,
where she got a comfortingly warm welcome from Janet: "The smile
which lit up her face when she saw me," Lina recalls, "lessened the
sternness of her thick, almost menacing eyebrows. 'Welcome, my
dear child,' she said."

For the moment, though, her future remained in limbo: the letter
Fanny had written expressing her wish that the Rosses adopt Lina
was, in the opinion of their English lawyer, "legally worthless," and
Maurice could reclaim his daughter if he saw fit. In the event, he
neglected even to try, probably out of genuine assent to the adoption
but perhaps also for fear of his sister's wrath. A few months after
Lina's arrival, he gave his formal blessing. "Aunt Janet waved the letter as if it were a flag of liberation and said: 'So that danger is over;

you are now our child and this is your home.'" Poggio Gherardo and its owners were to shape the rest of her life, which could scarcely have been more different from the one plotted for her by French nuns.

The readiness with which the Rosses agreed to take on parental duties is curious, considering their ambivalence (at best) toward Alick. In Janet's case there's a further layer of paradox: given her preference for male company over female, one might have expected her to be even less willing to make sacrifices for a niece. Why then did she rise so eagerly to the occasion? Again, her sense of family responsibility was strong, and her protective instincts had been aroused by Lina's predicament. Lina was also an appealing girl—bright, pretty, animated—and, at sixteen, already independent. But there may have been other factors at play. Nearing fifty and firmly rooted at last, Janet seems to have felt the allure of maternity as she hadn't at twenty. (While Lina continued to refer to her and Henry as "Aunt" and "Uncle"—or else the Italian "Zia" and "Zio"—the adoption technically made them her mother and father.) And with her distaste for designated roles, she no doubt preferred elective to obligatory guardianship.

The first order of business was to shore up Lina's education, thus far blinkered by convents. Just as Susannah Taylor had seen to Sarah's, Sarah to Lucie's, and Lucie—rather more haphazardly—to Janet's, so Janet would see to Lina's. Solicited for a reading list, Saint-Hilaire named Plato, Descartes, Bossuet, and Leibniz as the thinkers "qu'il faut étudier dans la jeunesse." To learn Italian and Latin, Lina was sent to Janet's friend Dr. Guido Biagi, head of the Laurentian Library,* while drawing lessons came courtesy of Carlo Orsi. Nor were her social graces neglected. Discontent with the fact that Lina had never learned to dance, Janet hired a retired ballerina to give her lessons, though these took an unforeseen course: "She taught me to dance the *tarantella*," Lina recalls, "and other Italian folk dances with great gusto, but an ordinary waltz was outside her category."

---

*Designed by Michelangelo but completed only after his death, the Laurentian Library is in a cloister of San Lorenzo and houses a collection of rare books and manuscripts, including many that belonged to the Medici.

To get into Florence for her various lessons, Lina often accompanied Janet in a carriage pulled by her "sturdy white mare." (This horse, Lina notes, "only caused trouble if she saw a pig; one day the mare met one in Via Cavour and was so unnerved she dashed on to the pavement and into a shop.") She also took the horse tram from Settignano, operated by the son of a Poggio Gherardo sharecropper, who sometimes let her take the reins. For a while she was permitted to ride her bicycle into town, but when it became apparent that the sight of a young lady on a bike—something rare in Italy at the time—was provocative to the local males, her guardians replaced it with a donkey cart. All in all she was granted, by the standards of the day, considerable freedom, and thrived on it. So completely did she shake off the ethos of the nunnery that she fell in love with the heroes of the Risorgimento, plastering her walls with portraits of the virulently anticlerical Garibaldi and Mazzini. By the time Janet mooted the idea of presenting her at court—in England, that is— Lina had become such a strident little republican that she flatly refused.

But such moments of friction were rare. During their first years together, Lina and the Rosses for the most part got along superbly, and nothing short of strong mutual love soon arose between them; they became a family not only on paper but in fact. On Lina's side, there was also immense gratitude: the Rosses had selflessly rescued her, and she was never to lose sight of her debt to them.

For Henry, Lina seems to have felt pure affection and admiration— neither *Castle in Italy* nor her letters have a bad word to say about him. Janet elicited much of the same, but Lina was also somewhat bewildered by her aunt's intensity, and her descriptions are often flecked with irreverence. "She considered it a great waste of time to wander around the gardens and farm without doing something useful," Lina remarks, "even if it were only to cut the big and evil-smelling beetles in half with her clippers." Janet's sense of the clock was more German than Italian—"Every afternoon at exactly the same time she put on her hat and strode off into the *poderi* to see what the peasants were doing"—and she was a creature of strict, frugal habits: each evening after dinner she would smoke precisely

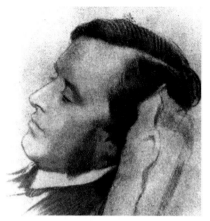

Alexander Duff Gordon, as portrayed
by G. F. Watts (Courtesy of Nigel, Hugh, and
Antony Beevor)

Sarah Austin (Courtesy of the Waterfield
Collection in the Archive of the British Institute
of Florence)

Lucie Duff Gordon,
as portrayed by
Henry Phillips
(Courtesy of the National
Portrait Gallery, London)

ABOVE: Janet at age sixteen, as portrayed by G. F. Watts (Courtesy of Nigel, Hugh, and Antony Beevor)

RIGHT: Janet at age eighteen, as portrayed by Henry Phillips (Courtesy of the Waterfield Collection in the Archive of the British Institute of Florence)

Henry Ross (Courtesy of Nigel, Hugh, and Antony Beevor)

The Marchese Lotteringo della Stufa, aka Lotto (Courtesy of Nigel, Hugh, and Antony Beevor)

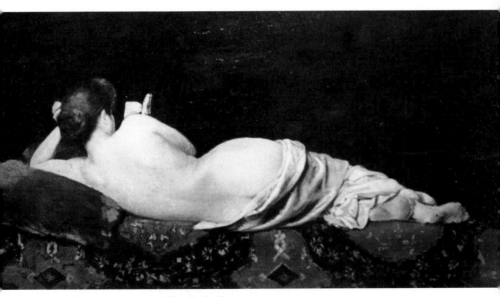

Janet, as portrayed by Carlo Orsi (Courtesy of Nigel, Hugh, and Antony Beevor)

Poggio Gherardo, as seen from the *bosco* (Courtesy of Nigel, Hugh, and Antony Beevor)

The Poodle Room (Courtesy of Nigel, Hugh, and Antony Beevor)

Agostino in his kitchen (Courtesy of Nigel, Hugh, and Antony Beevor)

Hauling grapes at Poggio Gherardo during the *vendemmia* (Courtesy of the Waterfield
Collection in the Archive of the British Institute of Florence)

Lina and Madge at Poggio Gherardo
(Courtesy of the Waterfield Collection in the Archive of
the British Institute of Florence)

Lina, as portrayed by G. F. Watts
(Courtesy of Nigel, Hugh, and Antony Beevor)

Henry, Lina, and
Janet at Poggio
Gherardo (Courtesy of the
Waterfield Collection in the
Archive of the British Institute
of Florence)

Aubrey Waterfield (Courtesy of
Nigel, Hugh, and Antony Beevor)

Aubrey and Lina in their ball
costumes, posing as Romeo and
Juliet (Courtesy of Nigel, Hugh,
and Antony Beevor)

Janet in her study, surrounded by mementos of family and friends (Courtesy of the Waterfield Collection in the Archive of the British Institute of Florence)

Kinta, Hugh, and Nigel Beevor, along with Garrow Waterfield, at Vincigliata

(Courtesy of Nigel, Hugh, and Antony Beevor)

Lina in Janet's study, some twenty years after Janet's death (Courtesy of Nigel, Hugh, and Antony Beevor)

half a cigarette, saving the other half for the next day. Yet she could be curiously inefficient: having never learned to multiply—there were, Lina observes, "amusing lapses in her education"—she used a drawn-out process of addition when doing the farm accounts. Lina was amused as well by Janet's dealings with sharecroppers and servants. These were mostly warm and relaxed, but there was the occasional dressing-down. In *Castle to Italy*, Lina bears witness to an especially comical one:

> One day our talk was interrupted by the angry tones of Beppe, our odd-job man, who was swearing loudly while watering the plants under the camphor tree: '*Porca Madonna!*' (Pig of a Madonna) he repeated in an angry voice. Although Aunt Janet was practically a free-thinker she felt strongly that people should respect their own religion. Beppe was summoned to come up to the balcony and was given a lesson.
>
> 'But everyone says it.'
>
> 'Now, Beppe,' said Aunt Janet, 'say at once, *Porca Padrona*' (Pig of a Mistress).
>
> 'But—but, *Signora Padrona*, I can't,' he wailed, looking horrified and hardly able to stand steady under her severe gaze.
>
> 'And yet, Beppe, you can speak like that of the Madonna—you a practicing Catholic. I am surprised at you; never let me hear you say it again.'
>
> She never heard it again from Beppe or from anyone else, for the story spread. She did not lose her temper with her dependents: she would open her eyes very wide and fix a steady look on the culprit which was quite enough to quell any sign of rebellion.

Though Janet sometimes talked down to Lina and mocked her liberal politics, she also made a point of bringing her into the adult social sphere, as per family tradition. For Lina, who'd been around Wilde and Whistler as a child but had then been deprived of such company, being introduced to the Rosses' enormous circle of friends was yet another boon, in some ways the biggest of all. Witty, affable, well-mannered, and confident, she was quite ready to join the grown-ups, a number of whom eagerly took her under their wings, just as Kinglake, Watts, and Caroline Norton had once done with Janet. And in one instance Janet and Lina took this family tradition a step further: as a pair, they made friends with another pair, a father and daughter with whom they became exceedingly close. It was a sort of intergenerational group friendship that brought out the best in everyone involved.

Back in 1882, Janet had been staying at Aldermaston—always a fertile source of new connections for her—when, after dinner, she was asked to sing some stornelli. "Rather unwillingly," she recalls, "I went to fetch my guitar, for it is uphill work to sing Tuscan folk-songs to an audience which does not understand a word you are saying. My guitar seemed to get flatter and flatter and my singing more Britannic as I looked at the unresponsive faces, when a voice behind me exclaimed *bene, brava*." The slight, frail, bearded man who'd applauded her was the writer John Addington Symonds. Janet had corresponded with him a few times, and his wife, Catherine, was the sister of Marianne North and the stepsister of Lucie's childhood friend Janet Shuttleworth. But the two had never previously met.

Born in 1840, Symonds was a former protégé of Benjamin Jowett at Balliol who'd gone on to become a respected popularizer of classical and Italian subjects; at the time Janet met him he was in the middle of his magnum opus, the seven-volume *Renaissance in Italy*, which bears comparison with Burckhardt's great survey. A married father of four and a friend to the likes of Leslie Stephen, Edmund Gosse, and Robert Louis Stevenson, he seemed a model Victorian literatus. Underneath, however, the man was a cauldron of conflicted emotion, and for one simple reason: he was gay to his fingertips.

After years of suppressing his desires, Symonds began acting on them—quite prolifically—in his late twenties, his wife having grudgingly agreed to countenance his affairs. The nervous ailments that had plagued him dropped away with his trousers, and he was easier in his skin from then on. Not that he was remotely well, for he still suffered from tuberculosis, which induced him to move to Davos. Restless in the Alps, he seized every chance to escape to Italy, especially to Venice, where he kept a lover and a pied-à-terre. Florence he claimed to find "detestable," but he was about to overcome his aversion.

After their meeting at Aldermaston, Symonds and Janet resumed their correspondence, and he came to Castagnolo at least once. In late 1889 he became one of the first overnight guests at Poggio Gherardo. The visit seems to have solidified or accelerated his friendship with Janet, for suddenly the two were thick as thieves, with volleys of letters flying back and forth and Symonds turning up in Florence on a regular basis.

Janet couldn't get enough of "my Historian," as she dubbed Symonds. ("The Historian," George Grote, had died, so the title was free.) His Italophilia and fondness for what he termed "Tuscan *Volks Lieder*" certainly counted, but it was more the wide span of his interests, and his virtuosity at leaping between them, that dazzled her. In his essay "Talk and Talkers," Stevenson declared Symonds, with his "various and exotic knowledge . . . and fine, full, discriminative flow of language," to be "the best of talkers," and Janet reached the same conclusion: "After listening to his brilliant talk, one felt as though cobwebs had been brushed away from one's brain." Clearly he had a good deal of intellectual respect for her as well, since he often solicited her opinion on his work, just as she asked for his on hers.

Yet the relationship was less cerebral than sentimental. Though Janet hugely admired Symonds's determination to live a full life in spite of his illness (he must have reminded her of Lucie in this regard), she also liked to cosset, nurse, and fret over him. "*La tiranna*," Symonds called her, with reference to her scolding ministrations, but he clearly relished the love and care. Despite their differences in temperament—Symonds was as highly strung as Janet was composed—they soon established an intimate rapport, as can be seen in a letter Symonds wrote just after one of his visits: already nostalgic for Janet's "hospitable feudal keep," he conjures up remembered images of the two of them "dreaming, gossiping, sauntering across a thousand fields with irresponsible feet of meditation, ventilating paradoxes, dissecting neighbours, over the wood fire in your dear drawing-room; while the presence of the Arno valley and the hills is always felt inside the house, adding a dignity and charm, not ours, to what we say."

Enhancing the friendship was the fact that a parallel one had sprung up among the younger generation. Symonds often brought his second-youngest daughter,* Madge, then in her early twenties, along to Poggio Gherardo. Her father's constant traveling companion, Madge had already collaborated with him on a book about life in the Swiss Alps, and seemed destined for a literary career. She also had a high vivacity that other women—including the young Virginia Stephen (later Woolf), who was to develop a crush on her—tended to find irresistible. Lina fell beneath her spell, and Madge, despite being five years older, returned her affection.

Janet took to Madge as well, and Lina and Symonds to each other, so that together they made a perfect foursome. Over the next few years they were often all together in Florence, but Madge sometimes came alone to Poggio Gherardo, and Lina would visit her in Davos or meet up with her elsewhere. When apart, Lina and Madge wrote each other letters at a furious clip. Madge's have been lost, but Lina's feature an appealing mix of drollery and puppy love: when not making sardonic (and often quite funny) remarks about mutual acquaintances, Lina plaintively rehashes her heart-to-heart talks with Madge in their secret spot in the bosco, near the poodle sarcophagus.

To Lina, Madge's friendship wasn't only flattering but horizon-expanding. This much became came clear in 1891, when she was invited to stay with Madge and Symonds at his pied-à-terre in Venice. Madge's closeness with her father had, Lina remarks, "developed her mind beyond her years," and going to museums with the two of them was an education in itself. "I remember my surprise when Mr. Symonds sat for hours each morning taking notes in front of an easel-picture by Tiepolo of the last communion of

---

*All four of Symonds's children were daughters. His eldest had died of tuberculosis in 1887. Her name happened to be Janet, and one can't help wondering whether Symonds's love for Janet Ross wasn't tinged or amplified by the coincidence.

St. Lucy . . . It then dawned on me that there is a real art in looking at pictures."

After Symonds retuned to Davos, Madge brought Lina to stay with her friend the Contessa Pisani, who bore a certain resemblance to Janet: half English by birth—her doctor father, Julius Millingen, had attended Lord Byron on his deathbed at Missolonghi—she'd married an Italian noble and taken over the Villa Pisani, near Padua, where she improved the gardens and oversaw the poderi, far more numerous than Poggio Gherardo's. The countess was, according to Lina, especially proud of her five hundred oxen. "It was thought a great privilege to be asked to have a calf named after one; Queen Victoria's daughter, the Empress Frederick, Sir Henry Layard, and Gladstone had been thus honoured, and while we were there two calves were named Maggetta and Linetta."*

Symonds, meanwhile, was discovering just how useful Janet could be, especially with regard to the biography of Michelangelo he'd embarked on. In addition to providing a cozy base for his research whenever he was in town, Janet went to the Alinari archives† to order photos of Michelangelo's works, which she then forwarded to Davos. She also had photographs taken of a supposed Michelangelo portrait belonging to the della Stufa family. (Apparently Lotto's relations took a sunnier view of her now that she was out of Castagnolo.) But her real coup was to remove an obstacle that had driven Symonds mad with frustration. In 1858 one of Michelangelo's descendants had bequeathed the artist's papers to the Casa Buonarroti, with the absurd proviso that access was to be denied "even to the learned, except in rare instances." Symonds, having gotten nowhere on his own, asked Janet for help. She paid a visit to Dr. Biagi, who exerted pressure in the right places, and before long Symonds was burrowing into the folios.

What he found there both startled him and confirmed his

---

*In 1893 Madge published a book about the Pisani family and their estate, *Days Spent on a Doge's Farm*. The countess took umbrage at some of Madge's characterizations and huffily withdrew her favors.
†Founded in 1852, Fratelli Alinari is the world's oldest photographic company.

suspicions. Michelangelo's nephew, it became clear, had systematically covered up his uncle's obsession with a young Roman noble, Tommaso de' Cavalieri, by feminizing the pronouns in his letters and sonnets (which as a result were thought to have been addressed to Vittoria Colonna). This wasn't the first time Symonds had encountered such whitewash. For twenty years he'd traded letters with Walt Whitman, often prodding him about the homoerotic subtext of his "Calamus" poems. Whitman had always lightly evaded these inquiries, but in 1890 Symonds pushed too hard, and the American shot back with an angry denial of Symonds's "morbid inferences." Disgusted by Whitman's cowardice, Symonds was now intent on setting the record straight—or, rather, setting it gay—when it came to Michelangelo.

One of the first people to learn of Symonds's bold plan for his biography was Janet. "I fear it will not be acceptable to the general reader," he confessed, "yet the time has come when the truth about Michelangelo must be told." Just how much of Symonds's private life was known to her is unclear. Before one of his first visits, he'd written to ask whether he might bring along a Venetian companion, described as follows: "He is an old peasant who has been with me for ten years. Just now I am really dependent on him while travelling." Janet must have drawn a conclusion or two when this "old peasant" turned out to be a dreamily handsome gondolier in his thirties. (Angelo Fusato, to give him his name, was Symonds's principal Italian lover.) Less prudish than many, she was probably unfazed by the fact of her friend's sexual preferences, though she might have been perturbed to learn of the full vigor of his activities. At any rate, he increasingly took her into his confidence as the biography neared completion. Sending her the proofs, he solicited particular comment on the twelfth chapter—the one in which he meant to detonate his bombshells. She advised a handful of small cuts and alterations, nearly all of which Symonds made. "The chapter will gain in dignity and not lose anything in point," he wrote, thanking her for the suggestions.

To Symonds's relief—his aim was to be truthful, not to shock— the biography, published in early 1893, was met with widespread

praise and, as he reported to Janet, "not a word of blame or outraged sense." One result of its success was an invitation to deliver a
lecture on Michelangelo in Florence that April. Exhausted from his
labors, Symonds couldn't face the prospect, but he also couldn't
turn down such an honor. He therefore wrote a lecture and asked
Janet to have it translated into Italian and read for him; she lined up
Enrico Nencioni, the same professor who'd once objected to the
way Britons "look down on us because there is no Michelangelo now
in Florence," but who admired Symonds's work. Meanwhile Symonds planned, entirely for rest and pleasure, a spring tour of southern Italy—including Leucaspide, to which Janet had gotten him
invited—with Madge and his faithful gondolier.

On April 19 the lecture was read. Though it went over well,
while clapping Janet unaccountably found herself seized by "a feeling of intense anxiety." That evening she got news that Symonds
had died in Rome, only hours before the lecture—"we had unwit-
tingly been applauding the words of a dead man." As she later learned,
he'd caught a respiratory infection a few days earlier. Despite the
attentions of his friend Dr. Axel Munthe,* then practicing in Rome,
Symonds, his lungs weakened by consumption, had quickly faded.
He was buried in the Protestant Cemetery, near Shelley and Trelawny, beneath an epitaph composed by Jowett.†

After attending to formalities in Rome, Madge made straight
for Poggio Gherardo and collapsed into the arms of Lina and Janet,
whose grief was almost as intense as her own. Eventually she
picked herself up and went on her way, but Poggio Gherardo and its

---

*Munthe (1847–1929) would go on to become world-famous as the author of *The Story of
San Michele*, an autobiography that takes its name from the villa he built for himself on
Capri.
†In a sense, Symonds's true monument is his body of posthumously published work about
being a gay man. Not long before his death he'd begun collaborating on a study of homosexuality with the psychologist Havelock Ellis, who credited him as coauthor of the pio-
neering *Sexual Inversion* (1897). During his last years he'd also written a secret memoir of
his homosexuality. Suppressed by his squeamish executor, Horatio Brown, it was finally
published in 1984, and is now considered a landmark of gay writing, one of the first and
most searching testaments of its kind. No doubt unbeknownst to Janet, parts of it were almost certainly written at Poggio Gherardo.

inhabitants were to go on playing an important role in her life for several years. Even after drifting away, she never forgot "Aunt Janet" (as she too had come to call her), and in 1922 she wrote a forty-page essay titled "Memoirs of Mrs. Janet Ross and of Life in a Florentine Villa." Though never published, it is one of the fullest accounts of its kind, and ends with a testimonial to Janet's softest, most human qualities. "In the shattering sorrow of my young days, namely after my Father's death in Rome," Madge writes, "I was brought by a friend one hot May night back to Aunt Janet's villa." After describing the enfolding care she received there, she concludes, "The world will remember Janet Ross as a rather domineering and commanding figure in the literary and social circles of her day. But some there are, who, like myself, will bless this great Victorian lady because of her hidden *tenderness*, and because of that deeper and serener *charity* which reaches the heart in its affliction."

—=≡፡Ө፡≡=—

While there was no replacing Symonds, Poggio Gherardo was hardly left desolate. Many friends—Lacaita and the Layards, among others—came to stay, and often wound up extending their visits because of the high grade of hospitality on tap. Financially pinched, Janet couldn't swaddle her guests in luxury the way richer colonists did, but she made up for it with an array of thoughtful touches. As an example of these, Madge mentions that she had her sheets hung out in a lavender-filled room, so that guests could enjoy a fragrant night's sleep. "To live under her roof," Madge remarks, "was to be carried back to the rule of some lady in the cinquecento."

But those who actually slept at Poggio Gherardo made up a small percentage of those who passed through its gates. Considerably closer to central Florence than Castagnolo, the house was easily reached by day-trippers. This was all to the good for Janet, who had no wish to isolate herself but was more put off than ever by mainstream colonial life. "I went into a tea-fight in Florence yesterday," she'd reported to Kinglake in 1889, "& I was astounded . . . at the extraordinary folly & stupidity of the people. I have registered a vow that I will go to no more social gatherings in Florence." Though she didn't entirely stick to this vow, for the most part she let Florence come to her.

It now began to do so on a weekly basis, for the Rosses had inaugurated their Sunday receptions. These weren't in the nature of a salon or conversazione, of the type held by Lady Walpurga Paget and Vernon Lee (who'd recently bought Il Palmerino, a villa below Fiesole). Neither explicitly intellectual nor dominated by any one set of people, they bore more resemblance to the "at-homes" of the earlier Victorians. Thrown almost every week for many years, they became an institution, and one whose renown spread well beyond Tuscany. Before long, British and American tourists with no direct connection to the Rosses were angling for an invitation. "The welcomed guests would boast of their success as though they had won a victory," Lina recalls. "One man sent by a mutual friend to see [Janet] is said to have rung the bell and then run away, his courage failing at the last moment."

Some courage was certainly needed, given Janet's unpredictability. She might warm to a guest right away, but she just as easily might, for no obvious reason, take a violent scunner against him. Fifty years earlier, Saint-Hilaire had commended Sarah Austin for the gentle way she policed her salon. Unconcerned with making enemies, her granddaughter observed no such tact. "Few could rival her in freezing with a look those she disliked," Lina comments.

But Janet's purpose in opening her door every Sunday afternoon was not, of course, to demonstrate her Medusa powers; she was as intent as any hostess on showing her guests a good time. A large and delicious buffet awaited them, along with plenty of Poggio Gherardo wine. There was always musical entertainment, with Janet performing stornelli and Carlo Orsi joining her for duets—"passionate love songs which touched some of their listeners to tears," in Lina's recollection. Cockie the cockatoo provided further diversion, clambering over people and jabbering away. In fine weather, guests would gather on the terrace and gush over the view, or else gaze at the Burmese goldfish. "Beautiful American girls with frocks worthy of Daisy Miller," writes Madge in her memoir of Janet, "would lean and watch the . . . fish in Mrs. Ross' pond (to say nothing of their own reflections and those of the rather languid young men who invariably followed in their train)." During the colder months they'd cluster indoors, where olive branches burning in the fireplaces gave off both heat and fragrance.

Another popular attraction at Poggio Gherardo was Janet's study, where she wrote and did her accounts. The room was crammed with memorabilia, from busts of Lacaita and Lord Lansdowne to drawings and family portraits by Thackeray, Watts, and Edward Lear; even the desk had associations, having previously belonged to Lucie. Still, the fascination exerted by the room on visitors (who often asked to see it) is rather perplexing, since none of its keepsakes was all that special. Clearly a level of interest had grown up around Janet and her ancestors, presumably in part because of *Letters from Egypt*, *Three Generations of English Women*, and *Early Days Recalled*, the last of which appeared in 1891. Yet there also seems to have been, now that the Victorian age was in its twilight, some nostalgia at work for its meridian splendors, which visitors found preserved not only in Janet's possessions but in her talk. "Visitors would gather round Aunt Janet listening enthralled to the stories of people she had known," Lina recalls. Her memory of having tea with the Berry sisters would be trotted out as the pièce de résistance.

But Janet had more than the past to trade on: she herself was the true cynosure of the receptions. When not singing, reminiscing, or giving tours, she would make outrageous statements and indulge her pet peeves. According to Lina, "She shocked people by saying there were three bores in Italian history: Saint Francis, Dante, and Savonarola." (Given that one still couldn't swing a cat in Florence without hitting a *dantista*, the second slur must have been especially provocative.) Above all, her sheer physical presence—not only her features but her bearing and attire—commanded attention. By this point she had a sort of everyday uniform, one that blended elegance with *padrona* practicality. "People still remember," writes Lina, "the impression she made on them in her white cashmere dress, its plainly cut bodice fastened by gold buttons, or else porcelain ones she had painted herself with exotic birds. She wore a black leather belt edged with silver round her waist from which hung a chatelaine with a watch, a leather memorandum book and a silver key to the three gates of the Villa." Madge speculates that her appearance "ensured the devotion" of her servants and sharecroppers, "for in Italy personal beauty is a talisman." At any rate, it floored many of her guests.

Not every reception was a success. "A few people trudged up in the rain last Sunday and endeavoured to admire the view through clouds," Lina wrote to Madge after one that fizzled. "A young lady with an impossible name and a face like a large macaw inflicted herself upon me." Usually, though, the gatherings caught fire to a degree, kindled in part by their own chanciness. There were a few regulars, but long-lost friends also had a way of turning up. The Duc de Chartres, for instance: meeting Lina for the first time, he recalled hunting with Janet back at Esher and "laughed in telling me she often took letters hidden in her hair from him and his brother to their friends in Paris." (Either these were very small letters or Janet had very large hair at the time.)

Among the complete strangers, many turned out to be dull, but some were memorable. Janet nowhere catalogs them, and if the Rosses kept a guest book it hasn't survived. But *Castle in Italy* and Lina's letters afford some humorous glimpses, especially of the once-prominent literary figures who trooped through Poggio Gherardo in the 1890s. One week brought Fergus Hume, a New Zealander whose self-published *The Mystery of a Hansom Cab* was the bestselling detective novel of its day. Another brought the even more popular Marie Corelli, described by one critic as combining "the imagination of a Poe with the style of a Ouida and the mentality of a nursemaid." Lina recalls that the notoriously vain novelist "expected to be fêted when she flitted into the drawing-room" and took umbrage when Janet ignored her, focusing instead on "a distinguished American lawyer whom she had enthroned in an armchair. Marie Corelli managed to insert herself near him and to start a conversation about literature and told him she had just finished writing her last book. He gave her a critical glance and said: 'And what do you write, Miss Corelli?' She seemed staggered by his ignorance of her fame."

Just as touchy was the newly appointed poet laureate of Great Britain, Alfred Austin, who had the misfortune of succeeding Tennyson. Pocket-sized in physiognomy and widely mocked for his bombastic verse, Austin was a giant in his own mind. At Poggio Gherardo he failed to find the flattery he craved: having rented a nearby villa, Austin dropped in repeatedly, but, according to Lina, "the visits were not a success," as "Aunt Janet always forgot that he was a poet."

One Sunday brought a blast, or at least a whimper, from the Anglo-Florentine past. Though Robert Browning had never been able to bring himself to return to Florence after Elizabeth's death, a few years after his own death in 1889 their son Pen came to town, and suddenly there he was at Poggio Gherardo, along with his aunt Sarianna Browning and his American wife, Fanny, an heiress whose fortune had allowed him to buy a colossal palazzo in Venice. As a child, Pen had been a Little Lord Fauntleroy, dolled up by his mother in ruffles and ribbons, and while he'd since found minor success as a painter he remained somehow pathetic—"Poor, grotesque little Pen," Henry James once wrote. As for his relationship with Fanny, it was a far cry from the celestial union of the Brownings. "They seemed to be an incongruous pair," Lina observes, "and I was not surprised when I heard that they had separated." All the same, Pen, like any child of famous parents, was invested with some of their aura, and to meet him was to catch an echo of an already legendary age.

―――•☼•―――

While it would be hyperbolic and inaccurate to call Poggio Gherardo the new Casa Guidi, over time it acquired a similar cachet. A Sunday jaunt to the castle became almost obligatory, part of the prescribed itinerary of the fin de siècle British visitor to Florence. And as more and more visitors rode out to take their chances with "the redoubtable Mrs. Ross" (as many now called her), she too started to take on the lineaments of legend. In a sense she'd become not the Elizabeth Barrett Browning but the Landor of her time, a picturesque "royal animal" valued as much for her ferocity as her charisma.

But where Landor had been all wild-eyed romance and delusion, Janet was eminently hardheaded and well informed. After a quarter century in town, she spoke Italian more or less perfectly, knew hundreds of Florentines from every walk of life, and had experience dealing with everything from phylloxera (a grapevine-ravaging pest) to *le lungaggini della burocrazia* (red tape). Along with her fearsomeness, her expertise—and her ready generosity in sharing it—became common knowledge: if one needed help with local matters, she was the person to ask. In 1892 this reputation for being comprehensively au fait led to one of the world's best-known authors becoming her neighbor.

Like Janet, Mark Twain had first seen Florence in 1867, on one of the side trips that punctuated his *Quaker City* cruise. (His account of the cruise, *The Innocents Abroad*, would make his name.) Mired in the company of prissy Congregationalists and hustled through town in less than two days, Twain thought little of Florence, and his equally perfunctory return visit in 1878 also left him indifferent. Then, fourteen years later, he finally gave it a fair shake. His financial blunderings having left him strapped for cash, Twain decided in 1891 to take his family for an open-ended stay in Europe, which at the time was far cheaper than the United States. After a bone-chilling winter in Berlin, he and his wife, Livy, sought a warmer refuge, and during a tour of Italy in the spring of 1892 Florence struck them as just the place. They planned to spend the summer nursing their various ailments at a German spa but to return to Florence in the fall, and to stay till the following summer.

For advice on property rentals, Twain turned to his friend Willard Fiske. A retired Cornell professor and librarian, Fiske had recently come into a large inheritance, which he used to snap up rare Danteana and to buy and refurbish the Villa Gherardesca, formerly owned by Landor. By the time of Twain's arrival, Fiske had gotten to know the Rosses, and had figured out that Janet was the go-to person in

such situations. He therefore brought Twain over to Poggio Gherardo. Twain, Janet recalls, "asked whether there was any villa to be
had near by, and from our terrace we showed him Villa Viviani,
between us and Settignano." She arranged for Twain and Livy to
see the house, which with its twenty-eight rooms was even bigger
than their Hartford mansion. Quoted a laughably low price, they
rented it on the spot, with the lease to begin in September.

In the Clemenses' absence, Janet hired servants for them and had
the house cleaned, stocked, and equipped. "When we got back three
or four months later," Twain writes in his autobiography, "everything was ready, even to the servants and the dinner. It takes but a
second to state that but it makes an indolent person tired to think of
the planning and work and trouble that lie concealed in it." In one
of his letters he goes into more detail: "Mrs. Ross laid in our wood,
wine and servants for us, and they are excellent. She had the house
scoured from cellar to roof, the curtains washed and put up, all beds
pulled to pieces, beaten, washed and put together again, and beguiled the Marchese [the villa's owner, presumably] into putting a
big porcelain stove in the vast central hall. She is a wonderful woman,
and we don't quite see how or when we should have gotten under
way without her." There was no payment or quid pro quo involved—
Janet had simply taken a liking to Twain and was happy to help
him out.

Once settled at the Viviani with Livy and two of his daughters
(the third remained in Berlin), Twain decided that, as he puts it in
his autobiography, "life at a Florentine villa is an ideal existence,"
and that the view from his terrace constituted "the fairest picture on
our planet." That picture included, in the near distance, "the imposing mass of the Ross castle, its walls and turrets rich with the
mellow weather stains of forgotten centuries." As with Janet's machicolations, Twain's turrets existed solely in his imagination, but
his false memory of Poggio Gherardo doesn't reflect a lack of acquaintance with the place. To the contrary, he stopped by often,
usually unannounced and in a state of befuddlement. "He considers P. Gherardo an office for general information," Lina wrote to

Madge, "& walks in at all hours of the day, generally entirely igno-rant of what he has come to ask until he pulls out a large notebook with the various ?? written down."

One day, to everyone's stupefaction, he showed up quite bald, shorn of his iconic mop. As Lina told Madge, he'd "shaved off his immense superabundance of hair . . . in order, as he quietly informed us, to learn the language." Famously dumbfounded by German, Twain was now struggling with Italian, and, as he explained to a *New York Times* reporter who asked him to "account for this muti-lation," he'd decided "to watch the natives and see if he could catch any peculiarity of theirs that might account for their capacity to master the language. Then he noticed their heads were all as smooth as billiard balls. Perchance his heavy crop prevented the tongue from filtering through. So he went straight to a barber." It didn't work. "Got my head shaved," Twain's diary tersely notes. "This was a mistake."

Amused by Twain's bumbling eccentricity, the Rosses invited him not only to their Sunday receptions but to smaller get-togethers. At one of these he met the Layards. "Old Sir Henry Layard was here the other day, visiting our neighbor Janet Ross," he wrote to a friend afterward, "and since then I have been reading his account of the adventures in his youth in the far East." At another gathering, according to Janet, he sang "some real negro songs; it was a revela-tion. Without much voice and with little or no knowledge of music (he played the bass notes with one finger) he moved us all in a won-derful way. It was quite different from what one had generally heard sung as 'negro melodies.'"

While the invalid Livy rarely joined Twain at Poggio Gherardo, his daughters often did. Lina preferred the twelve-year-old Jean ("We sat up in an ilex one afternoon and made great friends") to the morose Susy, who at twenty was closer to Lina in age. Yet she made an effort with both, and even brought Susy along to a ball in honor of the Duke of Aosta. "This ball was Susy Clemens' first experience of Italian society," she told Madge, "& it made a great impression on her American mind."

Twain himself had no interest in Italian society, and very little in the artistic treasures of Florence, as of Europe in general—"I *hate* the old Masters," he once confessed. More to his Missouri taste was the kind of farm talk to be found at Poggio Gherardo. Like any American, he was justly proud of his native sweet corn, whose praises he sang to Janet. When, in the spring of 1893, he had to make a quick trip to the United States to attend to business matters, he promised to send Janet seeds for what he called "real corn," as well as watermelon. A few weeks later, from Chicago, Twain forwarded her his correspondence with Secretary of Agriculture J. Sterling Morton, whom he'd asked to send her the seeds. Permitting himself the kind of ethnic persiflage no cabinet member would dream of putting on paper today, Morton had replied to Twain, "I am much pleased that you are become an agent for the introduction of corn as a food among the Italians, and it is to be hoped that by a vigorous effort on the part of the English lady who is to cultivate the cornfield and a strong appetite upon your part when the corn shall have been grown and boiled, this delicious food may be popularized among the deluded consumers of macaroni. The water-melon seeds are also sent, and will no doubt produce fruit calculated to inspire larceny among all the youthful *lazzaroni* [scoundrels] who may long for lusciousness." Soon afterward the seeds themselves arrived. Janet says nothing about the fate of the corn and is dismissive of the watermelon, which she found "not nearly as good" as similar Italian melons. Still, she was clearly tickled by Twain's little campaign—in *The Fourth Generation* she reproduces in full the correspondence related to it.

By May 1893 Twain was back in Florence, but only briefly, for in June he and his family returned to Germany. His nine months in town had been his happiest for a long time. Like Hawthorne at Villa Montauto, he'd found himself finally able to write fluently again: much of *Pudd'nhead Wilson* and *Tom Sawyer Abroad* were written at the Viviani, and he made progress on *Personal Recollections of Joan of Arc*. But his proximity to Poggio Gherardo, and the welcome he and his daughters found there, also made a difference to him.

For several years the Rosses had no American neighbors to equal Twain. But then a new pair came along, as different from Twain as chalk from cheese, and as redoubtable in their way as Janet.

———❧———

In May 1895 Florence was hit by a sizeable earthquake, and Poggio Gherardo suffered severe damage, including the collapse of its tower. To pay for repairs, Henry and Janet decided to sell a painting of theirs, a Madonna and child attributed to Alesso Baldovinetti. When they mentioned it to the writer Charles Dudley Warner, who was staying with Willard Fiske (and who, incidentally, had coauthored *The Gilded Age* with Twain), he recommended that they consult a young art historian of his acquaintance. The man came over to Poggio Gherardo and confirmed the attribution, paving the way for the Rosses to sell the painting for a handsome sum and start repairs. Little did they guess the role he would play in their lives, or in the colony at large.

Born Bernhard Valvrojenski in Lithuania in 1865, Bernard Berenson was a prodigy of assimilation, and of much else besides. Along with the rest of his poor Jewish family, he emigrated as a child to Boston, where his genius quickly declared itself. At Harvard he so impressed William James and others that he was admitted to the most exclusive Brahmin circles, his conversion to Christianity making him still more presentable. Sponsored by a series of admiring patrons, he spent several *Wanderjahre* in Europe, where he shook off his vague notion of becoming a novelist and realized that his true aptitude was for the study of those same Old Masters Twain claimed to hate. Before long he was not only writing authoritative books on the Italian Renaissance but refining the techniques of attribution and connoisseurship developed by Janet's friend Giovanni Morelli. So persuasive was he in his arguments for what was gold and what was dross, and so skilled at finding masterpieces for sale, that he was hired by the insatiable collector Isabella Stewart Gardner as her chief European buyer. At the time the Rosses met him he was, in fact, scouring the Continent for works that his client would later stuff into the Boston museum bearing her name.* Though he chafed at his arrangement with Gardner, which he felt to be mercenary and even Faustian, he profited hugely from it, and was on his way to becoming rich.

Besides his matchless acumen and knowledge, Berenson's art-world ascendancy was enabled by a secret weapon. Mary Costelloe, née Smith, hailed from a highly idiosyncratic—and, like Janet's, strikingly matriarchal—family of Philadelphia Quakers. Having shifted to Methodism, both her parents became revivalist preachers with large transatlantic followings; her mother, Hannah Whitall Smith, was especially popular and energetic, with fingers in the temperance movement and various other Christian pies. Despite all this holiness, they were intellectual Anglophiles, and after moving to a country house in Surrey, they were taken up by the likes of Oscar Wilde and George Bernard Shaw. One of their sons, Logan Pearsall Smith, became a respected belletrist, while their daughter Alys (alas for her) married Bertrand Russell.

As for Mary, born in 1864, she married Frank Costelloe, an Irish barrister and aspiring politician, with whom she settled in London and had two daughters. At first dedicated to advancing her husband's career, she became disillusioned with him, and on her second meeting with Berenson in 1890 her head was turned by his brilliance and vocational intensity. She began haunting museums across Europe with Berenson and picking up his connoisseurial skills. Such a quick study was she that her expertise soon approached his own, and he eagerly harnessed it: Mary became the virtual coauthor of his books and even wrote pseudonymous rave reviews of them. Gradually they fell in love, and in 1893 Mary left her husband and rented a villa near Fiesole, just down the road from Bernard's.†

They were an oddly sorted couple. Where Bernard was short and

---

*A number of these works had been coveted by Berenson's bitter rival Wilhelm von Bode, and it must have amused Berenson to hear how Henry Ross had dealt with the pushy German over *The School of Pan*.

†Strictly speaking, he was still "Bernhard" at this point—he didn't Anglicize his first name till World War I, as a protest against all things German. (His family had given up "Valvrojenski" in 1875, on arrival in the United States.)

lean, Mary was plumply Junoesque. Where he was dapper, fastidi-
ous, pedantic, testy, rather prudish, and given to excoriating sarcasm,
she was frumpy, warm, earthy, impulsive, and prone to romantic and
sexual infatuations. (This frank bohemian lustiness existed alongside her residual Quakerism, which dictated the use of archaic pronouns, and in her letters she would address Bernard as "thee" even
when confessing some new dalliance.) They were, inevitably, often
at loggerheads, yet also deeply intertwined at both an emotional
and a professional level.

At first the Rosses knew only B.B., as everyone called him. Because of the improper nature of their liaison, Bernard and Mary
were wary about appearing in public together. In houses like Il
Palmerino, where Vernon Lee held her rigorously highbrow conversazioni, they could relax in the knowledge that the prevailing mor-
als were as modern as the aesthetic theories. But the old guard
would, they feared, be less forgiving. Assuming the Rosses to be-
long to this camp, Bernard kept Mary out of the picture, establishing a single man's friendship with them. They knew many people in
common, and Berenson's strong historical sense made him appreciative of Janet's ancestry, just as his wide experience among willful vi-
ragos such as Lee and Gardner prepared him to take her character
in stride. He even admired her orchid paintings, which he described
to Mary as capturing "the movement and beauty of the flowers."
Henry also won him over, in particular with his Near Eastern tales;
after one long, hair-raising recital, a transported Bernard sat in si-
lence for a moment before declaring, "That is epic—it is Homeric."
He became a regular at their receptions, though he sometimes found
them tedious: Mary's diary records that one Sunday Bernard "called
on the Rosses, where he found a large miscellaneous company of
second rate celebrities boring each other to death. He escaped and
joined me on the road and we walked home discussing the eternal
question: '*Was ist die Kunst?*'"

After several years of hearing Bernard talk about the Rosses and
Poggio Gherardo, Mary became fed up with being excluded, and in
1897 Bernard finally brought her along to a reception. Janet, she later
recalled, "was noted for saying whatever she liked, and she began her

acquaintance with me by saying that she hated women—'Never trust a woman,' she sang out in her deep, mannish voice." Wisely, Mary didn't take the bait, and soon Janet was all geniality. A few weeks later, in fact, she went out of her way to put Mary at ease by telling an anecdote about the artists William and Evelyn De Morgan, who wintered in Settignano.* Janet had provokingly told Evelyn that she'd hosted "an illegally attached couple"—Bernard and Mary, that is—and Evelyn had pleaded with Janet not to mention it to her strait-laced husband. "Why? It's not contagious!" Janet had responded. Heartened by this gesture of support, Mary let her guard down completely, and from that point on she and Janet were firm friends.

While the advent of these two dynamic Americans was a blessing for Janet and Henry, it was even more of one for Lina. Twenty-three years old in 1897, Lina was setting out on her own literary career: the publisher J. M. Dent (of Everyman's Library fame) had commissioned her and Madge to write a book about Perugia for his "Medieval Towns" series. She traveled widely, sometimes on her own. At Poggio Gherardo, however, she was beginning to feel a bit stifled. The Rosses' friends, fond as she was of many of them, tended toward the geriatric, and she felt constrained by, as Madge puts it, "the (unspoken) rule of not seeing the queens of rival courts in Florence." Under these circumstances, Bernard and Mary came as a breath of fresh air; closer in age to Lina than to Janet, they had a youthful verve and an up-to-date sensibility despite their conservative tastes. The liking was mutual, and Lina quickly became a favorite protégée of theirs. "The friendship of Mary and B.B. made a great difference to my life," she recalls, "and I no longer felt the absence of parties and balls."

If nothing else, the friendship provided Lina with an extraordinary education in the Renaissance. She'd learned a good deal from both Symonds and the equally discerning Layard, with whom she'd once spent several weeks in Venice gorging on art. But nobody

---

*The painter Evelyn De Morgan (1855–1919) was a niece of John Roddam Spencer Stanhope and followed in his Pre-Raphaelite tracks, while William Frend De Morgan (1839–1917) was a ceramicist who often collaborated with William Morris. Today the couple's work can be seen at the De Morgan Centre in London.

compared to Berenson. Though sometimes malicious—Logan Pearsall Smith, who was often in Florence at this time, once watched him
lay traps for Lina and Madge, "leading them on to say silly things
about art, and then tearing them to pieces"—he was a patient teacher
and a singularly illuminating cicerone. Soon Lina was joining him
and Mary, along with Logan, Herbert Horne,* and others, on art
tours all over Tuscany. These had little in common with the standard itineraries. Instead, Berenson would lead the way into obscure
corners of the countryside, in search of forgotten masterpieces lan-
guishing in unsung chapels. "We need Art-students, men of sincerity and labor, who will not hesitate to go on their backs and knees,"
James Jackson Jarves had declared in 1853, and now here was his
fellow Bostonian not just crawling through the dust but identifying
with unprecedented precision what he found there. Lina was with
him at Empoli when "he discovered a little masterpiece" (she neglects
to say which), and she shared in his treasure hunter's jubilation. She
also took part in his and Mary's self-invented game of "conoshing"
(from the Italian *conoscere*, "to know"), which involved covering re-
productions of artworks so that only a single detail was visible—
a face, say, or a hand—and then trying to guess their identity. Despite
being at a hopeless disadvantage, Lina loved it.

Having had to accept minimal contact with her daughters back
in England as the price of running off with Berenson, Mary tended to
displace her strong maternal feelings onto anyone younger than herself, and Lina was one of the primary recipients. In particular, Mary
decided to take Lina's love life in hand. Tall and strong-featured, with
deep-set eyes and a determined-looking jaw, Lina was handsome if not
quite beautiful, and must have gotten her share of attention. A few of
the Rosses' friends had shown a tentative matrimonial interest in her,
among them the museum curator Sydney Cockerell and Tom Dibblee, an editor at *The Manchester Guardian*. (When Dibblee mooted
to Janet the possibility of his proposing to Lina, she sardonically

---

*Herbert Percy Horne (1864–1916) was an English architect, typographer, and antiquarian
who restored and lived in a Renaissance palazzo in Florence. After his death, the building
became the Museo Horne, which to this day displays his small but fine collection.

replied that Lina had better see Manchester first. He backed off.)
Lady Walpurga Paget, who'd helped engineer the match between the
Prince of Wales and Princess Alexandra of Denmark, dangled the notion of Lina marrying her son Ralph, but nothing came of it, nor of
Lina's infatuation with the the son of Janet's old friend Luigi Strozzi.
Now along came Mary, an incorrigible meddler. Recently she'd had
a fling with a young philosopher named Wilfred Blaydes. Forced
by Bernard to break it off, she tried to palm Blaydes off on Lina, who
wanted none of him. Undeterred, she began eyeing Lina as a potential mate for her brother—a ridiculous notion, since Logan, who
cared only for the life of the mind, was one of nature's own bachelors.

In point of fact, Lina didn't need Mary's help, for she'd found a
candidate of her own, and had set her cap squarely at him. Obedient
to stereotype, the course of love ran bumpily before smoothing out,
only to fetch Lina up against the glowering obstacle of Janet. For all
three inhabitants of Poggio Gherardo, a long traumatic melodrama
lay ahead, a web of heartbreak, conflict, death, grief, and blame that
gripped the castle like malign ivy.

In September 1897, during a visit to England, Lina went to stay
with the Rosses' friends Sir William and Lady Markby, where she
met a relation of theirs exactly her own age. Aubrey Waterfield had
recently graduated from Oxford and was just beginning his studies
at the Slade School of Art, with a view toward becoming a painter.
Tall, talented, and possessed of a chiseled handsomeness set off just
so by a studied dishevelment, he dealt Lina an instant *colpo di ful-
mine*. "A very fascinating 'Grifonetto' has disturbed my peace of
mind," she wrote to Madge. (Grifonetto Baglioni was a fifteenth-
century Perugian noble familiar to both women from their book
research.) The attraction seemed to be at least somewhat mutual, for
he invited her to stay at his parents' house near Canterbury.

The populous Waterfields—Aubrey was the youngest of seven—
were headed by a father who'd been a classicist and public school
headmaster before becoming a banker. They were a hot-tempered,

argumentative bunch, so much so that their residence, Nackington House, was often referred to as Naggington. They were, however, respectable, and not unknown to the Rosses, one of Aubrey's uncles having given Henry sound advice during the financial crisis of 1866. Even though Aubrey's feelings toward her were less than clear, Lina felt confident enough of his suitability to invite him to Poggio Gherardo the following spring.

Ominously, he managed to put Janet's back up even before they met by offhandedly changing his date of arrival at the last minute; Lina described him as "quite the most casual person I know," and careless informality didn't go over well with Janet. To this black mark were quickly added several more, for Aubrey also had a lazy insolence and the peacock manner of an Adonis—the contadini dubbed him "il Signorino Vanitoso." For her part, Janet declared him "quite hideous" and did her best to trip him up at every turn. Things soon got so uncomfortable for him at Poggio Gherardo that, like Boccaccio's lieta brigata, he decided to move on, staying instead with Mary, who was only too happy to insert herself into the situation. Lina was of course mortified, and also agonizingly unsure whether Aubrey's feelings for her were more than platonic.

Then, in late April, all ambiguity vanished. The couple had been invited to a Renaissance-themed ball at Palazzo Vecchio in honor of King Umberto and Queen Margherita. By this point Aubrey had returned to Poggio Gherardo (presumably Janet had agreed to suspend her hostilities), and he and Lina became excitedly absorbed in preparations for the event. Lina had noticed in a Leonardo painting a gown she wanted to copy, and after Aubrey did a sketch a dressmaker executed the design. Before the ball, Mary, accompanied by the visiting art critic Roger Fry, came by to help Lina primp, and was stunned at the final effect—"I never saw such a vision of beauty," she wrote in her diary, "brocade & jewels & her yellow hair all braided with pearls." Aubrey, meanwhile, was togged out as Dante, in a scarlet robe and a headdress.

The ball itself was ravishing; some of the men even gilded their hair, so that they looked "as if they had just stepped out of a fresco." At two in the morning the couple left Palazzo Vecchio for a moonlit carriage ride back to Poggio Gherardo, and Lina suddenly found her fantasy coming true: "Throwing caution to the winds, forgetting such things as £.s.d., Aubrey kissed me and we were engaged."

Ecstatic though she was, Lina knew better than to tell Janet and Henry the news, which was unlikely to go over well. She did, however, tell Mary, who a few days later invited the young couple over to her house, persuaded them to put their ball costumes back on, and had a friend of hers photograph them in poses suggestive of Romeo and Juliet, with Lina sitting in a window and Aubrey wooing her from below. It was clearly done for laughs, but Lina may have thought uneasily of that ill-fated Guelph girl at Poggio Gherardo, the one who'd died of grief after her Ghibelline paramour was butchered and whose supposedly haunted bedroom she now occupied. While Aubrey surely wouldn't come to such a sticky end (at least not on her account), they had to tread carefully, and the loose-lipped Mary must have been sworn and double-sworn to absolute secrecy.

Soon afterward Aubrey returned to England, but the lovers surreptitiously exchanged letters brimming with "golden plans for the future." Despite her fear of how the Rosses would react to these plans, Lina was flying high. The book Dent had commissioned, *The Story of Perugia*, had just appeared to good reviews. Her coauthor, Madge, was getting married in July—to William Vaughan, the headmaster of a public school near Bristol—and she, along with Vanessa Stephen (a cousin of Vaughan's), was to be a bridesmaid. After the wedding, George Frederic Watts was to paint a portrait of her in her Leonardo gown. All signs pointed toward a season of bliss.

On arrival in London, Lina received a letter from Aubrey coldly advising her to "look upon our days at Florence as a dream which could not be realized, for all he said had been a mistake and he no longer loved me." She staggered through the ensuing weeks, trying not to weep at the wedding and while Watts painted her in a dress that now symbolized her lost happiness.

When she returned to Italy in the fall, she tried to forget about

Aubrey by burying herself in work. Dent had asked her to write—this time on her own—a book on Assisi for his ongoing series, and she spent much of her time doing research there. But she couldn't escape the matchmaking propensities of Mary Costelloe, who, with "that fishy Waterfield" (as she termed him) out of the picture, was back in action. Mary's new nominee was Robert Trevelyan. Two years older than Lina, "Trevy," as he was called by his many friends (who included most of the Bloomsbury group and, later, E. M. Forster), belonged to a daunting family of statesmen and historians; the younger brother of George Macaulay Trevelyan, whose three-volume biography of Garibaldi is an underappreciated masterpiece, he was also a great-nephew of Lord Macaulay. He himself, however, was very much a black sheep, a long-haired, nature-worshipping, rhapsodizing poet with no regard for practicalities—or, for that matter, personal hygiene.

Though she complained that he stank "like a polecat," Janet had liked Trevy on their few meetings, and so had Lina, who'd traveled with him during one of Berenson's art tours. Now he was back in Florence, and Mary swung into Cupid mode. During a country walk one day with him and Lina, Mary deliberately lagged behind. As she'd hoped, the prospective lovers fell deep in conversation. Perhaps . . . But then Trevy, a fanatical nudist who couldn't resist jumping into any body of water he came across, noticed a pond just off the path, stripped, and dove in. As Lina wrote to Madge, the pond turned out to be filled with enormous frogs, "which, instead of being frightened, simply *made* for him, and drove him shrieking out of the water." Despite this ignominious rout, Lina was rather smitten by Trevy, and her interest seemed to be reciprocated. She was therefore taken aback when, out of nowhere, he announced his engagement to a Dutch woman, whom he later married.

By now thoroughly disgusted with men, Lina resolved to give them up, and to concentrate on strengthening her relationship with her aunt and uncle, which she'd let lapse somewhat during her turbulent year of romantic disappointments. In 1896 her father had died in a lunatic asylum, probably of tertiary syphilis, leaving Lina an orphan but for the Rosses.* They too were aging, especially Henry, who'd had two strokes. Recognizing how soon she might lose him, Lina found herself valuing his steadiness and low-key charm more than ever. Janet, whose skepticism toward Aubrey had proved to be well-founded, also grew in her estimation. And Poggio Gherardo, which she'd been itching to escape, again seemed a sanctuary, one where she could lick her wounds, regroup, and take comfort in being kind to Zio and Zia.

Though accidental, Lina's greatest service to her aunt at this time was to help bring about her most successful book. Since publishing *Early Days Recalled* in 1891, Janet had fallen into a lull; there'd been a new, expanded edition of *Three Generations of English Women,* and a translation of the memoirs of the Risorgimento commander Enrico della Rocca (published as *The Autobiography of a Veteran, 1807–1893*), but nothing original. Lina had become the prolific one. In 1899, while still at work on her Assisi book, she conceived the idea for yet another: a cookbook of Tuscan vegetable dishes. Dent, who'd been commissioning left and right, signed her up. Though Lina's plan for the book was unambitious—no cook herself, she meant to use the recipes of Giuseppe Volpi—she found it a chore, and was about to abandon it when Janet offered to take it over. Lina cheerfully agreed, and Janet, seizing on the project with her usual gusto, began quizzing Volpi about his repertoire of dishes and urging him to try out new ones. "The whole house reeks with recipes," reported Madge's sister Katharine Furse,† who came to visit during the experimentation process.

Completed in a matter of months, *Leaves from our Tuscan Kitchen, or How to cook vegetables* is a distinctly Rossian production, full of culinary arcana—"Fennel, dedicated to St. John, was believed to make the lean fat and to give the weak strength, while the root pounded

---

*Maurice's causes of death were listed as pneumonia and "general paralysis of the insane." Like Lina's mother, Fanny, he lived to forty-six. His death left Janet with no surviving siblings, for in 1877 Urania had died of tuberculosis at only nineteen.
†The youngest of Symonds's daughters, Dame Katharine Furse (1875–1952) earned distinction as a nursing administrator, in particular by founding the Voluntary Aid Detachment in 1909. Later she was a director of the Wrens (Women's Royal Naval Service).

with honey was considered a remedy against the bites of mad dogs"—
and forthright in tone: Janet makes no bones about her contempt
for British cooking and its criminally "plain-boiled" vegetables.
(She has especially hard words on the subject of cabbage, "the most
abused of vegetables.") The book gathers about two hundred recipes, including a few for pasta. Though most of the vegetables called
for in them were widely available in Britain at the time, some—
cardoons, sorrel, Jerusalem artichokes—must have seemed exotic to
readers.

So, indeed, must have the book itself, for nothing quite like it had
ever appeared on the British market. Along with Dorothy Daly's *Italian Cooking*, it seems to have been the first Italian cookbook in
English, and the cuisine it championed was a far cry from the stodgy
fare set forth in *Mrs. Beeton's Book of Household Management*, which,
though published four decades earlier, still had biblical authority.
Over the years, *Leaves* outsold all Janet's other books, and though
largely superseded, has rarely been out of print for long, with over a
dozen editions to date. Considered a minor but seminal classic of
Italian regional cuisine, it provided fodder for later, more professional food writers like Elizabeth David. The irony is that Janet
never made any of its recipes. "I know nothing about cookery," she
freely admits in *The Fourth Generation*, "never having even boiled
an egg in my life, though I *do* know if a dish is good or bad."

———※———

As a new century got under way, the success of *Leaves from our Tuscan Kitchen* was one pleasant surprise for Janet and the rest. Another was the fact that Bernard and Mary were about to become
their neighbors. Over the previous year the pair had become closer
than ever with the Rosses, as evidenced by Mary's diary entry
for her thirty-fifth birthday in February 1899:* "We ended up at
Poggio, with Lina, making a fiery procession through the olives.
Then we went in and had dinner, & I found a great bunch of orchids

———

*Almost too perfectly, Mary was born on Valentine's Day.

on my plate, & my health was drunk in champagne. Mr. Ross told me stories of crocodile-shooting on the Nile in the days before steamboats, and Mrs. Ross talked scandal to Logan & BB." In their own relationship, however, Bernard and Mary remained stuck in an awkward limbo, since Mary's husband refused to grant her a divorce. Finally, in late 1899, Frank Costelloe dropped dead, and Mary was free to remarry. Out of seemliness, she and Bernard decided to hold off for a year, but in the meantime they began to house hunt.

As chance would have it, John Temple Leader, by now in his nineties, was looking to lease a sixteenth-century villa that was part of his immense holdings. Called I Tatti, it was just downhill from Poggio Gherardo, and Bernard and Mary jumped on it. The house required extensive renovations, especially if it was to satisfy the finicky and luxury-loving Bernard, and soon there was a far larger squad of men hammering away at it than had ever worked at Poggio Gherardo. Experienced in these matters, the Rosses often gave help and advice, and as both the wedding and the move-in date neared they provided shelter as well: with Mary staying at I Tatti to supervise renovations, Bernard, who wanted to be on hand but also to keep things proper, spent a month at Poggio Gherardo. (The Rosses, he wrote to his sister, "are spoiling me and I fear when I return to Mary's housekeeping I shall be more inclined to be impatient with it than ever.") On December 29 they were married by the prior of Settignano in the I Tatti chapel, with the Rosses and a handful of others attending. Soon after, they moved into the villa, and a new era began.

Lina, meanwhile, had been burying herself in work. It had taken her barely a year to write *The Story of Assisi*, which appeared in 1900; running to almost four hundred pages, the book is an impressive accomplishment for a twenty-six-year-old amateur historian. Yet she remained single, and must have been starting to feel rather old-maidish. Then, in the spring of 1901, Aubrey resurfaced in Florence. After giving off mixed signals, he melted away again, but not for long. That July, back in England, Lina accepted an invitation to visit one of Aubrey's aunts, Tina Rate, supposedly to discuss a magazine assignment. On arrival she realized this was a ruse, for there was Aubrey, waiting. Claiming to have broken their engagement only because he couldn't support her, he said his father had recently died, leaving him a small inheritance, and that he was now finally in a position to marry. After making him squirm for a day, Lina accepted.

This time she knew she had to tell Janet and Henry, and that their reaction—especially Janet's—was bound to be less than enthusiastic; the bad impression Aubrey had made in Florence, his capricious treatment of Lina over the past four years, and her own impulsiveness were unlikely to be overlooked. After breaking the news in a letter, Lina nervously waited, as she put it to Aubrey, "for the thunder to travel across Europe to me."

The thunder, when it came, was even more deafening than she'd feared. Janet's first broadside was directed at Aubrey, who, in an attempt at preemptive mollification, had also written to her, assuring her that "I have £200 a year of my own which can be settled on Lina . . . and shall have £20,000 on my mother's death." Her response was scathing: "Neither my husband nor myself look with approval on Lina's engagement. She is quite unfit by tastes and education to be a poor man's wife . . . It is a sad thing for a marriage to depend upon your mother's death . . . You would have acted more honourably had you refrained from asking her to engage herself to you until you could say, 'I gain so much by the work of my own hands.'" To make matters worse, Janet discovered that Aubrey had exaggerated the size of his future inheritance: asked to investigate, William Markby learned that he would receive only £10,000.

Janet's fury erupted in a letter to Madge, who was ineluctably drawn into the fray: "W. is no more worthy of Lina than yr. cat wd be. He has nothing & is 'going to be' an artist . . . Lina is, I think you'll agree with me, the last person to marry a pauper. Had she written to me to say she was in love with him, I wd have said, very well, when he has a picture in the R.A. [Royal Academy], & sells one to a dealer, or a person who is *not* a relation or friend, then we will talk about an engagement." When Madge tried to stick up for Lina, Janet replied, "You don't know Lina if you think she can live a life of privation. What you write about her wonderful personality being above the ordinary ways and means of life is (forgive me) bosh." One can only imagine what Janet would have had to say about Aubrey's fanciful plan, described by Lina in a letter to Madge, to spend "a year in Japan for his painting."

As the summer wore on, Janet's onslaught intensified. "I have been bombarded by letters from Poggio, and they are of such a nature as to make me utterly wretched," Lina reported to Aubrey. "They implore, urge and entreat me to break off this 'miserable engagement.'" To her financial objections Janet now added a personal one. Henry had suffered a third stroke, the worst so far, and Janet claimed that Lina's behavior was impeding his recovery and pushing him toward the grave. "Poor Uncle Henry is *very* low," Janet told Madge. "This affair has taken all enjoyment of life from him. He talks of it unceasingly & even in his sleep it haunts him. It is a real wonder that Lina did not kill her uncle." Though wanting to remain loyal to Lina, Madge hadn't been especially taken with Aubrey the few times she'd met him, and under the force of Janet's propaganda she too now counseled Lina to throw Aubrey over. "I cannot do without Aubrey," Lina wailed in response, "and if we have not enough to marry on, there will certainly never be any question of marrying anyone else. Please do not add to my heavy depression by joining in the regular chorus that takes its rise from P.G. They wanted a 'brilliant match,' and I am sorry not to have been able to satisfy them on that point. Aunt Janet, never having been in love, can hardly be expected to enter into any romantic feelings on the subject."

But then Janet abruptly relented. "The Zia has turned out to be trumps at the eleventh hour," Lina wrote to Aubrey, "sending me a charming letter full of affection and desire to let the painful matter drop. I don't know what or who has wrought this miracle. The paragraph that pleased me is this: 'I desire to hear nothing more from Mr. Waterfield's solicitors or anyone else. I shall not mention his name again and we shall go on as before, you my dear child and I your old aunt.'" Probably assuming that Janet would soften toward Aubrey over time, Lina accepted the terms of the truce and returned to Florence in September.

On arrival, she found Henry stabilized but Janet in a state of high anxiety. Convinced that Henry didn't have long to live, she was adamant that he leave behind some sort of literary monument. For years she'd been urging him to write up his escapades in the Near East, but Henry, who was constitutionally inclined to hide his light under a bushel, had resisted. At one point Janet had even attempted to trick him into dictating the book. "Often friends deplored that all those tales of his early life in Turkey and Asia Minor should die with him," she writes in *The Fourth Generation*. "So we entered into a conspiracy. One or the other would drop in and lead him to talk, while I sat behind his chair and wrote down what he said." Not surprisingly, this proved ineffective, and the project seemed to be dead in the water. But then Henry found, in a chest of family papers recently sent from Malta, a bundle of letters he'd written to his sister between 1837 and 1857. "Here were all the tales we delighted in," Janet continues, "told in the same vivid picturesque words, and many others he had evidently forgotten." Henry scoffed at the idea of "such rubbish" being published, but Dent, who read the letters during a visit, found them compelling, and signed up yet another member of the family.* Janet promised Dent that she'd annotate the letters, write a preface, and extract an introduction from Henry.

This was the task in which Lina, returning to Poggio Gherardo, found her frantically caught up. In a letter to Aubrey, she described Janet as alternately typing and "running across the rooms to where that dear old man lies back in his chair, looking so dignified, so patient, with his beautiful hands folded on his knees. And those dreadful words of my Aunt's, 'I am racing death,' as she taps feverishly at her typewriter." Soon Lina was helping out as well, having been enlisted to write a short memoir of her uncle that would conclude the book.

Though Janet continued to disapprove of Lina's wedding plans, the two managed to get along over the next few months. Then, in March 1902, Lina made an unpleasant discovery. With Janet out of

---

*Janet herself had just done a second book for Dent, a large-format illustrated volume called *Florentine Villas* that covers twenty-three historic houses around the city.

the house one day, Lina decided to test the waters with Henry, whose opposition to her engagement had been more exclusively on financial grounds. "I told him what our income would be," she reported to Aubrey, "and he looked very surprised and said, 'But that is *not* what I was told,' which showed me that *someone* had not been quite accurate in their statements." Though Aubrey's true prospects weren't what Henry might have wished, he found them adequate, and said "it was much better I should marry the man I was fond of, provided there was enough to live on, than that I should marry a man I did not love who might be rich."

To Lina, all this came as a relief and a triumph, but not for long. When Janet realized that her dirty-tricks campaign had been exposed, she impenitently resumed open warfare against Aubrey and lashed out at anyone who dared defend him. "Aunt Janet is furious at everyone taking our side," Lina told Aubrey. "She now stands in an isolated and most undignified position."

Lina had been hoping to get married at Poggio Gherardo so that the ailing Henry might attend, but with Janet acting like a cornered cat, she and Aubrey would clearly have to tie the knot elsewhere. There was also some urgency. Dent had commissioned her to write, and Aubrey to illustrate, *The Story of Palermo*, and in order to finish the book on time—Dent wanted it done quickly—they would have to go to Sicily in the fall. To do so as an unmarried couple was out of the question, and they therefore began to plan a summer wedding in England. Lina's great-aunt Georgina Duff Gordon offered to host the reception, so long as it didn't conflict with the coronation of Edward VII, who'd acceded to the throne after Victoria's death the previous January and was due to be crowned on June 26.* The wedding date was fixed for July 1.

In April, Lina left Florence and went to stay with Madge near Bristol. While there she received alarming reports on Henry's health. "I can't go back—need I?" she wrote to Aubrey. "Is it my duty?" Fighting off the temptation to race back to Florence, she stayed

---

*In the event, the king fell ill with appendicitis three days before the coronation, which had to be postponed till August.

put, and on the first of July, as planned, she and Aubrey were married in a London church, with the Bishop of Rochester officiating. The reception had to be scrubbed at the last minute, Georgina Duff Gordon having come down with measles, but a boisterous party was held at Aubrey's flat instead.

The newlyweds then left for a long honeymoon in Devon. Some three weeks into it, they learned that Henry, after suffering a final stroke, had died on July 19. As Lina admits in *Castle in Italy*, during the final phase of her engagement she'd had a "a slight nervous breakdown," and the news of Henry's death left her wracked with not only grief but guilt. While logically she knew her wedding had in no way accelerated his demise, Janet's prophecy that Lina would kill her uncle rang in her head, and her failure to be at Henry's deathbed lay heavy on her conscience. "Too ill to make the journey in the heat of July or to cope with the tensions of Poggio Gherardo," she remained in England for the moment.

By chance, the very week Henry died *The Spectator* ran an advance notice for his *Letters from the East*, as the book had come to be titled (a deliberate echo, no doubt, of Lucie's *Letters from Egypt*). When it was published later that year, the character and talents of Henry Ross stood revealed at last. The earliest letters in the book were written when he was sixteen, but even these are startlingly mature—one would never guess his age from his lapidary descriptions of Ottoman life. Had he so chosen, he clearly could have become a first-class travel writer or narrative historian.

If the letters themselves showcase Henry's storytelling gifts, as well as his resourcefulness and immense sangfroid, Lina's epilogue gives a sense of other qualities: the "gentleness of his manner," his phenomenal memory (when challenged in argument he could riposte by quoting entire parliamentary speeches), his magic touch with plants and animals—"Even the gold-fish knew his footstep," she writes, "and rising to the surface of their pond . . . would wait for a daily gift of wafer." Lina had had, of course, a privileged view of the man and particular reason to be grateful to him, but nearly everyone who spent enough time with Henry for his subtleties to emerge came away impressed, if also tantalized by the air of terminal enigma that seemed to cloak him. "There was a certain mystery about him," Madge observed—a mystery that she, like others, found symbolized by his "enchanted fish."

Those fish would now have to get their wafers from someone else. For the moment, at least, it wouldn't be Janet. Losses had been mounting up around her over the previous years: Layard had died in 1894, Lacaita and Saint-Hilaire in 1895, and, all too prematurely, Carlo Orsi in 1898. But this was the worst one yet, of a painfulness that couldn't have been projected from the early days of her marriage, when, in her youthful brashness and flippancy, she'd taken Henry somewhat for granted. That had changed, slowly but surely, and she'd long since learned to appreciate him in full.

Though she restricts her lament in *The Fourth Generation* to a single sentence—"On July 19 my husband died, and the loss of the dear friend and companion of forty-two years left me more utterly lonely than I can say"—she admits that, after interring Henry's ashes at Trespiano Cemetery (by this point the English one was full), she broke down badly and fled to Bagni di Lucca, where she didn't leave her bed for seven weeks. Cared for by a kindly young doctor "who nursed me as though I had been his mother," she was eventually able to get back on her feet and limp home to Florence. With Henry in the grave and Lina estranged, Poggio Gherardo, the smallest of castles, must have felt as vast and desolate as the Escorial.

SIX

Aunt Janet

The life of Janet Ross can be seen as roughly falling into a large-scale ABA pattern. Her first twenty-five years, concluding with her arrival in Florence, form a distinct phase, one that might be labeled "Youth." Her next thirty-five form another—call it "Maturity." Finally came a second twenty-five-year phase, from 1902 till her death in 1927. This one might be referred to as "Widowhood," or else "Old Age." Certainly it was defined by Henry's absence and characterized by a host of diminishments, though she remained robust almost to the end. Yet neither of these tags is quite apt. Instead, her last quarter century is best thought of as her "Aunt Janet" phase. The first person to call her Aunt Janet had of course been Lina, but a few others, such as Madge and the Berensons, had taken to doing so as well. Now the custom spread.

Among the qualities that made Janet seem auntlike were her staunchness, forthrightness, venerability, and brisk blend of scolding and indulgence. Sometimes the title may have carried a hint of mockery, for she was becoming a parody of herself, her views ever more dogmatic, her tongue ever sharper, the knitting of her furious eyebrows ever more theatrical. But it also suited her altered relation to the world. Now less an actor than a (highly opinionated) spectator, she rarely made things happen, more often watched them unfold. One might therefore expect her last phase to be duller than the rest. In some ways, though, it's the most interesting of all. The lives of those around her became increasingly complex, entangled, dismal, absurd, and on occasion happy and noble. Vivid new characters arrived onstage. And history began to stir again. Beginning mildly enough, the century soon degenerated, a European war giving way to a menacing Italian revolution. By the time Aunt Janet reached her sunset years, Mussolini's Blackshirts were tightening their grip on Florence, and the colony was anxiously registering the first flickers of hostility—its own twilight had set in.

＝＝＝◎＝＝＝

Ironically, the one person to whom Janet truly was an aunt was also the person most alienated from her. In the months after Lina's wedding, in fact, Janet's animus toward Lina only hardened; as Mary Berenson put it in a letter to her mother,* Janet "magnified Lina into a monster of ingratitude and obstinacy."

The latest source of outrage was that staple of family discord, a contested will. In 1897 Henry had added a codicil under which Lina would have benefited had Janet predeceased him. Even though that hadn't happened, the codicil somehow became a point of dispute, with a resulting delay of probate. A series of misunderstandings between Lina and her solicitors sowed confusion, and led Janet to surmise that her niece was contesting the will, presumably in a spirit of vengeance.

In the fall of 1902, Lina and Aubrey returned to Italy, heading for Palermo. Tempted though she must have been to bypass Florence, Lina was determined to straighten things out with Janet. Mary, with her love of intrigue and genuine wish to see Lina and Janet reconciled, made a natural ally, and she offered not only to host the newlyweds but, before their arrival, to try to soften up "Aunt Granite," as they'd taken to calling her.

---

*Though she seems never to have met Janet, Hannah Whitall Smith was clearly fascinated by her, for Mary's letters to her mother routinely include the latest news and gossip from Poggio Gherardo.

After dropping her bags at I Tatti, Lina, heart in throat, walked uphill to her former home. To her surprise, she was received with feigned politesse, "as though," she wrote to Madge, "I had been Miss James from Florence making an afternoon call." Lina, who always dreaded confrontation, played along. The charade was repeated the following three days, on the last of which Aubrey joined her. Even this failed to provoke a reaction, Janet pretending that Aubrey was invisible. Neither he nor Lina had the courage to clear the air or bring matters to a head, and when they left for Palermo the next day, precisely nothing had been resolved.

Left to herself again, Janet began to get over the worst of her grief and to recover her joie de vivre. Two friends of the Berensons, the radical American journalist Hutchins Hapgood and his novelist wife, Neith Boyce, were brought to meet her in early 1903, and in her diary Boyce describes Janet as "full of vigor and dash . . . a fountain of scandal . . . Slaps her thigh whenever she tells a good story." Her appetite for travel and adventure also revived. For some years she'd been friends with a whimsical Prussian noble, Graf Fritz von Hochberg, who'd bought a nearby villa and renamed it Montalto, an Italianization of "Hochberg." One day in November 1903, Janet recalls in *The Fourth Generation*, "the door of my sitting-room flew open and Fritz appeared . . . Before I could say a word he exclaimed: 'I've sold Montalto, and you are to come with me to Egypt . . . You are to meet me at the station on Tuesday at midday.'" When she raised objections, the impetuous count swatted them aside, and the next thing she knew she was steaming southward from Genoa.

"He who drinks the waters of the Nile," an Egyptian proverb holds, "is destined to taste its sweetness again." In Janet's case the return was bittersweet, and not only because Egypt constantly put her in mind of Henry. Much had changed. "The sight of the statue of my old friend de Lesseps at the entrance of the harbour of Port Said made me feel rather sad, a feeling which increased when we landed and I found an evil-smelling, large, dirty town, instead of the pretty little place I remembered." As for Cairo, it was "so altered that I recognized nothing. The Ezbekieh had been built over, huge hotels had sprung up, and no donkeys were to be seen for hire.

I missed 'Come 'long, Ma'am, Gladstone, very good donkey,' or 'Here, lady, this Bismarck, good donkey.' " More melancholy still was the absence of old friends. "In vain I tried to find Hassan . . . my old donkey-boy, and in reply to enquiries at Alexandria I heard that my mother's faithful servant Omar had died some months ago."

Her spirits rose when Lord Cromer, the de facto ruler of Egypt,* came to make her acquaintance, but sank again in Luxor, where she found that the Maison de France had vanished and that no one could remember Sheikh Yussef, the kind imam who'd taught her mother Arabic. At Aswan she was given a tour of the recently completed Low Dam, and "could not help thinking how jealous the old Pharaohs would have been of that mighty work." But the disappearance of the abundant waterfowl she remembered from her first visit— geese, ducks, pelicans—depressed her further. "I was told that the Italians, who had been employed in thousands to build the great dam below Philae, had shot them all."

The plan was to continue upriver to Khartoum, but it had to be scrapped when von Hochberg came down with appendicitis. Once he was out of danger, Janet left him to recuperate in Aswan, heading back north on her own. Stopping at Luxor again, she at last found a measure of nostalgic satisfaction. "As I entered the hotel an old German gentleman asked me whether I was the daughter of Lady Duff Gordon." This turned out to be the explorer and ethnologist Georg August Schweinfurth, who brought her to meet a Coptic friend of his, a certain Todoros, who in turn gratefully told her that, as a child, he'd been taught English and German by Lucie—his father had been the one to foist an alabaster jar on the Rosses as they departed from Luxor in 1867. A few days later, Janet also managed to track down one of Lucie's former servants; now ancient, the man remembered Lucie fondly and summoned his extended family to meet her daughter.

Stirred by these encounters, Janet decided to look for Saoud, her groom during the Abu Nishab festival in 1863. After an exchange of telegrams, they linked up in Ismailia, a Suez Canal town. Saoud

---

*Ever since the Urabi revolt (1879–82), Egypt had been under tight British control.

salaamed deeply to "the Rose of Tel-el-Kebir" and invited her to go
hunting in the desert, "promising me a good horse and many ga-
zelles." She might have pounced on the offer had she not had to
hustle to Port Said to catch a boat home. Her account of their parting is one of the most frankly emotional passages in all her writings:
"How many memories the sight of Saoud called up. He and I were
almost the only ones left of those joyous days in the desert: de Lesseps and Guichard, my father* and my husband were dead. Saoud
was a middle-aged man, I was a white-haired old woman. Tears came
thick into my eyes as the train moved out into the station and I
waved a last farewell to Shaykh Saoud."

Returning to Florence, Janet was pleasantly surprised to find
Mark Twain back on the scene. His wife's health had deteriorated
further, and Twain thought a spell in Tuscany might do her good—
the winter they'd spent there a decade earlier had been mild and
sunny. This time, though, the weather was cold and damp, and Livy
continued to sink. Also less fortunate was their choice of houses.
Without Janet around to advise them, they'd made the mistake of
renting Villa di Quarto, cheerless, chilly, and so massive that, as
Twain wrote to William Dean Howells, "God himself couldn't start
through it on a given excursion and not get lost." Once the home of
Jérôme Bonaparte, it now belonged to the American-born Contessa
Massiglia, who proved to be a greedy, inattentive landlord; Twain,
with his penchant for bitter hyperbole, denounced her as "the lowest-
down woman on the planet."

Such was the state of affairs on Janet's return. Though she
couldn't extricate Twain from "Calamity House," as he'd dubbed it,
in May 1904 she held a luncheon for him, which the Berensons also
attended. A more improbable pairing than Mark Twain and Bernard
Berenson can scarcely be conceived, and one guesses that the afternoon was not a great success. At any rate, it appears that Twain and
Janet saw each other just this once. Twain withdrew into the miseries

---

*In 1864 Alexander had paid a brief visit to Egypt, and Janet, along with de Lesseps, had
taken him to see Tel-el-Kebir and the Suez Canal. The following year he published an account of his journey in *Macmillan's*.

of his villa, where, less than a month later, Livy died. He and Janet might have commiserated over their respective bereavements had he not immediately sailed home with his wife's body.

Janet, meanwhile, set out for England, where she hadn't been in several years. Still in the wistful mood induced by Egypt, she decided to visit George Meredith. They hadn't seen each other since crossing paths in Venice in 1866 but had stayed in touch, and at Janet's request Meredith had recently written an admiring profile of Lucie for a new edition of *Letters from Egypt*. Now seventy-six, he was at the height of his prestige, and his house at Box Hill, Surrey, had become a favorite pilgrimage destination. (In *A Backward Glance*, Edith Wharton memorably describes going to pay her respects with Henry James.) Janet made her own way to the shrine in July 1904. Though she found Meredith in poor shape physically, "the old fire and brilliancy were there, and we talked . . . about old times and old friends, most of them, alas, dead." One of the most illustrious of their mutual friends, George Frederic Watts, had died only days before, and Janet was able to report to Meredith on his moving funeral at St. Paul's. At the end of the visit Meredith alluded to his own fictional portrayal of Janet: " 'You have something of Rose in you still, my dear,' he said, smiling rather sadly as I got up to go; 'those were pleasant days.' " Rose Jocelyn, Rose of Tel-el-Kebir: she kept running into earlier incarnations of herself.

Back in Florence by fall, she settled at last into her former routines. She'd put her writing on hold after Henry's death, but now she picked it back up, publishing two books in as many years. The first was *Old Florence and Modern Tuscany*, a collection of essays that largely reprises *Italian Sketches* but also has several later magazine pieces, including the one written at Gladstone's suggestion, "*Mezzeria*, or Land Tenure in Tuscany." The second, commissioned by Dent, was *Florentine Palaces and Their Stories*, which consists of short histories of some seventy-five palazzi. Written from scratch in less than a year, this four-hundred-page book suffers from Janet's usual faults but also impressively displays her learning; few writers could have assembled so much dense fact in so little time.

Fewer still could have done so while managing a farm estate.

Except when she was out of town, Janet remained a daily presence in the poderi and supervised every vendemmia and olive harvest. She even added a new product to Poggio Gherardo's line: a vermouth made according to a secret Medicean recipe that, she claimed, a descendant of the family had given her. Sold at stores around Florence, the vermouth provided another source of income, as well as another treat for her friends abroad. (For years she'd been sending wine, olive oil, and sometimes even persimmons to Madge, Meredith, and others.)

Only in one way had Janet weakened. Though she seems to have given no thought to remarrying or striking up a romance—celibacy suited her just fine—in a sense she did allow herself to be seduced. Fortunato, her longtime butler and majordomo, had retired and been replaced by a certain Davide Torrini. Nobody else cared for this fawning yet officious little man, but to Janet he was a prince among servants. "If rung up during the night," she writes, "he would appear smiling, as though it was quite a pleasant experience to be called out of bed after a hard day's work." Once she would have scorned such toadying, but now she reveled in it. She also began to rely on what she took to be Davide's general competence and honesty: "Having been born a peasant, he could set me right if I did anything that might clash with the intricate laws of *mezzeria*, while at the same time my people [i.e., sharecroppers] were aware that he looked after my interests as though they were his own." It was a classic case of widow's dependency, reminiscent of Queen Victoria and her gillie, John Brown. Eventually Janet's "faithful David [*sic*]" would turn out to be rather less pure-hearted than Brown, but for the moment he could do no wrong.

If Janet uncharacteristically let her guard down around Davide, Lina continued to arouse her darkest suspicions. Had Lina settled in England, Janet could have huffily steered clear of her niece for the rest of her days. It was lucky, then, that Lina chose to keep one foot planted in Tuscany, where she couldn't be avoided forever.

After leaving Florence in late 1902, Lina and Aubrey had spent five months in Palermo working on their assignment and being introduced into Sicilian society by a rich and convivial friend of Janet's, Tina Whitaker,* who seems either not to have known or not to have cared that Lina had been blackballed by her aunt. In the spring of 1903 they returned to England, where, barely nine months after her wedding, Lina gave birth to a son, Gordon. ("Really I'm very glad it wasn't born sooner," Janet maliciously remarked to Neith Boyce on hearing the news. "People thought the marriage was being hurried on a good deal.")

Renting a house near Sandwich, Lina and Aubrey went back to their book. But then Dent, with his voracious demand for books about Italy, abruptly asked them to put the Palermo project temporarily aside and instead tackle *Rome and Its Story*, as he titled it. The part on ancient Rome was to be handled by another writer, Welbore St. Clair Baddeley, but Dent wanted Lina to do the longer part on Christian Rome, up to the sack of the city in 1527, and Aubrey to illustrate the entire book. Then came the kicker: he needed all this in three months. "I do not know why Dent was in such a desperate hurry," Lina comments, "unless he knew that another publisher was producing a book on Rome at the same time."

Just as Rome wasn't built in a day, to bang out a book on it in ninety seemed impossible, but the opportunity was too tempting to pass up. Parking their baby with relatives, the couple hastened to Rome and went furiously to work. Incredibly, they managed to complete the task on deadline, Lina writing nearly three hundred pages and Aubrey producing over a hundred illustrations. They had

---

*The daughter of General Alfonso Scalia, who'd fought with Garibaldi in Sicily, Tina Whitaker (1858–1957) married Joseph Whitaker, scion of an English family long involved in the Marsala wine trade. She trained as an opera singer, wrote several books, and entertained lavishly at Villa Malfitano, her home in Palermo. Her friends included Richard Wagner, King Edward VII, and Giuseppe Tomasi di Lampedusa, author of *The Leopard*. She seems to have met Janet through Lacaita, and her diaries include the following entry, set down after Lacaita's death in 1895: "Every year I have met Janet Ross and every year our friendship has been allowed to sleep on, nursed by our mutual esteem for Sir James Lacaita. Now that he is gone, it is all the stronger and will not break I think, so long as I do not mention the name of Ouida."

ample reason to be pleased with themselves, and their giddiness may have contributed to a fateful decision they made on the way back to England.

Seven years earlier, while still at Oxford, Aubrey had spent a vacation staying with the British consul in Genoa, Montague Yeats Brown, at his castle in Portofino.* Brown owned several other castles in the area, and Aubrey was curious to see a recent acquisition of his near the village of Aulla, in the remote Lunigiana region of Tuscany. The place made such an impression on him that he'd fantasized about living there ever since, and now, in late 1903, he took Lina to see it for herself.

Built in the sixteenth century and owned for many years by the locally powerful Malaspina family, the Fortezza della Brunella is not, like Poggio Gherardo, a castle only by courtesy title but a deadly serious, rather intimidating fortress, complete with a moat and walls up to eighteen feet thick. Perched atop a steep hill at the convergence of two rivers among the tightly clustered peaks of the Apuan Alps (a subrange of the Apennines), it enjoys a position at once impregnable and wildly dramatic.

For maximum effect, Aubrey brought Lina to the fortress at sunset. After walking its ramparts and taking in the eagle's-nest view they afford, Lina was dumbstruck. "Aubrey looked terribly sad," she recalls, "and asked in a pained voice: 'Lina, don't you like my castle?' . . . 'Yes, Aubrey,' I said, 'I am wondering how long it will take for two camp-beds to arrive from the Army and Navy Stores!' We laughed together in our joy and hurried down to the Post Office to write to Monty Brown for a lease of the Fortezza." Brown agreed, on dirt-cheap terms, and just like that the Waterfields committed themselves to a part-time residence (the plan was to split each year between Italy and England) of the utmost impracticality.

The difficulties began with location. Though less than twenty miles inland from the sizeable port of La Spezia, Aulla was a world apart, an isolated and primitive mountain burg that hadn't caught

---

*It was this same castle that Elizabeth von Arnim rented with some friends in 1921 and that inspired her novel *Enchanted April*. The film adaptation was shot there as well.

up to the nineteenth century, let alone the twentieth. As for the fortress, it was barely habitable. Not to be deterred, the Waterfields had local stonemasons repair several dangerously crumbling walls and got the place minimally furnished. Over time, Aubrey frescoed many of its walls and laid out a paradisal rooftop garden, complete with an ilex avenue and a latticework cupola overgrown with roses. A pulley system was devised so that food and drink could be hauled from the courtyard up to the garden, where on warm nights the Waterfields slept in hammocks. They even had a pet: as an obscure joke, Brown had given them a gazelle, which they kept in the moat along with some sheep and chickens.

Despite its remoteness, the fortress was soon pulling in almost as many visitors as Poggio Gherardo. Predictably, the nature-worshipping Robert Trevelyan made a beeline for it. (According to Lina, the local peasants "saw him walking with hurried footsteps, his untidy hair flying in the breeze, reciting poetry in a loud voice, and thought him mad.") So did Mary Berenson, who described it to her mother as "the most romantic and beautiful thing I have ever seen." "Lina and Aubrey are happy as kings in it," she added. Baroness Orczy, of *Scarlet Pimpernel* fame, and E. F. Benson, author of the triumphantly silly Mapp and Lucia novels, both came to inspect it. Some years later, D. H. Lawrence and his wife-to-be, Frieda, became frequent guests while living nearby. "When [Lawrence] saw Aubrey's frescoes . . . of hill-set castles and country scenes in the Lunigiana," Lina recalls, "he gave little squeaks of delight and wanted to set off at once to see those places and do some painting himself." Though Lina makes no mention of it, Aldous Huxley evidently stayed at the fortress as well, for the setting of his 1925 novel *Those Barren Leaves* is unmistakably based on it.*

---

*"The little town of Vezza stands at the confluence of two torrents that come down in two deep valleys from the Apuan mountains," the novel begins, and the house where the action unfolds, "the summer palace of the Cybo Malaspina," is said to be perched on "a bold promontory of hill" above town. When Huxley visited the fortress is unclear, but in the early 1920s the Waterfields often socialized with him at the Tuscan seaside resort of Forte dei Marmi, which for several years was his primary home.

Janet, however, kept her distance. While she was curious enough to send Davide to inspect the fortress—"Not a fit place for Christians," he reported—she herself refused to make the trip, no doubt in part because doing so would have signaled her forgiveness of Lina. Less grudge-holding than her aunt and saddened by their prolonged estrangement, Lina decided to take the initiative. In 1906 and 1907 she twice invited herself to Poggio Gherardo, the second time bringing four-year-old Gordon, in the hope that Janet would melt at the sight of him. The success of the visit can be judged from another of Mary's letters to her mother: "Aunt Janet says they came and forced themselves on her and she is dreadfully cross about it . . . She hates even their enchanting little boy." Thwarted, Lina again resigned herself to the split.

To an extent, Janet's surliness toward Lina and Gordon was inflicted on others as well; always rude, she was becoming more so as she aged, and her bad behavior must have cost her a certain number of friends, existing and potential. Most, however, put up with her ornery ways, and quite a few seem to have found them—within limits—amusing and even endearing. And so Poggio Gherardo once again hummed with visitors. The Berensons or Fritz von Hochberg might wander in at any moment. Sir William and Lady Markby came to stay every year. Janet's cousin Sir Cosmo Duff Gordon came several times with his glamorous wife, who had her own fashion house.* Alice Meynell (formerly Thompson), who'd been at Castagnolo with her sister, came at least once, and so did Katharine Furse, who reported to her mother that Janet was "just the same as ever, thanking God in a deep loud voice that some boring guest was leaving."

Always happy to see old friends, Janet hadn't lost her taste for new ones, and this period yielded a good crop of them. One was

---

*Lucy Christiana, Lady Duff Gordon (1863–1935), was the first British designer to achieve international prominence. Operating under the *nom de couture* Lucile, she had branches in Paris, New York, and Chicago, and dreamed up the "mannequin parade," a precursor of the runway show. Her sister was the risqué novelist Elinor Glyn.

Rev. Thomas Lindsay. Born a year after Janet, Lindsay was the principal of a theological college in Glasgow and the author of, among other books, an important work on the Reformation. In 1906 Janet met him at a party in Florence and liked him so much that she spontaneously invited him to come stay with her. Thereafter he became, like the Markbys, a yearly visitor. Despite being a minister and church historian, Lindsay was anything but dour or stuffy. In fact, Janet at first didn't realize he was a man of the cloth, since he wore no clerical collar. Learning of her oversight, she wrote to apologize for it, only to have Lindsay apologize in turn "for coming to you as a wolf in sheep's clothing; but I dislike uniforms of all kinds and never wear clerical collars out of Scotland. They are quite a nuisance in travelling. A clerical garb is a sort of placard, 'Enquire here for everything,' especially to ladies, who demand . . . the names of hotels, the proper tips to give, etc. etc." As his letter shows, Lindsay had an easy charm and humor, but he was also formidably learned, his knowledge and curiosity extending far beyond the ecclesiastical. To Janet, this blend of erudition and playfulness was always catnip— Kinglake, Symonds, and Lacaita had all had it—and she quickly came to count Lindsay among her most valued friends.

Coevals like Lindsay could hardly be expected to call her (or think of her as) Aunt Janet, but her younger new friends were quite happy to do so. Among them was Frank Crisp, a painter in his mid-twenties. Having won a traveling scholarship from the Royal Academy, Crisp was kicking around Italy in 1908, and one day he turned up at Poggio Gherardo bearing a letter of introduction. His modesty, geniality, and slight infirmity brought out Janet's caretaking side, and he too became an annual visitor. Impressed by his talent, Janet commissioned him to paint two portraits, one of herself and one of Mary's daughter Karin, which she presented to Mary as a gift. Though Mary held Crisp to be not untalented, she evidently didn't care for the portrait, since she put it in I Tatti's lavatory, to be hastily rehung in some more dignified spot whenever Janet came by.

Another new friend, the writer Edward Hutton, wasn't a visitor to Florence but a recent addition to the colony. An ardent Italo-

phile, he'd begun living part-time in Settignano's Casa di Boccaccio, once owned by Boccaccio's father, in 1901. Six years later
Hutton and Janet finally slipped into each other's orbits, and she
wasted no time in exerting her influence. Like Lina, Hutton had
been cranking out traveler's histories—*The Cities of Umbria* was just
one of his titles. Janet, still haunted by Symonds's early death and
convinced that overwork had been a cause, hoped to save this thirty-
two-year-old from the same fate. "I, with the authority derived
from age and white hair, stepped in and decreed a day's repose,
which generally consisted in much talk about Boccaccio, whose life
he was engaged in. In order to take him away from his desk I suggested that he, being an indefatigable walker, should explore the
country around Florence and write a book about the beautiful
walks, the wayside tabernacles, and the old-world villages." Rarely
has a suggestion been taken with such alacrity: only a year later Hutton published *Country Walks about Florence*. The book was dedicated to Janet, who, Hutton writes, "drew me out of the whirlwind."

A young visitor who failed to become a friend (it's hard to picture her doing so) was Virginia Stephen—the future Virginia Woolf,
that is. Janet had resumed her Sunday receptions, and one of these,
in May 1909, brought Miss Stephen to her doorstep, along with her
sister, Vanessa, and Vanessa's husband, Clive Bell; the three, who'd
been touring Italy, had presumably gotten wind of the event through
the Bloomsbury-connected Berensons. Afterward, in a letter to
Madge, Stephen wrote, "We had a tremendous tea party one day
with Mrs. Ross. She was inclined to be fierce, until we explained
that we knew you, when she at once knew all about us—our grandparents and great uncles on both sides." Though Stephen had no
way of knowing it, this was Janet in a nutshell, her pugnacity instantly vanishing at the mention of a common friend, to be replaced by genealogical enthusiasm. "She certainly looks remarkable,"
the letter continues, "and had typewritten manuscripts scattered
about the room . . . There were numbers of weak young men, and
old ladies kept arriving in four wheelers; she sent them out to look
at her garden. Is she a great friend of yours? I imagine she has had

a past—but old ladies, when they are distinguished, become so imperious."*

However distinguished and imperious, Mrs. Ross wasn't ready to rest on her literary laurels, and these years saw yet another burst of output. First, in 1909, came a book commissioned by Dent, *The Story of Pisa*, which traces the city's history across more than four hundred pages. Janet's real coup, though, was a book she'd conceived herself. The House of Medici, that ultimate Florentine dynasty, had inevitably cropped up in her writings from time to time, but she'd recently begun to consider it more closely, Hutton having asked her to help him gather the poems of Lorenzo the Magnificent.† Even though the task turned out to be "more laborious than I ever anticipated," since the poems were "scattered in many old and some modern volumes," she found her curiosity whetted, and decided to put together—this time on her own—a selection of the letters of Cosimo, Piero, Lorenzo, and their friends and relations. It was a fearsome endeavor, one that had her tunneling deep into archives, hunting for obscure pamphlets, puzzling out near-illegible manuscripts, and querying experts across Europe, to say nothing of translating hundreds of letters from fifteenth-century Italian; not even *The Land of Manfred* had been such a challenge.

Published in 1910, *Lives of the Early Medici, as told in their correspondence* is in many ways the most impressive and satisfactory of Janet's books. Previous Medici biographies, she notes in her preface, had been of a strictly public nature: "The men and women have disappeared, and we see instead the dexterous manipulators of tortuous Italian diplomacy, or the splendid patrons of art and literature." Her own, by contrast, is meant to provide a window on the "*vie intime*" of the family, "their doings within the home circle . . . their private loves and hates . . . In these old-world epistles Contessina

---

*Virginia Stephen amplified on these remarks in her travel diary. Though mostly rather cutting, the entry allows that Janet "has led a bold life" and that "there can be no question of her spirit."
†Though they began the project around 1907, their collection didn't appear until 1912, under the title *Poesie volgari di Lorenzo de' Medici, a cura di Janet Ross e di Edward Hutton*. Published by Dent, it has an English-language preface, but the poems themselves are in Italian only.

artlessly displays her household economies, Lucrezia reveals a fondness for bathing, Clarice quarrels with no less a tutor than Poliziano about the lessons he gave to her children, and the child Piero tells his father how he has studied hard . . . and proudly and persistently demands the pony promised as a reward for diligence." In the pages that follow, Janet skillfully strings together over a hundred letters, interlarding them with extensive commentary. Her design is essentially the same as in *Three Generations of English Women* (*Three Generations of Florentine Rulers*, she might have called the new book), but executed with considerably more care. Coming from the pen of a sixty-eight-year-old with no formal training, the book serves as a reminder that Janet, for all her weaknesses as an author, also had unusual strengths.

⸺⸺❖⸺⸺

If only because it marks the end of the Edwardian era, the year 1910 seems a good point to step back for a moment and consider the colony as a whole.

While the consular estimate that there were thirty-five thousand British subjects living in the area may have been inflated, it's a startling figure all the same, given that the population of Florence was only about two hundred thousand at the time, and that there must have been at least a few thousand Americans as well. In terms of sheer size, the colony had probably reached its zenith.

Certainly it had some noteworthy new members. There was, for instance, Arthur Acton, an English art and antiques dealer who'd moved to town in the 1890s and flourished as the principal buyer for the architect Stanford White (whose murder he later witnessed). In 1903 he married an American heiress, Hortense Mitchell, whose millions allowed him to acquire the Villa La Pietra and turn it into the ultimate Anglo-Florentine trophy house, stuffed to the rafters with paintings, sculptures, and objets of every description. With far more feeling for things than people, he wasn't an especially sympathetic or compelling figure, but his son Harold, born in 1904, was far more so, eventually becoming well known as an aesthete, a socialite, and a writer. Harold's memoirs provide many glimpses of the colonial world in which he grew up.

The year 1905 brought another American heiress, Mabel Dodge, who would later (by then having added Luhan to her name) found a colony of her own in Taos, New Mexico—one for the encouragement of artists and writers, that is. She and her second husband acquired the palatial Villa Curonia in Arcetri, near Bellosguardo, where she became friends with her neighbor Lady Walpurga Paget and hosted avant-garde figures like the poet Mina Loy, who also lived in Florence at the time, and Gertrude Stein, who often came to visit with her brother Leo, and who was inspired to write the typically unreadable *Portrait of Mabel Dodge at Villa Curonia*.

Another avant-gardist was the set designer and theatrical visionary Gordon Craig, who migrated to Florence in 1907. The following year he founded *The Mask*, an influential journal, and later established a theater school. Having recently broken off a relationship with Isadora Duncan, he became involved with a young writer named Dorothy Nevile Lees, who bore him a son, collaborated with him on *The Mask*, and wrote several books of her own, such as *Tuscan Feasts and Tuscan Friends* and *Scenes and Shrines in Tuscany*. With their affection for rural life and contadini, these bear a superficial resemblance to Janet's work, but are so moistly effusive as to fill one with admiration for the tough-mindedness of *Italian Sketches* and *Old Florence and Modern Tuscany*.

It was, in truth, a colonial period somewhat deficient in literary talent.* Not poets and novelists but art historians, dealers, and collectors were the dominant group, the one that set the tone and generated the most invigorating gossip and strife. A few years later, the writer Norman Douglas was to count "fifty squabbling art-coteries in that City of Misunderstandings," and if he exaggerated, it wasn't by much. Besides Berenson, Vernon Lee, and Herbert Horne, there was F. Mason Perkins, an American authority on Giotto; Maud Cruttwell, a historian who'd given yet more grief to Wilhelm von

---

*Ironically, the most celebrated Anglo-Florentine book from these years, *A Room with a View*, was by an author whose time in Florence, during three short visits, can be totaled in weeks.

Bode by challenging many of his Verrocchio attributions; and Charles Loeser, a wealthy collector who was on especially bad terms with Berenson (the two had been Harvard classmates and close friends but had rancorously fallen out). Observers of the endless feuds among this bunch often reached for medieval analogies. "The Guelfs and Ghibellines had been replaced by rival schools of art-historians," Harold Acton writes. "Between Berenson, Horne, Loeser and Perkins one never knew what fresh crisis had arisen." The English painter Sir William Rothenstein, who was commissioned to paint Berenson's portrait, recalls in his memoirs that there were "armed camps and fierce rivalries in Florence then, as in the past, but the fighting was far less bloody, concerned as it was with attributions rather than with Ducal thrones. Berenson, Horne, Loeser, Vernon Lee, Maud Cruttwell, all had their mercenaries—and their artillery." ("But," he continues, "there was other company to be enjoyed, away from the cognoscenti, notably that of Janet Ross.")

If skirmishing art historians imparted a flavor to colonial life, so, increasingly, did the overlapping homosexual contingent. The trial of Oscar Wilde in 1895 had sent a chill through every gay man in Britain, and had made relatively laissez-faire places like Florence look all the more attractive. One of Wilde's closest friends, the novelist Reggie Turner, was among those taking refuge; he struck the young Harold Acton—who would turn out to share his proclivities—as a "glittering Punchinello," and was widely beloved for his kindness and wit. Not that prejudice was lacking in the colony. It so happened that Henry Labouchère, author of the 1885 amendment under which many British homosexuals were prosecuted, had chosen Florence as his place of retirement in 1906. (Presumably he and Turner gave each other a wide berth in the Via Tornabuoni.) The businesslike Florentines, however, mostly seemed comfortable enough with the *stranieri invertiti*, as they were known. Unharassed and unpersecuted, both the gay subcolony and the "Sapphist" one—which included Lee, Cruttwell, and, to a degree, the bisexual Mabel Dodge—let its collective hair down, if not all the way, then at least an inch or two beyond what felt safe back home.

As for Florence as a whole, it largely remained the same affordable and convenient oasis it had been for decades. The real estate was still cheap, the Via Tornabuoni still full of kippers, marmalade, and proper tea. Colonists and tourists alike still flocked to Caffè Doney, as well as to newer gathering spots like Caffè Giubbe Rosse, in the recently completed Piazza Vittorio Emanuele II (since renamed Piazza della Repubblica). English speakers had two weekly newspapers to choose between, *The Florence Herald* and *The Italian Gazette*, neither of them as passionate as the Trollopes' *Tuscan Athenaeum* but widely read all the same. And the Gabinetto Vieusseux continued to be an invaluable resource. The novelist Arnold Bennett, who spent two months in Florence in 1910, was charmed by the library's trusting procedures: "I became a subscriber for 3 books for a month, 5 lire," he noted in his journal. "I signed my name in a big tome. No other formalities."

There were, to be sure, changes to the city, some of them jarring. Bennett was dismayed by its noisy new electric trams, which made stretches of the Lungarno unpleasant for walking, and was put out to find a "cinematograph theater" on the ground floor of an old palazzo. Florence now had streetlights, a handful of cars, and a bit of light industry alongside its traditional craftsmen's ateliers.

But the juggernaut of modernization had been slowed, thanks in part to the colony. In the late 1890s, it had appeared that the razing of the Ghetto and the Mercato Vecchio would be followed by more demolition; even the Ponte Vecchio was rumored to be under a death sentence. A preservationist group, the Società per la difesa di Firenze antica (Society for the Defense of Old Florence), sprang up to thwart the scheme. Working in conjunction with it were colonists such as Lee and Horne, who in 1898 mounted a vigorous campaign, in the London *Times* and elsewhere, against the ongoing *risanamento* (literally, "making healthy again"), as it was officially termed. An international outcry ensued. Florence's city council at first brushed aside these attempts at interference, but when Lady Walpurga Paget presented Prince Corsini, who headed the defense society, with a petition signed by ten thousand people—including Verdi, Kipling, Rodin, George Bernard Shaw, Sarah Bernhardt, and Theodore Roosevelt—the council was forced to abandon its plans.

The relationship between the colony and municipal authorities was not, however, always contentious; more often it was cooperative. In 1907, for example, the mayor asked Berenson to form a committee to oversee restoration of Ghirlandaio's frescoes in Santa Maria Novella. Even if Florentines sometimes bristled at foreign meddling, they couldn't deny that certain colonists were superbly qualified to help protect the city's patrimony.

Quick to butt into debates about preservation and city planning, the colony tended to ignore the hurly-burly of national politics. After the Battle of Adowa in 1896, when Italian forces were trounced by the Ethiopians, the writer Carlo Placci was so taken aback by the yawning indifference of his colonial friends that he burst out to Berenson, "You strange people, inhabiting hills and abstract ideas, how do you manage to exist outside of actualities?" The colony, its Risorgimento fervor having long since ebbed away, had relapsed into a cloud-cuckoo-land mentality.

For the moment it could afford to do so, given that Tuscany, while no longer a serenely cocooned grand duchy, had become only fractionally more hazardous since being absorbed into Italy. There were, however, portents of trouble ahead. The dreaded *sciopero* (strike), that bane of Italian life, became common in the 1890s. In 1898 nasty bread riots broke out in Milan and spread to other cities, including Florence. Two years later King Umberto was assassinated by Gaetano Bresci, a native Tuscan who'd emigrated to the United States and become an anarchist before returning home to level a blow against monarchy. It made for an ominous start to the new century.

These disturbances were accompanied, and to some degree produced, by a volatile ferment of new ideas. A dozen varieties of socialism sprang up like mushrooms, and in 1909 Filippo Tommaso Marinetti published his "Futurist Manifesto," adding a strain of combative iconoclasm to the mix—a strain particularly hostile to quaint museum-cities like Florence. Another belligerent, democracy-despising group of intellectuals, the Italian Nationalist Association, was largely based in Florence and held its first congress there in 1910. Spearheaded by eloquent polemicists like Giovanni Papini, Giuseppe Prezzolini, and Enrico Corradini, the Nationalists—a formative influence on the Fascists who followed them—poured their energies into a series of lively Florentine journals, culminating with *La Voce* (founded in 1908), which attracted many of the best writers and thinkers in the land.

There was, finally, the ineffable Gabriele D'Annunzio, an -ism unto himself. The most celebrated Italian writer of his day, D'Annunzio was also one of its most flamboyant characters, a swaggering, womanizing, bombastic would-be Übermensch. Beginning in 1898, he too based himself in Florence; in fact, he lived among the colonists near Settignano, having bought a villa adjacent to the one inhabited by his lover, Eleonora Duse, who happened to be Italy's most famous actress.

In 1910, D'Annunzio, deep in debt, fled to France to escape his creditors. His sensational return to Italy five years later was to mark a sort of symbolic pivot in the country's history, a turn toward darker waters. But all that lay, quite unimaginably, in the future. Despite the slight uptick in violence and the gathering swirl of radical ideas, Florence in 1910 remained essentially peaceful and harmonious, a place where Arthur Acton could collect his trophies and Mabel Dodge her guests; where Mina Loy could conduct experiments in poetry and Gordon Craig in theater; where art historians could whip up tempests in teapots and lesbians keep house together; where Reggie Turner could flutter along, scattering pearls of wit; and where Janet Ross could go on harvesting her olives and grapes.

⸺⸺⸺

With her farms producing nicely, her stock of friends replenished, and *Lives of the Early Medici* under her belt, Janet was perhaps doing better in 1910 than at any time since Henry's death. Less contented were her next-door neighbors. For the Berensons, the previous three years had been a period of sustained, sometimes hysterical turmoil. Though Janet was only minimally drawn into it, the Waterfields became more deeply enmeshed, and so did several significant new figures on the colonial scene.

Back in 1903, the Berensons' landlord, John Temple Leader, had finally died, leaving Vincigliata and the rest of his properties to his grandnephew, Lord Westbury. For four years nothing had changed, but in the fall of 1907 Lord Westbury decided to sell I Tatti. Having grown attached to the house, into which they'd already sunk a good deal of money, the Berensons were desperate to keep it. The asking price was high, by the standards of the day, and they had to scramble to raise enough cash. Luckily, a recent addition to Villadom, Henry White Cannon, happened to be a former president of the Chase National Bank, and he secured them a loan at an exceptionally low rate. By the end of the year I Tatti was theirs.

Like Poggio Gherardo, I Tatti came with two poderi. The Berensons weren't about to follow Janet's lead and try to run them, instead hiring a fattore. But if the agricultural side of the estate was of little interest to them, the house was a consuming obsession. By this point Bernard was an almost unrivaled figure in the art-history world, and, despite occasional cash-flow problems, rather rich. (Within a few years he would be richer still, thanks to his partnership with the wily and unscrupulous dealer Joseph Duveen.) He and Mary had also solidified their position as one of Europe's best-connected couples. As a result of all this, I Tatti was a hive of activity, half grand ducal court and half ministry, with dealers, restorers, and guests on the order of Edith Wharton and Hugo von Hofmannsthal constantly coming and going. "I receive like a dentist every morning and like a *femme du monde* every afternoon," Bernard joked. He and Mary needed a house appropriate to their station in life, which is to say one both exquisite and functional. They were to spend years realizing their dream, in the process repeatedly pushing their finances, marriage, and sanity to the brink.

The Italian architect hired to oversee the first round of renovations—which involved the addition of a library and several bedrooms to the house, as well as plumbing and electrical improvements—proved so incompetent that the Berensons fired him. They'd recently met a young English architect, Cecil Pinsent, who was attempting to establish himself in Florence. Though he had virtually no experience, the Berensons decided to put him in charge of the sprawling job. And if this showed dubious sagacity, their next move showed even less.

Back in 1906, Mary had arranged a motoring trip around Tuscany for her two daughters, Ray and Karin, and had asked her sister, Alys, to recommend two suitable young men to round out the party. The chaps Alys dispatched to Florence were the future economist John Maynard Keynes and Geoffrey Scott, a recent Oxford graduate and aspiring classicist. While the trip went well, no chemistry blossomed between the Costelloe girls and their companions, who were discovered to have homosexual inclinations.* Mary herself, however, developed a fixation on Scott, whose unprepossessing features—he was pale, lanky, fidgety, unkempt, and prone to boils—were offset by his first-rate mind and complex, intriguingly troubled character. Wanting both to give Scott a leg up and to keep him near, Mary proposed that he join forces with Pinsent, even though he had only the most elementary architectural training.

Bernard agreed, and in 1909 "the Artichokes," as he and Mary for some obscure reason called them, were loosed on I Tatti. Like that of true love, the course of renovation never runs smooth, and the two tyros were soon in over their heads. While bringing taste and imagination to the job, they bungled endlessly, to the point that certain snickering Anglo-Florentines began to refer to the ripped-open house as "Berenson's Folly." Bernard, with his short fuse and intolerance of error, would return from trips abroad and erupt in fury at the stupidities perpetrated in his absence. The Artichokes caught some of his wrath but Mary far more of it, in part because of Bernard's jealousy of Scott. Not that anything had actually happened between Mary and Scott, who was half her age (not to mention weight) and still unsure of his sexual orientation. Nor did Bernard have much right to complain: his prudishness having given way to compulsive skirt chasing, it was now he rather than

---

*Both of Mary's daughters did, however, end up marrying within the Bloomsbury circles frequented by Keynes and Scott: in 1911 Ray married Oliver Strachey, older brother of Lytton, and in 1914 Karin married Adrian Stephen, younger brother of Virginia.

Mary who routinely trampled the dictates of fidelity—the boot was on the other foot. Even so, he made her pay for her infatuation, and for the Artichokes' slow progress and missteps. On his frequent "black serpent days," as Mary termed them, he was a holy terror, spewing venom by the gallon.

To some extent, Janet was helpful to both Berensons throughout their travails, and during one especially disruptive stretch of the renovation they lodged at Poggio Gherardo for several weeks. But she also added to Mary's misery by criticizing and second-guessing her. Proud of her hands-on, low-cost transformation of Poggio Gherardo, Janet deplored the Anglo-Florentines' tendency to squander fistfuls of money on their estates without even understanding their ecology. In 1908, after taking Janet to visit the Dodges at Villa Curonia, Logan Pearsall Smith reported to his mother that Janet had found the house "absolutely hopeless & uninhabitable, & all [the Dodges'] improvements terrible . . . As we drove away she almost popped out of the carriage in her anxiety to point out walls that were sure to fall down & she counted at least 60 trees that were certain to die . . . She thoroughly enjoyed herself." Though she took no pleasure—or at least less—in the shortcomings of I Tatti, she didn't hesitate to point them out, and Mary came to fear "the all-seeing eye of Mrs. Ross," as she put it to her mother.

It may have been, in some small part, resentment at Janet's fault-finding, or even a hunger for payback, that prompted Mary to add a controversial new member to the renovation team. When she'd visited the Fortezza della Brunella, Mary had been struck—as was everyone—by Aubrey's magical rooftop garden, and now that she and Bernard were turning their attention to their own garden she decided to offer Aubrey a job working on it.

Since late 1907, when they'd last stayed at Poggio Gherardo, the Waterfields had continued to shuttle between Aulla and England, where they now had the use of Northbourne Court, a country house in Kent for which they paid only a peppercorn rent. By some measures, they were doing well: still happy with each other, still over the moon about the fortress and the rough-and-ready life they led there, still painting and writing prolifically. Lina, in fact, had published a book about their recent experiences, *Home Life in Italy: Letters from the Apennines*, with illustrations by Aubrey. But they were also struggling. Despite Aubrey's ability and fluency as a painter, he still refused to seek patronage or push his wares. Already strained, the couple's finances had been put under further pressure when Gordon was diagnosed with polio, which required expensive treatments, and by mid-1909 they were about to be put under still more, since Lina was pregnant again.

In short, things were turning out exactly as Janet had predicted, with the family living hand to mouth. Under these circumstances, Mary's proposal came as something of a godsend: a bit of income would trickle in, and Lina felt sure that this first, prestigious commission would lead to more of the same for Aubrey.

In November 1909, only weeks after Lina gave birth to John, her second son, Aubrey came to do an initial round of work at I Tatti, staying on-site. Geoffrey Scott seems not to have been involved in creating the garden, at least at this stage, but Pinsent was, and Aubrey's letters make clear that the architect was none too thrilled to have a new collaborator, especially given Aubrey's allegiance to the informal English aesthetic. (Pinsent preferred the rigorously geometric Italian style.) Predictably, the Berensons neglected to put either man in charge, though Aubrey and Pinsent managed to hammer out a modus operandi with each other. Equally predictable was Janet's reaction to it all: "Mrs. Ross's scorn knows no bounds," Mary sighed to her mother. "Asking a fool, who knows nothing of gardens, to come and make us one—a nice English cabbage-patch he will make of it!"

The following autumn Aubrey came back to I Tatti to resume the job. In his absence, Pinsent had won the Berensons decisively over to his school of thought, and Aubrey arrived to find his own plans shelved. "Full of fury," as Mary put it, "and determined to carry through his scheme," Aubrey sulked, brooded, and obstinately argued with his employers. Even Mary, who was as slow to rid herself of bothersome people as Janet was swift, might have dismissed him had Lina not happened to write in a panic from Aulla, saying that the leaky cistern at the fortress had run dry and pleading for temporary shelter at I Tatti. Softhearted as always, Mary offered her a cottage on the property, and suddenly the Berensons found themselves with the entire Waterfield tribe underfoot.

The timing was terrible. The prominent novelist Paul Bourget had recently published a novella, *La Dame qui a perdu son peintre*, featuring an art expert who is unmistakably modeled on Berenson—and who is disgracefully duped by a fake Leonardo. Whereas Janet had been able to shrug off *Friendship*, Bernard, his ego gargantuan and his professional reputation at stake, was apoplectic at being lampooned in a roman à clef. But this wasn't the worst of it, for the crowning fiasco of the renovation process had just occurred. The Berensons had chosen a French painter, René Piot, to fill the lunettes of their new library with frescoes depicting scenes from Virgil's *Georgics*. When Bernard, who'd been away, returned to I Tatti and first laid eyes on Piot's completed masterwork, he was confronted with a series of heavily eroticized shepherds disporting against a pastoral background rendered in the most garish of hues. Nearly fainting away, he ordered the monstrous frescoes covered over with canvas, then took to his bed. Mary reported him to be "on the verge of nervous breakdown."

He was certainly in no mood to have Aubrey's grievances put before him. But Robert Trevelyan, who was also staying at I Tatti and who was convinced of Aubrey's genius as a gardener, insisted on doing just that, doggedly prosecuting his friend's case. Afterward, Bernard fulminated that he didn't "want to see Trevy again for years, and Aubrey never." The next day Mary bit the bullet, telling Aubrey and Pinsent that she felt their collaboration had been a failure. For Pinsent, who already had other clients—he was to become Anglo-Tuscany's architect and garden designer of choice—it was a minor setback, but to Aubrey and Lina it was a painful blow.

To whatever extent Janet followed the debacle, she probably felt a mixture of disgust, Schadenfreude, and vindication; the Berensons had sometimes stuck up for Aubrey against her, but now his true colors had been exposed. Not surprisingly, Aubrey seems to have gone nowhere near Poggio Gherardo during these tense final months of 1910, and Lina, still in the doghouse, had only minimal contact with her aunt.

Lina was, however, on hand to witness one of the more telling and amusing moments of Janet's life. George Meredith had died the year before, and his son Will had just written Janet to ask whether he might borrow his father's letters to her, with a view toward including them in the collection he was assembling. In *Castle in Italy*, Lina describes what happened next: "She unlocked a small cabinet and took out some packets of letters, each tied up with blue ribbon. It seemed to me that my Aunt had not read them since receiving them, for she looked puzzled and suddenly exclaimed: 'Good God, my poet must have been in love with me!'" Coming from most people, such an expression of astonishment would be suspect, but coming from Janet it was almost certainly genuine. She was so devoid of romantic and sexual motivations that she tended to overlook them in others.

Meredith had been perhaps the last surviving figure from Janet's youth, and his death, sharply reminding her of Time's wingèd chariot, may have helped spur along a book she'd long been meditating. As early as 1889 she'd toyed with the idea of presenting her own life as a sequel to the lives documented in *Three Generations of English Women*. At the time, though, it seemed presumptuous—"I dare not pose as the 4th generation," she told Kinglake. Two years later, Symonds, after reading *Three Generations*, hit on the same notion, encouraging Janet to write about "the fourth generation" and predicting that such a book would have "the notable value of presenting a similar strain of family genius under the conditions of social evolution—the type altering with the alteration of environment." That same year she did in fact publish a work of autobiography, but it was the innocuously titled *Early Days Recalled*, which draws no explicit connections to her ancestors. Now, some two decades later, she felt ready to assert those connections, and to bring her story up to date.

Published in 1912, *The Fourth Generation* has a frontispiece by Frank Crisp that shows Janet at her desk, her back to the viewer, the wall in front of her filled with family mementoes. Her preface reinforces this hint of modesty and ancestral subordination: in it, Janet explains that she was urged to write the book by friends who "seemed to think that the story of my life ought to be linked in some way to that of my mother, grandmother, and great-grandmother." What follows is, at first, largely identical to *Early Days Recalled*, with only cosmetic changes.* But that book had taken Janet only to 1863. To carry the story forward to the present, she wrote over two hundred additional pages.

"Do not overload your book with letters," Rev. Lindsay had pleaded with Janet, urging her instead to give readers "plenty of yourself." Normally grateful for Lindsay's advice, she chose in this instance to ignore it, with the result that *The Fourth Generation* is crammed with letters and gives away almost nothing of an intimate nature. Few readers seemed to mind, for it was a considerable success, appearing on both sides of the Atlantic and going into five editions. There were a few quibbles from reviewers, but most were laudatory, focusing less on the book's clunky composition than on the remarkable woman behind it. "A new candidate for immortality has presented herself," gushed the critic for the *New-York Tribune*. "She is a woman who has lived every minute of her life . . . She lived in a brilliant world among brilliant people of whom she herself was surely one of the most brilliant." Writing for *The Observer*, Arthur Ransome (later to become famous for a series of children's books, Swallows and Amazons) captured Janet's peculiar majesty in an inspired, aptly overblown metaphor: "She seems to drive with immense skill and grace a twenty-in-hand composed indiscriminately of horses, dromedaries, camels, mules, poets, historians, painters, politicians and financiers." Together with one more volume for Dent—*The Story of Lucca*, also published in 1912—*The Fourth Generation* was the last book Janet wrote, and, whatever its defects, it stands as a fitting finale to her career as an author.

While the appearance and reception of *The Fourth Generation* gave a burnish to the year 1912, another, far more famous event cast

---

*A more substantial change was the addition of Meredith's letters. To Janet's annoyance, Meredith had denied her permission to print any of his letters in *Early Days Recalled*, presumably because he didn't want his infatuation with a mere teenage girl revealed. The fact that she was now able to print them suggests that Will Meredith had given his blessing, perhaps as a quid pro quo for her having dug the same letters out of her cabinet and provided them for his own book.

a pall over it. Sir Cosmo and Lady Duff Gordon had had the bad luck to book passage on the *Titanic*, and the good luck to survive its maiden voyage. Not, however, without repercussions. The Duff Gordons had escaped in a lifeboat that was only half full, and it was alleged that Cosmo had bribed its crew to hasten away from the sinking ship rather than trying to rescue more passengers. In May, he and Lucy were summoned to a government inquiry, where Cosmo faced a withering cross-examination in front of a large crowd, drawn by Lucy's fame and the frisson of scandal—not often was a British aristocrat charged with gross cowardice and depraved indifference to human life. Even though Cosmo hotly defended himself, explaining that the £5 he'd given to each crew member had been meant as charity rather than bribery, and even though the inquiry cleared him of any wrongdoing, the stigma remained. The whole affair caused immense distress not only to him and his wife but to his cousin: with her family pride, Janet was grieved and outraged to see Cosmo's name dragged through the mud.

Perhaps it was in part this reinvigorated, wagon-circling sense of family feeling that made Janet finally begin to soften toward Lina at the end of 1912. Needing to do some research in Florence and wanting to try yet again to mend fences with her aunt, Lina fished for an invitation to stay at Poggio Gherardo. To her surprise she got one, and to her even greater surprise she found herself made welcome. "My aunt is in an amiable mood and gracious to me," she wrote to her friend Maurice Headlam. "Of course we spar all day, but then we always did and she hates the worm that does not turn."

When Lina returned eighteen months later, the détente not only held but strengthened, though for a somewhat ironic reason. Lina had become a suffragette, and in so doing had enraged Aubrey's aunt Tina Rate, who threatened to cut her and Aubrey out of her will unless Lina relented. Aunt Janet was no more pro-suffragette than Aunt Tina—"A nice mess we will be in if women ever do get the vote," she taunted Lina in a letter. But she also loathed Tina Rate, and was tickled to hear that Lina had defied her. "Owing to At. Janet's detestation of Mrs. Rate," Lina wrote to Headlam from Poggio Gherardo in June 1914, "we have completely made up our quarrel of fourteen years* . . . She even listens to the mention of Aubrey's name and of my children without wrinkling her nose."

The quarrel was in fact less than completely made up, and never would be. But a corner had been turned, and the stage was set for aunt and niece to live under the same roof again. Even so, such a scenario would have been unlikely had history not nudged them into it—history, which in the summer of 1914 was about to have its way with everyone.

At first it seemed their common roof might be English. With unaccustomed bad timing, Janet was caught in Paris by the outbreak of war; she'd been on her way to London. When eventually she made it across the Channel, she decided to accept Lina's offer of refuge at Northbourne Court—an offer made palatable by the fact that Aubrey, whose mother had just died, was with his family in Canterbury.

Anxious about leaving Poggio Gherardo unsupervised in a time of crisis, Janet itched to return home, but she lacked a piece of documentation that was suddenly no longer optional: a passport. Luckily, Maurice Headlam, who was in government, managed to expedite the application process. By October, passport in hand, she was on her way south again.

Having declared its neutrality, Italy at this point remained on the sidelines, and it must have been a relief for Janet to be back there. But she was of course far from indifferent to the mounting horror of the Western Front. In particular, she worried over Frank Crisp, to whom she'd grown deeply attached and who was now in the mud of Flanders. All too soon, in January 1915, her worst fears were realized when Crisp was killed in action. Hutton cabled the news to Mary Berenson, asking her to break it to Janet. "It was one of the worst things I ever had to do," Mary wrote to her sister. "She

---

*A slight exaggeration on Lina's part: the quarrel, which began in 1901, had lasted thirteen years.

told me before that if he died she wanted to die too." Only a month earlier, Janet had endured another loss, the death (from natural causes) of Rev. Lindsay. Reeling under this double blow, she was in her worst state since being widowed, and both Berensons checked in on her frequently. After one visit, Mary wrote in her diary that Janet "sits all day by the fire, only stirring to make it up, and shuddering and wincing from time to time, as if someone had struck her."

So bereft and desolate was Janet that she took the extraordinary step of reaching out to Lina, albeit somewhat brusquely: "I am all alone," she wrote, "and you are all alone at Northbourne, so you had better come and stay with me." Lina was torn. Aubrey was about to join the Northants Yeomanry and be sent to France, and she wanted to be able to see him during his leaves; she also wanted to be able to see Gordon, who was at boarding school, during his vacations. "On the other hand," she writes in *Castle in Italy*, "East Kent was not a suitable place for younger children to be during the war . . . It was a great chance for Johnny, who was overgrown and delicate, to be in a warmer climate and have good food. There was no rationing in Italy then and in any case the farms of Poggio Gherardo supplied milk, wheat, oil, wine, vegetables, and fruit." After weighing the options, she took Janet up on her invitation. Except for a few hiatuses, she was to spend the rest of the war with her.

When Lina decided to go to Poggio Gherardo, John wasn't the only child whose welfare she had in mind. In 1911 she'd given birth to a daughter, Carinthia, nicknamed Kinta, who was now, in 1915, about to get her first taste of Italy. While she would never become quite as deeply involved with the country as Lina or Janet, her response to it was just as strong. This much is clear from *A Tuscan Childhood*, the excellent memoir she published almost eighty years later. Much of it evokes life at the Fortezza della Brunella, but it also has a good deal on Janet and Poggio Gherardo.

In Kinta's recollection, Janet was somewhat puzzling to a four-year-old. "I never quite understood," she writes, "why friends of all ages . . . addressed her as Aunt Janet when they were not related at all. Perhaps it was because she had assumed the rank of Great-Aunt-

General and they had fallen into step, half-dragooned and half-amused." Kinta herself wasn't the type to fall into step. An exuberant tomboy used to running wild (both Waterfields were lax parents), she soon raised Janet's hackles. Lina recalls Janet's impatience with Kinta, and the way "they used to look at each other in the manner of rival beauties." Kinta herself, however, soon found Janet to be "fair and painstaking with children. She thoroughly disapproved of the way my mother took little interest in our upbringing . . . And despite her rumblings of complaint to Mary Berenson about the way we were dumped at Poggio, I think she enjoyed our company. She was lonely in that huge house after Uncle Henry died."

As for Poggio Gherardo, Kinta loved it on sight. The Poodle Room served as her "very unusual nursery," the whole house seethed with dogs and birds, and the grounds and farms offered endless diversions. She and her brother spent their days romping with the children of Janet's servants and sharecroppers. When playing hide-and-seek, they'd slip into "the Ali Baba oil jars in the huge cellars that ran under the house." Another favorite game was to pretend they were condottieri, "wondering in excitement and fear whether this would conjure up the ghost of Sir John Hawkwood." All told, it was a world apart from the Kentish coast, where the din of battle, carrying across from Flanders, was not imaginary but unnervingly real.

But the war couldn't be kept at bay for long. Despite belonging to the Triple Alliance, Italy hadn't been obligated to fight alongside Germany and Austria, and it had refrained from doing so. One might have expected Italy to count itself lucky to be sitting out the conflict, especially after the delusional mass optimism of August 1914 gave way to the reality of interminable trench warfare. Somehow, though, the country managed to chafe at its neutral status. One reason was a vague but needling sense of its own deficiency. The disgrace of Adowa had been substantially canceled out in 1911, when Italy succeeded in wresting Libya from the Ottomans, but it hankered to test itself in a *real* war; until then, it would remain an unproven parvenu among nations. There were also more tangible goals. Ever since unification, Italy had longed to lay hold of *terre irredente* (unredeemed lands) such as Trieste and Trentino, where much of the population was ethnically Italian, and now perhaps it could take them from Austria as spoils of war. But that meant joining the right side . . . Finally, after much dithering, Italy decided to throw in its lot with the Entente Powers—France, Britain, and Russia—by signing the Treaty of London in April 1915.

Invidiously, the treaty was signed in secret, behind the backs of certain key players (to say nothing of the public). Bitter controversy erupted, with an antiwar faction coalescing around Giovanni Giolitti, the dominant politician of the previous decade. For a moment it seemed Italy's next war might be civil. "No one cared to be in Florence after sundown," Lina recalls, "as there were fights between different factions and crowbars were used as missiles." At just this moment, D'Annunzio returned from exile in France and began vociferously orating in favor of "intervention," as the euphemism went. In Lina's words, "He spoke in every city and sent a wave of impassioned patriotism throughout the country as no one else could have done." Simultaneously, a young agitator named Benito Mussolini, who'd recently launched an interventionist newspaper, whipped his own crowds into a fury. A Florentine friend of Lina's who was in Rome reported witnessing "ten thousand men marching through the city . . . shouting '*Mort'a* [Death to] *Giolitti*' in a rhythmic dirge." Faced with this kind of rabidity, the opposition soon crumpled, and on May 23 Italy declared war on Austria.

While Italy's decision to join the British side came as a relief to Janet and Lina, as to the rest of the colony, its entry into the war had immediate consequences. Within weeks, a large portion of Poggio Gherardo's sharecroppers had been conscripted into the army. The men "wept as they said good-bye to us," Lina writes, "and asked 'What will become of our fields, now that the harvest is near?'" Left with a sorely reduced labor force, Janet and Lina pitched in more than usual, helping to cut fodder and perform other tasks. Every pair of hands was needed, and even John and Kinta were called upon to help. Kinta recalls that Janet joined them "in the hardest task of picking up the fallen olives, even though she was well into her seventies. 'My back's tired,' I once complained after what seemed like hours of bending down. 'Nonsense, child,' she retorted. 'Mine's not, and I'm much older than you.' "

In actually having to inconvenience themselves somewhat (and not complaining about it), Janet and Lina were atypical of the colony, which in the early days of the war mostly went on cultivating its heavenly gardens as though not a thing had changed. Plenty of its members epitomized this insouciance—Arthur Acton, for instance—but one, a recent addition, stands out.

The daughter of an Anglo-Irish peer, Lady Sybil Cuffe had married William Bayard Cutting, a young, rich, brilliantly prospected product of the same New York gratin that nurtured Edith Wharton (who, indeed, considered him a dear friend). In 1902, barely a year after the wedding, Cutting had his first tubercular hemorrhage, and eight years later, just like Lucie Duff Gordon, he died in Egypt aboard a dahabeah. In 1911 his widow moved to Florence with her nine-year-old daughter, Iris, and rented the Villa Medici below Fiesole, which Scott and Pinsent helped her to spruce up. Soon she was consorting with the Berensons, and in 1914 she and Bernard began an affair—one that Mary claimed to condone, since it distracted her husband from his longtime mistress, Belle da Costa Greene, of whom Mary had grown intensely jealous.

Around the same time, Sybil struck up an acquaintanceship with Janet. In her memoirs, Iris* recalls, "Sometimes I drove over with my mother to Poggio Gherardo . . . to find old Mrs. Ross reckoning up her olive crop with an eye as shrewd and vigilant as that of any Tuscan farmer, and perhaps consenting, if in a good mood, to take us into the cosy clutter of her Victorian sitting-room," where the usual anecdotes about Thackeray and the rest would be told. That Janet tolerated Sybil for even a moment is surprising, as she embodied a style of tremulous, attention-craving femininity Janet despised. Utterly self-involved and hypochondriacal, she was notorious for fainting at the drop of a hat—"whenever she felt assailed by tedium," Kinta remarks—and Janet may have found her theatrics so

---

* Iris Origo, that is, though she wouldn't take on that name till some years later.

ridiculous as to be endearing.* For her part, Lina immediately hit it
off with Sybil; like Bernard, she found her smart and entertaining,
and didn't mind having to catch her when she swooned away. Before long Lina was a regular at Villa Medici.

"In my mother's ivory tower," Iris recollects, "the war was only a
distant rumble, an inconvenient and unpleasant noise offstage," and
she adds that the same held true in "many other villas inhabited by
foreigners on the Florentine hills." But Poggio Gherardo was, again,
an exception, and not simply because of its absent sharecroppers. To
a degree that put most of their neighbors to shame, first Lina and
then Janet were about to throw themselves into the war effort, each
drawing on her particular strengths to make a contribution.

Lina decided to focus her energies on strengthening the Anglo-
Italian relationship, which had been strained by the war. "The Socialists had great success," she notes, "in blaming England for their
hardships and for being the chief obstacle to a peace treaty; the
walls of towns and villages were plastered with the words *Mort'agli
Inglesi* [Death to the English] and Down with the War." To counter
such propaganda, she organized speeches in defense of the alliance
and collaborated with Janet's old friend Guido Biagi on a poster
touting its benefits; Biagi presented the poster to the mayor of Florence, and soon it was on walls all over town.

She also started to think in institutional terms. Even before the
war there had been talk in certain quarters about establishing some
sort of British center in Florence, and in 1916 Lina began taking
concrete steps toward one. At first it was no more than a library, for
which Lina obtained books and furniture—donated by, among others, the Berensons, Sybil Cutting, Arthur Acton, and Janet—along
with affordable space in central Florence. But enthusiasm for the
project quickly snowballed. John Buchan (author of *The Thirty-
Nine Steps*), who during the war held several high-level propaganda

---

*Not surprisingly, Sybil proved irresistible to parodists. Somerset Maugham's unflattering
short story "Louise" is thought to be based on her, and in Huxley's *Those Barren Leaves*,
the central character, Mrs. Aldwinkle—rich, voluble, socially ambitious—has been taken
for a caricature of her (though Lina suspected that Mrs. Aldwinkle was, in other ways, at
least in part a send-up of herself).

posts in London, was especially keen on it, and with his backing the library soon metamorphosed into the British Institute of Florence. In 1918 it was formally opened by Sir James Rennell Rodd, the British ambassador to Italy. The world's first British cultural institute abroad, it served as the model for the British Council. Lina would later receive the OBE for her role in launching it.

Even as Lina's cross-cultural campaign was succeeding, the Italian military one was close to collapse. The first two years of the war had been largely a stalemate, with Italian and Austrian troops holding each other in check along the Isonzo front. Then, in October 1917, came the Battle of Caporetto. Stiffened by a recent influx of German troops, the Austrians broke through and sent Italian forces reeling backward in disarray. In a scene reminiscent of Napoleon's retreat from Moscow, hundreds of thousands of soldiers and civilians stumbled across the countryside, bloody, starving, and desperate. By November 1917 some twenty thousand refugees had reached Florence, which struggled to cope with them.

Now it was Janet who rose to the occasion. Shocked and moved by the plight of the refugees, she established a committee to raise money for them; when the committee published a solicitation letter in the London *Times*, donors sent close to £1,000, which went toward basic provisions. She continued to aid the refugees through the rest of the war, even knitting sweaters for them, but her most strenuous efforts went toward helping her neighbors. As 1917 passed into 1918, life became dramatically grimmer and harder around Florence, which for the first time faced food and fuel shortages, as well as skyrocketing inflation. With their men either pinned down at the front or already dead, local women struggled both to feed their children and to keep them occupied, school hours having been curtailed. Janet therefore decided to establish a *doposcuola* (after-school program). After pulling a few strings, she was granted funding by the British government. The Berensons loaned her a building they owned in the hamlet of Ponte a Mensola, and some local ecclesiastics agreed to run the program, which was designed to feed and educate seventy children. "You will have often smiled thinking of [Janet] working in close alliance with priests, nuns & children,"

Lina wrote to Mary, who was away at the time. "She often laughs herself." It was a far cry from the ten village schools that Sarah Austin established on Malta, but coming from someone with no great affinity for children, it showed considerable altruism.

Janet herself often wrote to Mary during these bleak months, and her diligence in doing so represented another piece of charity. For Mary had recently suffered her own personal Caporetto. Typically, the disaster was in large part of her own making.

Odd from the start, her relationship with Geoffrey Scott had become still stranger. Even as Scott came into his own intellectually—in 1914 he published *The Architecture of Humanism*, a highly original book that retains a cult following to this day—he remained sexually and romantically tormented. By this point he seemed to be more straight than gay, and was falling in love (or so he convinced himself) with every woman in sight. While Mary had given up on claiming Scott for herself, she was still determined to keep him close; something about the man was addictive to her. Slipping into her favorite role of matchmaking confidante, she tried to steer him toward partners of her choosing, even encouraging his infatuation with her daughter Karin. But in early 1918 Scott took matters into his own hands, proposing to, of all people, Sybil Cutting, who accepted. Nearly everyone was appalled at the prospect of two such flighty, neurotic, self-absorbed souls joined in wedlock, but none quite like Mary; to Bernard, who'd only recently terminated his own dalliance with Sybil, she wrote of her "disgust that *both* my men should have been snatched away by that chatterbox." Her rage gave way to depression, and in March she tried to throw herself from a window in Paris. When a host of physical ailments—some apparently psychosomatic, others not—began to plague her as well, her daughter Ray brought her to England and installed her in a nursing home, where for months she lay helpless with agony.

Learning of Mary's dire state, Janet began writing to her much more frequently in the summer of 1918. This was her most concentrated epistolary output since her correspondence with Kinglake in 1889–90, as she herself observed to Mary: "It reminds me of dear

Eothen, to whom I also wrote every day from Castagnolo during his long illness." Where those earlier letters mixed solicitude with updates on the progress of Poggio Gherardo, these intersperse tender passages of morale-boosting with accounts of the deterioration of everyday life around Settignano. Food had become so scarce that there were "no more cats about, they have been eaten." Not having a cat of her own, Janet was spared the temptation, but she did decide to convert some of her menagerie into calories: "I've signed the death warrant of my pretty gold pheasants, & am going to eat them." Then came the Spanish influenza. Though less severe in Florence than certain other parts of Italy, the epidemic began picking off more and more of Janet's neighbors, and in October she was forced to close the doposcuola for fear of contagion.

Janet must have been tempted, like Boccaccio's lieta brigata, to shut herself up in Poggio Gherardo. Instead, she risked her own life to find homes for the many new orphans in the area. She also did favors for the absent Berensons, keeping an eye on their poderi and sending care packages to a sharecropper of theirs who'd become a prisoner of war. (She routinely sent such packages to her own people at the front.) She even intervened in a dispute on a nearby estate between a sharecropper and his fattore. The fattore, a "perfect *beast*," was trying to evict the sharecropper. Janet stepped in to reassure the frightened peasant and inform him of his wartime right not to be displaced, "particularly as the man has 2 sons at the front." "Like my mother," she remarked to Mary, "I hate injustice and always take the side of the oppressed." But her accounts of her deeds are nowhere self-glorifying. In fact, at no point in her life does she appear more admirable than during these awful last months of the Great War, as she works to put food on the table for Lina, John, and Kinta, to provide aid and comfort to those in need, and to help keep Mary's head above water.

Hard though the autumn was in Florence, at least there was good news from the battlefields to the northeast. After Caporetto, Italian forces had established a line behind the Piave River, reinforced by French, American, and British troops (including the XIV Corps, to which Aubrey was attached). In October 1918 the Allies mounted a triumphant offensive near Vittorio Veneto, and on November 3, under the Armistice of Villa Giusti, hostilities ceased. The Germans surrendered eight days later, and the war was over.

Not yet demobilized, Aubrey was initially seconded to the Allied Claims Commission and then—this time as a liaison officer—to an Italian contingent sent to Greek-occupied Smyrna (present-day Izmir, Turkey). Lina, meanwhile, stayed on at Poggio Gherardo till October 1919, when she returned to England with the children. Northbourne Court was no longer available, but Lina rented another house nearby. In 1921 Aubrey was released from service, and the family was reunited at last.

———

"We had been four years with [Janet] at Poggio," Lina comments, "and she had shown such great kindness, softening toward Kinta and showing affection to Johnny . . . For my part I was very sad for I realised that she would be lonely without us." Her prediction proved all too accurate. Arthritic and often ill, Janet didn't get out much, and she had fewer visitors than previously. The Berensons, to whom she would have turned for company, were rarely in town. While her servants and sharecroppers offered fellowship by day, her solitary nights must have seemed long, especially in winter. "I don't agree with you that uncongenial society is better than none," she wrote to Mary. " 'Meglio sola che mal accompagnata' [Better alone than in bad company] says the old proverb." No doubt she truly felt this way, since she was nothing if not self-sufficient. Still, a deep loneliness wells up in her letters to Mary and Lina.

Also clear from these letters is that life in Florence scarcely improved after the war, and in some ways became even worse. With the economy in shambles, basic supplies often vanished—"There is *no* sugar at present in Florence." Postal service became ever more erratic and expensive. Droughts were frequent, and in August 1920 a nearby artillery depot blew up, causing extensive damage—Poggio Gherardo had all its windows blown out. The city continued to be riven by strikes and protests, and the hodgepodge of groups jostling for power now included Mussolini's *fascisti*, with their policy of *squadrismo*, or gang violence and intimidation. "Bombs seem to be common as gooseberries now," Janet remarked.

Nor was this anarchy limited to the city. The countryside around Settignano, formerly so peaceful and welcoming, was plagued by theft and brigandage. In July 1920 Janet reported to Mary that a local church had been looted and its relics desecrated: "It seems the thieves could not get St Andrea's ring off, so they broke his finger & took that with the ring." The previous July she herself had been the victim of a crime, when fifty men from Ponte a Mensola showed up at her door and demanded, as she told Lina, "all my wine & oil & the gran turco [maize] for the cows," along with a horse and cart to haul it away. The following month, when she tried to shoo a hunter out of her bosco he pointed his gun at her and suggested she go back to England where she belonged.

At moments she contemplated doing just that, or at least getting rid of Poggio Gherardo, which became harder and harder to keep going on her small income and savings. "I am cutting down the great oak at the end of the wood, with sorrow, but the big trunk will make us 3 plows (cost 40 lire each) and the many boughs give us two cataste [cords] of wood (cost 450)," she told Lina, and to Mary she lamented having to let the remainder of Henry's orchid collection die off—it had become too expensive to maintain.

In one important way, however, she was spared the turmoil of the postwar years. All over Italy peasants were growing restive, and Janet's letters nervously chart the groundswell of agrarian mutiny. "'Mezzadria' is a thing of the past," she wrote to Lina in late 1920. "In Sicily the people are seizing the estates, in the North ditto, here the contadini are many of them up against the Padroni, who are selling the estates whenever they can." Ten days later she added, "Near Arezzo the contadini are proclaiming themselves masters of their poderi, & refusing to give anything to their Padroni." While she never voiced a fear that her own contadini might turn against her, it was a scenario that must have haunted her. Thankfully, it never came to pass; whatever their temptations toward rebellion, Poggio Gherardo's sharecroppers chose to leave well enough alone. Whether

Janet's uncommonly good relations with them over the decades helped retain their loyalty is impossible to say, but it seems likely.

Despite her growing reluctance to venture into Florence, Janet now and then took part in its half-revived social life, and some evocative names surface in her correspondence: "The other day," she informed Lina, "I made the acquaintance of Prince von Thurn & Taxis . . . he was at Duino when the Italians bombarded it." This was the owner of Duino Castle, which two years later was to be immortalized by Rainer Maria Rilke.

Her own much smaller castle was, moreover, still a magnet. In 1920 the future prime minister Harold Macmillan came to pay his respects to Janet while on honeymoon with his wife, the former Lady Dorothy Cavendish. The following year Alys Russell stayed at I Tatti for several weeks and spent much of her time with Janet, about whom she'd heard a great deal from Mary but whom she'd never met. It was a bad moment in her life, for her husband—by now a major philosopher—was about to divorce her in order to marry a twenty-seven-year-old. Touched by her suffering, Janet took to Alys immediately and insisted that she join the Aunt Janet club— no more saying "Mrs. Ross" for her. Though they saw each other only once or twice afterward, they remained on affectionate terms and exchanged the occasional letter.

Another emissary from I Tatti was Nicky Mariano. Half Italian and half Baltic-German, this fetching young woman had turned up in Florence before the war and charmed both Geoffrey Scott and Mary Berenson, who of course tried to push her into Scott's arms. The match might actually have come off had Nicky not gone to visit her sister in Russia in 1914. Trapped there for five years by war and revolution, she made it back to Florence only in 1919, at which point Mary swooped in to hire her as the I Tatti librarian. Over time she assumed various other duties as well, including that of serving as *maîtresse-en-titre* to Bernard. This development pained Mary but also came as a relief, since Nicky, who worshipped Bernard, was willing to devote herself entirely to meeting his fussy little needs, and now that he was being pampered like a sultan he was considerably less cross with Mary. "B.B. would be extremely happy married to Nicky, who would make him a more satisfactory wife than I have been," Mary noted in her diary.

What drew everyone to Nicky was her perfect temperament; sweet, unflappable, and fun, she was a woman about whom not even the most backbiting colonist could find a bad word to say. Janet, however, somehow contrived not to be disarmed by her, at least not initially. Mary had asked Nicky to keep an eye on Janet while she and Bernard were out of town. "It was not an easy task," Nicky recalls in her memoirs. "I tried hard to amuse her, with very tepid results. One day I tried to make her talk about her early days in Florence. She looked at me fiercely from under her bushy eyebrows and only said: 'If you had read any of my books you would not ask such foolish questions.'" (Much as Janet liked to regale listeners with tales of her youth, she had a curious resistance to being drawn out.)

Another kindness of Nicky's, and one for which Janet was truly grateful, was her habit of selecting and bringing over books from her employers' vast library. Janet's own shelves were stagnant and picked-over, and the frequent arrival of the book-bearing Nicky, like a doctor paying house calls, spurred her to experiment with new titles and authors. Conrad she found heavy going, and Henry James's letters seemed to her overly "involved and précieux," but she loved *Eminent Victorians*—"What a horrid fellow Cardinal Manning was," she remarked to Mary, "I always thought he was, now I know it"— and was captivated by Doughty's *Travels in Arabia Deserta*, with its elaborately throwback style and profound understanding of Bedouin life. "I actually said thank you in Arabic to Ida [her maid] yesterday, so full was I of Doughty," she told Mary. Reading the book must have brought Egypt, and especially the Abu Nishab festival, forcefully back to mind.

Another source of Egyptian nostalgia was the Berensons, who took an extended tour of the country beginning in the fall of 1921. Janet was, of course, full of advice and referrals, and Mary's frequent letters allowed her to track the Berensons' progress. The conjured image of Bernard riding a donkey made her laugh aloud, and in her return letter she expressed pity for whatever donkey Mary should happen to mount. (Though unhappy about her weight, Mary was a good sport when teased about it.) On hearing that Bernard was staggered by the sublimities of ancient Egypt, which he'd previously pooh-poohed, Janet replied, "I am delighted & rather amused at B.B.'s admiration for Egyptian art. When, now & then, I ventured to praise it, he looked so supercilious & bored that I held my tongue." Though mainly concerned for the Berensons' pleasure and safety, she didn't hesitate to ask for a favor, namely that they check on the condition of Lucie's grave. "If you have the time," she wrote when they reached Cairo, "do drive out one day & see what state her tomb is in." Mary, if not Bernard, clearly did so, for Janet wrote to thank her. "It is odd," she added, "what a hold [Lucie] has on people. A lady who was here a week ago told me some friends of hers had taken a lot of flowers to her grave after reading her Letters."

But the relatives about whom Janet mostly wrote to Mary during these months were not, like Lucie, dead and revered but living and (one of them) reviled. For she again found herself awash in Waterfields.

In the spring of 1921, Lina and Aubrey, burning to get back to Italy, had obtained an assignment to write and illustrate a feature on Italian villas and palazzi for *Country Life* magazine. The Fortezza della Brunella, which had been requisitioned as a garrison during the war, had more recently been turned into a shelter for those made homeless by a severe earthquake in the Lunigiana. Lina and Aubrey were therefore temporarily unable to use it as a base. Instead, they inflicted themselves, as well as Kinta and her governess, on Janet. (John was at boarding school back in England, while Gordon was at Oxford.)

By October they were all under Janet's roof, and she was venting to Mary nonstop about Aubrey's uselessness. "He was writing something," one indictment begins, "& I asked him why he did not type it. Answer: 'I have always refused to learn typing, or Lina would ask me to type her articles.' That paints him! How nice it will be to see his back." Though she mostly restrained herself from butting heads with Aubrey, she scored points where she could. Lina relates an anecdote that perfectly encapsulates the petty cold war of their relationship. One day Aubrey began to paint a branch of the magnolia tree on the terrace. Noticing this, Janet made disparaging remarks and suggested he desist. He ignored her and continued. But, Lina writes, "when he arrived next morning with his easel, he found that the whole branch he had been painting had been cut down. He gave up for he believed her quite capable of destroying the rest of the tree."

In December, to Janet's relief, Aubrey returned to England, in part because the *Country Life* assignment had fallen through. Lina, though, stayed on with Kinta and the governess. There now came a turning point in her life. Before arriving in Florence, she'd been commissioned by James Louis Garvin, the editor of *The Observer*, to cover the prolonged festivities commemorating the six-hundredth anniversary of Dante's death. ("Poor old Dante," Janet commented to Mary, "how bored he would be if he could hear and read all the rubbish people are howling and scribbling about him and his Beatrice.") Garvin himself happened to be in Florence that fall, and he came for dinner to Poggio Gherardo. Soon after, he decided to sack his Italian correspondent and offer the job to Lina, who'd clearly impressed him. For Lina, whose authorial interests had shifted from the past to the present, it was the chance of a lifetime, *The Observer* being one of the major British papers of its time and Italy being a hotbed of political strife and new ideologies.

She hit the ground running in early 1921, and was soon in the thick of things. By June 1922 she'd conducted the first of many interviews with Mussolini. As she recalls in *Castle in Italy*, Mussolini at first tried to use his repertoire of scowls and "curious grimaces" to impress or intimidate her, "but he only succeeded in making me want to laugh and I nearly choked in trying to suppress it. Of course he saw my amusement and with the swiftness of a good actor he dropped his bravado and changed his expression to one of friendly welcome as he shook hands with me."

A few months later she went to report on a Fascist rally in Cremona. Chatting with Mussolini beforehand, she twitted him about the Fascist anthem, "Giovinezza," of which she'd grown heartily sick. "My remark did not appear to annoy him; being musical, he was doubtless bored with it himself." After the rally, "Mussolini singled me out and asked if I had liked his speech. It was 'extraordinary,' I told him, using an adjective which often helped me when an awkward question was asked me. He turned to Cesare Rossi [one of his closest advisers] and told him to take care of me, but one look at his foxy face told me to lose myself in the crowd."

Then, in October, came the March on Rome. Lina, who'd left Rome for Florence just before, kicked herself for having missed out on the pivotal event of the Fascist takeover and thereby "let down *The Observer.*" Garvin, though, took it in stride and told her to carry on. At Florence's central station, she met up with pro-Fascist friends of hers returning from Rome. "Their train was garlanded with roses and they were in hilarious spirits although they had marched to Rome in pouring rain and their clothes were still damp. Their faces were radiant with joy and hope for the future. It was a moment of youth and Mussolini was leading them where they thought they wanted to go." Her own feeling was that "a terribly dangerous thing had happened," and her articles gradually became more critical of the new regime.

By now Kinta was no longer at Poggio Gherardo, having been sent back to England to attend boarding school. Unlike during the war, her most rewarding recent experiences hadn't taken place in the bosco and poderi but in the kitchen. In 1907 Giuseppe Volpi had retired and been replaced by a certain Agostino (surname unknown), previously an under-chef at I Tatti. "Such was his development as a master chef," Kinta writes, "that the Berensons, whenever they came to dinner, regretted their loss anew." Despite his virtuosity, Agostino was "the most modest of men," and very kind to Kinta. She spent much of her time watching him turn out delicacies like woodcock risotto, wild boar with chocolate, raisins, pine nuts, and vinegar, and *fragoline nelle ceste*, or raspberries in spun-sugar baskets. (Clearly Florence's food shortages were a thing of the past.) After six months of gorging on this kind of fare, she was brought up short by her English boarding school: "One glance, one sniff at the stodgy nursery food congealing on my plate in front of me was enough. With my mouth in my mind, I would dream of Agostino's delicate *fritti misti* . . . I nearly wept with longing." But she'd gotten a culinary education, or the beginnings of one, and a lifelong interest in cooking would result.

Lina, meanwhile, continued to base herself at Poggio Gherardo through most of 1922, after which she began staying there more irregularly, sometimes showing up alone and sometimes with Aubrey and one or more of her vacationing children in tow.

For over a year Aubrey filled in as the Italian correspondent for *The Manchester Guardian*, and he and Lina crisscrossed the peninsula in pursuit of stories. In 1923, when they went to Molinella, a village outside Bologna, to interview members of a Socialist collective who were being persecuted by the Fascists, they themselves were threatened, and briefly arrested.

The following year they were finally able not only to return to the Fortezza della Brunella but to buy it (presumably from the heirs of Monty Brown, who'd died in 1921). Around the same time, at a reception in Rome, they had an uncomfortable exchange with Mussolini, who liked to needle them in a half-joking, half-menacing manner about the Molinella incident. Lina reconstructs the scene in *Castle in Italy*:

> Mussolini paused as he drew near Aubrey and me. 'Do you still remember Molinella?' he asked.
>
> 'Who could forget it?' I was getting tired of this constant reference to that episode.
>
> 'What other serious thing have you been doing?' he asked—as much as to say, 'What mischief have you been up to?'
>
> 'We are buying the Fortress at Aulla,' I answered, laughing.
>
> 'Good gracious—English people buying an Italian fortress. This is serious and the State must look into the matter.'
>
> 'It is even more serious than you think,' Aubrey added, 'for the Fortezza dominates the road your Excellency takes when you travel from Rome to Milan.'

Despite all this jocularity, the Waterfields knew that their unflattering reportage—not to mention their friendships with dissident figures like Gaetano Salvemini and Giovanni Amendola—was irksome to the regime; Mussolini made this explicit when, some months later, he sent Lina "a message through the Prefect of Florence that I had better be careful what I wrote in *The Observer*." Their British passports would probably keep them from harm, but deportation was a real risk—an alarming one, given their attachment to Italy and hard-won ownership of the fortress.

Though Aubrey lost his post when the *Guardian* hired a permanent correspondent, Lina continued to report, with increasing sharpness, on the brutality of Fascism, which had reached new heights with the murder of the Socialist parliamentarian Giacomo Matteotti. Under the circumstances, it was brave of her to do so. In her readiness to annoy a foreign tyrant—Mussolini—on his own turf, she resembles her grandmother Lucie, who openly criticized Ismail in *Letters from Egypt*.

As for Lina's fellow Anglo-Florentines, few of them matched her defiance, and some were openly pro-Fascist. The majority played ostrich. "As foreigners we kept aloof," Harold Acton recalls. "My father continued to improve his garden and his collection of paintings, undisturbed." Mussolini, he adds, "was referred to as Mr. Smith or Brown." While few colonists were quite as blasé as Arthur Acton, most tried to go about their business and convince themselves that the Fascists, whatever their excesses, were just the chaps to put Italy back on the rails.

Such self-persuasion must have become more difficult after October 1925, when Florentine Blackshirts murdered eight liberals and Masons in broad daylight. And another shiver of fear must have run through the colony when, six months later, the deranged Violet Gibson tried to assassinate Mussolini in Rome, putting a bullet through his nose. (Lina witnessed the shooting.) Like Lady Sybil Scott, Gibson was an Anglo-Irish aristocrat, and Mussolini might have been expected to retaliate against her fellow Britons. But he didn't, and life went on.

Janet's own views fell somewhere between Lina's and the avoidant or rose-tinted ones typical of the colony. Early on she'd applauded the Fascists for their suppression of the Socialists, whom she loathed. Yet she soon realized they were no different from the local thugs who'd stolen her horse, cart, and agricultural products. Lina recalls the following incident, presumably from 1921: "One day . . . a group of young Black Shirts irrupted into Poggio and demanded money for 'the cause.' Aunt Janet met them in the corridor and ordered them not to smoke in her house. They put out their cigarettes. Yes, she would give them money but they must sign a receipt, which they did to her surprise . . . I think they were hypnotised by her eyes fixed upon them. She sent in their names to the Prefect of Florence who had them arrested." Increasingly skeptical of the Fascists, Janet also refused to be alarmed by them, remaining confident that, as she put it in a 1923 letter to Mary, they wouldn't "dare do anything to 'forestieri' [foreigners]." What they'd already done to their fellow Italians seemed to give her little pause.

Even if the political developments of the mid-1920s failed to rouse Janet, these years did see a final flowering of her energies. Not that they'd ever waned, but surviving the hardships of the postwar period had taken her full attention. Now, with everyday life in Florence less of a struggle, she could branch out again. In 1923 she put together a collection of the many fine letters written to her by Rev. Lindsay.* In the same year, for the first time in over a decade, she went to England, where she saw Will Meredith and the immunologist Sir Almwroth Wright, who'd stayed with her several times in Florence. Mary accompanied her on the journey, and persuaded her, against the advice of her doctor, to do the Paris-to-London leg by plane. "I induced Aunt Janet to fly," Mary exulted to Bernard, "and she thoroughly enjoyed it."

Above all, she made new friends. One was Count Umberto Morra, an amiable Piedmontese belletrist close to Bernard and Mary. (He would later publish the Boswellian *Conversations with Berenson*.) Janet's friendship with Morra was casual, but that with Filippo de Filippi became important to her. Born in 1869, de Filippi was one of the boldest Italian explorers of his day, best known for having led an expedition to Central Asia in 1913. About a decade later he moved into the Villa Capponcina, previously occupied by D'Annunzio, and met Janet, whom he persuaded to undertake an English translation

*The book, which was published under the title *Letters of Principal T. M. Lindsay to Janet Ross*, was the last to appear during her lifetime.

of the travel writings of Ippolito Desideri, an eighteenth-century Jesuit who was among the first Westerners to penetrate Tibet.* He also occasioned one of the great Rossian utterances. Lina, who overhead it, sets the scene. Janet was at work on a translation—presumably of Desideri—when de Filippi unexpectedly dropped by:

> "You are just the person I want, Filippo. Now what is the equator?"
>
> "It is an imaginary line circling the earth," he answered, much amused.
>
> "Imaginary line!" she repeated contemptuously. "I never heard of anything so ridiculous."

There had always been strange gaps in her knowledge, but this one, preserved into her ninth decade, has to be the most astonishing.

While Janet often had de Filippi, Morra, and others over to Poggio Gherardo, she had fewer overnight guests than in the old days. One of these, however, stands out, both for the fame he later achieved—more than anyone, he connects Janet to modern times—and for the droll record he left of her. He also happened to have a rather knotty relationship to her neighbors and extended family.

Forty-odd years before *Civilisation* made him a transatlantic television celebrity, Kenneth Clark was a newly minted Oxford graduate and a protégé of Charles F. Bell, head of Fine Arts at the Ashmolean Museum. In September 1925 Bell, an old friend of Janet's, went to stay with her and brought Clark along.

Clark's first taste of Janet's signature peremptoriness came right away. Bell had become ill during the journey, and on arrival was near collapse. As Clark recalls in his memoirs, "Mrs Ross looked at him with silent disapproval. 'I think he ought to go to bed,' I said. 'Bed! What nonsense! I've never spent a day in bed in my life.'" Bell crawled off to bed anyway, and the twenty-two-year-old Clark was

---

*Though Janet finished the translation before her death, for some reason it appeared only in 1932, under the title *An Account of Tibet: The Travels of Ippolito Desideri of Pistoia, S.J. 1712–1727*, with a preface by de Filippi.

left alone with his octogenarian hostess. "Being interested in history," Clark writes, "I was anxious to question this living document, and did so at my first dinner." Like Nicky Mariano, he got nowhere: "You'll find all that in my books" was her irritable response. After dinner he had a look at her personal copies of these books, then tried "to extract some marginalia from the author." Again he was stymied. He went to bed fed up with her, but the next morning he had an epiphany of sorts: "when . . . I went to find Mrs Ross, who, from a vantage point on the terrace, was superintending the work of her *contadini*, I felt that yearning for the long tradition of Mediterranean life . . . that has fascinated Northern man since Goethe."

Later that day Clark had another transformative experience. He and Bell had been invited for lunch at I Tatti, and Clark, who'd revered Berenson for years, couldn't wait to meet his idol. In the event, he was taken aback by Berenson's arrogance and conceived "the strongest possible dislike to him." But the antipathy was far from mutual. Poised and intellectually precocious to the highest degree, Clark made such an impression on Berenson that he was spontaneously offered a job: Would Clark help prepare a new edition of Berenson's book *Florentine Drawings*? Berenson was due to leave for Vienna the next day, and Clark, needing time to consider, promised to give him an answer on his return.

Clark spent another week at Poggio Gherardo, mulling over his future. Janet, he writes, "had made up her mind to like me"—a good thing, since Bell remained bedridden. Each night at dinner Clark knocked back a quantity of her vermouth and, full of Dutch courage, tried to loosen Janet's tongue. Eventually he cajoled her into serving up some morsels of gossip: "Like all Victorians of the upper class she resolutely disbelieved that anyone (except the eldest son) was the child of his or her father, and came out with some staggering deviations which would have amused historians of the Holland House set."*

After Bell recovered, Clark joined him on a tour of southern Tuscany and Umbria. When they returned to Poggio Gherardo a

---

*Centering on the third Baron Holland and his wife, this circle of Whig politicians and literati included several figures from Janet's youth, such as Samuel Rogers and Lord Macaulay.

few weeks later, Janet invited Clark to stay on for as long as he wanted, and offered him "the set of rooms . . . that had been occupied by John Addington Symonds." Evidently she was as taken by the young prodigy as Berenson.

Though Clark declined her offer, he did make plans to return to Florence in the spring, having finally agreed to live and work at I Tatti on a trial basis. During his one-month stay, he spent more time with Aunt Janet (as he was now permitted to call her), who told Clark that his "character had deteriorated since the previous autumn" but remained friendly. After a stretch back in England, Clark came to Florence yet again in the fall of 1926 and spent several months working at I Tatti and traveling with the Berensons around northern Italy. In January 1927 he rushed home to get married, then whisked his new bride, the former Jane Martin, off to Settignano, where Mary had arranged housing for the couple in a converted cloister; the immediate plan was for Clark to finish updating *Florentine Drawings*, but he was expected to stick around indefinitely, helping with other projects.

In his memoirs, Clark acknowledges that his decision to marry had produced consternation at both I Tatti and Poggio Gherardo: "The announcement pleased nobody. Nicky said to me, almost with tears, 'But Kenneth, we hoped you would have such wonderful affairs.' Mrs Ross said 'I don't know what he wants to get married for when he can live with me,' to which Mr Berenson replied 'There's no accounting for tastes, Aunt Janet.'" Clark also lays bare the awkward circumstances surrounding his engagement. Jane had previously been engaged to an Oxford friend of his. When this friend left to take up a job in Cairo, he asked Clark to keep an eye on his fiancée. It was, Clark writes, "a classic situation," and it played itself out in the expected way, though with a quintessentially English minimum of fuss: the dumped friend, according to Clark, "received the news without bitterness or resentment and is still a friend."

One detail Clark neglects to mention is that this friend, left anonymous in his memoirs, was none other than Gordon Waterfield. In 1925 Gordon had gone to Egypt to learn the cotton business, with a view toward joining an import firm in Manchester run

by one of his Waterfield uncles. Whatever show of good sportsman-
ship Gordon made, he can't have been unwounded, and the fact that
Kenneth and Jane were now ensconced in Settignano must have
rankled.

As for Janet, it's unclear when she learned of Clark's bride-
poaching and whether she held it against him. His biographer claims
that Lina and Aubrey had considered Jane a poor match for their
son, and if so their relief at the broken engagement might have been
shared by Janet. Yet Janet's behavior toward Jane on their first
meeting was less than gracious. Clark recalls being nervous when he
brought Jane to live near "two ogres' castles, I Tatti and Poggio
Gherardo." Berenson was as chilly toward her as he'd feared, but Janet was even worse: "The old dragon, in her best Ouida form,
would not speak to Jane at all, but led me off through the long suite
of rooms, leaving Jane with a canary." One suspects that Janet's
hostility toward Jane had less to do with Gordon than with her having stripped Clark of his carefree bachelordom.

The Clarks ended up spending two years in Settignano, and they
somehow braved several more meetings with Janet. But there can't
have been many, for she was dying.

———⊷⊶⊷———

When Janet's cancer was diagnosed and what form it took are unclear, but by the spring of 1927 she was noticeably failing.

Mary at first took the lead in caring for her, and when she
had to be out of town for a few weeks she arranged for Katharine
Furse to come watch over her. When Mary returned in May, she
found Janet so much worse that she summoned Lina, who'd been
on assignment in Naples. Except for one brief trip to Aulla, Lina
stayed at her aunt's bedside for the duration, which was agonizingly
protracted.

All through the scorching summer she hung on, sinking only to
rally again. Dr. Giglioli, who'd been her physician for twenty-five
years—it was he who'd attended her in Bagni di Lucca after Henry's
death—often came to check on her. After some fierce resistance, Lina

persuaded her to get a nurse as well; when the nurse arrived to take up her duties, Janet's first words to her were, "Take off that ridiculous cap!" Though Janet put up with the nurse's ministrations, she complained, as Lina reported to Mary, of feeling "like a hunted beast" and declared "that she meant to keep her independence to the last gasp." Stubbornly she beavered away at her last piece of work, namely a translation of the travel writings of Francesco Carletti, a Florentine merchant who circumnavigated the globe around 1600.* She also amused herself by lambasting "the usual bêtes noires in her old vigorous way," by swatting flies, and by scolding Lina for "not killing them properly. 'No good hitting them like that' she says."

Another source of pleasure was a letter mailed to her from Kashmir by the explorer and archaeologist Sir Aurel Stein, who'd just read *The Fourth Generation*. Where Mark Twain had once had American corn and watermelon seeds sent to her, Stein tucked some Himalayan wildflower seeds into his letter. "As [the seeds] pass the Suez Canal," he wrote, "they are to make my salaams to scenes of your equestrian exploits." Perhaps these exploits, along with other wind-in-hair memories of freedom on horseback, played through her mind as the cancer advanced.

By July she was so emaciated that her "Halim Pasha bangle" (as Lina terms it) would no longer stay on her wrist; she'd worn the bracelet continuously for sixty-six years, and was much upset at having to put it away. Over the following weeks she deteriorated rapidly, and on August 23 the end finally came. "I had gone out into the vineyards for a walk," Lina writes in *Castle in Italy*, "when the big bell in the tower rang for me to return. Aunt Janet had passed away very quietly."

The contadini were allowed to kneel and pray over Janet's body, but she'd been adamant about not having a religious service or funereal pomp of any sort. After she was cremated, Lina took the urn containing her ashes to Trespiano and placed it next to the one con-

---

*Her translation, *Voyages of Francesco Carletti, 1594–1602*, was published posthumously.

taining Henry's. And that was that. Even if Holman Hunt had been around to sculpt her an ornate tomb like his wife's, or Elizabeth Barrett Browning's, or any of the other gaudy Anglo-Florentine monuments in the English Cemetery, she wouldn't have wanted it. "What nonsense!" she would have said. "How ridiculous!"

Who was Janet Ross? Kenneth Clark describes her as "the most completely extrovert human being I have ever known," and as being so literal-minded that "she could not take in an abstract concept." The day before her death, Lina wrote the following in a letter to Mary: "Her life has been a starved one—its apparent fullness has consisted mostly of façade-dazzle." Lina wasn't given to such bleak conclusions, and this one should be taken with a grain of salt. Yet both Lina and Clark get at a fundamental truth: there was something stunted or incomplete about Janet. There are also moral charges to be leveled against her. She was often outrageously unfair to her own sex. Her treatment of Alick was nothing short of shameful, and her stubborn frostiness toward Lina in later years does not reflect well on her. "A wicked old lady," Mary wrote in her diary after hearing an especially vitriolic diatribe against Lina and Aubrey. Ouida of course thought her evil incarnate.

But the majority of remarks emanating from those who knew her are complimentary. Despite her cantankerousness and vindictive streak, she was recognized as being essentially large-hearted. In a short memoir of Janet written after her death, Mary stressed this point, adducing the intensity of Janet's grief after Frank Crisp was killed in 1915: "If anyone could have seen her, as I did, how she literally crumpled up, like a twisted piece of paper, and could have heard her groans of sorrow, they would never have questioned the warmth of her affection." Men tended to like her straightforwardness and lack of conventional femininity. In a letter to Edmund Gosse, Symonds described her as "a thorough *bon camarade*," and Meredith praised her for being "one of those rare women who don't find it necessary to flutter their sex under your nose eternally in order to make you like them." Nearly everyone admired her vigor and self-assurance; as her Anglo-Sicilian friend Tina Whitaker put it her diary, Janet was "a legend of physical and intellectual vitality and character." Many were struck as well by the richness of her past and her knack for evoking it. "There is no one from 1842 onward that Mrs. Ross has not known, and known well," Alice Meynell wrote in a letter from Poggio Gherardo, and Neith Boyce observes in her memoirs that Janet "links up to times already historical and brings them to life."

While many of Janet's qualities were evident from early childhood, they were hugely strengthened and refined by her later experience, and by living abroad in particular. Egypt enriched her, but it was Italy that brought out her full potential. To be sure, certain foreigners have become more completely assimilated into Italian life, amassed a greater knowledge of Italian history and culture, and spoken the language more impeccably. (Janet, Clark noted, "knew Italian perfectly but spoke it with a Churchillian defiance of accent.") But nobody has been more at ease with Italian society at every level. "Don't go with that awful tourist idea that Italy's only a museum," urges one of the characters in Forster's *Where Angels Fear to Tread*. "Love and understand the Italians, for the people are more marvelous." Though Janet would have scoffed at this sentimental injunction, she had an unforced affinity with Italians from all walks of life, and it's hard to picture anyone else going quite so seamlessly from, say, Dr. Biagi's office in the Laurentian Library to a sharecropper's podere, from light, bookish discussion of the early Medici to hard talk of a grape-menacing early frost.

Janet's rapport with peasants and ordinary working people was unusual in itself. The difference between her attitude and the casual Ruskinian disdain more typical of the colony can be gauged by means of a passage in John Lane's *In a Tuscan Garden* (1902) that warns aspiring garden-creators what to expect of the local labor pool: "Here, in democratic Tuscany, where the 'I am as good as you' spirit prevails, if you leave them alone for ever so short a time, you will find something has been done the direct opposite of what you wished and intended. Italians are the most conceited people on the face of the earth." Rather than noisome, Janet found the Tuscan spirit of presumed equality refreshing, and overall she held contadini in higher regard than counts—"If the gentlemen were half as good as the so-called lower classes," she once remarked to Kinglake, "things would go much better here."

Not that she was the least bit uncomfortable wielding power. "Aunt Janet is a great ruler," Madge wrote from Poggio Gherardo in 1912.* "Besides all her farms and farmers, she has thirty servants and labourers under her own thumb and she tells them all what to do and how to do it." According to Kinta, "The *contadini* on Aunt Janet's farms were said to have held her in such awe that none of them dared cheat on the *mezzadria* share-out." But her autocratic style was, in Kinta's words, "tempered by a matriarchal indulgence." A striking example was her custom, in later years, of summoning Giglioli whenever one of her sharecroppers was taken ill. "Fellow landowners," Kinta writes, "considered her most eccentric to send such a grand doctor." This generosity stemmed in part from a sense of noblesse oblige, but there was also an element of identification at play. In her agricultural instincts and hardheaded practicality, Janet was very much like the peasants who worked her land. "They appreciated each other's thrift, hers Scottish, theirs Tuscan," Harold Acton observes.

In the end, perhaps the most remarkable thing about Janet was her ability to find common ground with so many people despite her somewhat choleric and contrary nature. Another of Forster's exhortations (this one now a chestnut) comes to mind: "Only connect!" She did so, over and over and over.

---

*Madge's 1912 visit to Poggio Gherardo was her first since the 1890s, and the last she ever made. Her later life was far less fulfilling than Lina's: unhappy with her marriage and with playing the role of headmaster's wife (her husband worked his way up to the prestigious Rugby School), she lost her effervescence and wrote almost nothing, one exception being "Memoirs of Mrs. Janet Ross," which dates from about 1922. Making it only to fifty-six, she died in 1925—the same year, ironically, that Virginia Woolf immortalized her as Sally Seton in *Mrs. Dalloway*.

EPILOGUE
Legacies

G iven that the life of Janet Ross was full of novelistic scenes and motifs, it seems only appropriate that there was a posthumous twist, one taking the classic Victorian form of a disinheritance.

Despite her distant relationship with Alick, Janet had given the impression that she planned to leave him Poggio Gherardo. When her will was read, however, the castle turned out to have been bequeathed to John Waterfield, with a life interest for Lina.

After trading stocks for a time in the 1890s, Alick had become a tutor to the sons of a Russian grand duke in St. Petersburg. He'd come to Florence for Henry's funeral in 1902, which may have been the last time Janet saw him. After serving as an intelligence officer in the First World War, he'd moved to Vienna, then Budapest, where he'd worked for six years as a Reuters correspondent. Enraged at being cheated of Poggio Gherardo, he now challenged Janet's will before an English court. After losing the case in 1929, he returned to Hungary. Virtually nothing more is known of him, and the date and manner of his death remain a mystery.

Lina, who'd found Alick creepy on their few meetings, was only too pleased to have her son displace him as heir to Poggio Gherardo. Her own continued access to the castle was a great bonus, especially since Aulla made a poor base for her journalism. Though she and Aubrey kept the Fortezza della Brunella, Poggio Gherardo became their primary residence. Yet they faced difficulties beyond Alick's lawsuit. Money was tight and the estate in need of repairs. Most grating of all, Davide Torrini resisted their authority: according to Lina, he argued that she and Aubrey "knew nothing about farming" and wanted "the entire management of the property to remain in his own hands." Like many others, the Waterfields found Davide insufferable, but they could see no way to get rid of him without a fracas. Then came a stroke of exquisite luck. "One day," Lina writes, "I received a mysterious message from a Milanese merchant who had an office in Florence and asked me to come and see him. On his desk was a large bottle with a garish label depicting three towers, which were the newly invented crest of Davide Torrini. The merchant had been suspicious of the offer of vermouth from Davide and made inquiries." Davide had, in other words, been passing off Poggio Gherardo vermouth as his own brand. How long he'd been perpetrating the fraud is unclear, but Lina now had him dead to rights, and he "left without any trouble, for he had committed a serious penal offence."

Though she lacked her aunt's profound knowledge of agriculture, Lina kept the estate functioning, and even found lucrative new outlets (such as Fortnum & Mason) for its vermouth, which she learned to make. But she and Aubrey were still having trouble paying the bills, and in 1931 they decided to turn the castle into a finishing school for young ladies—the Poggio Gherardo School, they called it. In their brochure, the Waterfields declared that their chief aims were "to teach the rudiments of aesthetics" and "to train girls to use their eyes." ("Ruskin," they added, "taught insistently that one of the most difficult things in life is to learn to see.") The school caught on, with ten or twelve students attending at a time. Except for its strict rules—students were not allowed to go into town alone—it bore a resemblance to the year-abroad programs offered by so many colleges these days, in Florence and elsewhere. Students learned Italian history from Lina, the Italian language from a moonlighting University of Florence professor, drawing and art history from Aubrey, and cooking from Agostino. The Berensons gave them the run of their library, and Kinta, who was living with her parents at the time, took them on field trips all over Tuscany and Umbria in a big Fiat convertible.

Unlike her teenage passengers, Kinta enjoyed a measure of independence, and in *A Tuscan Childhood* she paints a somewhat racy picture of her life in the early 1930s, when she spent her free time carousing with "Florence's version of the Bright Young Things." Her days as a bachelorette came to an end in December 1933, when she married John ("Jack") Beevor, who worked as a lawyer in London. Returning favors the Rosses had done for them more than thirty years earlier, the Berensons insisted on having Jack stay at I Tatti before the wedding and on throwing a lavish dinner for him and Kinta. They were married by the mayor of Florence at the Palazzo Vecchio. After a skiing honeymoon in the Alps, they settled in London, though they frequently returned to Florence and Aulla on visits.

John Waterfield too was often in Italy during the mid-1930s, and Gordon briefly held a posting there. Having dropped the cotton trade for journalism, Gordon had worked for several years for *The Egyptian Gazette* and the London *Times* before joining Reuters and getting himself sent to Rome, along with his wife, Kitty, whom he'd married in 1929. Within a year he managed to so irritate the Fascist authorities that he was kicked out of the country, after which Reuters posted him to Paris. But he remained close to his parents and siblings, and had already begun to assume Janet's former role of family historian, publishing a biography of Lucie in 1937.

Lina, meanwhile, somehow avoided expulsion and continued reporting on Italy for *The Observer*. In 1934 she was in Venice for the very first meeting between Mussolini and Hitler, and the following year she attended the Stresa conference, which resulted in a short-lived pact between Italy, France, and Britain. But she and Garvin had long differed in their views on Fascism, and the Italian invasion of Abyssinia in October 1935 brought things to a head. "Garvin realised," she writes, "that the political gulf between us was too wide to bridge and terminated my work with *The Observer*." In another setback, she fell and broke her hip so badly that she had to lie in a plaster cast for three months. "All the family deities of Aunt

Janet's sitting-room look down upon me," she told Kinta, "and I feel so out of touch with their Victorian serenity I sometimes expect a voice from Aunt Janet's chair in the window to exclaim: 'How could you be so silly as to slip up and break your hip? I suppose you were wearing high-heeled shoes." She never healed completely and was lame for the rest of her life, getting about only on crutches.

In August 1939, at Gordon's urging, the Waterfields fled Italy. After three boring months in a cottage in Kent, they decided to go back, the Phoney War having lulled them into a false sense of security. "Right into the spring of 1940," Kinta writes, "they persuaded themselves they had done the right thing in returning to Tuscany." Then came the Nazi invasion of the Low Countries and France. That Italy might jump into the conflict suddenly seemed far likelier, and the Waterfields suspected that, as Lina puts it, "owing to our anti-Fascist opinions we would not fare well." A friend at the British embassy in Rome "promised to keep us informed of Mussolini's intentions under the cover of 'Grandmother's health.' During the next couple of weeks he sent us constant bulletins, and finally we received a telegram saying: 'Grandmother seriously ill and needs your presence.'" On June 9, one day before Italy's declaration of war, they caught the last train across the French border. "We realized our luck later, when we heard that Black Shirts had gone to Poggio Gherardo to arrest us and, not finding us, had hurried to Aulla feeling sure they would catch us there."

The Waterfields first found a house to rent near Oxford, then a flat in London. By way of Gordon, they already had two grandchildren, Michael and Harriet, and the war years brought them three more: Nigel Beevor and Garrow Waterfield, born within weeks of each other in 1941, and Hugh Beevor, born in 1943. Garrow was the son of John and his wife, Daphne, whom he'd married in 1939. Having been posted to Malta when Garrow was in utero, John hadn't yet met his son. He never would, for on Garrow's first birthday John was killed in action at age thirty-two, drawing his last breath on the island where Henry Ross had drawn his first. Lina merely states the fact of John's death in *Castle in Italy*, but her grief, like Aubrey's, was surely terrible. Two years later another blow fell, this time on Lina alone: Aubrey had been failing for some time, and in the spring of 1944 he died, age seventy.

A private man who left few written traces, Aubrey is difficult to appraise. Janet was by no means alone in disliking him. After hearing of his plan to buy the Fortezza della Brunella in 1924, Mary Berenson wrote in her diary that "the Great Interpreter of the Carraras"* (as she mockingly dubbed him) was "one of the most selfish men I ever knew . . . Lina is clearly the superior person, and the bread winner, but he sulks and scolds and insists on snatching her away to that remote place where he can paint pictures which no one will buy and she cannot do their journalism on which they live." Given that Mary's own husband was one of the most petulantly demanding men on the planet, this indictment is hard to dismiss. Aubrey was also, by all accounts, hot-tempered and martinetish. One of his students at the Poggio Gherardo School recollects that he threatened her with expulsion when he caught her with a color reproduction of a painting—such things were anathema to him. But his uncompromising aesthetic purity could, under the right circumstances, seem admirable. Nicky Mariano recalls a visit she and Bernard paid to him at the fortress in 1928: "Aubrey Waterfield, who tended to be peevish and dissatisfied at Poggio Gherardo . . . was at his best at Aulla, looking after his garden, painting his lovely flower compositions, and living the unconventional life he loved."

For her part, Lina seems to have taken Aubrey's inconsiderate ways and financial uselessness in stride. Theirs had been an impractical love match from the start, and the marriage was clearly successful in the main. "It is often said of my parents," Kinta notes, "that they had all the luxuries of life but none of the necessities." Such a state of affairs would never have suited Janet, but Lina was content with it.

As the war wound down, Lina's anxieties focused on Poggio Gherardo, which now, after John's death, belonged to her outright. She was much relieved when, in September 1944, Jack Beevor wrote

---

*Famous for their marble quarries, the Carrara Mountains are located to the south of Aulla but are visible from the fortress, and Aubey often painted them.

to say that it had suffered only cosmetic damage, even though the Germans had mounted a machine gun on the terrace during a recent battle. That winter, the castle was requisitioned by American troops, and Lina received an update on its condition from her friend Captain Roderick Enthoven. The Americans, Enthoven discovered, had painted over some of the frescoes in the Poodle Room so that they could project movies on one of its walls. After remonstrating with the officer in charge, Enthoven marched him down to I Tatti, where he showed Berenson a can of the offending paint. Not to worry, Berenson said: by chance, the Americans had used a kind of whitewash ideal for preserving frescoes. According to Kinta, the officer "was so overcome with relief and gratitude that B.B. called for some vermouth to fortify him."

Unlike the Waterfields, the Berensons had tried to ride out the war in Florence. But when the Germans took control of the city in September 1943, it became too dangerous for Bernard, as an anti-Fascist and a Jew by birth, to live in the open, and he took refuge in a nearby villa belonging to a diplomat of the Republic of San Marino, which enjoyed extraterritorial status. Mary, however, was too ill to be moved, and she remained at I Tatti under the care of Nicky's sister. A year later Bernard was able to return to I Tatti, where he found Mary in poorer health than ever. Over the following months she faded away, dying in March 1945, at age eighty-one.

For Lina, who'd been as fond of Mary as Janet, it was yet another painful loss, and she might have been expected to cut her ties to Italy, as a place too full of ghosts. But the country still exerted its old pull on her, and she began to contemplate a return. Bernard urged her to get back into journalism: "I doubt," he wrote, "whether England just now has another writer with such insight or such capacity for interpreting Italian affairs as you." Encouraged, she accepted an offer from Ian Fleming, future creator of James Bond, to serve as the Italian correspondent for *The Sunday Times*, and in January 1946, age seventy-one, she headed for Florence once again.

The welcome she received at Poggio Gherardo was moving in its warmth. "The peasants, men, women and children, all troop in to welcome me," she wrote to her friend Victor Cunard. "The older women kiss me, some weep talking of Johnny and Aubrey . . . They are beloved people and very loyal to our family." Even though the customs of mezzadria had been eroding for years, she found the estate's contadini atavistically eager to honor them. "My new *fattore*," she continued in her letter to Cunard, "expressed surprise at the devotion of these Tuscan peasants to their English *padroni*. He says mine are wonderful and would not let him cut down a truncated cypress or settle other matters '*finché non viene la padrona*' [until the padrona comes]." To her amazement, one contadino even asked her permission for his son to marry.

The estate itself, however, was in worse shape than she'd realized. During the recent fighting, the Allies had parked their armored cars in the poderi, causing extensive damage, and the castle had been so thoroughly looted that only a few pieces of furniture remained. Already hard-pressed to cover the expense of repairing, replanting, and restocking Poggio Gherardo, she was dismayed to learn that she'd have to pay heavy death duties on it to the Italian government. To make ends meet, she turned the castle into a sort of informal hotel, advertised by word of mouth. "In that post-war world of austerity and rationing," writes Kinta, who often came to stay, "the thought of good wine and perfectly cooked food fresh from the farms, as well as the peace of Poggio and its views across Florence, proved irresistible."

By 1950 the struggle to keep the estate afloat had become too much for Lina, and she put it on the market. Though determined that it not be broken up, she was, in Kinta's words, "taken in by a speculator," who retained the poderi for future sale (he later turned a large profit on them) and flipped the castle, along with a few surrounding acres, to a Catholic order that wanted to turn it into an orphanage. "How sad for me that you have left Poggio Gherardo," Berenson wrote to her. "I can't tell you how much I took it for granted that you would keep watch and guard there for ever."

She did, however, still have the use of the Fortezza della Brunella, which Aubrey had left to Gordon. The fortress had been substantially damaged during the war, by American artillery and the explosion of an ammunition train in the valley below (the town of Aulla had been flattened by the same blast), but by 1950 it had been repaired, and Lina moved back into it. While often visited by her children and grandchildren—who now included Antony Beevor, born in 1946—and friends like Gaetano Salvemini and Freya Stark,* then living in Asolo, she was often lonely, and the fortress, with its steep approach and sheer drops all around, was no place for a woman of her age and hobbled condition; just to get in and out of it, she had to be carried by two local men in (as Kinta describes it) "an improvised sedan chair made from a high-backed carver, with poles lashed to the arms." In 1952 she finally gave up on Tuscany and went to live with Kinta, who by that point was in Kent.

Kinta herself, however, maintained a relationship with the province, taking her sons to Aulla each summer. She also extended the connection between her family and that of Lady Sybil. After finally divorcing Geoffrey Scott in 1926, Sybil had married the man of letters Percy Lubbock, known for his friendships with, and thoughtful writings on, Henry James and Edith Wharton. ("That is the third of my friends she has annexed," hissed Wharton, who'd been close to Scott as well as Cutting.) In 1929 Aubrey had alerted the Lubbocks to a beautiful piece of land for sale on the Tuscan coast near Lerici, and after buying it they'd had Pinsent build them a house, Gli Scafari, where they'd spent a good part of the 1930s. Both had fled to Switzerland during the war, and Sybil had died there in 1943. After the war Lubbock had retired to Gli Scafari, where he was often visited by his stepdaughter, Iris. Her life had taken a different course. In 1924 she'd married a native Florentine, the Marchese Antonio Origo, and moved with him to La Foce, a large mezzadria estate in the Val d'Orcia region of southern Tuscany. Though she did not, like Janet Ross, involve herself much with the agricultural side of her estate, which she left largely to her husband, she was deeply committed to the well-being of its sharecroppers and their families, and had established a school for local children that went far beyond Janet's doposcuola program in scope, rigor, and longevity.

---

*Dame Freya Stark (1893–1993) was a sort of female Sir Richard Burton who explored and wrote about vast stretches of the Middle East.

In the early 1930s she'd begun to write the learned, elegant books—nearly all of them on Italian subjects—that would make her reputation. About the same time she'd had an affair with Gordon Waterfield, who'd once hoped to marry her. Though she'd broken it off after a few months, she remained friends with Kinta, who in the 1950s routinely brought her three boys from Aulla down to Gli Scafari, where they played with Iris's daughters, Benedetta and Donata.

Back in England, Lina published *Castle in Italy* in 1961. Three years later, having just reached ninety, she died. As with Janet, there are things to be said against her. Some of the same things, in fact: as Kinta remarks, "She had little time for other women and even less for children." Although, like Janet, she had many female friends, she preferred the company of men, especially those of intellect and power. In 1918, after celebrations for the birthday of King Emmanuel III, who'd succeeded Umberto, Janet reported to Mary that Lina had been "the only woman on the balcony of Pal.[azzo] Vecchio . . . with Prefect, Syndic, Generals, etc.," and being the only woman on the balcony, so to speak, was always a comfortable position for her. As for her attitude toward children, it's telling that in *Castle in Italy* she gets the year of birth wrong for two out of three of her own, namely John and Kinta.

Near the end of her life, Lina apologized to Kinta for her maternal neglect, but her sharpest pangs of remorse had to do with Janet and the rift between them, which was never entirely bridged. "My great regret," she writes, "is to have been tongue-tied at crucial moments when a few words might have cleared away much unhappiness. Aunt Janet was also loath to show her real feelings and I realised too late how much she loved me. She, too, never knew my feelings of love and admiration for her. A wall seemed to separate us at times and there was even a streak of Scottish dourness in both of us."

Whatever her emotional shortcomings (many of which were more generational then personal), there is also a great deal to be said in Lina's favor. She was mettlesome, enterprising, principled, loyal, and conscientious. Unlike Janet, she knew when to bite her tongue, and nobody deplored her manners. And where Janet was mostly concerned with the past and her family's place in it, Lina was, or least became, an engaged, well-informed, endlessly curious student of her own turbulent times. In 1954 Berenson—not one to pay compliments lightly—set down the following in his diary: "Lina through life has written on Italian politics, and has done it with such candor, such freedom from bile, that she won not only the respect but the confidence of Mussolini himself, and *a fortiori* of others to whom she was far less opposed." While this may be an exaggeration as far as Mussolini is concerned, Lina's journalism was clearly admired in its day, and one can only imagine the obstacles that, as one of the few women in the field, she had to overcome in producing it—Fascist Italy did not lack for male chauvinism. Like her aunt, she was nothing if not indomitable.

Ever since 1952, when Lina had returned to England, the Fortezza della Brunella had been kept up and watched over by Vittorio and Maria Chiodetti, an Aullese couple who'd long worked for the Waterfields in various capacities. But in 1977 they retired, and Gordon decided to sell the fortress to the comune of Aulla, which stripped it of all Aubrey's embellishments and turned it into a natural history museum.*

With the fortress and Poggio Gherardo out of its hands, the family no longer held real estate in Tuscany. But its sense of connection to the province, and to Aunt Janet, remained strong. In 1973 Gordon's son Michael Waterfield, a chef, had edited and illustrated a new edition of *Leaves from our Tuscan Kitchen* for Penguin—"I'd always been interested in my great-great-aunt Janet," he writes in his preface, "having heard about her adventurous life from my family"— and he continued to cook from its recipes at his restaurant in Kent, The Wife of Bath, which for years was considered one of Britain's best. Gordon himself, meanwhile, became increasingly obsessed with his ancestors. In the 1940s he'd published two more books—

---

*It remains a natural history museum to this day, but unfortunately not a good one, its paltry exhibits of ill-stuffed woodland creatures looking forlorn and ridiculous in their austere fortress setting.

one about the Fall of France, the other about his wartime experiences in Africa, the Middle East, and Asia—but had subsequently moved into broadcasting, taking charge first of the BBC's Eastern service and then of its Arabic service. After his retirement in 1963, he began writing again, and the books from this second phase included a biography of Layard, a new edition of *Letters from Egypt*, and, finally, a biography of Janet that he failed to get published before his death in 1987.

Instead, the final word on Janet came from Kinta, who published *A Tuscan Childhood* in 1993, just two years before her own death at eighty-four. Six years after that, in 2001, Nigel Beevor, acting on behalf of the extended family, donated the family's papers, along with miscellaneous related material, to the British Institute of Florence. Gathering the correspondence of everyone from Sarah to Kinta and presided over by an institute founded by Lina, the Waterfield Collection symbolizes the family's seven generations of continuity, and its four of close involvement with Tuscany.

⸺⸺⸺

At the time of Janet's death, there were, Kinta recalls, "many predictable remarks about it being the end of an era," and no doubt some of these were made from an Anglo-Florentine perspective. The colony was, however, far from finished.

Even while Janet was still around, it had put aside the last of its postwar doldrums. In 1924 it received the social equivalent of a hood ornament when the legendary Edwardian concubine Alice Keppel came to town with her trivial husband, George.* Settling into the Villa dell'Ombrellino in Bellosguardo for her last twenty-three years, Mrs. Keppel was so staunchly British that she had Cecil Pinsent plant her a garden in the shape and colors of the Union Jack,

---

*Kinta recalls that George Keppel, "a cousin of Aunt Janet and my mother," would "appear in Doney's wearing his panama hat and try to persuade the girls to go for a ride in his red Lancia sports car, followed by a swim in the pool at the Ombrellino . . . Once we agreed as a joke. He took photographs of us there in our Jantzen swimming-costumes . . . We all knew that he was longing to take more 'artistic' poses."

and the more insular and retrograde elements of the colony rallied around her.

By contrast, the literary scene of the 1920s was cutting-edge and raffish. Aldous Huxley lived in Florence for several years. So did D. H. Lawrence, whose first stay in 1919 had yielded a partially Florentine novel, *Aaron's Rod*, and who returned in 1926 for a longer sojourn, renting a villa near Ouida's old home in Scandicci. (In 1928 the Waterfields had him over for lunch at Poggio Gherardo.) Though he never quite lived in town, C. K. Scott Moncrieff, prince of translators, shuttled between Florence and Pisa for several years.* Then there was Norman Douglas, whose best-known books are set in Capri and Calabria but who often spent months at a time in Florence. Douglas resembled Landor in his outrageousness, only with the difference that he was openly pedophilic. (Harold Acton recalled that on a walking tour of Chianti he took with Douglas and Scott Moncrieff, Douglas tried to fondle boys in every village along the way.) Hugely charismatic, he was sought out by Huxley, Lawrence, and others, and presided over riotous evenings at cheap Florentine *osterie*. Also part of this crowd was Giuseppe "Pino" Orioli. A kind of Florentine Sylvia Beach, Orioli operated both a bookstore and a small press, and when *Lady Chatterley's Lover* ran afoul of British censors, he ventured to publish it, as Beach had done with *Ulysses*. His friendships with Lawrence and the rest are charmingly described in his memoir *Adventures of a Bookseller*.

In the early 1930s, under the influence of Fascist xenophobia, Florence began to shake off some of its colonial trappings; Kinta cites as an example a shop in the Via Tornabuoni that changed its name from Old England to Giovane Italia (Young Italy), even though it "went on selling tartan rugs and Oxford marmalade." Few took these minor suppressions as a cue to leave, for the city remained fundamentally welcoming. But after 1935, when British Foreign Secretary Anthony Eden led the charge to impose sanctions against Italy for its behavior in Abyssinia, the mood became rougher and more

---

*It is a curious fact that Scott Moncrieff's great translation of Proust's *À la recherche* was mostly produced not in France but in Italy.

threatening. Franco Zeffirelli recalls that Fascist provocateurs would sometimes whip students up into an angry mob and then herd it toward the Via Tornabuoni.

Intimidated, a portion of the colony left in the later 1930s. But many held their ground. "The established Anglo-Florentine," Iris Origo notes, "felt himself to have become as much a part of city life as any Tuscan," and if he happened to be pro-Fascist, he probably refused to believe that Mussolini could ever be such a thankless brute as to eject him. Yet on June 10, 1940, British citizens awoke to find themselves declared enemy aliens and given only a few days to pack their bags.

While the colony was never remotely the same again, after the war its embers kindled back to life with surprising speed. Mixed in with the old-guarders like Lina, trying to pick up where they'd left off, was a modest company of new arrivals. The Australian historian and war correspondent Alan Moorehead, who spent two years in the city, describes its postbellum appeal in his memoir *A Late Education*: "Florence in the nineteen-forties was the perfect balm to assuage six years of war. The tourist horde had not yet arrived, one could rent a villa for next to nothing in the hills above the town, and it was a wonderful thing after so much destruction and ugliness to live quietly in the midst of the most civilized landscape in Europe." Also lured to the city was the young novelist Francis King, who went on to write several novels set in the colonial milieu (Janet's name pops up in one of them), as well as *Florence: A Literary Companion*. In his introduction to that book, King recalls "being entertained by members of the 'community,' often elderly and often eking out impoverished and improvident lives in once sumptuous but now dilapidated villas." As these fossils reminisced, "with a typically Florentine mixture of tolerance and malice," about everyone from Ouida and Henry James to Aldous Huxley and Norman Douglas, he "felt the literary past of Florence to be constantly interpenetrating with its present."

Not everyone found the place as soothing as Moorehead or as stimulating as King. There was, for instance, Sinclair Lewis, who did little during his several years in town but drink himself into the grave and scratch out a weak satire, *World So Wide*, about American expatriates in Florence. But most found the city's enduring reputation as a paradise of wordsmiths well deserved. Robert Lowell and Elizabeth Hardwick, who came to town in 1950 for what was supposed to be a one-week visit, ended up staying six months, and they weren't alone in their dawdling.

For many of these Johnnies-come-lately, almost the first order of business was to head out to I Tatti and pay their respects to the Master. Bernard Berenson was in his prime. Already rather famous before the war, he was now an outright celebrity, his peerless sophistication and exquisite lifestyle standing for a lost world of cosmopolitan high culture; as Moorehead puts it, he was "like the one piece of brittle china that miraculously escapes the blast in a bombed house." More than ever, I Tatti was a sort of Camelot, attracting everyone from Jacqueline Bouvier to Vivien Leigh and Laurence Olivier; even Harry S. Truman was curious enough to make the pilgrimage. While all this adulation did nothing to curb Berenson's vanity, he'd mellowed under Nicky Mariano's regimen of selfless cosseting, and Moorehead (whom he warmly befriended) and others found him less acerbic than kindly and paternal. He died only in 1959, at the age of ninety-four. Kinta happened to arrive for a planned visit a day or two after his death, and was puzzled to find I Tatti "besieged by television crews"—she'd been traveling with Nigel in rural Tuscany and hadn't heard the news.

For several years after Berenson's death the colony went without a figurehead. Then, in 1962, Harold Acton's widowed mother died and he inherited La Pietra. At Eton and Oxford, Acton's exotic upbringing, along with his literary precociousness, had made him a sensation among his peers, who included George Orwell, Cyril Connolly, Evelyn Waugh, and Graham Greene. After college he'd faltered, finding success neither in poetry nor prose. Living in China before the war and Naples after, he'd occasionally returned to Florence. Now, like a prodigal son, he finally settled in the city of his birth, turning out a series of books on local subjects—including, à la Janet, one on Tuscan villas—and presiding over La Pietra, which replaced I Tatti as a symbol of Anglo-Florentine fine living. As debonair as Berenson and nearly as cultured, Acton himself became something of an icon. Though occasionally accused of arrant snobbishness and cultivation of royalty (Princess Margaret and Prince Charles both came to visit), he was also widely liked and admired, and not just by the British—the comune of Florence made him an honorary citizen.

When Acton died in 1994, he was described as the last of his breed. Two other prominent colonists, Joan Haslip and Sir John Pope-Hennessy,* happened to die in the same year, and to those who cared about such matters the coincidence seemed telling: in some hard-to-define yet unmistakable way, the colony was finished. "The tide of foreign residents had ebbed while the tourists multiplied," Acton observed on returning to Florence in the mid-1960s, and the ratio had only shifted further in the same direction over the following three decades. Nobody replaced the Brownings, the Trollopes, the Berensons, the Actons, the Rosses and Waterfields. In the Via Tornabuoni, Caffè Doney went out of business and the little tartan-and-marmalade shops gave way to designer boutiques. There are still hundreds, if not thousands, of anglophones about, but the sense of a colony, of a city within the city, has vanished. Perhaps the most striking proof yet of this decline came in 2011, when the British consulate, which (except for a hiatus during World War II) had existed for over five centuries, closed its doors. Matteo Renzi, the mayor of Florence, expressed sadness at the loss of an institution with "a very unique and beautiful history," one no longer deemed necessary in "the era of EasyJet and Ryanair."

⊰⊱

What was the Anglo-Florentine colony? A mere soap bubble, or else a unique and significant cross-cultural phenomenon—it depends on one's point of view.

---

*Haslip (1912–94), who grew up in Florence—as a child she knew Janet a bit—and returned in later life, was a respected and prolific biographer, while Pope-Hennessy (1913–94) was a distinguished art historian and museum director who spent his last eight years in the city.

Like Janet Ross, it had its share of detractors. Huxley was especially withering: to him, Florence was "a third-rate provincial town, colonised by English sodomites and middle aged lesbians," and the colony itself "a sort of decayed provincial intelligentsia." Mary McCarthy, who spent over a year in town in the mid-1950s working on *The Stones of Florence*, found that "the foreign colony's notion of Florence . . . was bookish, synthetic, gushing, insular, genteel, and, above all, proprietary." Other epithets could easily be piled on. The colony had, despite its size, a suffocating fishbowl smallness, and was largely composed of pensioners, remittance men, and twittering flocks of widows and spinsters—*gli scorpioni*, as they were known in Zeffirelli's day. It also had a cheapening effect on the city. The firebrand critic Giovanni Papini made this case succinctly in 1913: "Florence is put to shame by the fact that it . . . does not live off the honest earnings of its living citizens, but off the indecent and miserly exploitation of the genius of its ancestors and the curiosity of foreigners . . . Half of Florence lives directly off the backs of foreigners, and the other half lives off those who live off foreigners." Of course Papini was thinking of foreigners in general, many of them tourists rather than residents. But the fact remains that the colony was a mainstay of the economy, and that there was something inherently uncomfortable, even degrading, about once-mighty Florence being so dependent on it.

Valid though these objections are, the colony also deserves a defense. Even those like Huxley who claimed to abhor it got more out of it than they cared to admit. For one thing, it gave them something to jeer at, to kick against, and to study like a petri dish— "that little simmering social pot," as Henry James phrased it. These dissenters, who would have gone elsewhere if they'd truly wanted to avoid their own kind, were drawn to the colony in spite of themselves, as by a guilty pleasure, and in a sense they belonged to it willy-nilly; the colony had a preponderance, a critical mass, such that few could totally escape it.

Most, however, had no wish to flee. The colony allowed them to have the best of both worlds, to wallow in foreign pleasures without feeling cut off from home. ("Everyone on earth that you almost want to see turns up in Florence, and you do see them and are glad of it," an astonished Robert Lowell wrote in 1951.) It also provided them with an interpretive community: if they wanted to learn more about a church, a painter, a historical episode, even a genus of wild-flower, some colonial authority on the subject would be happy to take them by the sleeve and expatiate. Overall, the colony generated a thickness of association that did more to enhance the experience of being in Florence than to taint or undermine it.

Perhaps most important, the colony gave more to Florence than it took. McCarthy denigrates its "sickly love" for the city, and she has a point. But that love was no less true for being saccharine and possessive. The colony helped preserve and protect Florence, helped the world understand and appreciate its treasures, and helped re-store one of the great cities of Europe to its former eminence. "Mud angels" was the term coined for the thousands of volunteers from around the globe who rushed to dig Florence out and clean it up after the devastating flood of 1966. One might also loosely apply it to the colony, which, so to speak, left its muddy footprints across the City of Lilies but also stood guard over it and tried to bring its halo back up to full wattage.

—————

In recent years, the cult of Florence has largely been supplanted by the cult of Tuscany. Not that the capital's popularity has waned, but a rhapsodic mania for the rest of the province has taken hold. Where Miss Honeychurch thought of Florence as a "magic city," today's visitor is bound to seek—indeed, to expect—enchantment in Chianti or some other stretch of countryside.* And if that visitor is so smit-ten (and well-heeled) that she decides to buy property and make a new life for herself, she is likely to want to emulate the natives,

---

*This shift can be observed among the high and mighty as well. Whereas Queen Victoria once took her vacations in Florence, it's now almost de rigueur for British prime ministers to take theirs in "Chiantishire." Blair went so often that he acquired the nickname "Tuscan Tony," and in the riot-torn summer of 2011 David Cameron was criticized for renting a pricey villa just down the road from one owned by the rock star Sting.

observing their seasonal rituals and getting her hands dirty. Then maybe she'll write a book about her adventures, one in the tradition of *The Hills of Tuscany: New Life in an Old Land*, *Vanilla Beans & Brodo: Real Life in the Hills of Tuscany*, and, of course, *Under the Tuscan Sun*.

Which isn't to suggest that there's anything wrong with all this; after all, the authors of these books have harmlessly found happiness for themselves and shared it with thousands of readers. There are, however, interesting differences between them and Janet Ross. Some have to do with altered actualities: mezzadria having been outlawed in 1982 and contadini in the old sense of the word no longer existing, today's rural colonists primarily interact not with poor, illiterate, superstitious, custom-bound peasants but with more or less prosperous, educated, worldly folk like themselves. But others are a matter of attitude and perspective. For the followers of Frances Mayes, *toscanità*, or Tuscanness, is a sublime set of virtues to be studied, celebrated, and aspired to, and when they pick olives, say, or repair a stone wall, or cook a traditional dish, they are aware of themselves as (they hope) partaking of it. As a result, both their actions and the pleasures they derive from them tend to seem scripted and self-conscious. For Janet, by contrast, the notion of toscanità held no inherent romance. Her appreciation of things Tuscan was consequently more discriminating, and the satisfactions she took from helping to manage Castagnolo, and then from overhauling and running Poggio Gherardo, were entirely organic and spontaneous.

This doesn't make her superior. Some of Tuscany's best qualities were, in fact, wasted on Janet, beginning with its landscape: according to Kinta, she was "proudly impervious to the scenery around her," and she would mock anyone who went into raptures over it. She also happened to arrive at a time when Tuscany's rural life was little known to outsiders, which meant that there was no bandwagon to jump aboard, no interposing body of stereotypes and clichés to color her experience. All the same, there's something bracing and instructive about her example. If our current collective obsession with Tuscany is another version of the "sickly love" of the

Anglo-Florentines, Janet's was a healthy love—measured, skeptical, informed, slow-building, and ultimately deeper and more rewarding for all that realism.

—◦—

A few years ago I spent two days visiting colonial houses, monuments, and curiosities with a Florentine friend who shares my interest in them.

Tootling around in her tiny car, we went first to the English Cemetery, in the Piazzale Donatello. Originally nestled up against the city walls, the cemetery is now hemmed in by a traffic circle whose incessant roar banishes tranquillity. It is, however, in far better shape than in previous years, thanks to the efforts of Julia Bolton Holloway, a medievalist and nun who has made the restoration of the cemetery her personal mission, and who lives on-site as its caretaker. Led by Holloway in her pale blue robes, we toured the dense collection of famous graves. Even the most ostentatious, such as Elizabeth Barrett Browning's, are of modest size, and some are simplicity itself: Landor's consists of a plain slab laid in the ground, though one dignified by an epitaph from Algernon Swinburne, who commands Florence to "keep safe" Landor's "dedicated dust."

Later that day we went to La Pietra, which now belongs to New York University. Part of the villa has been turned into classrooms, but much of it remains a virtual museum, its rooms crammed with a dizzying array of artifacts. My friend, who sometimes teaches at the villa, was able to slip me into Harold Acton's palatial bedroom, where I was oddly moved to see that the books he'd had on his bedside table at the time of his death had been left undisturbed.

We then drove out to Lastra a Signa, looking for Castagnolo. After questioning several locals who'd never heard of it, we found one who had, and who pointed us in the right direction. Though now converted to apartments and surrounded by newer houses, the villa still had, to my pleasant surprise, a tumbledown charm, its yellow stucco crumbling away under a drapery of vines. There was nobody around to interrogate. Glancing at the doorbells, I was excited to see that one bore the name Pianetti della Stufa—a descendant of Lotto, clearly. I rang it several times, but no one answered.

That evening we walked around Bellosguardo, which, with its prodigious greenery, remains very much a slice of heaven. Stopping at the gate of Villa dell'Ombrellino, we peered though. There were no signs of life, but we rang the buzzer anyway, and after a minute or two a voice sounded from the intercom. My friend, who as an architectural historian is expert at talking her way into strangers' houses, made the case for admitting us. The voice issued a curt assent, the gate clicked open, and we entered. The scene was one of vaguely sinister desolation. The house looked unused, and the grounds were in sorry shape, their plants withered, their statues bird-spattered, their eponymous metal *ombrellini* (parasols) rusty. A chill went up my spine as I thought of the villa's latter-day history. After both Alice and George Keppel died in 1947, it was inherited by their notorious daughter, Violet Trefusis, a stormy petrel if there ever was one. Ambivalent about Florence, she came and went over the following decades. Then, on Christmas Eve 1971, she left her primary home in Paris and returned one last time to the villa, where over the next two months she starved herself to death, "surrounded," as one biography puts it, "by statues, empty fountains, and dead flowers." My friend felt the chill too, and we hastened back to the gate, only to find it locked. The grounds were enclosed by an unclimbably tall fence, and whoever had let us in had never appeared, though presumably he was somewhere in the house. I felt an absurd stab of panic, as though we were trapped in the plot of a Gothic novel. After a short search we found an unlocked smaller gate and escaped through it, but those moments of seeming captivity had ruffled us both.

The following day we headed toward Settignano. Near Ponte a Mensola we pulled over to look at a roadside plaque commemorating anglophone writers who'd found "accogliente ospitalità e ispirazione" (welcoming hospitality and inspiration) in the "circostanti colline celebrate dall'arte di Giovanni Boccaccio" (surrounding hills celebrated in the art of Boccaccio). The list of names, which follows no obvious principle of organization, runs as follows: Leigh Hunt, Charles Armitage Brown, Janet Ross, John Addington Symonds, Edward Hutton, Mark Twain, Frederic H. Trench,* and Bernardo [*sic*] Berenson.

Many of Villadom's houses can now be rented out by the day for private functions. Just so, when we stopped at the Villa Viviani (where Mark Twain and his family had lived), we found it being set up for a wedding, and we were allowed to take only a quick peek at its domed reception room, so big and imposing that Twain, by his own account, "tried many names for it: the Skating Rink, the Mammoth Cave, the Great Sahara." At John Temple Leader's Castello di Vincigliata, where we went next, preparations were also under way for some sort of event, and my friend had to lobby longer and harder to get us inside. Finally we were permitted to walk through the place, which is patently artificial but seductive and rather wonderful nevertheless.

After pausing outside Vincigliata to note a plaque commemorating Queen Victoria's visit in 1888, we backtracked toward Florence a bit, and soon were at the main gate of Poggio Gherardo.

The busts of the four seasons still sat atop the gate's pillars, one of which had a cracked, inset marble sign reading "È proibito cacciare nei possessi di Poggio Gherardo": no hunting. I smiled, thinking of Janet's fearless confrontations with poachers in the hungry, semilawless years during and after the Great War; some had ignored her, but others had been unnerved by her fluent invective and fled the bosco.

Immediately inside the gate was a modern house, and more houses followed—much of the estate's land has been converted into a sort of suburban development. But when we got to the top of the hill, there stood the castle, looking much as it does in old paintings and photographs, except for the basketball court now alongside it. We called out, and a jovial-looking, middle-aged man emerged. When I explained the reason for our visit, he nodded vigorously—he knew all about the Rosses. Poggio Gherardo is now owned, he

---

*Frederic Herbert Trench (1865–1923) was an Irish poet and playwright who lived in the area for several years beginning in 1914.

informed us, by the Rogationists of the Heart of Jesus, a small Catholic order, and is used as a boys' home. Dressed in jeans and a T-shirt, he himself wasn't a priest but some sort of lay handyman or caretaker. He was the only person around, the boys apparently being off on an excursion. At any rate, he offered to show us around, and we stepped inside.

When Kinta visited the castle one last time in the early 1990s, she found that its charm had vanished beneath the "bleak hygiene of a modern ecclesiastical institution," and her description still held. One room had been turned into a chapel of breathtaking hideousness. No trace of Pippo the poodle remained, nor of any other embellishment. On one wall hung a portrait of Annibale Maria di Francia, founder of the Rogationists, who died two months before Janet in 1927 and was canonized in 2004. On another wall was a picture of the Virgin Mary, with a motto beneath: IO SONO LA PADRONA DI QUESTA CASA (I am the mistress of this house). I could easily imagine Janet's reaction to this new padrona, and to the whole transformation of her house; though by no means anti-Catholic, she had a strong distaste for convents, Mariolatry, and the garish side of the Church. I struggled not to laugh.

Back outside, though, I found that fewer changes had been wrought. The terrace, while poorly kept, was still rather enchanting, and so was the view of Florence, despite the suburban buildup on its perimeter. Just to the south lay Coverciano, a soccer complex where the Italian national team trains. Walking around to the north side of the house, I could partially make out I Tatti, which is now the Harvard University Center for Italian Renaissance Studies, and where I had an appointment the following day to look at the Berensons' papers.

While it was easy enough to imagine the Rosses and their friends strolling around the castle itself, just as my friend and I were doing, the poderi were another matter. Where were they, exactly? Where were the olive press, the tinaia, the stable for the Val di Chiana oxen, the cottages of the contadini? I suddenly thought of a passage in Iris Origo's book of essays *A Need to Testify* in which she tells of her first meeting—in London—with Virginia Woolf: ' "Tell me,' said Virginia, 'what does it *feel* like to wake up in the morning on a Tuscan farm?'" Instead of trying to answer, Origo suggested that Woolf come see La Foce for herself, and the following autumn she did so, along with Vita Sackville-West. "Vita found inspiration in our white oxen," Origo adds, "for some of the best lines in her English Georgic, *The Land*." Poggio Gherardo had never had, even in Janet's day, anything like La Foce's rural isolation, and it was nowhere near as big. But it did have the distinct atmosphere of a preindustrial Tuscan farm, and that could never be recaptured. If I wanted, I could go stay at one of the many *agriturismo* bed-and-breakfasts that have cropped up all over Tuscany, but I wouldn't wake up to the sound of peasants singing stornelli while they worked, or of them bickering with their padrona.

As we left Poggio Gherardo, I thought of another passage, this one from *A Tuscan Childhood*. With regard to the castle's Burmese goldfish, Kinta writes that Janet

> used to breed them and give them away to friends. Harold Acton still has some of their descendants at La Pietra. A less fortunate pair was presented to Charles Bell . . . to take back to Oxford by train. The journey was long and slow, and the two goldfish began to gasp in distress, so when the train halted at Pisa, Bell dashed out of the station to buy a bicycle pump. He then spent the rest of the journey pumping away to aerate the water, and they survived the ordeal.

Perhaps, I reflected, trying to conjure up life at Poggio Gherardo and the lost world of the Anglo-Florentines is like trying to transport exotic fish from one country to another, only without a pump. Then again, so is any attempt to revive the past.

APPENDIX: JANET ROSS AS
EGYPTIAN CORRESPONDENT

While the life of Janet Ross is, biographically speaking, largely a straightforward, open-book affair, it does have its puzzles. Of these, none is harder to sort out than the one surrounding her supposed authorship of several dozen articles for *The Times* in 1863–64. Was she or was she not the paper's true Egyptian correspondent? As I made plain in the third chapter, it is my firm belief that she wrote (or in one case co-wrote) most if not all of the articles. My reasons for believing this will be laid out momentarily. First, however, let us consider a scholarly exchange that sheds a good deal of light on the matter.

In the Summer 1994 issue of the *Victorian Periodicals Review*, Jean O'Grady, a Canadian independent scholar, published a piece called "The Egyptian Correspondent of the *Times*" that identifies Janet Ross as the author of the articles and goes on to provide an overview of the Trading Company controversy.

Then, in the Spring 1995 issue of the same journal, Eamon Dyas, Group Records Manager at *The Times*, published "The Mystery of the Egyptian Correspondent of the *Times*," which argues that Henry, not Janet, wrote the articles. At first glance his evidence seems irrefutable. Digging in the paper's archives, Dyas had unearthed nine letters from Mowbray Morris to Henry Ross, including one in which

Morris confirms Henry's appointment as Egyptian correspondent. As Dyas points out, these letters contradict Janet's claim to have been appointed by Morris. Dyas goes on to cite several other pieces of evidence, including the fact that Janet, in her 1902 edition of *Letters from Egypt*, amplified a previously published letter of Lucie's from May 1863 to include the following sentence: "[Janet] is Times correspondent and does it very well." Though he doesn't say so, Dyas clearly suspects Janet of having fabricated the sentence in order to bolster her claim of authorship.

Finally, in the Spring 1996 issue of the journal, O'Grady published "More Egyptian Correspondence," a response to Dyas. Though she admits to having initially been rattled by Dyas's display of evidence, she goes on to maintain that Janet was, "to some extent, the *de facto*, though not the *de jure*, correspondent of *The Times*." She then produces a trump card of her own. At that time, many of Lucie's manuscript letters were in the possession of Kinta Beevor. Just before Kinta's death in 1995, O'Grady had written to her and asked her to check on the May 1863 letter that Dyas had singled out for skepticism. Although Kinta could find only a transcription of the letter in question, "made by an unknown hand," she was able to report that it did in fact include the crucial sentence about Janet being the *Times* correspondent. Furthermore, Kinta reported, the letter—addressed to Sarah Austin—included a sentence that had never appeared in any edition of *Letters from Egypt*: "I must finish Janet's Times letter [i.e., article] for her as she has to go to a wedding." (Lucie had been staying with the Rosses in Alexandria at the time.) As O'Grady remarks, this is "as close as one can hope to get" to conclusive proof.

Now for my own views. To begin, I agree with O'Grady that the existence of those two sentences in Lucie's letter constitutes very strong proof. This proof would, admittedly, be even stronger if the letters were in Lucie's own hand. But neither are they in Janet's, and it would be ludicrous to hypothesize that Janet arranged for some third party to write them and insert them in the manuscript record; besides, had she done so, she surely wouldn't have included the sentence about Lucie finishing her article for her. As O'Grady points out, there's also nothing inherently suspicious about the fact that Janet added that other sentence ("She is Times correspondent and does it very well") to her edition of *Letters from Egypt*. The book had never been conceived as a comprehensive record of Lucie's correspondence—a judicious selection, rather—and Janet felt perfectly free to take all sorts of liberties with it, restoring certain passages and expurgating others.

As for Janet's claim in *The Fourth Generation* that Morris proposed that she serve as the new Egyptian correspondent for *The Times*, it is manifestly untrue. My hunch, though, is that her fib was unconscious. She wrote *The Fourth Generation* almost fifty years afterward, and in the interval she'd probably managed to convince herself that Morris *had* offered her the job—memory does tend to burnish things.

In short, it would appear that Morris thought Henry was writing the articles when they were actually being written by Janet. Beyond those two sentences in Lucie's letter, what reason is there to draw such a conclusion? For one thing, Henry was always a reluctant writer, particularly for publication; he was also swamped with work and would surely have been loath to take on more. Janet, meanwhile, had too much time on her hands and was eager to have a go at writing.

But to me the most compelling evidence is the simple fact that Janet told her friends she was the new Egyptian correspondent. While prone to exaggeration, she was no liar or fantasist, and it is inconceivable that she would grossly deceive venerated friends such as Meredith and Kinglake (whose letter congratulating her on the job appears in *The Fourth Generation*); besides, she had no motive for doing so. It is, of course, entirely possible that Henry wrote some of the articles, or co-wrote them with Janet. (Even Dyas admits this latter possibility: "There is enough evidence in some of the dispatches to suggest two hands at work.") We know, after all, that Lucie contributed to one of them. And it seems likely that Henry fed Janet information, especially for the articles that mention the Trading

Company. So my best guess is that the Rosses took a rather casual and cavalier attitude toward the job from the start, dividing the labors from month to month however it suited them; that they pulled the wool over Morris's eyes; and that, in the end, it was Janet who wound up doing most of the composition.

NOTES

Besides Janet Ross's two works of autobiography, *Early Days Recalled* and *The Fourth Generation*, and her family biography *Three Generations of English Women*, the main source for this book is the Waterfield Collection at the British Institute of Florence, which holds not only the papers of Janet Ross and her family but the manuscript of Gordon Waterfield's unpublished biography, the tellingly titled "Aunt Janet: Her Friends and Victims" (introduction by Harold Acton). I feel compelled to say a bit about this manuscript. Though it ventures little in the way of context or analysis, "Aunt Janet: Her Friends and Victims" constitutes an invaluable assemblage of facts and anecdotes about Janet Ross, one that helped me fill in many gaps and pointed me toward obscure sources that I might otherwise have overlooked. Gordon Waterfield was an admirably thorough researcher, and I am much indebted to him.

Given my extensive use of these same few sources, it would be otiose to provide numbered citations. Instead, I will list the additional sources for each chapter, and also specify the origin of certain quotes and facts.

INTRODUCTION: POGGIO UNTOPPLED

I drew on Harold Acton's *Memoirs of an Aesthete* and *More Memoirs of an Aesthete*, Giuliana Artom Treves's *The Golden Ring: The Anglo-Florentines, 1847–1862*, Olive Hamilton's *Paradise of Exiles: Tuscany and the British*, Francis King's *Florence: A Literary Companion*, David Leavitt's *Florence, A Delicate Case*, and Iris Origo's *Images and Shadows*.

3   "As in the twilight . . . I came in sight of the broken-down garden walls and scorched fields": The quote is from Bernard Berenson's *Rumor and Reflection*.

5   In 1910 the British consul in Florence estimated that there were thirty-five
      thousand British citizens living in and around the city: The figure is cited in
      Olive Hamilton's *Paradise of Exiles: Tuscany and the British.*
8   But if she was, in the words of Sir Kenneth Clark . . . "a well-known terri-
      fier": The quote is from Clark's *Another Part of the Wood: A Self-Portrait.*
8   she wielded her power from what Twain termed a "stately castle": The quote
      is from the *Autobiography of Mark Twain, Vol. 1.*
9   "In contrast with the average foreign resident," Harold Acton remarks of
      Janet, "her energy and enterprise seemed phenomenal": He does so in his
      introduction to Gordon Waterfield's "Aunt Janet: Her Friends and Vic-
      tims."

CHAPTER ONE: A DYNASTY OF SORTS

I drew on Rosemary Ashton's *Thomas and Jane Carlyle: Portrait of a Marriage*,
Peter James Bowman's *The Fortune Hunter: A German Prince in Regency En-
gland, The Collected Letters of Thomas and Jane Welsh Carlyle*, ed. Charles Rich-
ard Sanders and Kenneth J. Fielding, Katherine Frank's *A Passage to Egypt: The
Life of Lucie Duff Gordon*, Lotte and Joseph Hamburger's *Troubled Lives: John
and Sarah Austin* and *Contemplating Adultery: The Secret Life of a Victorian
Woman*, Josephine Kamm's *John Stuart Mill in Love*, Bruce Mazlish's *James and
John Stuart Mill: Father and Son in the Nineteenth Century*, Michael St. John
Packe's *The Life of John Stuart Mill*, George Paston's *Little Memoirs of the Nine-
teenth Century*, and Gordon Waterfield's *Lucie Duff Gordon in England, South
Africa and Egypt.*

19   According to the diarist Henry Crabb Robinson, who sat in on the class, the
      students could not attend to the matter of his lecture from anxiety for the
      lecturer: Quoted in Lotte and Joseph Hamburger's *Troubled Lives: John and
      Sarah Austin.*
26   Janet Shuttleworth's younger stepsister, Marianne North, was especially in
      awe of Lucie, and later wrote of her mesmerizing "grand eyes and deep-toned
      voice": She did so in *Recollections of a Happy Life.*

CHAPTER TWO: SUCCESSIONS

I drew on Alice Acland's *Caroline Norton*, Katherine Frank's *A Passage to Egypt:
The Life of Lucie Duff Gordon*, Ivor Forbes Guest's *Napoleon III in England*, Althea Hayter's *A Sultry Month: Scenes of London Literary Life in 1846, The Letters
of George Meredith*, ed. C. L. Cline, Ann Monsarrat's *An Uneasy Victorian: Thackeray the Man*, Siegfried Sassoon's *Meredith*, Lionel Stevenson's *The Ordeal of
George Meredith*, Gordon Waterfield's *Layard of Nineveh* and *Lucie Duff Gordon
in England, South Africa and Egypt*, David Williams's *George Meredith: His Life*

and Lost Love, and the entries on A. W. Kinglake, Eliot Warburton, and Austen Henry Layard in the *Oxford Dictionary of National Biography*.

32   In person, Kinglake was shy but engaging—"delicious, sweet . . . as urbane and deferential as Emerson" was how Henry James described him: See *Henry James Letters, Vol. 2: 1875–1883*, ed. Leon Edel.

36   "A nice leg of mutton, my Lucie, / I pray thee have it ready at three": Thackeray's poem is quoted in Katherine Frank's *A Passage to Egypt: The Life of Lucie Duff Gordon*.

42   But Meredith was interested in her as more than a babysitter: he was, as one of his biographers puts it, "more than a little in love with Janet Duff Gordon": The biographer in question is Lionel Stevenson, author of *The Ordeal of George Meredith*.

CHAPTER THREE: SITTI ROSS

I drew on Edwin de Leon's *The Khedive's Egypt*, Lucie Duff Gordon's *Letters from Egypt*, *Flaubert in Egypt: A Sensibility on Tour*, ed. Francis Steegmuller, E. M. Forster's *Alexandria: A History and a Guide*, Katherine Frank's *A Passage to Egypt: The Life of Lucie Duff Gordon*, A. W. Kinglake's *Eothen*, David S. Landes's *Bankers and Pashas: International Finance and Economic Imperialism in Egypt*, Florence Nightingale's *Letters from Egypt: A Journey on the Nile, 1849–1850*, ed. Antony Sattin, John Pemble's *The Mediterranean Passion: Victorians and Edwardians in the South*, Marguerite Power's *Arabian Days and Nights*, Max Rodenbeck's *Cairo: The City Victorious*, Anthony Sattin's *Lifting the Veil: British Society in Egypt, 1768–1956*, the diaries of William S. Thayer (University of Virginia Library), and Gordon Waterfield's *Lucie Duff Gordon in England, South Africa and Egypt*.

61   a friend likened her to "a salmon which swims up river to spawn and then swims out to sea again": The friend is quoted anonymously in Lina Waterfield's *Castle in Italy*.

69   the twenty-odd articles she wrote have been said to constitute "the best journalistic record of the Egypt of the period": The quote is from David S. Landes's *Bankers and Pashas: International Finance and Economic Imperialism in Egypt*.

INTERMEZZO: THE ANGLO-TUSCANS

I drew on Giuliana Artom Treves's *The Golden Ring: The Anglo-Florentines, 1847–1862*, Lady Blessington's *The Idler in Italy*, Van Wyck Brooks's *The Dream of Arcadia: American Writers and Artists in Italy, 1760–1915*, Christopher Duggan's *The Force of Destiny: A History of Italy Since 1796*, Kate Field's "English Authors in Florence" and "Last Days of Walter Savage Landor," Olive Hamilton's *Paradise of Exiles: Tuscany and the British* and *The Divine Country: The British in Tuscany, 1372–1980,* Christopher Hibbert's *Florence: The Biography of a City* and *Garibaldi and His Enemies,* George Stillman Hillard's *Six Months in Italy,* Richard Holmes's *Footsteps: Adventures of a Romantic Biographer* and *Shelley: The Pursuit,* Leigh Hunt's *Autobiography of Leigh Hunt,* Henry James's *William Wetmore Story and his Friends,* Johanna Johnston's *The Life, Manners, and Travels of Fanny Trollope: A Biography,* Francis King's *Florence: A Literary Companion,* Jacob Korg's *Browning and Italy,* Austen Henry Layard's *Autobiography,* Michael Levey's *Florence: A Portrait,* R.W.B. Lewis's *The City of Florence: Historical Vistas and Personal Sightings,* Rosalie Mander's *Mrs. Browning: The Story of Elizabeth Barrett,* Leslie A. Marchand's *Byron: A Biography,* John Pemble's *The Mediterranean Passion: Victorians and Edwardians in the South,* Gary Scharnhorst's *Kate Field: The Many Lives of a Nineteenth-Century American Journalist,* Francis Steegmuller's *The Two Lives of James Jackson Jarves,* R. H. Super's *Walter Savage Landor: A Biography,* George Macaulay Trevelyan's *Garibaldi's Defence of the Roman Republic, Garibaldi and the Thousand,* and *Garibaldi and the Making of Italy,* Thomas Adolphus Trollope's *What I Remember,* Elihu Vedder's *The Digressions of V.,* Brenda Wineapple's *Hawthorne: A Life,* the entries on Henry Elliott, Seymour Kirkup, and Thomas Adolphus Trollope in the *Oxford Dictionary of National Biography,* and the full run of *The Tuscan Athenaeum.*

93   as one scholar notes, "when the Italians brought back to Italy the pictures that Napoleon had carried away they left Fra Angelico's 'Coronation of the Virgin' behind," along with works by Cimabue, Giotto, and even Botticelli: The scholar in question is Van Wyck Brooks, writing in *The Dream of Arcadia: American Writers and Artists in Italy, 1760–1915.*

96   Dostoyevsky wrote, with reference to the French and British, of being unable to "conceive of why these people, *who had money to get away with,* would voluntarily stay in such a hell": Dostoyevsky is quoted in *Tuscany: An Anthology,* ed. Laura Raison.

CHAPTER FOUR: LA PADRONA DI CASTAGNOLO

I drew on Eileen Brigland's *Ouida, the Passionate Victorian,* Lady Elizabeth Butler's *An Autobiography,* Sergio Camerani's *Vita fiorentina attraverso i secoli: Vol. 3, Cronache di Firenze capitale, Unfolding the South: Nineteenth-Century British Women Writers and Artists in Italy,* ed. Alison Chapman and Jane Stabler, Vineta Colby's *Vernon Lee: A Literary Biography,* Leon Edel's *Henry James: The Middle Years,* Katherine Frank's *A Passage to Egypt: The Life of Lucie Duff Gordon,* A. C. Gissing's *William Holman Hunt: A Biography,* Olive Hamilton's *Paradise of Exiles: Tuscany and the British,* Augustus Hare's *The Story of My Life,* Christopher Hibbert's *Florence: The Biography of a City,* John A. Huzzard's "George Meredith and the Risorgimento," *Henry James Letters, Vol. 3: 1883–1895*, ed. Leon Edel, *Traveling in Italy with Henry James*, ed. Fred Kaplan, Francis King's *Florence: A Literary Companion*, the papers of A. W. Kinglake (Cambridge University Library), Michael Levey's *Florence: A Portrait*, R.W.B. Lewis's *The City of Florence: Historical Vistas and Personal Sightings, Firenze 1815–1945: un bilancio storiografico*, ed. Giorgio Mori and Piero Roggi, John Julius Norwich's *Paradise of Cities: Venice in the 19th Century*, Iris Origo's *The Last Attachment*, Lady Walpurga Paget's *In My Tower* and *Scenes and Memories*, John Pemble's *The Mediterranean Passion: Victorians and Edwardians in the South*, Monica Stirling's *The Fine and the Wicked: The Life and Times of Ouida*, Henry Jones Thaddeus's *Recollections of a Court Painter*, Marcello Vanucci's *Firenze Ottocento*, Elihu Vedder's *The Digressions of V.*, Gordon Waterfield's *Lucie Duff Gordon in England, South Africa and Egypt*, Charles Weld's *Florence: The New Capital of Italy*, and the entries for James Lacaita and George Frederic Watts in the *Oxford Dictionary of National Biography*.

119 "Now, the Cascine is to the world of society what the Bourse is to the world of trade," Charles Lever wrote in the 1840s: He did so in his novel *The Dodd Family Abroad*.

124 By the time of her death, Lucie had become something of a celebrity— "Egypt's most famous invalid," as one scholar puts it: The scholar in question is John Pemble, writing in *The Mediterranean Passion: Victorians and Edwardians in the South*.

124 her old friend Heine, who'd spent twelve years stoically wasting away in Paris on what he called his "mattress-grave," and who, as one biographer writes, was "an obligatory stop for visitors from beyond the Rhine": The biographer in question is Ernst Pawel, writing in *The Poet Dying: Heinrich Heine's Last Years in Paris*.

128 "In no other work," one scholar contends, "is the never-never land of classical antiquity . . . so idyllically re-created": The scholar in question is Frederick Hartt, writing in *History of Italian Renaissance Art*.

129 As National Gallery archives reveal, in 1866 Boxall had been sent by the previous director, Sir Charles Eastlake, to look at *The School of Pan*: It was Gordon Waterfield, not I, who checked in the archives.

143 one biographer claims that "marriages were ruined, engagements broken, lifelong associations smashed to smithereens—all in the cause of *Friendship*": The biographer in question is Eileen Brigland, writing in *Ouida, the Passionate Victorian*.

CHAPTER FIVE: CASTLE ROSS

I drew on Sarah Benjamin's *A Castle in Tuscany: The Remarkable Life of Janet Ross*, the papers of Bernard and Mary Berenson (Villa I Tatti), *Mary Berenson: A Self-Portrait from Her Letters and Diaries*, ed. Barbara Strachey and Jayne Samuels,

Katie Campbell's *Paradise of Exiles: The Anglo-American Gardens of Florence*, Vineta Colby's *Vernon Lee: A Literary Biography*, Phyllis Grosskurth's *The Woeful Victorian: A Biography of John Addington Symonds*, Fred Kaplan's *The Singular Mark Twain*, the papers of A. W. Kinglake (Cambridge University Library), Henry Ross's *Letters from the East*, Ernest Samuels's *Bernard Berenson: The Making of a Connoisseur*, Meryle Secrest's *Being Bernard Berenson*, Barbara Strachey's *Remarkable Relations: The Story of the Pearsall Smith Family*, *The Memoirs of John Addington Symonds*, ed. Phyllis Grosskurth, Margaret ("Madge") Symonds's unpublished "Memoirs of Mrs. Janet Ross and of Life in a Florentine Villa" (Waterfield Collection), Laura Trevelyan's *A Very British Family: The Trevelyans and Their World*, *Autobiography of Mark Twain*, vol. 1, ed. Harriet E. Smith et al., *Mark Twain's Letters*, ed. Albert Bigelow Paine, Lina Waterfield's *Castle in Italy*, and the entry on John Temple Leader in the *Oxford Dictionary of National Biography*.

191 Marie Corelli, described by one critic as combining "the imagination of a Poe with the style of a Ouida and the mentality of a nursemaid": The critic in question is James Agate.
195 Twain was now struggling with Italian, and, as he explained to a *New York Times* reporter who asked him to "account for this mutilation," he'd decided "to watch the natives": The reporter's article appeared on April 10, 1904, under the headline "Mark Twain to Reform the Language of Italy."

CHAPTER SIX: AUNT JANET

I drew on Harold Acton's *Memoirs of an Aesthete*, Walter L. Adamson's *Avant-Garde Florence*, Kinta Beevor's *A Tuscan Childhood*, Arnold Bennett's *Florentine Journal, 1st April–25th May 1910*, the papers of Bernard and Mary Berenson (Villa I Tatti), *Mary Berenson: A Self-Portrait from Her Letters and Diaries*, ed. Barbara Strachey and Jayne Samuels, *The Modern World of Neith Boyce: Autobiography and Letters*, ed. Carole DeBoer-Langworthy, Carolyn Burke's *Becoming Modern: The Life of Mina Loy*, Katie Campbell's *Paradise of Exiles: The Anglo-American Gardens of Florence*, Kenneth Clark's *Another Part of the Wood: A Self-Portrait*, Martin Clark's *Modern Italy 1871–1982*, Robert Clark's *Dark Water: Flood and Reflection in the City of Masterpieces*, J. M. Dent's *The Memoirs of J. M. Dent*, Christopher Duggan's *The Force of Destiny: A History of Italy Since 1796*, Richard M. E. Dunn's *Geoffrey Scott and the Berenson Circle*, Phyllis Grosskurth's *The Woeful Victorian: A Biography of John Addington Symonds*, Olive Hamilton's *Paradise of Exiles: Tuscany and the British*, Christopher Hibbert's *Florence: The Biography of a City*, Francis King's *Florence: A Literary Companion*, David Leavitt's *Florence, A Delicate Case*, Nicky Mariano's *Forty Years with Berenson*, Caroline Moorehead's *Iris Origo: Marchesa of Val d'Orcia*, Nicholas Murray's *Aldous Huxley: An English Intellectual*, Iris Origo's *Images and Shadows*, Bernd Roeck's *Florence 1900: The Quest for Arcadia*, William Rothenstein's *Men and Memories*,

Ernest Samuels's *Bernard Berenson: The Making of a Legend*, Meryle Secrest's *Being Bernard Berenson* and *Kenneth Clark: A Biography*, Christopher Seton-Watson's "British Propaganda in Italy 1914–1918," Barbara Strachey's *Remarkable Relations: The Story of the Pearsall Smith Family*, Raleigh Trevelyan's *Princes under the Volcano: Two Hundred Years of a British Dynasty in Sicily*, Lina Waterfield's *Castle in Italy*, John Woodhouse's *Gabriele D'Annunzio: Defiant Archangel*, *The Diary of Virginia Woolf, Vol. 3, 1925–30*, ed. Anne Olivier Bell, and *The Letters of Virginia Woolf: Vol. 1, 1888–1912*, ed. Nigel Nicolson and Joanne Trautmann.

222 [Tina Whitaker] seems to have met Janet through Lacaita, and her diaries include the following entry, set down after Lacaita's death in 1895: "Every year I have met Janet Ross": Selections from her diaries—including the two sentences I quote in the footnote—appear in Raleigh Trevelyan's *Princes under the Volcano: Two Hundred Years of a British Dynasty in Sicily.*

227 Virgina Stephen: The diary has been lost, but a typed copy survives, and it is quoted in an appendix to *The Diary of Virginia Woolf, Vol. 3, 1925–30*, ed. Anne Olivier Bell. (The appendix is to an entry on the death of Geoffrey Scott in August 1929. Woolf recalls that in 1909 she met Scott for the first time in Florence; they had lunch, and "afterwards we went to a party at Mrs. Ross's.")

233 the writer Carlo Placci was so taken aback by the yawning indifference of his colonial friends that he burst out to Berenson, "You strange people, inhabiting hills and abstract ideas": Quoted in Ernest Samuels's *Bernard Berenson: The Making of a Connoisseur.*

237 Logan Pearsall Smith reported to his mother that Janet had found the house "absolutely hopeless & uninhabitable": Quoted in Meryle Secrest's *Being Bernard Berenson.*

262 " 'You are just the person I want, Filippo. Now what is the equator?' ": This version of the anecdote is from Lina Waterfield's *Castle in Italy*. However, it also appears, in somewhat different form, in Kenneth Clark's *Another Part of the Wood: A Self-Portrait*. Clark claims that Janet was at work translating *An Account of Tibet* when "she came on the word Equator. 'Equator, what on earth is that, my dear?' she asked me. 'It's an imaginary line drawn round the earth, Aunt Janet.' 'Imaginary line; what nonsense, I shall leave it out.' " Given that *Castle in Italy* was published thirteen years before *Another Part of the Wood*, it seems likely that Clark read about the incident in Lina's book and then, years later, somehow misremembered it as having occurred in his own presence, with himself in the role of de Filippi. Or perhaps he simply poached it.

269 Madge wrote from Poggio Gherardo: The identification of Madge with Sally Seton, as mentioned in the footnote, has been made by a number of scholars. For instance, Nigel Nicolson, in his introduction to *The Letters of Virginia Woolf: Vol. 1, 1888–1912*, writes, "It was to Madge, 13 years older than herself,

that Virginia first opened her heart about her literary ambitions, and Madge who became Sally Seton in *Mrs. Dalloway*."

EPILOGUE: LEGACIES

I drew on Harold Acton's *More Memoirs of an Aesthete*, Walter L. Adamson's *Avant-Garde Florence*, Kinta Beevor's *A Tuscan Childhood*, the papers of Bernard and Mary Berenson (Villa I Tatti), Katie Campbell's *Paradise of Exiles: The Anglo-American Gardens of Florence*, Robert Clark's *Dark Water: Flood and Reflection in the City of Masterpieces*, Mark Holloway's *Norman Douglas: A Biography*, Ian Hamilton's *Robert Lowell: A Biography*, Olive Hamilton's *Paradise of Exiles: Tuscany and the British*, Christopher Hibbert's *Florence: The Biography of a City*, Francis King's *Florence: A Literary Companion*, David Leavitt's *Florence, a Delicate Case*, James Lord's *Some Remarkable Men: Further Memoirs*, *The Letters of Robert Lowell*, ed. Saskia Hamilton, Nicky Mariano's *Forty Years with Berenson*, Mary McCarthy's *The Stones of Florence*, Alan Moorehead's *A Late Education: Episodes in a Life*, Caroline Moorehead's *Iris Origo: Marchesa of Val d'Orcia*, Nicholas Murray's *Aldous Huxley: An English Intellectual*, Iris Origo's *Images and Shadows* and *A Need to Testify*, Giuseppe Orioli's *Adventures of a Bookseller*, Ernest Samuels's *Bernard Berenson: The Making of a Legend*, Meryle Secrest's *Being Bernard Berenson*, Lina Waterfield's *Castle in Italy*, John Worthen's *D. H. Lawrence: The Life of an Outsider*, Franco Zeffirelli's *An Autobiography*, and the entries on Harold Acton, Violet Trefusis, and Gordon Waterfield in the *Oxford Dictionary of National Biography*.

275 One of [Aubrey's] students at the Poggio Gherardo School recollects that he threatened her with expulsion: The student in question is Rosalys Coope, who went on to become an architectural historian, and who described the school (and Aubrey's temper) to me by phone.

278 "That is the third of my friends she has annexed," hissed Wharton: Quoted in Caroline Moorehead's *Iris Origo: Marchesa of Val d'Orcia*.

282 Harold Acton recalled that on a walking tour of Chianti he took with Douglas and Scott Moncrieff, Douglas tried to fondle boys in every village along the way: Acton described the incident to his friend James Lord, who set it down in *Some Remarkable Men: Further Memoirs*.

285 Matteo Renzi, the mayor of Florence, expressed sadness at the loss of an institution with "a very unique and beautiful history": Quoted in *The New York Times*, April 26, 2011.

286 The firebrand critic Giovanni Papini made this case succinctly in 1913: "Florence is put to shame": Quoted in Walter L. Adamson's *Avant-Garde Florence*.

290 over the next two months [Violet Trefusis] starved herself to death, "surrounded," as one biography puts it, "by statues, empty fountains, and dead

flowers": The biography in question is Phillipe Jullian and John Phillips's *Violet Trefusis: A Biography, Including Correspondence with Vita Sackville-West*. I did not consult the biography directly, but rather borrowed the quote from the entry on Trefusis in the *Oxford Dictionary of National Biography*.

BIBLIOGRAPHY

FAMILY

Beevor, Kinta. *A Tuscan Childhood.* New York: Pantheon, 1993.

Duff Gordon, Alexander. "A Trip to the Isthmus of Suez." *Macmillan's Magazine,* March 1865.

Duff Gordon, Lucie. *Last Letters from Egypt, to which are added Letters from the Cape.* Ed. Janet Ross. London: Macmillan, 1875.

———. *Letters from the Cape.* London: F. Galton, 1864.

———. *Letters from Egypt, 1863–1865.* Ed. Sarah Austin. London: Macmillan, 1865.

———. *Letters from Egypt.* Revised and with a memoir by Janet Ross and a new introduction by George Meredith. London: R. Brimley Johnson, 1902.

———. *Letters from Egypt.* Ed. Gordon Waterfield. London: Routledge and Kegan Paul, 1969.

Ross, Henry James. *Letters from the East.* London: J. M. Dent, 1902.

Ross, Janet. *Early Days Recalled.* London: Chapman and Hall, 1891.

———. *Florentine Palaces and Their Stories.* London: J. M. Dent, 1905.

———. *Florentine Villas.* London: J. M. Dent, 1901.

———. *The Fourth Generation.* London: Constable, 1912.

———. *Italian Sketches.* London: K. Paul, Trench, 1887.

———. *The Land of Manfred.* London: John Murray, 1889.

———. *Leaves from our Tuscan Kitchen, or How to cook vegetables.* London: J. M. Dent, 1899.

———. *Leaves from our Tuscan Kitchen, or How to cook vegetables.* With an introductory note by Michael Waterfield. London: Penguin, 1973.

———. *Lives of the Early Medici, as told in their correspondence.* London: Chatto and Windus, 1910.

———. *Old Florence and Modern Tuscany*. London: J. M. Dent, 1904.

———. *The Story of Lucca*. London: J. M. Dent, 1912.

———. *The Story of Pisa*. London: J. M. Dent, 1909.

———. *Three Generations of English Women: memoirs and correspondence of Susannah Taylor, Sarah Austin, and Lady Duff Gordon*. London: John Murray, 1888.

———. *Three Generations of English Women: memoirs and correspondence of Susannah Taylor, Sarah Austin, and Lady Duff Gordon: a new, revised, and enlarged edition*. London: T. Fisher Unwin, 1993.

Ross, Janet, ed. *Letters of Principal T. M. Lindsay to Janet Ross*. London: Constable, 1923.

Ross, Janet, trans. *An Account of Tibet: The Travels of Ippolito Desideri of Pistoia, S.J., 1712–1727.* London: G. Routledge and Sons, 1932.

———. *The Autobiography of a Veteran, 1807–1893*, by Enrico della Rocca. New York: Macmillan, 1898.

———. *Voyages of Francesco Carletti, 1594–1602*. London: G. Routledge and Sons, 1931.

Ross, Janet, and Edward Hutton. *Poesie volgari di Lorenzo de' Medici, a cura di Janet Ross e di Edward Hutton*. Edinburgh: J. M. Dent, 1912.

Waterfield, Gordon. "Aunt Janet: Her Friends and Victims." Unpublished manuscript, c. 1987.

———. *Layard of Nineveh*. London: John Murray, 1963.

———. *Lucie Duff Gordon in England, South Africa and Egypt*. London: John Murray, 1937.

Waterfield, Lina. *Castle in Italy*. London: John Murray, 1961.

———. *Home Life in Italy: Letters from the Apennines*. London: Methuen, 1908.

———. *The Story of Assisi*. London: J. M. Dent, 1900.

Waterfield, Lina, and Welbore St. Clair Baddeley. *Rome and Its Story*. London: J. M. Dent, 1904.

Waterfield, Lian and Margaret Symonds. *The Story of Perugia*. London: J. M. Dent, 1898.

Waterfield Collection. British Institute of Florence.

NONFAMILY

Acland, Alice. *Caroline Norton*. London: Constable, 1948.

Acton, Harold. *Memoirs of an Aesthete*. London: Methuen, 1948.

———. *More Memoirs of an Aesthete*. London: Methuen, 1970.

Adamson, Walter L. *Avant-Garde Florence*. Cambridge, MA: Harvard University Press, 1993.

Artom Treves, Giuliana. *The Golden Ring: The Anglo-Florentines, 1847–1862*. Trans. Sylvia Sprigge. London: Longmans, Green, 1956.

Ashton, Rosemary. *Thomas and Jane Carlyle: Portrait of a Marriage.* London: Chatto and Windus, 2002.

Benjamin, Sarah. *A Castle in Tuscany: The Remarkable Life of Janet Ross.* Millers Point, Australia: Pier 9, 2006.

Bennett, Arnold. *Florentine Journal, 1st April–25th May 1910.* London: Chatto and Windus, 1967.

Berenson, Bernard. *Rumor and Reflection.* New York: Simon and Schuster, 1952.

———. *Sunset and Twilight: From the Diaries of 1947 to 1958.* New York: Harcourt, Brace and World, 1963.

Berenson, Bernard, and Mary Berenson. Papers, 1880–2002. Harvard University Library, Villa I Tatti.

Berenson, Mary. *Mary Berenson: A Self-Portrait from Her Letters and Diaries.* Ed. Barbara Strachey and Jayne Samuels. New York: W. W. Norton, 1983.

Blessington, Marguerite, Countess of. *The Idler in Italy.* London: H. Colburn, 1839.

Bosworth, R.J.B., *Mussolini's Italy: Life Under the Fascist Dictatorship, 1915–1945.* London: Allen Lane, 2005.

Bowman, Peter James. *The Fortune Hunter: A German Prince in Regency England.* Oxford: Signal, 2010.

Boyce, Neith. *The Modern World of Neith Boyce: Autobiography and Letters.* Ed. Carole DeBoer-Langworthy. Albuquerque: University of New Mexico Press, 2003.

Brigland, Eileen. *Ouida, the Passionate Victorian.* New York: Duell, Sloan and Pearce, 1951.

Brooks, Van Wyck. *The Dream of Arcadia: American Writers and Artists in Italy 1760–1915.* New York: E. P. Dutton, 1958.

Burke, Carolyn. *Becoming Modern: The Life of Mina Loy.* New York: Farrar, Straus and Giroux, 1997.

Butler, Lady Elizabeth. *An Autobiography.* London: Constable, 1902.

Camerani, Sergio. *Vita fiorentina attraverso i secoli: Vol. 3, Cronache di Firenze capitale.* Florence: Leo. S. Olschki, 1971.

Campbell, Katie. *Paradise of Exiles: The Anglo-American Gardens of Florence.* London: Frances Lincoln, 2009.

Carlyle, Thomas, and Jane Welsh Carlyle. *The Collected Letters of Thomas and Jane Welsh Carlyle.* Vols. 5–9. Ed. Charles Richard Sanders and Kenneth J. Fielding. Durham: Duke University Press, 1977.

Chapman, Alison, and Jane Stabler, eds. *Unfolding the South: Nineteenth-Century British Women Writers and Artists in Italy.* Manchester: Manchester University Press, 2003.

Chaney, Edward. "Acton, Sir Harold Mario Mitchell (1904–1994)." *Oxford Dictionary of National Biography.* Ed. H.C.G. Matthew and Brian Harrison. Oxford: Oxford University Press, 2004.

Clark, Kenneth. *Another Part of the Wood: A Self-Portrait.* London: John Murray, 1974.

Clark, Martin. *Modern Italy, 1871–1982.* London: Longman, 1984.

Clark, Robert. *Dark Water: Flood and Reflection in the City of Masterpieces.* New York: Doubleday, 2008.

Colby, Vineta. *Vernon Lee: A Literary Biography.* Charlottesville: University of Virginia Press, 2003.

Courtney, W. P. (rev. Elizabeth Baigent). "Warburton, Bartholomew Elliott George [pseud. Eliot Warburton], 1810–1852." *Oxford Dictionary of National Biography.*

Crane, David. *Lord Byron's Jackal: A Life of Trelawny.* London: HarperCollins, 1998.

Cust, L. H. (rev. David Robertson). "Kirkup, Seymour Stocker (1788–1880)." *Oxford Dictionary of National Biography.*

De Leon, Edwin. *The Khedive's Egypt.* London: Sampson, Low, Marston, Searle, and Rivington, 1877.

Dent, J. M. *The Memoirs of J. M. Dent.* London: J. M. Dent and Sons, 1928.

Dentler, Clara Louise. *Famous Foreigners in Florence 1400–1900.* Florence: Bemporad Marzocco, 1964.

Dickens, Charles. *Pictures from Italy.* London: Bradbury and Evans, 1846.

Donadio, Rachel. "Britain to Close a Consulate with a View." *New York Times,* April 26, 2011.

Duggan, Christopher. *The Force of Destiny: A History of Italy Since 1796.* London: Allen Lane, 2007.

Dunn, Richard M. *Geoffrey Scott and the Berenson Circle.* Lewiston: Edwin Mellen Press, 1998.

Dyas, Eamon. "The Mystery of the Egyptian Correspondent of the *Times.*" *Victorian Periodicals Review* 28, no. 1 (Spring 1995).

Edel, Leon. *Henry James: The Middle Years.* London: Rupert Hart-Davis, 1963.

Fantoni, Marcello. *Gli anglo-americani a Firenze.* Rome: Bulzoni Editore, 2000.

Field, Kate. "English Authors in Florence." *The Atlantic Monthly,* Dec. 1864.

———. "Last Days of Walter Savage Landor." *The Atlantic Monthly,* Apr.–June 1866.

Flaubert, Gustave. *Flaubert in Egypt: A Sensibility on Tour.* Ed. Francis Steegmuller. Boston: Little, Brown, 1972.

Forster, E. M. *Alexandria: A History and a Guide.* London: Whitehead Morris, 1922.

Frank, Katherine. *A Passage to Egypt: The Life of Lucie Duff Gordon.* Boston: Houghton Mifflin, 1994.

Gissing, A. C. *William Holman Hunt: A Biography.* London: Duckworth, 1936.

Grosskurth, Phyllis. *The Woeful Victorian: A Biography of John Addington Symonds.* New York: Holt, Rinehart and Winston, 1964.

Guest, Ivor Forbes. *Napoleon III in England.* London: British Technical and General Press, 1952.

Hamburger, Lotte, and Joseph Hamburger. *Contemplating Adultery: The Secret Life of a Victorian Woman*. New York: Fawcett Columbine, 1991.

———. *Troubled Lives: John and Sarah Austin*. Toronto: University of Toronto Press, 1985.

Hamilton, Ian. *Robert Lowell: A Biography*. New York: Random House, 1982.

Hamilton, Olive. *The Divine Country: The British in Tuscany, 1372–1980*. London: André Deutsch, 1982.

———. *Paradise of Exiles: Tuscany and the British*. London: André Deutsch, 1974.

Hare, Augustus. *The Story of My Life*. Vol. 4. London: George Allen, 1900.

Hartt, Frederick. *History of Italian Renaissance Art*. New York: Harry N. Abrams, 1969.

Hayter, Althea. *A Sultry Month: Scenes of London Literary Life in 1846*. London: Faber and Faber, 1965.

Hibbert, Christopher. *Florence: The Biography of a City*. London: Viking, 1993.

———. *Garibaldi and His Enemies*. London: Longmans, Green, 1965.

———. *Mussolini: The Rise and Fall of Il Duce*. London: Longmans, 1962.

Hillard, George Stillman. *Six Months in Italy*. London: John Murray, 1853.

Hodgkin, E. C. "Waterfield, (Ottiwell Henry) Gordon (1903–1987)." *Oxford Dictionary of National Biography*.

Holmes, Richard. *Footsteps: Adventures of a Romantic Biographer*. London: Hodder, 1985.

———. *Shelley: The Pursuit*. London: Weidenfeld and Nicolson, 1974.

Holloway, Mark. *Norman Douglas: A Biography*. London: Secker and Warburg, 1976.

Howells, William Dean. *Indian Summer*. Boston: Ticknor, 1886.

Hutton, Edward. *Country Walks about Florence*. London: Methuen, 1908.

Hunt, Leigh. *Autobiography of Leigh Hunt*. London: Smith, Elder, 1850.

Hutton, Laurence. "Literary Landmarks of Florence." *Harper's Magazine*, Nov. 1896.

Huxley, Aldous. *Those Barren Leaves*. London: Chatto and Windus, 1925.

Huzzard, John A. "George Meredith and the Risorgimento." *Italica* 36, no. 4 (Dec. 1959).

James, Henry. *Henry James Letters, Vol. 2: 1875–1883*. Ed. Leon Edel. Cambridge, MA: Belknap, 1875.

———. *Henry James Letters, Vol. 3: 1883–1895*. Ed. Leon Edel. London: Macmillan, 1981.

———. *Traveling in Italy with Henry James*. Ed. Fred Kaplan. New York: William Morrow, 1994.

———. *William Wetmore Story and his Friends*. Boston: Houghton Mifflin, 1903.

Johnston, Johanna. *The Life, Manners, and Travels of Fanny Trollope: A Biography*. New York: Hawthorn, 1978.

Kamm, Josephine. *John Stuart Mill in Love*. London: Gordon and Cremonesi, 1977.

Kaplan, Fred. *The Singular Mark Twain*. New York: Doubleday, 2003.

King, Francis. *Florence: A Literary Companion*. London: John Murray, 1991.

Kinglake, A. W. *Eothen*. London: J. Ollivier, 1844.

———. Papers of Alexander William Kinglake (1809–1891) [Add. MS 76333]. Cambridge University Library.

Korg, Jacob. *Browning and Italy*. Athens: Ohio University Press, 1983.

Landes, David S. *Bankers and Pashas: International Finance and Economic Imperialism in Egypt*. Cambridge, MA: Harvard University Press, 1958.

Lane, John. *In a Tuscan Garden*. London: The Bodley Head, 1902.

Layard, Austen Henry. *Autobiography and letters from his childhood until his appointment as H. M. ambassador in Madrid*. Ed. W. N. Bruce. London: John Murray, 1903.

Leavitt, David. *Florence, a Delicate Case*. New York: Bloomsbury, 2002.

Lee, Sidney (rev. H.C.G. Matthew). "Leader, John Temple (1810–1903)." *Oxford Dictionary of National Biography*.

Levey, Michael. *Florence: A Portrait*. Cambridge, MA: Harvard University Press, 1996.

Lewis, R.W.B. *The City of Florence: Historical Vistas and Personal Sightings*. New York: Farrar, Straus and Giroux, 1995.

Listri, Pier Francesco. *Firenze e la Toscana di Yorick*. Prato: Edizioni Del Palazzo, 1985.

Lord, James. *Some Remarkable Men: Further Memoirs*. New York: Farrar, Straus and Giroux, 1996.

Lowell, Robert. *The Letters of Robert Lowell*. Ed. Saskia Hamilton. New York: Farrar, Straus and Giroux, 2005.

Mander, Rosalie. *Mrs. Browning: The Story of Elizabeth Barrett*. London: Weidenfeld and Nicolson, 1980.

Marchand, Leslie A. *Byron: A Biography*. New York: Alfred A. Knopf, 1957.

Mariano, Nicky. *Forty Years with Berenson*. New York: Alfred A. Knopf, 1967.

"Mark Twain to Reform the Language of Italy." *New York Times*, Apr. 10, 1904.

Matthew, H.C.G. "Elliot, Sir Henry George (1817–1907)." *Oxford Dictionary of National Biography*.

Mazlish, Bruce. *James and John Stuart Mill: Father and Son in the Nineteenth Century*. London: Hutchinson, 1975.

McCarthy, Mary. *The Stones of Florence*. New York: Harcourt Brace, 1959.

Meredith, George. *Diana of the Crossways*. London: Chapman and Hall, 1885.

———. *Evan Harrington*. London: Bradbury and Evans, 1861.

———. *The Letters of George Meredith*. Ed. C. L. Cline. London: Oxford University Press, 1970.

"Miscellaneous Notes." *Bulletin of Miscellaneous Information (Royal Botanic Gardens, Kew)* 1917, no. 2 (1917).

Monsarrat, Ann. *An Uneasy Victorian: Thackeray the Man*. London: Cassell, 1980.

Moorehead, Alan. *A Late Education: Episodes in a Life*. London: Hamish Hamilton, 1970.

Moorehead, Caroline. *Iris Origo: Marchesa of Val d'Orcia*. London: John Murray, 2000.

Mori, Giorgio, and Piero Roggi, eds. *Firenze 1815–1945: un bilancio storiografico*. Florence: Le Monnier, 1990.

Murray, Nicholas. *Aldous Huxley: An English Intellectual*. London: Little, Brown, 2002.

Nightingale, Florence. *Letters from Egypt: A Journey on the Nile, 1849–1850*, ed. Antony Sattin. London: Weidenfeld and Nicolson, 1987.

North, Marianne. *Recollections of a Happy Life*. Ed. Mrs. John Addington Symonds. London: Macmillan, 1892.

———. *Some Further Recollections of a Happy Life*. Ed. Mrs. John Addington Symonds. London: Macmillan, 1893.

Norwich, John Julius. *Paradise of Cities: Venice in the 19th Century*. London: Viking, 2003.

O'Grady, Jean. "The Egyptian Correspondent of the *Times*." *Victorian Periodicals Review* 27, no. 2 (Summer 1994).

———. "More Egyptian Correspondence." *Victorian Periodicals Review* 29, no. 1 (Spring 1996).

Origo, Iris. *Images and Shadows*. London: John Murray, 1970.

———. *The Last Attachment*. London: John Murray and Jonathan Cape, 1949.

———. *A Need to Testify*. London: John Murray, 1984.

Orioli, Giuseppe. *Adventures of a Bookseller*. London: R. M. McBride, 1938.

Ouida. *Friendship*. London: Chatto and Windus, 1878.

Packe, Michael St. John. *The Life of John Stuart Mill*. London: Secker and Warburg, 1954.

Paget, Lady Walpurga. *In My Tower*. London: Hutchinson, 1924.

———. *Scenes and Memories*. New York: Charles Scribner's Sons, 1912.

Paston, George. *Little Memoirs of the Nineteenth Century*. London: G. Richards, 1902.

Pawel, Ernst. *The Poet Dying: Heinrich Heine's Last Years in Paris*. New York: Farrar, Straus and Giroux, 1995.

Pemble, John. *The Mediterranean Passion: Victorians and Edwardians in the South*. London: Oxford University Press, 1988.

Power, Marguerite. *Arabian Days and Nights*. London: Sampson, Low, 1863.

Raison, Laura. *Tuscany: An Anthology*. London: Cadogan, 1983.

Rodenbeck, Max. *Cairo: The City Victorious*. London: Picador, 1998.

Roeck, Bernd. *Florence 1900: The Quest for Arcadia*. Trans. Stewart Spence. New Haven: Yale University Press, 2009.

Rothenstein, William. *Men and Memories*. London: Faber and Faber, 1931.

Samuels, Ernest. *Bernard Berenson: The Making of a Connoisseur*. Cambridge, MA: Harvard University Press, 1979.

———. *Bernard Berenson: The Making of a Legend*. Cambridge, MA: Harvard University Press, 1987.

Sassoon, Siegfried. *Meredith*. London: Constable, 1948,

Sattin, Anthony. *Lifting the Veil: British Society in Egypt, 1768–1956*. London: J. M. Dent, 1988.

Scharnhorst, Gary. *Kate Field: The Many Lives of a Nineteenth-Century American Journalist*. Syracuse: Syracuse University Press, 2008.

Secrest, Meryle. *Being Bernard Berenson*. New York: Holt, Rinehart and Winston, 1979.

———. *Kenneth Clark: A Biography*. London: Weidenfeld and Nicolson, 1984.

Seton-Watson, Christopher. "British Propaganda in Italy 1914–1918." In *Inghilterra e Italia nel '900*. Florence: La Nuova Italia Editrice, 1973.

Steegmuller, Francis. *The Two Lives of James Jackson Jarves*. New Haven: Yale University Press, 1951.

Stevenson, Lionel. *The Ordeal of George Meredith*. New York: Scribner, 1953.

Stirling, Monica. *The Fine and the Wicked: The Life and Times of Ouida*. New York: Coward-McCann, 1958.

Strachey, Barbara. *Remarkable Relations: The Story of the Pearsall Smith Family*. London: Victor Gollancz, 1980.

Super, R. H. *Walter Savage Landor: A Biography*. New York: New York University Press, 1954.

Sweetman, John. "Kinglake, Alexander William (1809–1891)." *Oxford Dictionary of National Biography*.

Symonds, John Addington. *The Life of Michelangelo Buonarroti*. London: J. C. Nimmo, 1893.

———. *The Memoirs of John Addington Symonds*. Ed. Phyllis Grosskurth. New York: Random House, 1984.

Symonds, Margaret. *Days Spent on a Doge's Farm*. London: T. Fisher Unwin, 1893.

———. "Memoirs of Mrs. Janet Ross and of Life in a Florentine Villa." Unpublished manuscript, 1922. Waterfield Collection.

Taylor, Clare. L. "Trefusis, Violet (1894–1972)." *Oxford Dictionary of National Biography*.

Tedder, H. R. (rev. H.C.G. Matthew). "Lacaita, Sir James Philip (1813–1895)." *Oxford Dictionary of National Biography*.

Thaddeus, Henry Jones. *Recollections of a Court Painter*. London: John Lane, 1912.

Thayer, William Sydney. Papers of William Sydney Thayer 1835–95. University of Virginia Library.

Trevelyan, George Macaulay. *Garibaldi and the Making of Italy*. London: Longmans, Green, 1911.

———. *Garibaldi and the Thousand*. London: Longmans, Green, 1909.

―――. *Garibaldi's Defence of the Roman Republic*. London: Longmans, Green, 1907.

Trevelyan, Laura. *A Very British Family: The Trevelyans and Their World*. London: I. B. Tauris, 2006.

Trevelyan, Raleigh. *Princes under the Volcano: Two Hundred Years of a British Dynasty in Sicily*. London: Macmillan, 1972.

Trollope, Thomas Adolphus. *What I Remember*. London: R. Bentley, 1887–89.

The Tuscan Athenaeum. Nos. 1–13 (Oct. 30, 1847–Jan. 22, 1848). New York Public Library.

Twain, Mark. *Autobiography of Mark Twain*. Vol. 1. Ed. Harriet E. Smith et al. Berkeley: University of California Press, 2010.

―――. *Mark Twain's Letters*. Ed. Albert Bigelow Paine. New York: Harper, 1917.

Vanucci, Marcello. *Firenze Ottocento*. Rome: Newton Compton Editori, 1992.

Vedder, Elihu. *The Digressions of V*. Boston and New York: Houghton Mifflin, 1910.

Weld, Charles Richard. *Florence: The New Capital of Italy*. London: Longmans, Green, 1867.

Williams, David. *George Meredith: His Life and Lost Love*. London: Hamish Hamilton, 1977.

Wineapple, Brenda. *Hawthorne: A Life*. New York: Alfred A. Knopf, 2003.

Woodhouse, John. *Gabriele D'Annunzio: Defiant Archangel*. Oxford: Clarendon Press, 1998.

Woolf, Virginia. *The Diary of Virginia Woolf, Vol. 3, 1925–30*. Ed. Anne Olivier Bell. London: Hogarth, 1980.

―――. *The Letters of Virginia Woolf: Vol. 1, 1888–1912*. Ed. Nigel Nicolson and Joanne Trautmann. London: Hogarth, 1975.

Worthen, John. *D. H. Lawrence: The Life of an Outsider*. London: Allen Lane, 2005.

Zeffirelli, Franco. *An Autobiography*. New York: Grove, 1986.

ACKNOWLEDGMENTS

First off, a great big thanks to my editor, Jonathan Galassi, for seeing the virtue of this book before I wrote it and for deftly improving it once I did. I'm also grateful to the rest of the FSG staff, especially Miranda Popkey, who expertly guided me through the production process and cheerfully answered all my dumb questions.

I'd be nowhere without my wonderful agent, Irene Skolnick, who stuck with me through my missteps and provided just the right mix of encouragement and reality. As for Irene's former colleague Erin Harris, I grope for the right superlatives to heap on her; suffice it to say that few people combine such sharp literary judgment with such nice manners.

For many biographers, "keepers of the flame"—zealously protective widows, descendants, and executors, that is—are a source of torment and frustration. My experience was precisely the opposite: Antony, Hugh, and Nigel Beevor were endlessly patient and helpful, whether pointing me toward materials, fielding inquiries, or commenting on my manuscript. My understanding of their enviably colorful family would be far less complete without them.

Alyson Price, archivist of the British Institute of Florence, was another godsend. Going far beyond the call of duty, she not only facilitated my use of the Waterfield Collection in a highly professional manner but weeded errors from my manuscript (her knowledge of the Anglo-Florentine colony easily exceeds my own) and helped me with various errands and bits of sleuthwork.

To Grazia Gobbi Sica I owe an incalculable debt. Throughout my research visits to Florence, she housed me, fed me, chauffeured me, entertained me, and was a constant source of fun and kindness. For all this alone I count myself beyond lucky. Yet Grazia also happens to be a leading authority on the Anglo-Florentines, which made her not only my friend and hostess but a conspirator of sorts. Not even John Addington Symonds, the most pampered of Janet Ross's guests, had it so good.

While a number of people were generous enough to comment on my manuscript, no one zeroed in on the wobbles and infelicities of my prose like Jeremy Axelrod. As an editor myself, I know smart edits when I see them. A tip of the hat!

Beatrice Sica and Gregory Dowling were also very helpful as manuscript vetters, especially where all things Italian are concerned. Thank you.

Rosalys Coope allowed me to pick her brain about the Poggio Gherardo School, which she attended, and in so doing opened a special window on my chosen little patch of the past.

In addition, I'm grateful to the following people for their assistance and support, by turns archival, technical, and moral: Will Brewer, Artemis Cooper, Ilaria Della Monica, Jeff Greggs, Herb Leibowitz, William Logan, Benedetta Origo, Eric Ormsby, Giovanni Pagliarulo, Alyssa Varner, Susan Yankowitz, and David Yezzi.

INDEX

PERMISSIONS ACKNOWLEDGMENTS

Quotations from the Waterfield Collection appear by permission of the Archive of the Harold Acton Library at the British Institute of Florence.

Quotations from the unpublished diaries of William Sydney Thayer appear by permission of the University of Virginia Library.

Quotations from *The Papers of Alexander William Kinglake (1809–1891)* [Add. MS 76333] appear by permission of the Syndics of Cambridge University Library.

Quotations from the unpublished diaries of Mary Berenson appear by permission of the Camphill Village Trust and Biblioteca Berenson, Villa I Tatti—The Harvard Center for Italian Renaissance Studies, courtesy of the President and Fellows of Harvard College.

Quotation from the unpublished diary of Bernard Berenson appears by permission of Biblioteca Berenson, Villa I Tatti—The Harvard Center for Italian Renaissance Studies, courtesy of the President and Fellows of Harvard College.